The Wage Curve

The Wage Curve

David G. Blanchflower and
Andrew J. Oswald

The MIT Press
Cambridge, Massachusetts
London, England

© 1994 Massachusetts Institute of Technology
All rights reserved. No part of this book may be reproduced in any form by any electronic or mechanical means (including photocopying, recording, or information storage and retrieval) without permission in writing from the publisher.

This book was set in Palatino by Asco Trade Typesetting Ltd., Hong Kong and was printed and bound in the United States of America.

Library of Congress Cataloging-in-Publication Data

Blanchflower, David.
   The wage curve / David G. Blanchflower and Andrew J. Oswald.
     p. cm.
   Includes bibliographical references and index.
   ISBN 0-262-02375-X
   1. Wage—Statistical methods.   2. Unemployment—Statistical methods.   I. Oswald, Andrew J. II. Title.
HD4915.B6   1994
331.2'1—dc20   94-8882
                                     CIP

To our wives,
Sian and Coral

Contents

Preface

Work on this monograph began in 1987. The project was originally to be a single paper on the role of local unemployment in British wage determination, but we started to believe that there was a more general finding to be uncovered. Our first analysis of data from the U.S. Current Population Survey—dating to a 1989 visit to the National Bureau of Economic Research—gave such apparently similar conclusions to those we had for Britain that it seemed sensible to look at other nations. That led to the multi-country International Social Survey Program study described in a later chapter, and to an attempt to check the U.S. and British estimates on samples as large and varied as possible. With more than a little help from friends around the globe, Korean, Canadian, and Australian data eventually were acquired. At the same time, other economists began to let us know that they were replicating the key result using their own nations' data. What seemed initially to be a puzzling uniformity came to look like a relationship worth documenting as systematically as possible.

Because a long time has elapsed since the beginning of the research project, we have an unusually large number of people to thank. The first acknowledgments, however, go to two institutions. The Centre for Labour Economics (now the Centre for Economic Performance) at the London School of Economics (LSE) funded our work and fostered our interest in the determinants of pay and unemployment. Its influence contributed to the macroeconomic theme within this book. The National Bureau of Economic Research (NBER) in Cambridge, Massachusetts, provided help and a forum for suggestions. Its influence contributed to the book's emphasis on empirical microeconomic methods. The monograph is an attempt to blend these two different traditions.

It would not be an exaggeration to say that hundreds of economists have given us comments and ideas. Special thanks go to Richard Freeman, whose LSE public lectures helped mold the project at an early stage, and who has provided encouragement and insightful criticism. He placed his bets earlier than anyone else. Richard Freeman, George Johnson, and Larry Katz provided valuable written comments on a version of this work discussed, under the title International Wage Curves, at an NBER conference.

The results in this book have been presented at approximately fifty university seminars and conferences across various continents. Each presentation led to a set of hastily jotted notes summarizing people's criticisms. They now fill a large box—the mix of paper colors and headings a testimony to nations' varied tastes in stationery. Next to each name is written the gist of the point (as perceived by us at that time). Some points occur again and again, and we have tried, no doubt imperfectly, to tackle them in the chapters to come. We are grateful to those who sent us detailed written comments.

It is not possible, unfortunately, to say thank you to everyone who contributed. Nevertheless, for their help and suggestions, we are pleased to be able here to express our thanks particularly to John Abowd, Joe Altonji, Josh Angrist, Richard Arnott, Lanny Arvan, Mark Beatson, Joan Beaver, Brian Bell, Sonia Bhalotra, David Blackaby, Olivier Blanchard, Becky Blank, Fran Blau, John Bauer, Gary Becker, Mark Bils, Richard Blundell, Steve Bond, Alison Booth, George Borjas, Simon Burgess, Ed Butchart, Lars Calmfors, David Card, Alan Carruth, Louis Christofides, Andrew Clark, Meghnad Desai, Bill Dickens, Richard Disney, Per-Anders Edin, Peter Elias, Paul Evans, Hank Farber, Nils Gottfries, Peter Gottschalk, Bob Gregory, Alan Gustman, John Haltiwanger, Simon Hands, Peter Hart, David Hendry, Andrew Hildreth, John Hoddinott, Steinar Holden, Bertil Holmlund, Sergi Jinenet, Larry Kahn, Meir Kohn, Alan Krueger, Richard Layard, Eddie Lazear, Thomas Lemieux, Jonathan Leonard, Assar Lindbeck, Karl-Gustaf Lofgren, Steve Machin, Tom MaCurdy, Thierry Magnac, Jim Malcomson, Alan Manning, Nancy Marion, Ken Mayhew, Steve Matusz, Barry McCormick, Bruce Meyer, Kevin Murphy, David Newbery, James Oswald, Martin Paldam, John Pencavel, Craig Pennington, Torsten Persson, Hashem Pesaran, Maire Nic Ghiolla Phadraig, Edmund Phelps, Steve Pischke, Chris Pissarides, Chang Rhee, Asbjorn Rodseth, Sherwin Rosen, Bob Rowthorn, Peter Sanfey, Christoph Schmidt, John Schmitt, Eric Simpson, Dennis Snower, Bob Solow, David Soskice, Mark Stewart, Paul Storer, Coen Teulings, Bob Topel, Hege Torp, the late John Vanderkamp, Steve Venti, Susan Vroman, Joachim Wagner, Ian Walker, Rudolph Winter-Ebmer, Frank Wilkinson, Frederik Wulfsberg, and Alex Zanello.

Brian Bell, Ed Butchart, and Craig Pennington of Oxford University and Matt Downer, John Stock, Jeff Sweeney, Bill Wilson, and Wendy Wolford of Dartmouth College provided invaluable research assistance. For fine secretarial help, we thank Tricia Cornelius, Margy Powell, Jill Walters, and Candy Watts. Tim Bartik and Larry Katz generously made available their data on variables suitable for instrumenting regional U.S. unemployment rates. Much of this book was written at Dartmouth College, and we thank the members of the Economics Department for their help and comments. David Avery and Hebe Quinton, from the Dartmouth Kiewit Computer Center, gave invaluable help with what must have seemed an insatiable need for computing assistance. They always dealt with us with a smile. A Rockefeller grant from the Department of Economics at Dartmouth is also gratefully acknowledged. Thanks are due to the members of the Oxford Institute of Economics and Statistics, and the director, Steve Nickell, for their hospitality. The institute's research library is one of the most helpful in the world. It was a pleasure to work with Terry Vaughn of The MIT Press.

A book like this one has to explain the details of most calculations that have been done. This makes a few of the chapters look more complicated than they really are. If the people on whom we have computerized records all linked hands, the line would stretch from California to New York. The computations reported in this book were completed at Dartmouth College using an IBM 4381-14 32m system running SPSS v.4 under VM/ESA 1.0. We had access to 8 gygabytes of storage capacity. Over 20,000 connect hours were used during the last four years of this project, consuming around 9,000 CPU hours. At commercial rates this represents a computing cost of approximately $2,000,000.

Many readers will want to get through to the monograph's punchlines, which are simple ones, without having to pore over regression equations and appendixes. We hope, too, that some of those who pick up this book will be undergraduates, nonspecialists, or lay readers who want to know what research economists do. The book's structure has been designed to try to help these readers. Most of the technical discussion can be skipped without impairing the flavor of the product. The key material is summarized in the main chapters' concluding sections, and these are kept deliberately brief. If you have only an hour, and like your fare unsalted, you might find it best to skim through chapter 1, and then read the short concluding parts to chapters 2 to 8. Finally, chapter 9, particularly the italicized list of findings, can be read. If you have only twenty minutes, and so must have your fare raw, you might want to read chapter 9 and glance through the rest. If you have only five minutes, look up our telephone numbers.

The term 'wage curve' was chosen for simplicity. We considered calling the relationship the wage-unemployment curve but thought that too long-winded. It began life as a cross-section pattern, in the Workplace Industrial Relations Survey of 1980, and grew.

This research was supported by the Economic and Social Research Council (UK).

1   Introduction

This book uses data from many countries to explore the workings of the labor market. It attempts to document the existence of an empirical "law" of economics. The law features two of the variables that most interest policymakers, namely, the level of unemployment and the level of wages.[1] These are linked, it is argued here, by a curve or formula described by figure 1.1. Because the wage curve is not part of conventional economics, most of the chapters to come are designed as collections of new evidence for it. Data on approximately three and a half million people, from twelve countries, are used in the analysis. Secondary evidence, drawing upon others' recent work, is also discussed. Some of this covers further nations.

The relationship captured in figure 1.1 raises obvious questions. What does this curve mean? Is it not unrealistic to believe in laws of behavior in a subject such as economics, which studies human beings? How, in a field where experiments are almost impossible, could there be any convincing scientific basis for this wage curve? Why does the figure look like a Phillips curve with the vertical axis mislabeled? How does the relationship fit into existing knowledge? What causes the curve? What, if anything, does all this imply for policymakers and their economic advisers?

These are some of the questions tackled in the next several hundred pages. The book's modus operandi is to draw upon random samples of workers and establishments from various nations. It uses the same statistical methods on each sample and aims to demonstrate that these international samples all reveal approximately the same curve. This book describes the search for a common pattern in data. To be convincing, such an approach needs data of high quality. In the natural sciences such data would

---

1. The term "wage" should be taken here to mean the level of real earnings per unit of work. The empirical research described in later chapters uses a variety of measures of the nominal wage, and usually includes year dummies to allow for aggregate price-level movements.

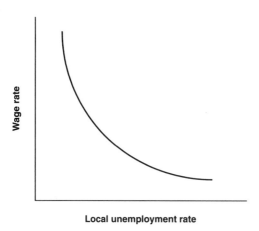

Figure 1.1
The wage curve

normally be collected as part of controlled experiments, and a proposition would not normally be thought of as proved until many different investigations replicated the essential finding. However, much science, especially medical science, proceeds in a less orderly way. A good example is the discovery—usually attributed to the Oxford researcher Sir Richard Doll— that smoking raises the probability of contracting lung cancer and other diseases. This fact emerged from an examination of survey information on British individuals. The data contained a "natural experiment": some people smoked and some did not. With the help of simple statistical methods, it could be shown that, other things being constant, there seemed to be a relationship between smoking and ill-health. Since then the same pattern has, of course, emerged in many other studies, and most Western governments have brought in policies to discourage smoking. Doll's discovery provides an illustration of how non-experimental methods can uncover relationships.[2] Although the topic covered in this book is far from those tackled in medical science, there are certain similarities in the underlying methods.[3]

2. Ferry (1993) records that Doll's research was stimulated by the need to explain the rise in lung cancer in Britain between the wars, and that Doll's original hunch—before the data came in—was that car exhaust fumes, and not cigarette smoking, were the likely cause.
3. The analogy will not be exact, because the book studies an effect from the environment surrounding individuals. Moreover, although the monograph has large samples by the standards of modern economics, the key statistical role will be played by a smaller number of regional observations.

This study is principally an examination of the role that local unemployment plays in pay determination—where causality is to be thought of as running from the amount of joblessness to the level of wages. The research crosses the three fields of labor economics, macroeconomics, and regional economics. In a sense, regions are treated as mini-economies. This provides many more units of observation than in conventional macroeconomics. A later chapter on the United States, for example, focuses partly upon fifty states through the 1980s rather than on ten aggregate time-series data points. Some of the issues of spatial economics are then impossible to avoid.[4] How does the fact that people can migrate from New Mexico to New Hampshire, or from Aberdeen to Aberystwyth, fit into the picture? What shapes the cross-section structure of the main labor market indicators? These topics are discussed later. Occasionally the analysis looks at industries rather than regions, but the underlying idea, that of uncovering the links between unemployment and earnings by using disaggregated information, remains the same.

Other economists have pointed to the potential that disaggregated data offer to analysts concerned with aggregate behavior. Layard and Bean (1990:159), for example, have argued that there is little power in aggregate time-series to discriminate between competing macroeconomic theories: "There is, however, a wealth of disaggregated and microeconomic data which can be brought to bear." Similar sentiments are expressed by Margo (1993). His topic is the Great Depression and its causes. The author puts forward the idea that, although the depression years are a premier example of a macroeconomic event, researchers in the field should try more often to do disaggregated analysis. Margo cites two principal benefits. First, less-aggregated data would provide "many more degrees of freedom than the decade or so of annual observations associated with the depression" (Margo, 1993:41). Second, he suggests, work at a lower level of aggregation can reveal aspects of economic behavior that lie hidden in the aggregate time-series. Bils (1985), too, advocates the study of microeconomic-level data on pay flexibility. Although he does not examine the effect of disaggregated measures of unemployment, nor study any country other than the United States, Bils' approach has similarities with that pursued throughout the forthcoming chapters. One purpose of this book is to try

---

4. This is reminiscent of Lindbeck (1989:300): "The enormous differences in unemployment rates between regions *within* national economies suggest that aggregate unemployment within a country cannot be well understood without a realistic analysis of the reasons why unemployed people do not move to areas with better employment prospects."

to contribute to the emerging but still-unconventional view that macro-economic questions can be analyzed with microeconometric methods.[5]

Subsequent chapters contain another methodological theme. It is that economists in the 1990s are among the first researchers to have at their disposal microeconomic data of a genuinely internationally comparable kind. This provides the current generation of economists with an advantage denied to earlier analysts. The book exploits, among other sources, the International Social Survey Program. This is a multicountry collaborative project, described in sources such as Jowell et al. (1989), in which survey teams from a dozen nations asked the same questions of random samples of individuals from each of the countries. Assuming that difficulties of common translation can be overcome—perhaps not an insurmountable obstacle when asking respondents about objectively measurable items such as income or numbers of years of education—a data set of such a kind endows social scientists with a statistical resource of value. Comparable data across nations offer a natural test-bed for scrutinizing theories. This is because deep explanations of economic and social behavior are presumably those that are common to peoples with different histories and institutions. The book's focus on internationally equivalent microeconomic data sets is unusual in the 1990s, but it may come to seem orthodox to those who write in the early part of the twenty-first century.

The empirical chapters in the book are based upon information on approximately three and a half million people from a dozen countries. The size of sample varies dramatically from one country to another. The years sampled also vary. For the United States, for example, the later analysis draws upon the Current Population Surveys from 1964 to 1991. This provides a sample of approximately one and three quarter million U.S. workers. Some completed their interview survey sheets in the 1960s; others did so a quarter of a century later. A similarly large sample is available for South Korea. This country's Occupational Wage Surveys of 1971, 1983, and 1986 offer the investigator information on approximately 1.4 million employees. At the other end of the spectrum, this book also reports results for countries such as Switzerland and Norway. These data are from the International Social Survey Program, and come from the late 1980s. In this case the samples are of less than three thousand people in each country.

---

5. Summers's (1991) paper on scientific illusion describes other difficulties caused by placing too much reliance upon macroeconomic data. Rayack (1987) gives further results like those of Bils.

For each person, from each country, the data sets record the individual's level of pay, and his or her personal characteristics. In most instances, the name of the region in which the worker lives is also recorded in the data set. It is well known that the rates of unemployment vary widely from one region to another and from one country to another. This book's analysis matches those unemployment rates to the sampled individuals. In other words, if Ms. X of San Francisco is known to be earning $12,000 per year in 1981, the unemployment rate in California in that year can be merged into the data set and treated as a variable that is potentially relevant in "explaining" the level of Ms. X's pay. For Great Britain, similarly, the sample might include information on Mr. Y working in Edinburgh in the year 1974. The 1974 unemployment rate for Scotland, therefore, can be added to the data set as a possible influence upon Mr. Y's remuneration in that year. Repeating this process many times gives information on a large number of workers' pay levels and, in each case, an associated unemployment rate in the person's region. Some people live in areas of high unemployment; others are surrounded by little joblessness. This variation offers useful statistical information.

What emerges from the data is a pattern linking pay and unemployment. Just as in the case of smoking and lung cancer, it is necessary to control for many other factors (such as age and gender) when performing the calculations. Once this is done, a locus of points is visible. This takes the form of a downward-sloping convex curve in wage/unemployment space. *A worker who is employed in an area of high unemployment earns less than an identical individual who works in a region with low joblessness.* The nature of the relationship appears to be the same in different countries. The wage curve in the United States is very similar to the wage curves in, for example, Britain, Canada, and Norway. As a crude characterization of the data—the details are spelled out in later chapters—the wage curve is described by the formula

$$\ln w = - 0.1 \ln U + \text{other terms,}$$

where $\ln w$ is the log of the wage, $\ln U$ is the log of unemployment in the worker's area, and the other terms in the equation are control variables for further characteristics of the worker and his or her sector. The equation, which seems to hold in each country, implies that the unemployment elasticity of pay is -0.1. A hypothetical doubling of unemployment is then associated with a drop in pay of 10% (that is, a fall of one tenth).

There is another way to think about this finding. When treated in the way just described, the data provide a method for the calculation of an index of wage rigidity or inflexibility. The concept of wage "stickiness" has long been central to much of macroeconomics. It has proved harder, however, to agree on a measure of wage inflexibility. The analysis developed later can be seen as offering such a measure. The responsiveness of workers' remuneration to the state of the labor market is captured by the coefficient on log unemployment in an equation for log earnings. Later results suggest that it is approximately the same (at −0.1) in each of the twelve countries considered. This uniformity seems remarkable. Despite sometimes dramatic institutional differences, countries exhibit much more uniformity in wage flexibility than has been thought. Put more technically, the unemployment elasticity of pay appears to be the same across nations.[6]

A brief glance at the relationship plotted in figure 1.1 conjures up thoughts of the curve identified by Phillips (1958) using nine decades of British aggregate data.[7] The Phillips curve, however, is not the concern of this book. The textbook construction is purportedly a locus linking the rate of change of wages to the level of unemployment. The present focus is different.[8]

1. The Phillips curve was proposed as a disequilibrium *adjustment* mechanism. The wage curve described in this book is instead to be thought of as an equilibrium locus that is not, in any useful sense, a description of temporary phenomena or of transitory dynamics.

2. The Phillips curve links changes in pay to the unemployment rate. The wage curve links the pay-level itself to the degree of joblessness.

3. The Phillips curve is traditionally estimated on macroeconomic data.[9] The wage curve is estimated primarily here on microeconomic data.

---

6. The conventional wisdom, as in the special supplement to *Economica* 1986, at the time of writing (based on time-series results) is that countries have very different degrees of wage flexibility. The editors' introduction concludes that "wages seem to be more responsive... in economies that are more corporatist in nature" (*Economica*, 1986:S19).

7. Yet Pigou (1927:201) pointed out that for the period before World War I there was a "distinct negative correlation between rates of real wages and quantities of unemployment." Pigou's statement is about levels of pay, not rates of change.

8. Some commentators have had difficulties here (see Paldam 1990, for example), so it may be useful to re-emphasize that the wage curve is not a Phillips curve.

9. This huge literature includes Phillips (1958), Christofides, Swidinsky and Wilton (1980), Desai (1975, 1984), Gilbert (1976), Gregory (1986), Grubb (1986), Laidler and Parkin (1975), Lipsey (1960), Manning (1993), Paldam (1980), Phelps (1967), Sargan (1964), Sparks and Wilton (1971), and Wadhwani (1985). Sargan (1964), in a sense, estimated an aggregate time-series wage curve.

Nevertheless, it would be misleading to view later results as divorced from the tradition that Phillips began. His underlying concern, to understand the macroeconomic influence of joblessness upon wage-setting, is continued in this book. Moreover, modern error-correction models integrate short-run dynamics and long-run equilibrium. They suggest that it is valuable to specify Phillips-style equations in a way—namely with a wage-level term on the right—in which the steady-state can exhibit a connection between wage levels and unemployment levels. Despite efforts in later chapters, only a little evidence is found for the idea that wage (level) equations have a significant autoregressive component. In other words, lagged dependent variables often enter this monograph's microeconometric earnings equations with a coefficient close to zero. Later results are consistent with the belief that it is the omission of suitable control variables—including those for fixed effects—that leads to spuriously large coefficients on lagged dependent wage variables. The idea of a Phillips curve may be inherently wrong.

In a recent review article Johnston (1992) drew attention to the difficulty that modern applied econometrics has had in producing robust and believable conclusions. His prose is pointed. "One impression which surfaces repeatedly in any perusal of applied work is the fragility of estimated relationships. By and large these relationships appear to be time-specific, data-specific and country- or region-specific. Why should one expect otherwise?" (Johnston 1992:53). If this is the opinion of an experienced econometrician, it is possibly unsurprising that theorists pay little attention to empirical work. Chapters 2 through 9 are designed, daunting though the task, to try to do better.

The book will not say a great deal about so-called insider-outsider models or about hysteresis in unemployment. These ideas have been popularized by Blanchard and Summers (1986), Carruth and Oswald (1987a), Cross (1988), Gottfries and Horn (1987), R. G. Gregory (1986), Solow (1985), and perhaps especially Lindbeck and Snower (1986, 1987, 1988a, 1988b). A contribution made by this way of thinking is that it has helped economists to face up to the fact that unemployment seems to be more persistent than simple models would ever have predicted. It might be argued, however, that some of the popularity of these models is more for linguistic than substantive reasons. The terms "insiders" and "outsiders" evocatively describe what happens in the world–they are never forgotten once heard in a seminar–rather than necessarily explain it. Real evidence, barring brute stylized facts, has been in short supply.[10] The book's findings fit into the broad spirit of the approach, but they do not offer evidence for the hypothesis of hysteresis in unemployment.

If figure 1.1 holds empirically, its causes need to be decoded. This book considers a number of possible theoretical explanations for the curve.

Most economists react to an empirical phenomenon by reaching initially for supply-and-demand analysis. Could a framework of that kind explain the wage curve of figure 1.1? At first glance it could not. Unemployment in the neoclassical model of the labor market is given by the difference between supply and demand. If the wage exceeds the market-clearing level, the numbers of individuals who wish to supply their labor exceeds the number firms wish to employ. Unemployment results. The higher the wage, the greater the degree of unemployment. In a framework of the textbook kind, where unemployment is the gap between a supply curve of labor and a demand curve for labor, wages and unemployment are positively associated. This is the reverse of the curve in figure 1.1.

The demand-and-supply model of the labor market cannot be dismissed quite this easily. Unemployment might be viewed as a voluntary choice by workers. Many commentators have pointed out that this is difficult to square with the apparent distress shown by people when they lose their jobs. Nevertheless, there is a long tradition in economics that questions the usefulness of the concept of involuntary unemployment. Thus a possible way to make figure 1.1 consistent with a demand-and-supply analysis is to suggest that the curve in the figure is some kind of labor supply function. The key assumption then is, of necessity, that unemployment is in some sense the negative of employment. There is a precise way to make the argument. If the potential labor force is fixed at some number greater than the level of employment on a labor supply curve, unemployment does not have to be thought of as a gap between supply and demand. It could, in principle, be viewed as the gap between labor supply and a fixed labor force.

Logical difficulties spring up here. In particular, the unemployed, according to this definition, are not part of the labor supply curve. They are not offering their labor for sale. This seems inconsistent with the technical definition of unemployment used by most government survey agencies, and perhaps runs counter to common sense. However, neoclassical analysts are still likely to see figure 1.1 as something akin to a labor supply function.

---

10. Despite their titles, Blanchflower et al. (1990) and Nickell and Wadhwani (1990) are really about something else, namely, the existence of rent-sharing.

One possibility is that figure 1.1's wage curve is a mismeasured version of the upward-sloping supply curve of labor found in most textbooks.

The possibility of a labor-supply interpretation of the wage curve of figure 1.1 is considered in detail later in the book. This is done by comparing the explanatory power, within a wage equation, of unemployment and conventional measures of the supply of labor. If unemployment is a mismeasured version of a normal labor supply relationship, it should perform statistically less well than supply variables such as the participation rate or the employment/population rate. Empirically, however, it does not. The evidence given in this book does not offer support for the idea that the negative correlation between pay and unemployment is explained by a labor supply curve. The book argues that the demand-and-supply framework is the wrong way to think about the labor market. As Robert Solow's 1989 lectures at Berkeley suggest, there seems to be something special about labor as a commodity and therefore about the labor market itself (Solow 1990:3).

If the competitive-market model gives an unconvincing rationalization of the wage curve, noncompetitive accounts of the labor market have to be considered. In a bargaining model, a high degree of joblessness in the surrounding labor market might be expected to reduce the ability of workers to claim a large share of the surplus to be divided. Noneconomists probably think such an idea too obvious to be worth pondering, but economists are required to outline the mechanism at work. A possible story is that outside unemployment frightens workers. This is because if something goes wrong, and the bargaining reaches permanent impasse, the individual workers involved will need to obtain other jobs. Finding jobs is likely to be harder when the local labor market is depressed. Therefore, although some details of the process here remain cloudy, rising joblessness might be thought to spawn declining levels of pay. A variant on this species of explanation relies on the explicit assumption of a trade union that worries about both its employed members and its unemployed members. High unemployment means that more of its members are likely to be without work, and that an employed member who is dismissed or laid-off will have difficulty finding new employment. An increase in unemployment may then tilt the union's preferences towards a greater concern with the number of jobs. If this implies a reduced concern for pay, or at least a slightly smaller weight on the target of high remuneration for union members, a lower negotiated level of pay might result.

Although a bargaining or union approach might thereby render intelligible the pattern in the data in figure 1.1, it could be viewed as inappropriate in many settings outside Western Europe and even in some industrial sectors within that part of the globe. Unionism is not pandemic. In the United States, in particular, the great majority of those who hold jobs do not belong to a trade union. This does not make bargaining theory irrelevant, but it raises some doubts about its pertinence.

Another way to provide an intellectual rationale for the wage curve is by appealing to efficiency wage theory. This approach is intrinsically nonunion, so it is potentially suitable for economies that are more like the United States' than Sweden's. The well-known characteristic of efficiency wage analysis is that firms set pay in an environment where the wage influences productivity. Shapiro and Stiglitz (1984) is an archetypal case. In equilibrium, firms try to maximize profits and workers choose how hard to work. If the costs of shirking at work are low, employees put in little effort. The outside rate of unemployment plays a role, because it determines the ease with which a sacked worker can get another job. In a highly depressed labor market, employees are frightened of losing their jobs, and so put in high effort even if pay is comparatively low. Put differently, a marginal rise in unemployment leads to a corresponding marginal fall in the level of wages. The reason is that firms can reduce pay slightly while maintaining a motivated workforce. Unemployment is a discipline device: when it is high the generosity of workers' remuneration can be low. Hence there is an efficiency wage interpretation of figure 1.1's pattern.

A further possibility exists; it is a half-way house between a union model and competitive theory. A "labor contract" model might be able to explain the negative correlation between wages and unemployment. In some versions of labor contract theory, wages and employment are positively correlated. A contract curve slopes upward in wage/employment space because when the wage rate is high it is sensible for the workers and their firm to ensure that as many as possible of those in the labor pool have jobs. To those economists raised on neoclassical labor demand theory, this argument may have a strange ring to it. Should not employment be low when the price of labor is high? In this contractual framework, the answer is that it should not. An efficient labor contract maximizes the joint welfare of employer and employees. Unemployed workers contribute only a little to the surplus earned by the combination. The higher the level of pay, the more desirable it is, from the combination's point of view, to have extra individuals in work and fewer individuals drawing unemployment benefit. An upward-sloping contract curve here acts as a quasi-supply curve. It is, therefore, worth considering as another potential source of a negatively inclined relationship between pay and unemployment. There is a variant on this. Consider a situation in which demand shocks occur randomly and the firm has to design a remuneration package that will both make it money and attract sufficient employees. If the firm dislikes risk, it will wish the wage to rise in good times and to fall in bad times. When there is a boom, many workers are employed. In a slump, some are laid off. There is the basis here for a model in which pay and unemployment are negatively related.

The wage curve in these labor-contract theories is not truly a causal relationship. The variables' apparent interdependence is a trick of the eye. This approach therefore suffers one of the disadvantages of the competitive demand-and-supply apparatus. It is inherently about employment rather than unemployment. To be convincing, an additional step is required.

It has been argued for at least two decades (since Phelps et al. 1970) that convincing macroeconomics requires an explicit microeconomic foundation. The last twenty years have witnessed a wave of such attempts, and the most recent, real business cycle theory, is closer to pure microeconomics than to any traditional macroeconomic model. The research project described in the chapters of this book is in one sense a descendant of the theoretical current that began as a search for microeconomic foundations. In another sense, however, it departs from convention. Later chapters are dominated by inductive rather than deductive reasoning. They are driven by a hunt for empirical regularities at the individual level that might be able to inform judgments about economy-wide interconnections. If later chapters contribute to the microeconomic underpinnings of macroeconomics, they do so in a more empirical way than has been considered usual.

There is a final and more general issue that is tackled—perhaps imperfectly and in a way that may seem to some to be arcane—throughout the ensuing several hundred pages. This is the old and difficult question, "what is the most appropriate macroeconomic model of the economy?"

During the years of this project, theoretical macroeconomics has begun to change. A generation of models has sprung up in which an aggregate wage curve (in this book's terminology) is the primary distinguishing feature. The exact history of this research current is discussed in Layard, Nickell and Jackman (1991) and Phelps (1990, 1992, 1993, 1994). Influential contributions include Rowthorn (1977),[11] Shapiro and Stiglitz (1984), Layard and Nickell (1986), the 1990 *Scandinavian Journal of Economics* sym-

---

11. Rowthorn's work is the earliest we know of, except for Marx's *Capital*, which Rowthorn cites. Rowthorn (1977) argues that it is the wage share that depends negatively upon the amount of unemployment, but the basic conception is the same.

posium issue, and Phelps's early work. Rowthorn (1977:237) talks of the level of demand as a "discipline" that leads to consistency between workers' desire for higher wages and firms' desire for lower wages, and of equilibrium as requiring "the creation of a permanent reserve of unemployed labour ... higher than the frictional amount envisaged by the monetarists." Layard and Nickell (1986) neatly term this process the battle of the markups. A textbook introduction to these ideas is contained in Carlin and Soskice (1990). The gist of all this work is that, in the 1980s, "a surrogate employment supply curve, or equilibrium wage curve, was born" (Phelps, 1992:1004). A review by Michael Woodford (1992:396) describes the new theories succinctly:

All of these imply that labor market equilibrium (i.e., a state in which expectations are fulfilled and transacting parties correctly understand the aggregate state of the economy) lies at the intersection of the derived labor demand curve with a surrogate labor supply curve that lies to the left of, and is flatter than, the true Marshallian labor supply curve.

A recent overview by Lindbeck (1992) adopts the same approach and uses the assumption that there is a wage-setting curve, different from conventional atomistic supply, that slopes upwards in real-wage/employment space. Another model in which a central part is played by the same form of wage equation is the fairness approach described in Akerlof and Yellen (1990).

As Shapiro and Stiglitz (1984) and Layard and Nickell (1986) make clear, the novel aspect of these models is not their assumptions about labor demand, which are the standard ones. Rather, it is that the models replace the conventional labor supply curve with a wage-fixing function. This allows the theories to explain, or at least to be consistent with, both involuntary unemployment and the paradoxical fact—noted by Greenwald and Stiglitz (1993) and others—that real wages fluctuate little over the cycle while the long run supply of workers appears to be close to vertical. The crucial constituent part in this way of thinking is a negatively sloped curve linking the level of pay to the level of unemployment.

In summary, this monograph considers the theoretical idea that wages and local unemployment are linked by a downward-sloping curve, and it attempts to demonstrate that approximately the same curve is visible in the microeconomic data of many nations. Every country seems to have a "wage curve." The notion that there exist empirical laws in social science is, to put it at its mildest, an unconventional one. Nevertheless, most of this book is designed to show that the pattern of a wage curve can be detected in random samples of individuals and establishments in the United States, Great Britain, South Korea, Canada, Austria, Italy, the former Federal Republic of Germany, Switzerland, Ireland, Norway, Netherlands, and Australia. The book also summarizes corroborative secondary results on countries such as Japan, Sweden, the Côte d'Ivoire, and India. Later chapters consider possible explanations for the curve. These include the idea that it is an efficiency wage no-shirking condition, a contract curve, a bargaining power locus, or a scatter of disequilibrium points. The book argues that the wage curve is not a labor supply curve. It endeavors, more broadly, to demonstrate how microeconomic data can be used to tackle macroeconomic questions. The book's purpose is to document a fact and to suggest that much conventional thinking is wrong.

2

Previous Research on Wages and Unemployment across Space

It is a good morning exercise for a research scientist to discard a pet hypothesis every day before breakfast. It keeps him young.

Konrad Lorenz (1966)

2.1 The First Generation

Economists' thoughts about the spatial distribution of wages and unemployment were especially influenced by three papers published at the beginning of the 1970s. These were Harris and Todaro (1970) in the *American Economic Review* and Hall (1970, 1972) in the *Brookings Papers on Economic Activity*. The papers argued that regions with high unemployment would also be ones with high wages. The central idea of these authors is a version of Adam Smith's concept of compensating differentials. Regions with high unemployment are less desirable places to live, other things constant, because it is relatively difficult to find a job there. In a free society, workers can live in any region they choose. Hence, to keep people in an area that has some unpleasant feature, the area has also to have an off-setting advantage. High wages can play that role.

Harris and Todaro (1970) begin their paper by describing a "curious" economic phenomenon taking place in Africa. Despite significant levels of urban unemployment, there is continuing migration from rural areas to the cities.[1] This fact, Harris and Todaro argue, is difficult to explain with conventional economic models. Such models are built around the assumptions of full employment and wage flexibility. Unemployment should therefore be fleeting. Moreover, where it exists, wages should be visibly falling.

---

1. Greenwood (1975) is a survey of the economics of migration, and reveals that the data often fail to show what neoclassical models predict.

Their solution, the Harris-Todaro model, has become famous. It now plays the premier role in understanding the wage and unemployment patterns across regions in developing countries, and is also widely used, as later sections will show, in the analysis of regional unemployment within developed nations. The authors construct a very special framework. It has two sectors: one is a rural region producing an agricultural good and the other an urban region producing a manufactured good. Each sector has a fixed capital stock. Agriculture has a fixed supply of land. Land is not an input in the manufacturing half of the economy. Employment is the only variable input, and it is in fixed supply in the economy as a whole. Firms are price-takers. There is a competitive labor market in agriculture, where the wage equals the value of the marginal product of labor. In the manufacturing sector, however, it is assumed that wages are completely inflexible. The wage is taken to be equal to an exogenously determined number. This number is supposed to be fixed by "institutional" forces. Urban firms then choose their employment levels optimally, equating the value of the marginal product of manufacturing labor with the exogenous rate of pay.

This model could, in principle, generate an equilibrium without any unemployment. Because the agricultural wage is flexible, it could be bid down until all joblessness disappears. Harris and Todaro design their framework so that this does not happen. They assume that migration occurs between the sectors until the wage in agriculture is equal to the "expected wage" in the urban sector. The expected urban wage is the exogenous urban wage multiplied by the probability of getting an urban job. This implicitly assumes a number of facts not explained very fully by the authors.

1. Those who are unemployed in the urban sector receive zero income. Hence the second term in the implicit expected-income formulation is zero. Workers moving into the city have some chance of earning a wage plus one minus that chance of getting zero income.

2. Everyone who wants an urban job must first live in the urban area. Those living in the rural region cannot apply for an urban job.

3. Any individual who migrates to the urban area has some probability of getting a job. That probability is given by the ratio of employment in manufacturing to the stock of employed and unemployed people living in the urban region. Every urban dweller has the same chance of employment.

4. Workers are risk-neutral and so care only about expected income.

These four assumptions are, of course, extreme. Numbers 1 and 4 are restrictive but are not crucial to the authors' argument. Numbers 2 and 3 cannot be accepted as lightly.[2]

The crucial step in the Harris-Todaro logic is that migrants must first pass through the pool of unemployed urban workers. The authors have a vision of a changing world where employees are constantly leaving their employers. Those employers re-hire from the stock of unemployed workers plus employed workers. An individual who lives in the rural region, but who wants an urban job, must move to the city. He or she is at first without work, and lives on money saved from earlier rural employment. Urban jobs are advertised and the migrant applies for them. Eventually he or she gets a job offer. That job does not last forever. The individual then moves back into the stock of jobless workers and waits. Eventually another job comes along. It, too, subsequently ends. This process continues. Equilibrium has the feature that the expected income of an urban dweller is exactly equal to that of a rural dweller. The rural worker earns a low wage without ever being laid off; urban employees earn a high wage for some of the time and are laid-off on zero income for the rest of the time.

In work done separately, Hall (1970) tackles the same underlying issue. His paper contains no explicit model, but does have some intriguing data. The paper begins by plotting 1965 unemployment rates for twelve U.S. cities against 1969 unemployment rates in those cities. The data lie along an upward-sloping line with a gradient of approximately unity. Hall believes that this persistence indicates a degree of structural unemployment that is not easily explained by conventional models. The author's next step is to plot wages against weeks of unemployment. He does this for cities in 1966, producing separate graphs for white males, black males, white females, and black females. The graphs for females are not obviously informative: the scatters take no clear form. For men, however, the data are modestly supportive of the idea of a positive relationship between city pay and city unemployment. Hall's explanation is that "the existence of unemployment in his labor market is a distinct advantage to the employer" (Hall 1970:381), because it reduces quits and thus saves on training and hiring costs. Hence, Hall argues, there is an indeterminacy in the equilibrium in the labor market of a city. High wages and high unemployment counterbalance one another in equilibrium. In a depressed area, firms' costs are low, so they can afford to pay well.

---

2. Fields (1975), however, shows that it is possible to relax the assumptions somewhat and still get the basic Harris-Todaro result.

This theme is taken up in more detail in Hall (1972). The author is again concerned to understand the relationship between an area's pay and its unemployment rate. He begins with a list of ideas that economists would believe to be important. They are that both workers and firms are free to migrate, that wages rise faster in cities with tight labor markets, that cities face random demand shocks, and that different areas have different intrinsic amenities. Hall's analysis, like that of Harris and Todaro, assumes that the expected return to a migrant must equal the income available elsewhere. The expected income, or return, is assumed to equal the wage multiplied by one minus the unemployment rate (that is, the wage times the chance of a job). Then, because in long-run equilibrium each city must offer the same expected income, pay and unemployment will be positively correlated in a cross-section of cities. This captures worker behavior. Hall suggests that there is another relevant locus, namely, a relation between pay and joblessness that stems from employer behavior. The author argues that high unemployment induces high productivity and that this generates, through the equality of the wage with the productivity of labor, another upward-sloping curve linking the wage rate to the unemployment rate. Unemployment in the outside labor market is assumed to help the individual employer by holding down the level of quits.

Hall's model for an individual city is therefore given by the intersection of two curves in wage/unemployment space. Both curves slope up. One describes the requirement that each city offer workers the same expected income. The other describes the requirement that each city offer firms the same expected returns. Hall assumes that there is a unique equilibrium given by the curves' intersection point. Differences in factors such as climate mean that different cities will have different equilibria. Hence real cities will not have identical unemployment rates. Instead, Hall suggests, observed points will lie between and close to the upward lines of the theory.

The next step in Hall (1972) is an examination of the cross-section relationship between the real wage rate and the fraction of the year the average worker is unemployed. As in Hall (1970), this is for twelve cities in 1966. The raw data are shown in table 2.1.

These data come from two regression equations. A wage equation is first estimated, for individual data, in which the independent variables include a set of personal characteristics and dummy variables for the twelve cities. Nominal wages by city are then taken to be the anti-logs of the coefficients on the city dummies. These are deflated by an official index for city price

Table 2.1
Unemployment and wage rates for twelve U.S. cities in 1966

City	Unemployment rate (%)	Real wage	Nominal wage
Washington, D.C.	2.4	3.39	$3.39
Houston	2.4	3.13	$2.87
Chicago	2.6	3.22	$3.32
Cleveland	2.6	3.03	$3.12
Baltimore	2.9	3.25	$3.02
Pittsburgh	3.0	3.19	$3.08
Philadelphia	3.3	3.25	$3.23
Detroit	3.3	3.71	$3.65
St. Louis	3.3	2.98	$3.00
New York	4.2	3.06	$3.33
San Francisco	4.4	3.48	$3.73
Los Angeles	4.5	3.42	$3.45

Source: Hall 1972, p 735.

levels. An equivalent regression method is used to produce the data on city unemployment levels.

Hall plots these data. There is no obvious pattern in the graph of real wages against percent of the year unemployed. The twelve observations, one for each city, make up an almost circular shape (Hall 1972: fig. 2). However, estimating a least-squares line through them produces a positive gradient with a t-statistic of approximately unity. The author accepts that this is weak evidence for the theory's predictions, but offers some experiments. First, use of the official published unemployment rate—instead of the rate derived from a regression—improves the t-statistic to approximately 1.5. Second, switching to the nominal wage and the derived unemployment rate produces a t-statistic of approximately 1.2. Third, a reasonably strong result is obtained by regressing the nominal wage on the official unemployment rate. A t-statistic of just over 2 is produced by this method.

Given the weakness of Hall's statistical results, and the small size of his sample, it is not surprising that his Brookings Panel discussants were critical. Aaron Gordon argues in the published conference remarks that Standard Metropolitan Statistical Area (SMSA) data do not support the idea that areas' unemployment rankings remain the same. He points out that Detroit, for example, had the highest unemployment in 1961 but was near the median in 1964. Gordon also questions the uncertain fit of the relationship between wages and unemployment. He claims that the results are unconvincing. The second discussant of the paper, Charles Holt, is less critical and points to the fruitful theoretical contribution of Hall's analysis. He does, however, suggest that Hall's model is unsuited for an understanding of cyclical changes in unemployment.

The next influential contribution was by Reza (1978). This paper was important because it provided evidence that Hall's (1972) finding was not merely the product of his tiny 1966 data set. Reza begins by repeating the Hall model: there is taken to be an upward-sloping locus for workers and another for firms. Again the data of the world are assumed to lie around a line in between each locus. Reza points out that in principle it is inadequate to estimate simultaneous equations by ordinary least squares, and discusses orthogonal regression estimators. Nevertheless, his main results use OLS and estimate a log wage equation with log unemployment as a regressor.

Reza uses eighteen SMSAs as his regions. He includes the twelve areas that incorporate Hall's cities (New York, Los Angeles-Long Beach, Chicago, Philadelphia, Detroit, San Francisco-Oakland, Washington, Pittsburgh, St. Louis, Cleveland, Baltimore, Houston, Boston, Minneapolis-St. Paul, Dallas, Cincinnati, Milwaukee, and Buffalo). The variable on pay is calculated in two different ways. One takes total per capita earnings by region from 1970 to 1972. The other calculates regional personal income per capita, which includes wages and salaries, net rental income, dividends, interest, and government and business transfer payments. These data include the years 1967 and 1970–1974. Each of the two forms of pay variable is converted from per capita to per worker by multiplying by the ratio of population to employment. Real income and real earnings statistics are calculated by deflating the nominal figures by a Bureau of Labor Statistics (BLS) "budget" or price index. Reza's results show that the cross-section relationship between wages and unemployment is positive. He is not clear about the source of the unemployment data, but it is presumably the BLS SMSA count. All regressions use eighteen observations, and no mention is made of additional control variables, so it appears that the only extra component is the intercept. In each year, and for all pay variables, the coefficient on log unemployment is positive. The t-statistics on unemployment vary for the case of the nominal income equation from 1.88 to 2.96, and for the case of the real income equation from 0.68 to 2.70. The use of earnings data reduces the t-statistics somewhat, but in some years the unemployment variable is significant at the 5% level. Like Hall, perhaps paradoxically, Reza finds that nominal pay works better than real pay in the estimation. The author's conclusion is that unemployment and wages are positively related across space.

Another paper using U.S. data appeared that year. Behman (1978) takes data from twenty-seven states, over the years 1970 to 1975, and estimates unemployment and real wage equations. These are pooled equations with 162 observations; they include year dummies but not state dummies. Equations are also estimated for the labor force participation rate of married women, and for the labor force participation rate of teenagers. A four-equation system is estimated by two-stage least squares. Unemployment data come from the Current Population Survey. The real wage data are calculated by dividing the average nominal hourly earnings of manufacturing workers by the BLS budget data for a four-person family.

As with its precursors, the study's identifying assumptions are probably open to dispute. A set of compositional, migration, tax, and unemployment insurance variables are omitted from the wage equation. This is presumably to identify the wage equation, where the unemployment variable is treated as an instrumented regressor. Unfortunately, most of the independent variables in the wage equation could be viewed as endogenous. Labor productivity, which the author finds to be highly significant, is one example. Leaving aside difficulties of specification, Behman's chief result is that the state unemployment rate enters insignificantly in the wage equation. She concludes, "the unemployment rate ... should be positively related to real wages if there is wage flexibility. As seen ... this hypothesis is rejected" (Behman 1978:172). Such a conclusion is perhaps unwarranted. The point estimate of unemployment in the wage equation is, in fact, positive. The hypothesis being tested by Behman is the null of a zero coefficient on unemployment, and her failure to reject that may not be informative. However, although identification is problematic, Behman's work certainly offers little support for the Hall hypothesis.

It seems obvious at the intuitive level that the spatial structure of wages must depend upon the distribution of inherent amenities across regions. Roback (1982) formalizes this idea and explores it empirically.[3] Her model assumes that firms and workers are mobile and that they locate wherever is most advantageous. Some regions are inherently attractive. They must offer, in equilibrium, wage rates and land rental rates that exactly off-set their natural advantage. Roback assumes that the representative firm is a price-taker producing with a constant returns-to-scale technology. The inputs are labor and land.[4] The firm's profit is a decreasing function of wages and of land rents; the worker's utility function is an increasing function of

---

3. Browne (1978) contains further discussion.
4. It might be thought a logical weakness to assume constant returns and fixed land.

wages and a decreasing function of rents. The region has to provide the going market-levels of profits and utility. Hence there is a unique wage and rent combination that satisfies the requirements of equilibrium. It is given by the intersection, in a two-dimensional diagram with wage and rent as the axes, of a downward-sloping firms' iso-profit contour with an upward-sloping workers' indifference contour. Different areas have different inherent amenities (such as climate) and thus different factor prices.

Roback's (1982) empirical work estimates wage and land rental rate equations for the United States. The wage equations rely on weekly earnings data from the 1973 Current Population Survey (CPS). A sample of males over age eighteen is used. This provides information on 12,000 individuals distributed across ninety-eight major cities. External data on city characteristics are grafted on to the CPS data set. These variables include the crime rate, the unemployment rate, the degree of air pollution, the population growth rate and density, and climate. Roback's variables work strongly in an earnings equation. Moreover, all have the signs expected of them if the variables capture compensating differences across space. Wages are high in regions with a high crime rate; they are low in regions with many sunny days per year. The local unemployment rate enters positively, but not in a statistically significant way, into her wage equation. This study appears to offer support for the general idea that there are compensating differentials across areas, although it does not convincingly demonstrate the role of unemployment in that process.

The idea that regional wages might be positively correlated with regional unemployment is based ultimately on Adam Smith's notion of compensating differentials. The ability of workers and firms to migrate is what underpins this relationship. If, however, migration is costly, agents are likely to see it as an investment. They will be inclined, therefore, to calculate the expected or "permanent" returns and costs. An article by Adams (1985) is one of the early attempts to face up to this and to study the relation between pay and permanent unemployment rates.

Adams (1985) begins by constructing a theoretical model of wage and employment determination. It is a contract model in which firms are subject to random demand shocks. Layoffs occur in bad states of nature. Employees who lose their jobs receive unemployment insurance, but this does not replace the full value of the wage. The replacement ratio is the level of unemployment insurance relative to the level of pay. Adams shows that, conventionally, if the job package must offer some going market-utility level of workers, the wage will be an increasing function of the probability of unemployment and a decreasing function of the replacement ratio. Underlying the analysis is the usual requirement that in a spatial equilibrium each region has to provide the same expected utility.

Adams's work draws upon the U.S. Panel Study of Income Dynamics (PSID) covering 1970 to 1976. There are approximately two thousand workers in each year of the sample. The author merges PSID data with information on published unemployment insurance replacement ratios, derived data on the cyclical sensitivity of industry output, published long-run unemployment rates by state, and published industry unemployment and output growth rates. The latter measures are motivated by the author's concern to allow for the existence of risk-sharing between firms and workers. The crucial regional unemployment rate is calculated as the five-year average of the state unemployment rate centered on the particular year. Hence the 1973 variable, say, is the mean rate for 1971 to 1975. In cross-sectional earnings equations, Adams shows that this average unemployment variable enters positively and significantly, with an elasticity of approximately 0.2. Therefore, other things constant, a state with double the average unemployment rate will have a wage approximately 20% higher. The earnings equations include conventional personal controls. They also include the industry growth and unemployment rates and the state unemployment replacement rate. The latter enters negatively, as predicted by the theoretical model. Interestingly, the current industry unemployment rate is negative in the earnings equations. It has an elasticity of -0.09 in the full sample. This means that a doubling of the industry unemployment rate is associated with a 9% drop in the wage level.

The same issue of the Quarterly Journal of Economics that published Adams (1985) contained a second paper on the same topic. Marston (1985) applies Current Population Survey data through the 1970s. He initially specifies a model of the Harris-Todaro and Hall variety in which wages and unemployment are tied together by a locus with a positive gradient. The author's next step is to show that, using SMSA regions, area unemployment rates' disequilibrium components do not persist for long. This conclusion emerges from estimating autoregressive unemployment equations in which it is possible to distinguish temporary from permanent movements. Marston argues that shocks that disturb the steady-state relationship among regions' unemployment rates tend to be eliminated within a year. The author believes that this adjustment is the result of speedy labor mobility. He suggests that the main influence on observed unemployment rates is the persistent one of regional amenities and pay levels.

Marston estimates probit equations for whether or not individual workers in the sample had a job. These unemployment probit equations give similar results to simple OLS equations. The paper presents estimates for approximately half a million individuals in 1970. The independent variables include a set of individual characteristics and a set of area characteristics. The former are age, gender, race, whether a household head, number of young children, family income, and education. It is the latter, however, that are the key to the author's analysis. These area characteristics are the real wage in the region, variables for amenities such as climate and clean air, and the unemployment insurance replacement-rate in the region. The real area wage enters positively and significantly in the joblessness probits. Marston concludes that the central prediction of the compensating differentials model is confirmed. The signs of the amenity and unemployment insurance variables are also as predicted by that theory.

A more explicitly dynamic model has been developed by Topel (1986). In his paper, he attempts to capture both permanent and transitory effects of labor market shocks. A fairly complicated framework is set out in which there are many different cohorts of workers with different experience levels. Production uses all cohorts; they are imperfect substitutes for one another. Firms are profit-maximizers. A competitive market is assumed. The equilibrium is characterized as the allocation that maximizes the economy's expected real net output. Workers choose among different regions, all of which must offer the same expected utility in long-run equilibrium. Migration is assumed to be costly. Hence workers' choices of locales are investment decisions. Because Topel assumes that different cohorts of workers have different mobility costs, his model predicts that the least-mobile will have the most volatile wage rates. This is because, for them, demand shocks cannot be accommodated as easily by migratory flows. In the model:

1. wages are higher in a region, the higher is the future cost of migration;
2. a rise in expected future demand will reduce current wages.

These properties follow from the fact that employees are more easily attracted to areas which are either going to boom or are, if necessary, easy to migrate out from.

Topel (1986) studies a sample of approximately 80,000 prime-aged males from the Current Population Surveys of 1977–1980 (each of which refers to the year before the survey date). Wages are defined by dividing the ratio of annual earnings by reported weeks worked. Local labor markets are taken to be the fifty states of the United States. A number of labor market variables are calculated. First, regressions are estimated for each state's unemployment on a quadratic time trend. The residuals from these fifty regressions are then used as measures of area demand shocks. Topel is aware that this method is open to the severe criticism that employment movements might by supply-determined. Second, these state employment shocks are used to create weighted averages of forecasts of state disturbances derived from autoregressive time series models. This method provides "expected" demand changes. Third, individual-level measures of the probability of unemployment are derived from the sample. These come from maximum likelihood estimates using as regressors a set of variables including industry, personal, and state characteristics. Fourth, by drawing upon information about unemployment insurance laws in different states, Topel creates a measure of imputed unemployment-income per person.

Equations are then estimated by Topel with the logarithm of weekly earnings as the dependent variable. The personal control variables are education, experience and race. Year dummies are also included. The other demand and unemployment variables are the state employment growth rate, current state employment disturbances, predicted and unpredicted state disturbances, and the probability of unemployment interacted with the state level of unemployment-income replacement rate. All of these enter the regressions in the predicted way. Demand shocks are associated with wage movements. Fast-growing states have higher pay levels. Expected booms, however, are associated with lower wage levels. This, Topel believes, confirms the model's predictions. A high probability of unemployment is only weakly correlated with wages, but the relationship becomes strongly significant once the unemployment probability is weighted by the generosity of unemployment benefit. Consistent with the theory of compensating differentials, the relationship is positive.

By the middle of the 1980s, therefore, there was comparatively little controversy about the spatial forces acting upon unemployment and pay. The framework of Harris and Todaro (1970) and Hall (1970, 1972) had become orthodox theory. High regional pay went with high joblessness in that region.

2.2 The Next Generation

A paper by Blackaby and Manning (1987) was one of the first studies in the United Kingdom to estimate microeconometric wage equations with local

unemployment as an independent variable.[5] It mixes Phillips curve estimation and Mincer-style earnings equations. The former relies on aggregated
regional data, for the regions of Great Britain, across the years 1964 to
1984. Familiar Phillips-style results are generated. The rate of wage change
appears to depend upon the level of unemployment, the rate of change of
unemployment, and the rate of change of prices. However, the authors also
report earnings *level* equations estimated on 7,288 observations for white
male employees in 1974. The data are drawn from the General Household
Survey. This classifies people into ten regions and provides information on
the individuals' characteristics. The principal specification regresses earnings on schooling, experience, experience squared, marital status, number
of weeks worked in the previous year, a set of 23 industry dummies, and
the log of the unemployment rate in the individual's region. The coefficient
on unemployment is -0.16. Because of the logarithmic form, this is a
measure of the cross-section unemployment elasticity of pay. The t-statistic
on unemployment exceeds 10. The equation's R^2 is 0.62, and the other
variables are well-determined.

The authors extend their analysis to other data in Blackaby and Manning
(1990c). Although they mention that the Harris-Todaro-Hall view might be
expected to hold if workers are mobile, the paper's findings run counter to
this expectation. It applies U.K. microeconomic data from the 1975 General
Household Survey and the 1982 General Household Survey. No attempt is
made to examine Phillips curves. Instead the authors estimate Mincer-style
annual earnings equations on 7,288 males for the first year and 4,666 males
for the second year. The control variables include schooling, experience,
marital status, number of weeks worked, industry dummies, occupational
dummies, and the log of the unemployment rate in the individual employee's region. The latter enters negatively and significantly with an elasticity of -0.13 in 1975 and -0.19 in 1982. The authors also experiment
with the inclusion of regional measures for the extent of long-term unemployment and for the cost-of-living by area. These are significant but reduce only slightly the estimated unemployment elasticity of pay. Blackaby
and Manning (1990c:524) conclude that "the general finding of a negative
association between earnings and unemployment is not ... consistent with

---

5. This section describes published research done up until the early 1990s. For the sake of
logical consistency, it tries to exclude most studies done in response to the claims made in
early reports (such as Blanchflower and Oswald (1990b)) of this monograph's results. They
are discussed later. Recent empirical research on wages across space includes Holzer (1991)
and Montgomery (1992), but they do not focus upon the effects of the local unemployment
rate.

the competitive hedonic wage model of labor markets." Blackaby and Manning (1990a, 1990b) contain further results that confirm the negative effect of regional unemployment upon regional earnings. They also tentatively suggest that individuals who have been unemployed for a long time cease to exert downward pressure on pay.

To compare the flexibility of pay in Great Britain and the United States, Freeman (1988a) looks at regional data. He estimates unemployment equations for sixty-one British counties and fifty U.S. states. The log of county/state pay enters positively in each case. It is statistically insignificant in Great Britain and statistically significant in the United States. Both regressions are single cross-sections for 1985; both include controls for education and the proportion of workers employed in manufacturing industry. Freeman also estimates wage equations using time-differenced data. For the period 1970 to 1985, the change in regional pay is negatively correlated with the change in regional unemployment. The t-statistic in the British case is over 3; in the U.S. case it is approximately 1.3. Freeman's conclusion is that the United States does not appear to have a more flexible labor market than its neighbor on the other side of the Atlantic. His empirical work also seems to suggest a radical difference between estimating levels equations across space compared to change equations, and the existence of a negative pay/unemployment relationship once the investigator has controlled for fixed regional effects.

A country with a more centralized bargaining system, Sweden, is studied in Holmlund and Skedinger (1990). Holmlund and Skedinger calculated the determinants of wage "drift," namely, the extent to which local wages drift above nationally-agreed rates of pay. To do this the authors focus on a single sector, the wood industry. This covers the production of lumber and of wooden products such as furniture. Regional data are pooled over sixteen years. The authors regress region-specific pay upon region-specific unemployment rates and various region-specific and aggregate tax and price variables. One representative result (Holmlund and Skedinger, 1990: table 3) is based on a sample of seventy regions from 1969 to 1985, producing approximately 1,200 observations. Local unemployment, entered in two different ways, is negative but not highly significant. These regressions control for regional fixed effects and linear time trends. Holmlund and Skedinger argue that measurement error is likely to bias down the t-statistics on the local unemployment variables, and so instrument with the national unemployment rate and a measure of relative labor cost by region. The result is a better-defined negative effect of area unemployment upon area wages.

One of the most ambitious attempts to analyze regional labor markets in Britain is Pissarides and McMaster (1990). In this study, cross-sections from 1961 to 1982 were pooled. Pissarides and McMaster did not work directly with microeconomic data but rather with published regional-average statistics. One slightly unusual feature of the analysis is that the South-East and East Anglia—two rather different areas—are combined into one region. Northern Ireland is excluded from the analysis. This gives the authors nine regions by twenty-two years, and they estimate pooled migration equations and pooled wage equations. In the latter case, the dependent variable is the change in the region's wage relative to the nation's wage. The independent variables are lagged relative wages, changes and levels of relative unemployment (both current and lagged), and the lagged change in the relative wage. Regional dummies are also included where significant. Year dummies are omitted. This can be justified by the fact that regional variables are measured relative to the national levels. Pissarides and McMaster estimate wages in a dynamic specification to try to uncover the difference between short-run adjustment and long-run equilibrium. Their error-correction specification is estimated using ordinary least squares (OLS). The wage variable is average hourly earnings of male manual workers over age twenty-one. The unemployment variable covers all workers.

Pissarides and McMaster find that changes in a region's relative wage are correlated with its unemployment movements. A rise in relative unemployment induces in the short-run a fall in relative pay. They describe this as "perverse" (Pissarides and McMaster, 1990:823) and suggest that it is a form of Phillips curve effect. Their main concern is the estimation of the steady-state relationship between regional pay and regional joblessness, and for that they set all change terms in their equation to zero. This yields a positively sloped equation between the level of relative wages and the level of relative unemployment. Pissarides and McMaster conclude that, in the long run, a region which has unemployment one percentage point above the national average will have a wage 3.2% above that in the nation as a whole. This result is, in the authors' eyes, the expected one, because the Harris-Todaro locus should ensure that there are compensating pay differentials in areas with high joblessness. The model indicates that adjustment towards this long-run equilbrium proceeds very slowly—taking decades rather than years.

Canadian evidence is contained in Card (1990b). His empirical analysis is based on a sample of 1,293 labor contracts.[6] These are negotiated settle-

---

6. Further results, which include strike variables as regressors, are described in Card (1990a).

ments between 280 firm-union bargaining pairs spanning the sixteen-year period between 1968 and 1983. Although the main purpose of the study is not to explore the regional interactions between wages and unemployment, it reports first-differenced real wage equations in which the provincial unemployment rate (also first-differenced) is included as a regressor. For some provinces, Card is forced to use the national Canadian unemployment rate. Using OLS and instrumental variable methods, and a variety of specifications, the author finds a statistically significant negative effect from the rate of unemployment. The coefficient appears to be stable across specifications. Christofides and Oswald (1992) give fairly similar results on a different sample (these are described in chapter 8).

One of the most extensive studies of regional labor markets is that done by Bartik (1991). He uses data from the 1980 to 1987 March editions of the U.S. Current Population Survey. The data in the author's statistical analysis are for adult males, between age twenty-five and sixty-four, who live in eighty-nine metropolitan statistical areas (MSAs) chosen by Bartik as having sufficient observations to enter the data set. A random subsample of 100 individuals per year was drawn, for each area, for the forty-four MSAs included in the eight March CPS tapes. For the remaining forty-five MSAs that were only identified on the two 1986 and 1987 tapes, all individuals were included. The pooled data set was then of 44,000 observations, covering the eighty-nine small regions over eight years. Twenty-five MSAs offered information on local consumer prices.

Unlike early U.S. investigators in the field, Bartik (1991) controls for unchanging area characteristics. He eliminates these regional fixed effects by estimating all the microeconometric regressions in his book using differenced data. Each variable is defined as the deviation from the MSA mean. Moreover, the author includes in all micro estimating equations a set of demographic controls and time dummies. The former are variables such as education, experience at work, race, and family size. These, too, are entered as deviations from means.

Bartik (1991) does not study the effect of unemployment across space. Instead his concern is the interplay between wages and employment. A representative result (Bartik, 1991: table 6A1.4) is that in an OLS real wage equation the local employment level enters positively with a *t*-statistic of a little over two. Many variants on this basic finding are presented, using different definitions of the wage variable and sometimes different data. Bartik estimates that, in micro data, a one percent employment upward shock leads to a 0.26 of 1% rise in real pay.[7] This estimate changes slightly if a long set of lagged employment variables are used as explanatory variables. Allowing for eight lags on metropolitan area employment, the impact of a unit shock is estimated to be 0.17 rather than 0.26. Bartik (1991:152) argues that local growth raises wages, but that some of the effect decays over time ("presumably due to in-migration"). The author concludes that this wage effect works not through higher pay within an occupation but through individuals' quicker promotion up a wage hierarchy. Promoted individuals, in his view, are able to keep their better-paying jobs even in the long-run. The empirical results in Bartik (1991) suggest that employment growth in an area has especially large (positive) effects upon the pay of blacks and young workers.

Because he is conscious that employment and wages may be determined endogenously, Bartik estimates some wage equations using two-stage least squares. For this he needs an instrument that shifts labor demand but is uncorrelated with disturbances in the wage equation (which the author views as a kind of labor supply curve). Bartik uses as an instrument the share effect from a shift-share analysis of each metropolitan area's employment. In other words, the author first calculates which industries grew disproportionately in each region. These differences from the national average are then viewed as indicators of regional deviations of labor demand from the national average. Current and lagged values are shown to predict well the endogenous employment variable. Using this form of instrumental variable in a wage equation, Bartik shows that long-run two-stage least squares (2SLS) estimates are not significantly different from long-run OLS estimates. Both methods predict the same increase in pay in response to a local employment rise. However, the 2SLS coefficient's standard error is approximately equal to the size of the coefficients, so the t-statistic on pay is only approximately unity. The author argues that the point estimate should be taken more seriously than the small t-statistic. Nevertheless, this seems a potentially critical weakness, because the key variable loses significance.

The theoretical interpretation favored by Bartik is that his analysis reveals the importance of hysteresis in the labor market. The mechanism is the following. Imagine that labor demand rises in an area. Because of an initial shortage of labor, employers relax their hiring standards. Jobs then become filled more quickly. This "forced" hiring and promotion leads to

---

7. In private correspondence with us, Tim Bartik estimates that the implied unemployment elasticity of wages in his study is roughly −0.1.

faster skill acquisition. There are long-run gains in the form of improved human capital. Wages are thereby permanently raised. According to this intellectual account, booms deliver wage hikes. Rates of pay never drop back to their original levels. As the author is aware, the exact process is not easy to justify theoretically. Although Bartik mentions efficiency wage theory (fairly briefly), it is not clear whether he sees this as the explanation for the apparent rejection of competitive analysis.

A similar kind of study has been done by Eberts and Stone (1992). The authors examine the determination of pay and employment using U.S. data from the Current Population Surveys from 1973 to 1987. Wage regressions are estimated for each year. After controlling for standard personal characteristics, skill-adjusted wage differentials are obtained as the estimated coefficients on a set of twenty-one dummy variables for different metropolitan areas. The empirical work is restricted to twenty-one SMSAs (out of a possible forty-six) to ensure consistent time-series information on employment levels. Wage estimates for each area are converted to deviations from the average by subtracting the national average wage in the relevant year. Eberts and Stone (1992) estimate a first-difference wage equation on pooled data. The explanatory variables include year dummies and a set of six lagged levels of employment. Three of these are negative and three are positive. The cumulative response, in steady-state equilibrium, is 0.2 with a t-statistic greater than two. Inverting this, Eberts' and Stone's estimate of the long-run wage elasticity of labor supply is approximately five. This is one of the highest labor supply elasticities ever recorded in an econometric study.[8] The authors also estimate a labor demand curve, which has a wage elasticity of -1. There is no attempt to allow for simultaneity, although the authors suggest that identification is achieved through the use of lags.

Eberts' and Stone's (1992) results imply that demand shocks have permanent effects upon the level of pay in an area. A rise in demand at first causes wages to overshoot, reaching a peak after approximately five years. Wages decline subsequently, but stay above their original level. Although the authors do not discuss it, this behavior appears to be inconsistent with a competitive model in which different areas are individually wage-takers.

A paper conceptually like that of Pissarides and McMaster (1990) is Blackaby and Manning's 1992 study of regional earnings and unemployment. To try to distinguish between long-run and short-run effects, the authors estimate an error-correction model of regional wage and unem-

---

8. For example, those listed in Pencavel's (1986) survey are much lower.

ployment determination. Their data are for the ten standard regions of Britain for the years 1972 to 1988. One unconventional feature of the empirical analysis is that the independent variables are measured relative to their national averages, whereas the dependent variable in the wage equation is not. The wage variable uses gross weekly earnings for males. These raw statistics are corrected for composition effects by weighting them by the size of different industrial employment levels within each region. An "expected" earnings figure is thereby generated. This is the wage that a region should be paying, after allowing for its particular industrial mix, if its workers earn at exactly the national average rate. The dependent variable in the estimated earnings equations is the rate of change of the deviation of the log of actual wages from expected wages. Blackaby's and Manning's (1992) appendix notes that similar results were obtained when the industry weighting was not done. Hence the reported equations are very close to a specification in which all variables are measured relative to a national average.

Blackaby and Manning (1992) estimate wage equations and unemployment equations. The equations include as explanatory variables the proportion of unemployed people in the region who have been out of work for more than a year, the average regional house price, the consumer price index in the region, and the level of per-capita GDP. Because wages and unemployment are assumed to be endogenously determined, exclusion restrictions are required for the estimation. The authors assume that regional GDP does not enter the wage equation, and that cost-of-living variables do not enter the unemployment equation. Lagged values of regional variables are also used as instruments. Both the wage and unemployment equations are estimated by instrumental variable methods; these specify the dependent variable as a rate of change; they include current and lagged explanatory variables, both in levels and changes.

The results in Blackaby and Manning (1992) hint that wages and unemployment are linked in a complex way. First, an increase in unemployment acts in the short-run to reduce earnings within the region. Approximately half of the wage effect comes through in the first year. Second, wages depend upon the degree to which unemployment is long-term. The variable for the proportion of unemployed people who have not worked for at least the previous year enters positively in the wage equation. Blackaby and Manning include a variable defined as "the unemployment rate minus the long-term unemployment rate." This is intended to capture the Layard and Nickell (1986, 1987) and Nickell (1987) idea that only the short-term unemployed affect wages (perhaps because the long-term unemployed are discouraged and stop applying for jobs). The variable enters significantly negatively. A variable for the long-term unemployment proportion is positive and significant. These conform to Layard's and Nickell's predictions. Third, in the unemployment equation the wage is estimated to have a positive effect, in the long run, upon the degree of joblessness in a region. The authors conclude that this is evidence for a neoclassical labor demand curve. They note in a footnote that it could be a Harris-Todaro locus, but cannot rationalize such an interpretation with the negative slope found in the long-run in the wage equation.

In a recent paper Blanchard and Katz (1992) study the dynamics of labor markets across U.S. regions. They construct two models. The first assumes full employment, a downward-sloping labor demand curve in each region, demand shocks, and migration by firms and workers toward favorable areas. The second allows for unemployment by adding an extra equation, which states that a region's relative wage is a decreasing linear function of the region's relative unemployment rate. The authors do not explain where this equation comes from, nor what economic mechanism underlies it. In other respects, however, the modeling has conventional neoclassical features. In the model, an adverse shock to relative labor demand increases unemployment in the short run. Wages fall. There is then out-migration of workers (who want to get away from low pay and high joblessness) and in-migration of firms (who seek the extra profits provided by low wage rates). These migration flows help to restore the regions' unemployment and wage levels. Blanchard's and Katz's model has no hysteresis, so shocks have no long-run effects on unemployment or workers' remunerations. Although Blanchard and Katz do not discuss it in detail, the model appears to have the Harris-Todaro feature that long-run regional pay is positively correlated with long-run regional unemployment (to see this, set migration to zero in the third of the equations on p. 21 of Blanchard and Katz 1992).

Blanchard and Katz (1992) examine postwar data on the states of the United States. The data show that, in a cross-section of fifty states, the relative unemployment rate in 1975 is a poor predictor of the relative unemployment rate in 1985. A scatter diagram reveals no pattern, and the regression line has a slope of 0.03 with a t-statistic of 0.2. The authors report that a stronger correlation exists for other choices of time period. Between 1970 and 1990, for example, the regression coefficient is 0.41 with a t-statistic of 3.8. The tests favor the view that there is a permanent component to the spatial unemployment structure of the United States. Impulse response functions, based on AR(2) unemployment equations for each state, suggest that relative unemployment rates return to their mean after six to ten years. Wages, they find, are much slower to return to their mean value. Using average hourly earnings of production workers in manufacturing, and an AR(4) structure with fixed effects for each state, Blanchard and Katz suggest that a unit shock continues to have an effect on pay of 0.2 after twenty years have passed.

Figure 10 on page 39 of Blanchard and Katz (1992) provides interesting information about the long-run relationship between joblessness and pay. The figure plots twenty-year average wages and twenty-year average unemployment, for each of fifty states, over the period 1970 to 1990. The scatter of 50 points lies around an upward-sloping line. The regression coefficient is positive, with a t-statistic of 3.1, and the R^2 is 0.16. This is consistent, as the authors note, with the relation identified by Hall (1970) on his much smaller sample. Hall, of course, uses current rather than average unemployment. The dynamic correlation between wages and employment points to quite a different relationship, however, and the authors' calculations indicate that recessions create wage falls. In a vector autoregressive system, estimated with pooled 1952 to 1990 data, and allowing for state dummies, a negative employment shock generates a decrease in pay. A downward shock to employment also raises unemployment. Blanchard and Katz (1992) calculate the implied inverse co-movement of wages and unemployment in a somewhat different way to that presented here. In a private communication dated 22d September 1993, Blanchard and Katz estimated for us that their unemployment elasticity of pay, using the definition in this book, is approximately -0.05. A 1 percentage point rise in unemployment from 5% to 6% reduces pay 1%.

A final paper that is relevant here, but is of a different kind, is Jones (1989). The author finds that local unemployment enters negatively and significantly in estimated equations for the reservation wage. His analysis draws upon cross-section data on 1096 unemployed individuals in Great Britain in 1982. This was a recession year in which the mean local unemployment rate in the author's data is 14%. Individuals in the sample were asked, "What is the lowest amount in take-home pay you would be prepared to accept from a new job?" The answers were grouped into ranges. Using mid-points of these, Jones estimates a log reservation wage equation using as controls a set of personal characteristics. These characteristics include the log of past earnings and the log of current unemployment benefits. The author reports OLS and instrumental variable estimates. The coefficient on the level of local unemployment varies from -0.005 to -0.018, with most estimates closer to the latter. The author does not report an elasticity. At the reported mean, if -0.01 is taken as a reasonable central estimate of the author's coefficient, it appears that the regional unemployment elasticity of reservation pay is -0.14.

2.3 Conclusions

Until recently there was consensus about the way in which wages and unemployment are related across space. High-unemployment regions, orthodox theory says, will be high-wage regions. If they were not, people would leave in large numbers, for workers would not tolerate repeated joblessness unless compensated by good pay once employed.

Although the broad concept of compensating differentials dates back at least to Adam Smith, its application in this area was stimulated by Harris and Todaro (1970). The same idea, that pay and unemployment ought to be positively correlated across geographical areas, is presented in Hall (1970, 1972). Unlike Harris and Todaro, Hall has in mind a developed economy setting, and presents data as well as theory. The positive slope found in Hall's analysis of a small sample of U.S. cities was subsequently replicated by other Americans. Reza (1978), Adams (1985), and Marston (1985) all discover a positive and significant relationship between what workers earn in a region and the rate of unemployment in that region. Behman (1978) and Roback (1982) obtain a positive correlation, but one that is not statistically significant. Topel's (1986) results, although of a different kind, are also consistent with the theory that regions offer compensating differentials.

By the end of the 1980s, this accord had begun to crumble. Evidence had started to emerge that regional wage and unemployment rates were negatively correlated.[9] In a series of papers, Blackaby and Manning (1987, 1990a, 1990b, 1990c, 1992) find apparently powerful evidence for some form of negative spatial relationship between joblessness and workers' remuneration. Their data are from Great Britain. Freeman (1988a) offers complementary results for the United States and British results at a more disaggregated level than presented by previous analysts. Card (1990a, 1990b), using data on Canadian union contracts, obtains findings that look somewhat like Freeman's. Holmlund and Skedinger (1990) for Sweden, and Jones (1989) for U.K. reservation wages, are similar. Pissarides and

---

9. This statement refers to unemployment and wage *levels*, and not to regional Phillips curves.

McMaster (1990) argue that in the United Kingdom the short-run impact of a rise in regional unemployment is to depress pay. In the long run, however, they suggest that the two are positively correlated. With the help of much larger data sets, Bartik (1991) and Blanchard and Katz (1992) obtain evidence that the Harris-Todaro view of U.S. regional labor markets is, at the very best, incomplete.[10] These findings are not easily reconciled with the textbook model of the labor market.

---

10. Blanchflower and Oswald (1990a, 1990b) and Blanchflower et al. (1990) also find evidence for a negative unemployment effect in wage equations. More complete statements of these results are given later, so they are not summarized in this chapter. Some other authors' post-1990 papers are discussed in later chapters.

3   Theoretical Issues

In the case of the labor market, our preoccupation with price-mediated market clearing as the natural equilibrium condition may be a serious error.

Robert Solow (1986)

This chapter questions the central theoretical idea in the orthodox work described in the previous chapter. It develops models in which wages are negatively related to the local rate of unemployment. The analysis can be viewed as an attempt to understand the supply half of the scissors that describes labor market equilibrium. Orthodox demand-and-suppply theory, however, plays only a small role in this chapter. This is because, as will become clear, one of the underlying ideas in this book is that the competitive model of the labor market is probably an inadequate framework for the study of pay and unemployment.[1]

The theoretical tradition begun by Harris and Todaro (1970) has built upon the notion that, across space, wages and unemployment are to be thought of as positively related. Yet there are four broad reasons to predict the reverse—that high unemployment will be associated with low pay.

1. The first reason can be found in so-called contract models of the labor market. These suggest that observed wage and employment combinations may be points on an upward-sloping efficiency locus. The intuitive idea is that when pay is high it is a waste of resources to leave workers idle. A contract curve might therefore be expected to generate a downward-sloping curve in a diagram with wages and unemployment as the axes.

---

1. This view may be controversial. The February 1992 symposium issue of the *Quarterly Journal of Economics*, for example, has ten papers on wage determination and inequality, but none uses noncompetitive theory.

2. A second argument follows efficiency wage theory in stressing the role of unemployment as a motivator. In a booming labor market, firms may have to pay well to ensure that individual workers, who know that there are many other jobs open to them, exert enough effort at work. In a depressed labor market, where workers are keen to hang on to their existing jobs, employers can pay low wages. Again a downward-sloping curve results.

3. The third reason recognizes that workers have little bargaining power when surrounded by extreme levels of joblessness. It will be difficult in such circumstances for employees to find another good job; employers, when they come to the bargaining table, know that. This rationale fits well with union and other bargaining theories and even, more generally, with Marxist accounts of the role of the reserve army of the unemployed. It provides another rationale for a negative association between wages and local unemployment.

4. A fourth possibility builds upon the idea of persistent disequilibrium (this is the kind of model in McCormick and Sheppard, 1992). If the labor market adjusts sluggishly, non-equilibrium states may routinely be observed, and these may trace out a negatively inclined set of points in wage and unemployment space. Slumps, on this view, generate both depressed pay and depressed employment opportunities. Such an account is reminiscent of the Phillips curve, and overlaps somewhat with labor contract theory. Although it might be thought to confuse the distinction between low wages and falling wages, this disequilibrium view needs to be considered.

Despite first appearances, these four lines of argument do not preclude a role for some form of Harris-Todaro locus. They suggest only that, by thinking predominantly of the role of compensating differentials within an exclusively competitive model, the existing regional literature may be incomplete. Later sections draw upon aspects of Harris and Todaro (1970) and Hall (1970, 1972), but also attempt to show why those papers can be misleading.

3.1 A Labor Contract Model of the Wage Curve

3.1.1 Preliminaries

This section constructs a contract model of the labor market in which workers are paid a competitively determined level of utility. The conditions for a downward-sloping cross-section relationship between pay and unemployment are explored. Although later sections discuss the way in which noncompetitive rent-sharing models can generate a "wage curve" relationship, this segment of the chapter largely eschews noncompetitive assumptions.[2] Because traditional classical models of the labor market have difficulty predicting the existence of unemployment, the analysis takes as its starting point the kind of model introduced by Baily (1974) and Azariadis (1975), in which contractual relationships are an optimal response to immobility and product market uncertainty. The terminology of the chapter will follow the idea of a distribution of wages and unemployment across regions. However, all of the results can be rephrased as propositions about wage and employment distributions across industrial sectors, or across other kinds of disaggregated structures (for example, different occupations or different countries). The applicability of the models will therefore be wider than might at first be apparent.

It is useful to begin with the commonplace observation that real countries are not perfectly homogeneous. Each falls naturally into different regions, and these regions are typically dissimilar from one another. California is like neither Massachusetts nor Alaska. Scotland is different from the London conurbation. The north of Italy is unlike the mezzogiorno of the south. For the purpose of the analysis, these regional variations can be divided into at least four economic types:

1. different nonpecuniary features (intrinsic niceness or lack of it),

2. different technologies,

3. different probabilities of demand shocks,

4. different unemployment benefit levels.

Although it is possible to construct an analytical framework in which these are incorporated simultaneously, it is simpler and more efficient to examine them one at a time. The next four sections treat (1) to (4) in turn. Later sections consider criticisms of the contract approach.

3.1.2   Regions with Different Nonpecuniary Characteristics

Imagine an economy divided into many geographical regions. Assume that these areas differ in only one way: they offer varying nonpecuniary utility

---

2. Labor contract theory is usually viewed as a variant on competitive theory, because workers earn no rents.

levels to those people who live there. Some regions, in other words, are pleasant, while others are unpleasant. It is possible to think of all kinds of reasons why these variations might arise. Difference in climate is perhaps the most obvious possibility; another might be differing degrees of congestion; a third could be differences in the scenic quality of the environment. Although not essential for the analysis to come, it will be convenient to think of these differences as exogenous.[3]

Assume that, at the start of any period, each individual must choose where to live, and that he or she can, at this stage, move costlessly to whichever region is thought most likely to provide the highest (pecuniary plus nonpecuniary) utility. After this point, however, assume that it is prohibitively costly to move again during the time period. This is an abstraction from the real world of constantly migrating individuals; but it captures, in a simple way, the fact that moving regions is possible but too costly to do often.

Assume that individuals all wish to work. They get utility from income and from the nonpecuniary aspects of their environment. Those who are employed in region j have utility

$$u = u(w) + \phi(j), \tag{3.1.1}$$

where $u(w)$ is an increasing concave function of wage w, and $\phi(j)$ is nonpecuniary utility, which is a function of the identity of the region. The regions can be thought of as ordered by the size of their ϕ. Thus if j^0 is the region with the lowest nonpecuniary utility, assume that $\phi(j^0)$ is the lowest value of ϕ in the economy. Similarly, assume that $\phi(j^1)$ is the value in utility units of living in the economy's nicest region. The additive separability in (3.1.1) is an extreme but useful assumption.

Assume that those who are unemployed receive unemployment benefits from an outside source like the government. Thus someone without a job in region j has utility

$$u = u(b) + \phi(j), \tag{3.1.2}$$

where b is unemployment benefit. This formulation implicitly makes two assumptions. First, as in equation (3.1.1), the utility function is additively separable in (benefit) income and nonfinancial rewards. Second, the size of the non-pecuniary returns to being in a region is independent of whether the individual works or is unemployed. Because b will be taken as fixed throughout the initial analysis, it is worth noting that it can be interpreted

---

3. This is obviously not true of congestion. The chapter returns to this issue.

as the exogenous value of full-time leisure. It is then possible to dispense with the assumption that there are government unemployment benefits. A later section considers the case where benefit levels (or values of leisure) vary geographically.

Each region is assumed to have one representative employer. This firm is a price taker and uses only workers' labor to manufacture a single product. Each region has the same technology, and workers are equally productive everywhere. The firm's ex post profit is taken to be

$$\pi = \theta f(n) - wn, \tag{3.1.3}$$

where θ is the exogenous product price, $f(n)$ is an increasing concave production function, w is the wage rate, and n is the number of employees. Ex ante, however, there is uncertainty about the price (or demand shock) θ. Assume it is described by a known density function $g(\theta)$. The firm's expected profits are therefore

$$E\pi = \int [\theta f(n) - wn] g(\theta) \, d\theta. \tag{3.1.4}$$

Most of the analysis will assume that firms are risk-neutral, so that (3.1.4) is the employer's maximand. Assume, at this stage, that every region has the same $g(\theta)$.

Consider a region with m inhabitants, all of whom are willing to work. If only n people are employed at wage w, the remaining $m - n$ receive unemployment benefit b. Consider the position before the state of nature occurs. Assuming individuals are identical, the expected utility of each is, for a given level of demand θ,

$$\hat{u} = \frac{n}{m} [u(w) + \phi(j)] + \left(1 - \frac{n}{m}\right) [u(b) + \phi(j)], \tag{3.1.5}$$

namely, a convex combination of the utility from having a job and the utility from being unemployed. Because n and w may be functions of the demand variable, the representative worker's expected utility, and thus (3.1.5), could be written more fully as

$$Eu = \int \left\{ \frac{n}{m} [u(w) + \phi(j)] + \left[1 - \frac{n}{m}\right] [u(b) + \phi(j)] \right\} g(\theta) \, d\theta \tag{3.1.5*}$$

where it is assumed that $n \leq m$, so that employment in a region cannot exceed its population. For notational simplicity, equation (3.1.5*) has not written out n and w explicitly as functions of θ.

In equilibrium, each region of the economy must offer the same expected utility to its inhabitants. If that were not true, migration would occur until some regions were empty or the inter-regional utility differences were eliminated. This does not mean that, at any point, an individual in region r' receives the same utility as a person in region r''. Region r' may have had a luckier draw from the distribution $g(\theta)$; Mr. A in region r'' may be unemployed. It is only on average that regions need be equally attractive. If the economy's going expected level of worker utility is $\bar{u}$, any region j must offer $\bar{u}$. Thus, in terms of equation (3.1.5*),

$$Eu \geq \bar{u} \qquad \text{for all } j \tag{3.1.6}$$

with strict equality in equilibrium. Workers spread themselves evenly across space. For maximum simplicity, think of an economy as divided into a set of equally sized regions. Hence m is constant across areas.

Each region's employer attempts to maximize its expected profits. To do so it has to solve the following problem: choose $w(\theta)$ and $n(\theta)$ to

$$\text{Maximize} \int [\theta f(n) - wn]g(\theta)\,d\theta \tag{3.1.7}$$

$$\text{subject to} \int \left\{ \frac{n}{m}[u(w) + \phi(j)] + \left(1 - \frac{n}{m}\right)[u(b) + \phi(j)]\right\}g(\theta)\,d\theta \geq \bar{u} \tag{3.1.8}$$

This is a version of the implicit contracts discussed in Azariadis (1975) and Baily (1974). The firm and workers implicitly agree on a state-contingent wage level and a state-contingent employment level. These provide the maximum return to the employer while simultaneously offering at least as high a utility level as available to workers in another region. Workers who consent to work in region j are therefore assured, for any particular demand shock θ, of some implicitly agreed wage and employment level. Those who are unlucky enough to be unemployed, after θ occurs, are by assumption unable to move regions during the period. They are the jobless.

The maximization problem takes a simple isoperimetric form. Hence attach a noncontingent multiplier, λ, to the constraint and form the Lagrangean

$$L = \int [\theta f(n) - wn]g(\theta)\,d\theta$$

$$+ \lambda \int \left\{ \frac{n}{m}[u(w) + \phi(j)] + \left(1 - \frac{n}{m}\right)[u(b) + \phi(j)]\right\}g(\theta)\,d\theta \tag{3.1.9}$$

The firm thereby chooses a wage schedule and an employment schedule. Each are functions, $w(\theta)$ and $n(\theta)$, defined for every possible demand-level, θ. The first-order conditions for a maximum include

$$\frac{\partial L}{\partial w(\theta)} = -1 + \lambda u'(w)\frac{1}{m} = 0 \qquad (3.1.10)$$

$$\frac{\partial L}{\partial n(\theta)} = \theta f'(n) - w + \frac{\lambda}{m}[u(w) - u(b)] = 0 \qquad (3.1.11)$$

These can be written more intuitively as

$$u'(w) = \frac{m}{\lambda} \qquad (3.1.12)$$

$$\frac{u(w) - u(b)}{u'(w)} = w - \theta f'(n). \qquad (3.1.13)$$

Equations (3.1.12) and (3.1.13) are the conventional equations of contract theory. The nonpecuniary advantages of an area have dropped out of each equation. Conditions (3.1.12) and (3.1.13) are of importance to the model. The first defines the equilibrium wage. Because m and λ are both constant, the marginal utility of income to a worker, $u'(w)$, is also constant. Hence

$$w(\theta) = w \qquad (3.1.14)$$

$$= \text{a constant independent of } \theta. \qquad (3.1.15)$$

This is the wage rigidity result of implicit contract theory. Intuitively, workers are risk-averse while firms are not, so the optimal labor contract takes the form of a steady wage in which firms insure their employees from fluctuations in product demand. The result does not mean that every region pays the same, but that each region's wage rate is independent of current selling prices in the output market.

The equation (3.1.13) is an implicit function that defines the relationship between wages, employment, and the state of product demand. It appears both in contract theory and in the theory of efficient trade union bargains (McDonald and Solow, 1981, for example).[4] Equation (3.1.13) can be thought of as a contract curve in wage-employment space. It defines a

4. Recent literature on models of unions includes Calmfors and Horn (1986), Carruth and Oswald (1987b), Farber (1986), Oswald (1982, 1985), Pencavel (1984, 1985, 1991), and Solow (1985). Booth (1994) gives an overview.

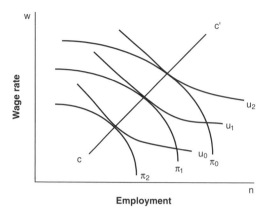

Figure 3.1
The contract curve cc'

locus of tangency points between workers' indifference curves and the employer's indifference, or iso-profit, curves.

Equation (3.1.13) is sketched in figure 3.1. Labelled as cc' in the diagram, it has a positive gradient, so that higher wages are associated with higher levels of employment. The figure is drawn for a fixed product price shock, that is, a given θ. In principle, the diagram could have a third dimension for selling prices, θ.

To derive the algebraic properties of (3.1.13), write it as a function

$$n = n(w, b, \theta), \tag{3.1.16}$$

which requires merely that $f'(n)$ is monotonic in employment. The derivatives of this employment function are

$$n_w = \frac{[u(w) - u(b)]u''(w)}{\theta f''(n)[u'(w)]^2} > 0 \tag{3.1.17}$$

$$n_b = \frac{u'(b)}{u'(w)\theta f''(n)} < 0 \tag{3.1.18}$$

$$n_\theta = -\frac{f'(n)}{\theta f''(n)} > 0. \tag{3.1.19}$$

Along the locus of efficient points, therefore, employment, n, is an increasing function of the wage rate, w, and of the product price level, θ, and a decreasing function of the unemployment benefit level, b. Figure 3.1 illustrates the first of these three relationships.

Some intuitive explanation of (3.1.13) comes from rewriting it in the following way:

$$\frac{u(w) - u(b)}{u'(w)} \qquad + \qquad [\theta f'(n) - w] = 0 \qquad (3.1.20)$$

the net gain to workers,   the net gain to the
in real income units,   employer from taking
from taking on one   on one extra employee
extra employee

The firm and its workers can be thought of here as a single unit trying to maximize joint utility. When employment increases by one person, there are two effects on the whole unit's income. First, one worker's utility rises from $u(b)$ to $u(w)$. Second, the employer's revenue increases by $\theta f'(n)$ and its costs by w. Therefore, when the above equation holds, the gains to the firm/workers unit have been exhausted. The benefit from employing another individual, from the pool of m possible workers, is zero. The model assumes that this process is at work in each geographical area.

Up to this point the analysis has been concerned largely with wages and employment inside a region. But the focus will be its implications for the cross-section pattern of wage rates, employment levels, and unemployment levels. These are captured in three propositions.

PROPOSITION 1.1   Regions have different wage and unemployment levels. High-*j* regions (that is, attractive ones) have low wage rates.

Proof   It is intuitively obvious that nicer places must, in a steady state, have worse wage and unemployment levels than unpleasant places. To show in a formal way that regions cannot have the same wage and unemployment rates, assume the reverse, to establish a contradiction. Consider two regions, *i* and *k*. Assume that $\phi(k) \neq \phi(i)$, so that the regions differ in their nonpecuniary attributes. By the assumption of identical wage and employment levels, and the requirement that each region offer individuals expected utility $\bar{u}$, it follows that

$$\bar{u} = \int \left\{ \frac{n}{m}[u(w) + \phi(i)] + \left(1 - \frac{n}{m}\right)[u(b) + \phi(i)] \right\} g(\theta)\, d\theta \qquad (3.1.21)$$

$$= \int \left\{ \frac{n}{m}[u(w) + \phi(k)] + \left(1 - \frac{n}{m}\right)[u(b) + \phi(k)] \right\} g(\theta)\, d\theta \qquad (3.1.22)$$

By subtraction, therefore,

$$[\phi(i) - \phi(k)] \int \left\{ \frac{n}{m} u(w) + \left(1 - \frac{n}{m}\right) u(b) \right\} g(\theta) \, d\theta = 0 \tag{3.1.23}$$

or simply

$$\phi(i) = \phi(k). \tag{3.1.24}$$

This is the required contradiction.

To establish the second part of Proposition 1.1, which is intuitive, again assume the reverse in order to get a contradiction. Hence assume that the wage in region k exceeds that in region i, and that $\phi(k) > \phi(i)$. Because employment, by (3.1.17), is increasing in the wage, this implies that employment in k exceeds employment in i. It follows immediately that region k has lower unemployment, and so offers higher expected utility than i, which contradicts the requirement that both offer $\bar{u}$.

A more valuable result is encapsulated in the following.

PROPOSITION 1.2   There is a negatively sloped function (a "wage curve") linking wages and unemployment across regions.

Proof   By Proposition 1.1, high-j regions (that is, regions with nice nonpecuniary attributes) pay lower wages than less pleasant regions. By the contract curve equation, and especially (3.1.17), there is a positive association between pay and employment within any region. Moreover, regions in this framework have the same benefit levels and demand shocks. Thus region j's unemployment rate can be defined as

$$U^j = m - n(w^j, b, \theta) \tag{3.1.25}$$

where by equation (3.1.17)

$$\frac{\partial U^j}{\partial w^j} < 0. \tag{3.1.26}$$

This demonstrates that low-wage regions have high unemployment rates, and vice versa.

There is an implicit assumption that should be brought out here. It is that the price or demand shock is common to all regions: it is a kind of uniform macroeconomic shock. If different regions had different draws from the density function of shocks, the wage curve would intermittently disappear from the cross-section data (if, say, attractive regions were, by chance, all hit by a slump specific to them). The instantaneous cross-section relationship between wages and unemployment is therefore negative. This is one

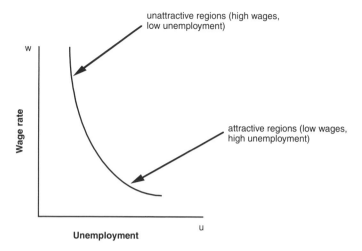

Figure 3.2
The wage curve across regions

theory of a downward-sloping relationship such as in figure 3.2 (which can be redrawn as figure 3.3). However, a special version of the old idea of a positive association between unemployment and pay levels—the compensating-differentials argument—is correct ceteris paribus in the long run.

PROPOSITION 1.3   Holding nonpecuniary characteristics constant, there is a positively sloped function linking wages and expected unemployment.

Proof   Workers in a region must be offered

$$\bar{u} = \int \left\{ \frac{n}{m}[u(w) + \phi] + \left(1 - \frac{n}{m}\right)[u(b) + \phi] \right\} g(\theta)\, d\theta \tag{3.1.27}$$

where ϕ is nonpecuniary utility. By optimal firm behavior, the wage is independent of θ. Hence the expression can be rewritten

$$\bar{u} = [u(w) + \phi] \int \frac{n}{m} g(\theta)\, d\theta + [u(b) + \phi]\left[1 - \int \frac{n}{m} g(\theta)\, d\theta\right] \tag{3.1.28}$$

$$= [u(w) + \phi](1 - U^e) + [u(b) + \phi]U^e, \tag{3.1.29}$$

where U^e is the expected rate of unemployment in the region, defined as

$$U^e \equiv 1 - \int \frac{n}{m} g(\theta)\, d\theta. \tag{3.1.30}$$

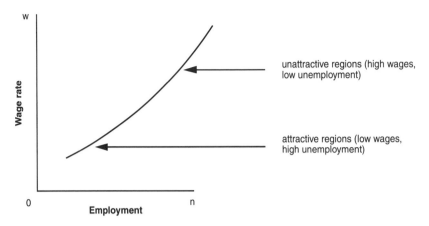

Figure 3.3
The curve in wage-employment space

Holding $\bar{u}$, ϕ, and b constant, therefore, the relationship between changes in wages and changes in expected unemployment is, from (3.1.29),

$$0 = u'(w)[1 - U^e]\,dw + [u(b) - u(w)]\,dU^e. \qquad (3.1.31)$$

The slope of this generalized Harris-Todaro condition is

$$\frac{dw}{dU^e} = \frac{u(w) - u(b)}{u'(w)(1 - U^e)} > 0, \qquad (3.1.32)$$

which establishes the necessary positive correlation.

Why does the curve in Proposition 1.2 slope down? The first point to be made is that unemployment does not "cause" wages, nor wages the level of unemployment. Rather, pay and joblessness are determined in a simultaneous system, driven by θ, the demand shock, and the characteristics of the region. The locus of efficient points is described by

$$w - \frac{u(w) - u(b)}{u'(w)} = \theta f'(n) \qquad (3.1.33)$$

so an increase in the wage reduces the value of the left-hand side of this equation, partly because it lowers the marginal utility of income, the denominator of the second term on the left. Hence, to maintain equality, the right-hand side must also decline. This requires an increase in employment, thereby driving down the marginal product of labor. To put it differently, in a region where the wage level is high, it is inefficient to have a lot of the region's inhabitants unemployed. The optimal outcome for firms and workers—the two sides are to be thought of here as a single unit with collaborative interests—is to raise employment as the wage increases, because the opportunity cost to having unemployed people is large when rates of pay are high. Unattractive regions must offer high wage levels, ceteris paribus. These regions, therefore, exhibit low unemployment and high pay. Others have high unemployment and low pay.

3.1.3   Regions with Different Probabilities of Boom and Slump

Regions can differ in another, and fundamental, way. They can have different chances of boom and slump. More formally, some regions may have better probability distributions of demand shocks than others. To be able to analyze this it is necessary to define how one probability distribution can be "better" than another. Loosely speaking, better will be taken to mean that there is more weight in the upper tail of the distribution of demand shocks.

Let θ be a demand parameter which, as before, can be thought of as the exogenous selling price of the firm. Assume that the economy is divided into many regions. Denote the probability distribution of θ in the most favored region as the density function $h(\theta)$. On average this region has the highest selling prices: in this sense it is the most prosperous region. Denote the probability distribution of θ in the least favored region as $s(\theta)$. On average, this region has the smallest positive demand shocks, and is thus, put loosely, the most depressed region in the economy. Assume that demand can vary from $\theta = 0$ to $\theta = 1$, so that the support of the distributions of $s(\theta)$ and $h(\theta)$ is the unit interval. Figure 3.4 sketches the idea.

The economy is taken to have a continuum of regions, indexed by r. Define the composite function

$$g(\theta, r) = rh(\theta) + (1 - r)s(\theta) \qquad (3.1.34)$$

as the density function of demand across the different parts of the economy. Thus each region's distribution is a convex combination of that in the worst and best regions. Although this parameterization is not necessary for the main conclusions, it simplifies the model.

Assume that the cumulative density functions for the best and worst regions are $H(\theta)$ and $S(\theta)$. Thus

$$H(\theta) = \int_0^\theta h(x)\,dx \qquad (3.1.35)$$

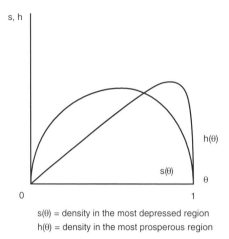

s(θ) = density in the most depressed region
h(θ) = density in the most prosperous region

Figure 3.4
Possible probability distributions of demand in the best and worst regions

$$S(\theta) = \int_0^\theta s(x)\, dx. \tag{3.1.36}$$

Assume also that

$$H(\theta) \le S(\theta) \qquad \text{for all } \theta. \tag{3.1.37}$$

Thus, for any level of demand, it is true that there is less accumulated weight in the left-hand tail of the distribution in the "good" region than the "bad" one. Those regions in between the top and bottom ones have cumulative distribution

$$G(\theta, r) = rH(\theta) + (1 - r)S(\theta), \tag{3.1.38}$$

so that for r' and r'', where $r' > r''$,

$$G(\theta, r') - G(\theta, r'') = (r' - r'')[H(\theta) - S(\theta)] \le 0 \tag{3.1.39}$$

Thus high-r regions have more favorable demand distributions. Condition (3.1.39) will be required later. In passing it is worth noting the continuous version, given differentiability,

$$G_r(\theta, r) = H(\theta) - S(\theta) \le 0. \tag{3.1.40}$$

The basic structure of the model is the same as in the previous section. Thus it is assumed that workers make their migration choices at the beginning of the time period; that each region receives m workers and offers them expected utility $\bar{u}$; that firms in region r employ $n(r)$ individuals at wage $w(r)$ to produce $f(n(r))$ output, leaving $m - n(r)$ unemployed people to get unemployment benefit b. Regions pay differently and have different employment levels. To concentrate on the effect of differing probability distributions of θ, it is assumed that in other ways regions are alike.

The employer in region r acts as though solving the following constrained maximization problem:

$$\underset{w, n(\theta)}{\text{Maximize}} \int [\theta f(n) - wn]g(\theta, r)\, d\theta \tag{3.1.41}$$

$$\text{subject to } \int \left\{ \frac{n}{m}u(w) + \left[1 - \frac{n}{m}\right]u(b) \right\}g(\theta, r)\, d\theta \geq \bar{u} \tag{3.1.42}$$

Assigning a multiplier, λ, to the constraint, the first-order conditions are once more

$$w: \ -1 + \lambda \frac{1}{m}u'(w) = 0 \tag{3.1.43}$$

$$n(\theta): \ \theta f'(n) - w + \frac{\lambda}{m}[u(w) - u(b)] = 0. \tag{3.1.44}$$

so

$$w - \theta f'(n) = \frac{u(w) - u(b)}{u'(w)}, \tag{3.1.45}$$

which is the same efficiency condition as in the previous section. In other words, the equation implicitly defining the relationship between wages and employment is unaffected by the assumption that different regions have different probability distributions. This is because the solutions are state-contingent.

The following result can be established.

PROPOSITION 1.4   There is a negatively sloped curve linking wages and unemployment across regions. Regions with more favorable distributions of demand shocks pay lower wages.

Proof   The proof of the first part of this proposition is immediate from (3.1.45), for that condition implicitly defines an employment function

$n(w, \theta, b)$. Hence unemployment in region r is

$$U^r = m - n(w^r, \theta, b). \tag{3.1.46}$$

As established in equation (3.1.17) of the previous section, $n(w, \theta, b)$ is increasing in w, so that unemployment is inversely related to the wage rate. To complete the proof, however, requires that the wage in region r' be shown to be lower than in region r'', where, as earlier, r' is the region with the more favorable demand distribution, and r'' the region with the less favorable one.

To simplify the proof it is helpful to assume that there exists across a continuum of regions a differentiable wage function $w(r)$. A later section replicates the proof, in a more long-winded way, for discrete regions and a nondifferentiable wage relationship.

High-r regions have the most favorable demand distributions. To obtain a contradiction, assume $w'(r) \geq 0$. Because each region must offer $\bar{u}$ expected utility, it is necessary that

$$0 = \frac{\partial \bar{u}}{\partial r} = \frac{w'(r)}{m} \int \{u'(w)n + [u(w) - u(b)]n_w\}g(\theta, r)\, d\theta$$

$$+ \frac{1}{m} \int [u(w) - u(b)]ng_r(\theta, r)\, d\theta \tag{3.1.47}$$

As has been established earlier,

$$n_w = \frac{[u(w) - u(b)]u''(w)}{\theta f''(n)[u'(w)]^2} > 0. \tag{3.1.48}$$

Therefore, for (3.1.47) to be zero, it is necessary (given the assumption of $w'(r) \geq 0$ for the second of the two right hand side terms of (3.1.47) to be negative. This implies that

$$\int n(\theta, w, b)g_r(\theta, r)\, d\theta \leq 0. \tag{3.1.49}$$

Integrating by parts,

$$\int n(\theta, w, b)g_r(\theta, r)\, d\theta = \int -n_\theta(\theta, w, b)G_r(\theta, r)\, d\theta, \tag{3.1.50}$$

noting that $G(1, r)$ and $G(0, r)$ are both independent of r, because they are respectively equal to unity and zero. The right hand side of (3.1.50) is of crucial sign. First,

$$n_\theta = -\frac{f'(n)}{\theta f''(n)} > 0. \tag{3.1.51}$$

Second, by the earlier (3.1.40),

$$G_r = H(\theta) - S(\theta) \leq 0 \tag{3.1.52}$$

Thus the right-hand side of (3.1.50) is positive, which contradicts (3.1.49). This completes the proof that high-r regions cannot have high wages. Equation (3.1.45) then guarantees that wages and unemployment are inversely related.

3.1.4   Regions with Different Productivities

A third way in which regions may vary is in their ability to produce goods efficiently. The most obvious example is that some regions have natural resources cheaply available while others have none. Most agricultural activities rely on particular configurations of climatic conditions; effective hydroelectric schemes require certain kinds of rivers; the transportation of raw materials is more costly in mountainous terrain. Regions thus differ in their intrinsic productivity.

To stay within the broad framework used earlier, assume that regions are identical except in their ability to produce output. Let region k have production function $kf(n)$, where k is a positive productivity constant and $f(n)$ is an increasing and concave production function. Regions here are implicitly ordered by their productive capability. The lowest-k is the least effective at producing output with a given quantity of employment.

Using now-conventional notation, the value of the representative firm's output is $k\theta f(n)$, where θ is the exogenous selling price or demand shock. Thus the employer in region k must choose a wage and employment combination to solve the following problem:

$$\underset{w(\theta),n(\theta)}{\text{Maximize}} \int [k\theta f(n) - wn]g(\theta)\,d\theta \quad \text{s.t.}$$

$$\int \left[\frac{n}{m}u(w) + \left(1 - \frac{n}{m}\right)u(b)\right]g(\theta)\,d\theta \geq \bar{u} \tag{3.1.53}$$

As usual the first-order conditions include the requirements that

$$w = \text{a constant independent of } \theta \tag{3.1.54}$$

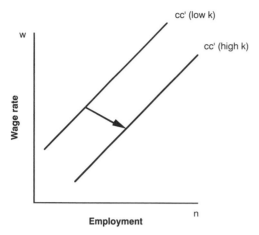

Figure 3.5
The effect of an increase in productivity (k)

$$\frac{u(w) - u(b)}{u'(w)} = w - k\theta f'(n). \tag{3.1.55}$$

Differentiating implicitly with respect to productivity in the second of these (implicitly relying on equation 3.1.54),

$$\frac{\partial n}{\partial k} = -\frac{f'(n)}{f''(n)k} > 0. \tag{3.1.56}$$

Employment is higher, other things constant, in regions with greater productivity.

As in earlier sections, equation (3.1.55) defines within figure 3.5 an efficiency locus in wage-employment space. This has a positive gradient, and is shifted to the right—by the result just proved—whenever there is a rise in intrinsic productivity, k.

The following less obvious result can be proved.

PROPOSITION 1.5   High-k regions (that is, highly productive ones) have low wages.

Proof   Assume not, to get a contradiction. Thus assume that high-k areas have high levels of pay. Assume also, for simplicity, that this can be represented as a differentiable function $w(k)$. It is straightforward to extend the proof to the discrete case.

Region k offers

$$\bar{u} = \int \left[\frac{n}{m} u(w(k)) + \left(1 - \frac{n}{m} \right) u(b) \right] g(\theta) \, d\theta \tag{3.1.57}$$

so that the derivative with respect to k must be

$$0 = \int n_k \left[\frac{u(w) - u(b)}{m} \right] g(\theta) \, d\theta + u'(w)w'(k) \int \frac{n}{m} g(\theta) \, d\theta. \tag{3.1.58}$$

As shown, $n_k > 0$. Hence $w'(k) > 0$ is a contradiction, because the right hand side of (3.1.58) is then unambiguously positive.

Is there a negatively sloped wage curve in wage-unemployment space? Write unemployment as

$$U = m - n(w, k, \theta, b), \tag{3.1.59}$$

where the n function is equation (3.1.55). Differentiating this unemployment equation with respect to k,

$$\frac{\partial U}{\partial k} = -n_w w'(k) - n_k. \tag{3.1.60}$$

Unfortunately, because $w'(k)$ must be negative, this can take either sign.

What can be shown is:

PROPOSITION 1.6   Holding constant the level of regional productivity, there is a negatively sloped curve linking wages and unemployment.

Proof   This follows from the usual result that

$$\frac{\partial U}{\partial w} = -n_w < 0. \tag{3.1.61}$$

In conclusion, in this variant of the model there may not be a negative correlation between wages and unemployment in the cross-section data. Controlling for regional productivities, however, does generate such a relationship.

3.1.5   Regions with Different Levels of Unemployment Benefit

In a country such as the United States the level of unemployment compensation varies by region. Some states pay more generously, and for a longer period, than others.

When benefit, b, varies by geographical area, it is not possible to prove that there must always be a reduced-form "wage curve." To see why the previous kinds of proof go wrong, assume that there is a differentiable positively sloped function, $w(b)$, linking the wage rate to the benefit level. To try for a contradiction, which would ensure that high-benefit regions have low wages and high unemployment, differentiate throughout the requirement that

$$\bar{u} = \int \left[\frac{n}{m} u(w(b)) + \left(1 - \frac{n}{m} \right) u(b) \right] g(\theta) \, d\theta \tag{3.1.62}$$

to give

$$0 = u'(w)w'(b) \int \frac{n}{m} g(\theta) \, d\theta + \frac{1}{m} [u(w) - u(b)] \int n_b g(\theta) \, d\theta$$

$$+ u'(b) \int \left(1 - \frac{n}{m} \right) g(\theta) \, d\theta + \frac{1}{m} w'(b) [u(w) - u(b)] \int n_w g(\theta) \, d\theta. \tag{3.1.63}$$

The now-standard proof by contradiction breaks down, because one of the terms on the right hand side is negative:

$$\frac{1}{m} \int n_b g(\theta) \, d\theta < 0. \tag{3.1.64}$$

This can be established by checking that the usual first-order condition applies,

$$\frac{u(w) - u(b)}{u'(w)} = w - \theta f'(n,) \tag{3.1.65}$$

with derivative

$$\frac{\partial n}{\partial b} = \frac{u'(b)}{u'(w) f''(n) \theta} < 0. \tag{3.1.66}$$

Another method leads to an explanantion for this. Totally differentiating (3.1.62) and (3.1.65), bearing in mind that the wage is not state-contingent, gives

$$0 = \frac{1}{m}[u(w) - u(b)]\,dn$$

$$+ \left[u'(w) \int \frac{n}{m} g(\theta)\,d\theta \right] dw + u'(b)\left[1 - \int \frac{n}{m} g(\theta)\,d\theta \right] db \qquad (3.1.67)$$

$$0 = \theta f''(n)\,dn - \frac{u''(w)[u(w) - u(b)]}{[u'(w)]^2}\,dw - \frac{u'(b)}{u'(w)}\,db \qquad (3.1.68)$$

Substituting out the db terms, the condition for the derivative of employment with respect to the wage to be positive is that dn/dw is less than or greater than zero as the expression

$$\frac{n}{m}\left[\frac{w}{\theta f'(n)} - 1 \right] + \frac{1}{m} \int \frac{n}{m} g(\theta)\,d\theta \qquad (3.1.69)$$

is greater than or less than σ, where σ is the elasticity $-f''(n)n/f'(n)$. This condition is hard to interpret intuitively.

Thus there may or may not be a regional wage curve when benefits vary across areas. The reason appears to be the following. An area with generous unemployment compensation offers greater expected utility to individuals, other thing constant, than other areas. Inequality cannot hold in long-run equilibrium, so there must be some off-setting negative characteristic. One possibility is that unemployment is high because firms implicitly take advantage of the high unemployment benefits in their region. If this effect is sufficiently strong, it may so lower the region's expected utility that the wage rate must be large to restore the going level of expected utility. In this case the regions with high benefit levels have high wages and high unemployment. Then a negatively sloped wage curve does not exist.

Nevertheless, there is one familiar outcome.

PROPOSITION 1.7   Holding constant the level of regional unemployment benefit, there is a negatively sloped wage curve linking wages and unemployment.

Proof   Because unemployment is $U = m - n$, the proposition is established by the fact that, as usual, the locus defined by (3.1.65) has a positive gradient in wage/employment space.

According to this variant of the analysis, a cross-section econometric study might not find a negative correlation between wages and unemployment in the raw data. Controlling for regional benefit levels, however, would lead to an inverse relationship.

3.1.6 Contract Models with Private Unemployment Insurance

All of the previous sections implicitly assumed that firms made no payments to the unemployed. As has been known since at least 1981 (see Grossman and Hart, 1981), this is a sub-optimal form of contract that has important implications for predicted behavior. The counter-argument is that it appears to be the one observed most commonly in reality. Oswald (1986a), for example, documents the fact that the majority of U.S. union contracts have no private unemployment benefit provision. Unemployment insurance is almost certainly even rarer in the non-union sector.[5]

The existence of a "wage curve" relationship depends sensitively, in a contract model, upon the assumption of no private unemployment insurance. Consider the model of section 3.1.2, for example, in which nonpecuniary attributes generate a wage curve across regions. When firms can make a payment β to workers who lose their jobs, the optimization problem for the firm in region j is

$$\underset{w(\theta), n(\theta), \beta(\theta)}{\text{Maximize}} \int [\theta f(n) - wn - \beta(m - n)]g(\theta) \, d\theta \qquad (3.1.70)$$

$$\text{s.t.} \int \left\{ \frac{n}{m}[u(w) + \phi(j)] + \left(1 - \frac{n}{m}\right)[u(\beta + b) + \phi(j)] \right\} g(\theta) \, d\theta \geq \bar{u} \qquad (3.1.71)$$

Again forming the Lagrangean, with a multiplier λ on the constraint, leads to the first-order conditions

$$\beta(\theta): \ -(m - n) + \lambda\left(1 - \frac{n}{m}\right)u'(\beta + b) = 0 \qquad (3.1.72)$$

$$w(\theta): \ -1 + \frac{\lambda}{m}u'(w) = 0 \qquad (3.1.73)$$

$$n(\theta): \ \theta f'(n) - w + \beta + \frac{\lambda}{m}[u(w) - u(\beta + b)] = 0 \qquad (3.1.74)$$

By combining the first two,

$$\beta = w - b \qquad (3.1.75)$$

---

5. Oswald and Turnbull (1985) report an even greater lack of private unemployment insurance in the United Kingdom.

w = a constant independent of θ.   (3.1.76)

Hence β is a payment with two characteristics. First, it is exactly the difference between unemployment benefit and the workers' wage. Therefore it makes those without jobs as well off as those working. Individuals are completely insured against lay-off. Second, like the wage rate, the amount of private unemployment benefit, β, is independent of the size of the demand shock, θ.

The third first-order condition, (3.1.74), can be simplified. Because $w = \beta + b$, it becomes

$$\theta f'(n) = b. \qquad (3.1.77)$$

Hence, employment, n, is independent of the wage rate, w. The contract curve is vertical. Because the number of the workers in the region is constant, unemployment is the same as in other regions. There is no negatively sloped wage curve.

Another way to look at this is to note that, whenever employers offer private full insurance to their workers, the wage must be the same across all regions (given a common b). Because $w = \beta + b$, the expected utility constraint becomes

$$\bar{u} = \int \left[\frac{n}{m} u(w + \phi) + \left(1 - \frac{n}{m}\right) u(b + \beta + \phi) \right] g(\theta) \, d\theta$$

$$= u(b + \beta + \phi) \int g(\theta) \, d\theta$$

$$= u(b + \beta + \phi). \qquad (3.1.78)$$

This is true for both of the earlier variants of the model (Section 3.1.3 and 3.1.4) once private unemployment insurance is incorporated, because (3.1.78) is independent of productivity and the distribution of θ. Equation (3.1.75) implies that $u(b + \beta + \phi) = u(w + \phi)$ across regions, in other words that, given $\phi = 0$, each region pays the same wage. There is then no downward-sloping relationship between wages and local area joblessness.

In conclusion, the models described in earlier sections all change in important ways once private unemployment insurance is incorporated. The models no longer generate a wage curve as a cross-section relationship across regions. Although not theoretically satisfactory, one practical objection to this might be that private unemployment insurance is empirically rare.

3.1.7   Two Further Points

There are two notable criticisms of earlier analysis. First, it might be considered implausible that real firms are risk-neutral. Second, the models have not incorporated the fact that firms may be mobile, and should, in general equilibrium, receive the same expected profit in each region. There are replies to these objections. It is straightforward to demonstrate that the derivation of the negative cross-section relationship between pay and unemployment goes through for the case in which employers are risk-averse. To show this, assume the firm has a strictly concave utility function, $v(\pi)$, defined on profits. Assume that $v(.)$ is differentiable. The model with non-pecuniary differences across regions can then be reformulated as

$$\text{Maximize}_{w(\theta), n(\theta)} \int v(\theta f(n) - wn) g(\theta) \, d\theta$$

$$\text{s.t. } \int \left\{ \frac{n}{m} u[(w) + \phi] + \left(1 - \frac{n}{m}\right)[u(b) + \phi] \right\} g(\theta) \, d\theta \geq \bar{u} \qquad (3.1.79)$$

Where λ is a multiplier, therefore, the first-order conditions include:

$$w(\theta): \; -v'(\pi) + \lambda u'(w) \frac{1}{m} = 0 \qquad (3.1.80)$$

$$n(\theta): \; v'(\pi)[\theta f'(n) - w] + \frac{\lambda}{m}[u(w) - u(b)] = 0 \qquad (3.1.81)$$

Combining these to eliminate λ,

$$\theta f'(n) - w + \frac{u(w) - u(b)}{u'(w)} = 0. \qquad (3.1.82)$$

Thus, crucially, $v'(\pi)$ drops out. Equation (3.1.82) is exactly the relationship derived in earlier models.

This result means that the existence of firm risk-aversion leaves unchanged the earlier argument for a wage curve. Regions offering low wages, because they have high nonpecuniary advantages, will have low levels of employment and thus high levels of unemployment. As is well known, the existence of risk-aversion eliminates the optimality of a wage rate that is independent of θ, demand. Thus the wage will be state-contingent here.

The second objection is of a different character, but it also can be countered. It is true that the models in previous sections allow for the possibility that firms in different regions earn different levels of expected profit. Unless it is reasonable to assume persistent supernormal profits, firms should therefore migrate to the highly profitable regions. This has been left out of the analysis.

The simplest response relies on the plausible assumption that firms have to pay fixed costs $c(j)$, where j is the region. The primary fixed cost is likely to be the rental price of the land. Expected profit is now

$$\int [\theta f(n) - wn]g(\theta)\,d\theta - c(j), \tag{3.1.83}$$

and this can be equated across regions, without affecting the argument for a wage curve, by an appropriate set of c's across space. Perhaps the natural interpretation is that firms' entry to an area bids up the price of land. Land, being in inelastic supply within a region, increases in value until the return from running a business in a previously profitable region is just equal to that in a region that began as less profitable. This argument ensures that the earlier sections' findings generalize to an equilibrium in which both firms and workers are mobile.

3.1.8   A More General Version of Proposition 1.4

This section, which is a form of appendix, proves Proposition 1.4 for the nondifferentiable case. In order to show that regions with favorable $g(\theta)$ distributions must have lower wages than those with less favorable $g(\theta)$ densities, assume not, in order to try to establish a contradiction. Thus assume, for regions r' and r'', where the former has the better distribution of θ,

$$u(w^{r'}) > u(w^{r''}), \tag{3.1.84}$$

that is, that workers in regions with more favorable demand shocks have higher pay. The following algebra establishes the contradiction.

Region r offers its workers expected utility

$$\bar{u} = \int \left\{ \frac{1}{m} n(\theta, w^r, b)[u(w^r) - u(b)]g(\theta, r) \right\} d\theta + u(b). \tag{3.1.85}$$

The difference in expected utility between regions r' and r'' must be zero. Define the difference as

$$D(r', r'') \equiv \int \left\{ \frac{1}{m} n(\theta, w^{r'}, b) [u(w^{r'}) - u(b)] \right\} g(\theta, r') d\theta$$

$$- \int \left\{ \frac{1}{m} n(\theta, w^{r''}, b) [u(w^{r''}) - u(b)] \right\} g(\theta, r'') d\theta \qquad (3.1.86)$$

It will be convenient to multiply through by m, the numbers in each region, and to take the utility terms out of the integrals (they are, as usual, independent of θ).

Thus write the difference between regions as

$$mD(r', r'') = [u(w^{r'}) - u(b)] \int n(\theta, w^{r'}, b) g(\theta, r') d\theta$$

$$- [u(w^{r''}) - u(b)] \int n(\theta, w^{r''}, b) g(\theta, r'') d\theta. \qquad (3.1.87)$$

To show that this is positive, and thus to establish a contradiction, a number of calculations are needed. First, define the following variables:

$$\eta \equiv [u(w^{r'}) - u(b)][n(\theta, w^{r'}, b) - n(\theta, w^{r''}, b)] \qquad (3.1.88)$$

$$\psi \equiv u(w^{r'}) - u(w^{r''}) > 0 \qquad (3.1.89)$$

Because n_w, the derivative of employment with respect to the wage, is given by

$$n_w = \frac{[u(w) - u(b)] u''(w)}{\theta f''(n) [u'(w)]^2} > 0 \qquad (3.1.90)$$

it follows that

$$n(\theta, w^{r'}, b) - n(\theta, w^{r''}, b) > 0. \qquad (3.1.91)$$

Hence both $\eta \geq 0$ and $\psi \geq 0$. Second, substituting both η and ψ into equation (3.1.87), allows us to write

$$mD(r', r'') = \int \eta g(\theta, r') d\theta + \psi \int n(\theta, w^{r''}, b) g(\theta, r') d\theta$$

$$+ [u(w^{r''}) - u(b)] \int [n(\theta, w^{r''}, b) g(\theta, r') - n(\theta, w^{r''}, b) g(\theta, r'')] d\theta. \qquad (3.1.92)$$

Thus the whole expression is positive if the last of these terms is positive.

By integration by parts,

$$\int [n(\theta, w^{r''}, b)g(\theta, r') - n(\theta, w^{r''}, b)g(\theta, r'')]\, d\theta$$

$$= -\int n_\theta(\theta, w^{r''}, b)[G(\theta, r') - G(\theta, r'')]\, d\theta \tag{3.1.93}$$

As shown earlier, $n_\theta > 0$. Moreover

$$G(\theta, r') - G(\theta, r'') \le 0, \tag{3.1.94}$$

by the requirement that region r' have the more favorable demand distribution. Therefore (3.1.92) is unambiguously positive, which establishes the necessary contradiction.

3.1.9   The Contract Approach: Conclusions

This section has described a type of neoclassical theory of the "wage curve" that does not rely on the existence of labor-market rents. It develops an analytical framework in which the behavior of atomistic maximizing individuals leads to a negatively sloped cross-section relationship between wages and unemployment. Although the discussion has been of pay and joblessness across geographical regions, the analysis can be applied to other disaggregations, such as industries or occupations.

Why do high unemployment rates accompany low wage rates? The primary reason, according to the models developed here, is that optimal behavior by firms and workers traces out a contract curve that slopes upwards in wage/employment space. The idea of such a contract curve, or efficiency locus, is a very old one. Leontief (1946) suggested a unionized construct of this sort, and McDonald and Solow (1981) expanded upon his theme. Although it may not have been quite as widely recognized, the same equation emerges from the nonunion contract models of Baily (1974) and Azariadis (1975). These authors do not discuss the concept of a contract curve across regions, nor provide empirical evidence for their models. In numerous details, moreover, the analysis in the chapter differs from that in these articles. Nevertheless, the underlying idea is the same.

The chapter visualizes an economy divided into different regions. Workers are free, at the start of the period, to move to whichever area they find most attractive. Once settled, they are assumed to find it prohibitively costly, within the period, to move again. There is uncertainty about demand. Because all firms must offer the same level of expected utility to workers, individuals spread themselves evenly across space. Once the uncertain level of demand is realized, firms hire workers and produce output. Not all regions hire in identical numbers, so unemployment differs across regions ex post. Wages, too, vary geographically. The analysis explores four reasons, and so develops four variants of the overall model. These reasons are (1) different nonpecuniary advantages across regions, (2) different interregional probability distributions of demand, (3) different productivities in the various regions, and (4) different regional unemployment benefit levels. It has been shown how each, in slightly different ways, can lead to a wage curve. For example, if some areas are intrinsically nicer places to live than others, they will pay lower wages in long run equilibrium (defined as a position in which there is no incentive for migration). Because it is optimal for wage-employment combinations to lie on an efficiency locus with a positive gradient, these low-wage regions will have low employment. By the requirement that workers spread themselves evenly across regions, the unemployment rate is higher in these areas. Thus a declining cross-section curve is traced out.

3.2   An Efficiency Wage Framework

3.2.1   A Model with Nonpecuniary Differences

This section's purpose is to write down an explicitly noncompetitive theory. It sets out a multi-region efficiency wage model that is consistent with, and offers a possible conceptual framework for the analysis of, a "wage curve." According to this model, even when workers are free to migrate between regions, the contemporaneous cross-section correlation between pay and unemployment will be negative rather than, as is sometimes asserted, positive. Within this framework the crucial relationship corresponds to a no-shirking condition of the kind in, for example, Shapiro and Stiglitz (1984).[6]

This section sets out a model in which a downward-sloping curve in wage-unemployment space is derived from optimizing behavior. The reason for the negative gradient is that unemployment frightens workers and,

6. Akerlof and Yellen (1990), Bowles (1985), and Phelps (1990) also contain functions similar—at the aggregate level—to what is described here as a wage curve. Their papers are variants on the same efficiency wage theme. Interesting new work includes Arvan (1993) and MacLeod, Malcomson, and Gomme (1994). An innovative paper by Jackman, Layard, and Savouri (1991) is one of the few to have thought about how to analyze noncompetitive wage-setting over space.

in consequence, firms find that in recessions it is feasible to pay their employees less well. The model is constructed in a way in which, contrary to Harris and Todaro (1970), wages and unemployment are negatively rather than positively related. To understand why the upward-sloping Harris-Todaro relationship is misleading it is useful—as in chapter 2—to recall that, in reality, migration is a costly process that takes place in a world with random demand shocks. Then shocks that are perceived as temporary need not induce migration, and another kind of association may shape the data.

The theoretical framework allows workers to migrate across regions, but assumes that it is not possible to do so instantly. Unemployed individuals do not immediately attempt to migrate: they migrate only if one region offers a better expected utility than another. This realistic assumption of costly, rational, far-sighted migration decisions effectively decouples current pay and current unemployment, and so bypasses the positive gradient of the Harris-Todaro relationship. One version of the model goes further: it shows that regions that differ only in nonpecuniary attractions may have the same wage curve and nothing that corresponds to a visible positive wage-unemployment relationship. This is possible, for example, if one region is inherently attractive and, to ensure consistency with a zero-migration equilibrium,[7] therefore offers both low pay and high unemployment. Another region, say, pays well and has low unemployment, but is an inherently unattractive place. The result is a negatively inclined wage function even in long-run equilibrium.

Consider an economy consisting of just two regions. The following assumptions are made about region 1, and, with small modifications, about region 2.

A.1 Assume that workers are risk-neutral, and get utility from income and disutility from effort. Define the wage as w and the level of on-the-job effort as e. Assume that utility equals the difference between income and effort, so that utility is

$$u = w - e.$$

A.2 Assume that effort at work, e, is a fixed number determined by technology, but that individual employees can decide to "shirk" and exert zero effort. If undetected by the firm, these individuals earn wage w and have

---

7. To use the useful term coined in Jackman, Layard, and Savouri (1991).

$e = 0$, so that $u = w$. They are then better off than employees who provide effort.[8]

A.3 An individual who shirks runs the risk of being detected. Designate as δ the probability of successfully shirking, that is, of escaping detection. Assume that anyone caught shirking is fired, and has then to find work elsewhere (at required effort e). Let the expected utility of a fired worker be $\bar{w}$. Define it

$$\bar{w} = (w - e)\alpha(U) + b[1 - \alpha(U)].$$

This is a convex combination of $w - e$, the utility from working at the required effort level, and of b, which is defined as the income value of unemployment benefit plus leisure. The function $\alpha(U)$ measures the probability of finding work, and how that is affected by the level of unemployment, U, prevailing in the local labor market.

A.4 Assume that there is a constant rate of break-up, r, of firms. In steady-state equilibrium, total new hires in the local economy are $\alpha[l - n]$, where l is working population and n is employment, and

$$rn = \alpha[l - n].$$

Unemployment is $U \equiv 1 - n/l$, so

$$r = \frac{r}{U} - \alpha.$$

This defines a function $\alpha(U)$ with derivatives:

$$\alpha'(U) = -\frac{r}{U^2} < 0$$

$$\alpha''(U) = \frac{2r}{U^3} > 0.$$

Thus the probability of finding a job, α, is a convex function of unemployment, U.

A.5 Equivalent conditions hold in the second region. The wage there is ω and the level of unemployment benefit is β. The unemployment rate in the second region is μ.

A.6 The second region differs from the first in that both workers and non-workers enjoy a non-pecuniary benefit, ϕ, from living in the region.

---

8. This discreteness assumption, that there are only two effort levels, can be dropped. Phelps (1990, 1992), for example, works with a continuous effort function.

Their utility is thus $u = \omega - e + \phi$ when working, and $u = \beta + \phi$ when unemployed.

A.7 Each region is affected by shocks to the demand for labor. The shock variable is denoted s in region 1, with a density function $g(s)$. The shock variable in region 2 is σ, with density of $h(\sigma)$. These shocks could be thought of as exogenous movements in real input prices, but other interpretations are possible.

A.8 Workers are free, between periods, to choose to live in whichever region they prefer. They cannot migrate during a period.

The assumptions given above describe a form of efficiency-wage model. The model's key characteristic is that employers must pay a wage that is sufficently high to induce employees not to shirk. In equilibrium, workers must be behaving optimally in their effort decisions, and firms must be behaving optimally in their wage-setting. Regions differ in their non-pecuniary attractions: one of the two is a nicer place to live than the other. Excluding degenerate equilibria, however, each region must offer workers the same level of expected utility. This condition defines a zero-migration equilibrium.

A number of results can be proved.

PROPOSITION 2.1   Each region has a downward-sloping convex wage curve. If both regions have the same level of unemployment benefit (so $b = \beta$), they have a common wage curve given by the equation:

$$w = e + b + \frac{e\delta}{(1 - \delta)[1 - \alpha(U)]}.$$

Proof For a no-shirking equilibrium, the expected utility from not shirking must equal that from shirking. Thus in region 1

$$w - e = \delta w + (1 - \delta)\{(w - e)\alpha(U) + b[1 - \alpha(U)]\}, \tag{3.2.1}$$

which simplifies, after manipulation, to

$$w = e + b + \frac{e\delta}{(1 - \delta)[1 - \alpha(U)]}. \tag{3.2.2}$$

In region 2, in which individuals receive a utility supplement ϕ, the no-shirking condition is

$$\omega - e + \phi = \delta(\omega + \phi)$$

$$+ (1 - \delta)\{(\omega - e + \phi)\alpha(\mu) + (\beta + \phi)[(1 - \alpha(\mu)]\} \tag{3.2.3}$$

so that the ϕ terms cancel from both sides, leaving a wage equation

$$\omega = e + \beta + \frac{e\delta}{(1 - \delta)[1 - \alpha(\mu)]}. \tag{3.2.4}$$

If $b = \beta$, equation (3.2.2) is identical to equation (3.2.4), and the two regions have the same wage equation. It is straightforward to verify that, along the curve defined by (3.2.2), the equilibrium wage is a declining function of the unemployment rate. The convexity of this wage curve follows from the convexity of the $\alpha(U)$ function and can be checked by differentiation.[9]

PROPOSITION 2.2   There exists involuntary unemployment in equilibrium.

Proof   In equilibrium, the no-shirking condition, equation (3.2.1), must be satisfied. Assume zero involuntary unemployment, in order to try to establish a contradiction. With full employment of this kind, $\alpha(U) = 1$, namely, the probability of being rehired is unity. Then equation (3.2.1) collapses to the requirement $\delta e = 0$. This is a contradiction, because both δ and e (parameters for the detection technology and effort) are strictly positive, and so establishes the required result.

More intuitively, equilibrium necessitates that wages in each region be just enough to dissuade employees from shirking. This requires that the expected utility from shirking be no greater than that from working at effort e. Because the second region's nonpecuniary attractions, ϕ, are available both to the employed and the unemployed, the condition for no-shirking is independent of ϕ. Thus, as long as there is no difference in unemployment benefit levels (or, more generally, the utility available to the jobless), each region has the same equation for its no-shirking condition. This common equation traces out a convex negatively-sloped locus linking

---

9. The derivatives are

$$\frac{\partial w}{\partial U} = \left(\frac{e\delta}{1 - \delta}\right)[1 - \alpha(U)]^{-2}\alpha'(U)$$

$$\frac{\partial^2 w}{\partial U^2} = \left(\frac{e\delta}{1 - \delta}\right)\{[1 - \alpha(U)]^{-3}[\alpha'(U)]^2 + [1 - \alpha(U)]^{-2}\alpha''(U)\}.$$

The first is unambiguously negative, given the assumption that $\alpha'(U) < 0$, namely that higher unemployment levels diminish the unemployed worker's chance of finding a job. A sufficient, but not necessary, condition for the second derivative to be positive is that $\alpha''(U)$ be positive. This is the requirement that the probability of being hired is a convex function of the unemployment rate.

the wage, w, to the unemployment rate, U. When unemployment is low, for example, firms pay high wages to ensure that workers value their jobs sufficiently not to shirk. Unemployment has to act as a kind of deterrent, and therefore must be involuntary.

PROPOSITION 2.3   Assume that both regions have the same level of unemployment benefit. (1) Then, for a zero migration equilibrium, they must face different distributions of demand shocks, and exhibit different wage/unemployment patterns. (2) Region 1 has a higher expected wage than region 2.

Proof   For a zero-migration equilibrium, each region must offer the same level of expected utility to workers. The expected utility of a migrant into region 1 is

$$\int \{(w - e)\alpha(U) + b[1 - \alpha(U)]\}g(s)\,ds, \tag{3.2.5}$$

and of a migrant into region 2 is

$$\int \{(\omega - e + \phi)\alpha(\mu) + (\beta + \phi)[1 - \alpha(\mu)]\}h(\sigma)\,d\sigma. \tag{3.2.6}$$

where for simplicity these assume the worker had been sacked for shirking (this is inessential). Given identical unemployment benefit levels $b = \beta$, and identical distributions of demand shocks $g(.) = h(.)$, these two expressions cannot be equal. The difference between them would be $\phi > 0$. In equilibrium, therefore, the regions must exhibit different wage/unemployment patterns, and this establishes the first part of the proposition.

To demonstrate that the expected wage in region 1 is higher than the expected wage in region 2, it is necessary to prove that

$$\int wg(s)\,ds > \int \omega h(\sigma)\,d\sigma. \tag{3.2.7}$$

Zero migration requires:

$$\int \{(w - e)\alpha(U) + b[1 - \alpha(U)]\}\,g(s)\,ds$$

$$= \int \{(\omega - e + \phi)\alpha(\mu) + (\beta + \phi)[1 - \alpha(\mu)]\}h(\sigma)\,d\sigma \tag{3.2.8}$$

The two no-shirking conditions (one for each region) are

$$w - e = \delta w + (1 - \delta)\{\alpha(U)(w - e) + [1 - \alpha(U)]b\} \tag{3.2.9}$$

$$\omega - e + \phi = \delta(\omega + \phi)$$
$$+ (1 - \delta)\{\alpha(\mu)[\omega + \phi - e] + [1 - \alpha(\mu)](\beta + \phi)\}. \tag{3.2.10}$$

Rearranging, and integrating both sides of each of these equations,

$$\int \left(w - \frac{e}{1 - \delta} \right) g(s)\, ds = \int \{\alpha(U)(w - e) + [1 - \alpha(U)]b\} g(s)\, ds \tag{3.2.11}$$

$$\int \left(\omega - \frac{e}{1 - \delta} + \phi \right) h(\sigma)\, d\sigma$$

$$= \int \{\alpha(\mu)[\omega + \phi - e] + [1 - \alpha(\mu)](\beta + \phi)\} h(\sigma)\, d\sigma \tag{3.2.12}$$

By equation (3.2.8), the left hand sides of these must be equal:

$$\int \left(w - \frac{e}{1 - \delta} \right) g(s)\, ds = \int \left(\omega - \frac{e}{1 - \delta} + \phi \right) h(\sigma)\, d\sigma, \tag{3.2.13}$$

which simplifies, noting that the integral of $eg/(1 - \delta)$ equals the integral of $eh/(1 - \delta)$, to

$$\int wg(s)\, ds - \int \omega h(\sigma)\, d\sigma = \phi > 0. \tag{3.2.14}$$

If Proposition 2.3(1) were false, the two regions would have identical wage and unemployment outcomes. But, because region 2 is intrinsically attractive (it offers nonpecuniary benefit ϕ), all workers would attempt to migrate there. In equilibrium, therefore, region 2's attractions must be exactly counter-balanced by inferior wage and unemployment combinations.

To illustrate these ideas, figure 3.6 sketches two no-shirking conditions. Curve I represents the locus along which occur the wage-unemployment combinations for regions with identical unemployment benefit levels. Repeated random shocks produce different points on the curve. To ensure a zero-migration equilibrium, the intrinsically more attractive region 2 must be characterized more often by points in the lower right-hand portion of the wage curve, which implies worse wage and unemployment combinations. Equilibria in the less attractive region 1 must more usually occur in the upper left-hand segment of the wage curve—so that workers are willing to live there. This is captured algebraically in Part (2) of the proposi-

Figure 3.6
Two wage curves (Region II here has a higher level of unemployment benefit than region I.)

tion, which states that, because of its inherent disadvantages, the first region must on average offer higher wages than region 2. Equation (3.2.14) shows that, in this world of risk-neutral people, the size of the regional gap in expected wages will equal the value of the nonpecuniary difference between the regions. This accords with intuition.

The previous result establishes that the nice region pays less well, on average, than the unattractive one. The next two propositions concern the chances of a job in these regions.

PROPOSITION 2.4   Assume that the two regions have the same level of unemployment benefit. Then, if the the no-shirking condition is sufficiently close to linear, region 1 has a lower expected rate of unemployment than region 2.

Proof   By continuity, this need only be proved for the strictly linear case. Let the common wage curve in the regions be

$$w = c - mU \tag{3.2.15}$$

$$\omega = c - m\mu \tag{3.2.16}$$

so that from Proposition 2.3

$$\int Ug(s)\,ds - \int \mu h(\sigma)\,d\sigma = -\frac{\phi}{m} < 0. \tag{3.2.17}$$

The weakness of Proposition 2.4 is that it appeals to a case that is intrinsically unlikely. The algebra generates an inherently curved relationship between pay and unemployment. A more general conclusion is the following.

PROPOSITION 2.5   Let q be the relative probability of having a job, defined as $q = \alpha/(1 - \alpha)$. Then, if both regions have the same level of unemployment benefit, expected q is higher in region 1 than region 2.

Proof   Using equations 3.2.2 and 3.2.4, and Proposition 2.3's equation (3.2.14), the difference between the regions' expected wage rates can be written as

$$\frac{e\delta}{1 - \delta}\left\{\int \frac{1}{1 - \alpha(U)}g(s)\,ds - \int \frac{1}{1 - \alpha(\mu)}h(\sigma)\,d\sigma\right\} = \phi > 0. \qquad (3.2.18)$$

After manipulation, this implies

$$\int \frac{\alpha(U)}{1 - \alpha(U)}g(s)\,ds - \int \frac{\alpha(\mu)}{1 - \alpha(\mu)}h(\sigma)\,d\sigma > 0, \qquad (3.2.19)$$

which proves that expected $q = \alpha/(1 - \alpha)$ is greater in the first region.

This framework can be used to demonstrate why a simple Harris-Todaro locus might never be visible in regional data. There will be a logical equivalent to the upward-sloping curve discussed in the existing literature; but it will not link actual pay to actual unemployment. In the model just described, the positive relationship is between "permanent" values of the two variables. It could be said, loosely, that there is a locus with positive gradient tying together the expected wage and expected unemployment.[10]

Consider a world where two regions differ only in inherent amenities. Figure 3.7 is the sketch of a case where a statistical analyst would never observe a simple Harris-Todaro line. There is a nasty region with low amenities. There is also a nice region (with high ϕ). Because amenities enter in an additively separable way, each region has the same no-shirking equation. Workers in the attractive region have to suffer some pecuniary disadvantage to off-set the utility they enjoy from the inherent attractions of the area. If they did not, no other region would be inhabited. In figure 3.7, the nice region has harsher "business cycles." In other words, demand shocks make the region vibrate left and right along the south-east segment of the curve. Typical outcomes are marked as crosses. Exceptional circumstances might take this nice region temporarily up into the upper left-hand part of figure 3.7. But that is the more normal home of the nasty region. Its

---

10. The reason the statement is loose is that the expected wage is positively related to the expectation of a nonlinear function of unemployment.

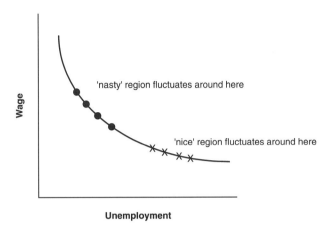

Figure 3.7
A sketch of an equilibrium where no Harris-Todaro locus would be visible in the data

demand fluctuations move it around points like the dots marked. In this way, a long-run regional equilibrium, where both areas are inhabited, can be sustained. Each of the two areas offers the same expected utility to individuals. Pleasant regions, on average, must endure higher unemployment rates and lower wage levels than regions with a poorer amenities. In this model, all the data points observed by a statistical analyst lie on a downward-sloping curve.

Consider, next, geographical differences in the utility from being without work.

PROPOSITION 2.6 Assume that the regions have different levels of unemployment benefit. Then the wage curve in the high-benefit region lies vertically above that in the low-benefit region.

Proof Because the no-shirking condition is

$$w = e + b + \frac{e\delta}{(1 - \delta)[1 - \alpha(U)]},$$ (3.2.20)

the level of unemployment benefit, b, is a vertical shift parameter in a graph of the wage equation in wage/unemployment space. This result follows from the fact that the level of unemployment benefit (or value of full leisure) is an intercept variable in the no-shirking-condition defining equilibrium. As would be expected intuitively, therefore, in a region with higher benefits to those who are unemployed, firms must set higher wage rates if they are to discourage shirking.

PROPOSITION 2.7   The results generalize to models with an arbitrary number of regions.

Proof   A non-shirking condition will hold for each region. Mathematically, the separability of ϕ in the wage equation ensures that, because an equivalent non-shirking condition can be written down for each area, the results generalize to an arbitrary number of regions. The positions of the different wage curves are determined by the size of the different unemployment benefit levels.

An intuitive summary of the model's structure can be given in the following way. In this form of efficiency wage framework, a high level of regional unemployment is associated with a low level of regional wages. High unemployment makes an employee keen to keep a job because it will be difficult to find another. Other things being constant, therefore, these employees are reluctant to shirk at work, for fear they will be detected and dismissed. Knowing this, firms need pay only low wages to extract the required level of effort from workers. Fear of unemployment then "disciplines" workers. If unemployment is low, employers have to offer high wages. If they do not, employees are likely, realizing that it will be easy to find another job if dismissed, to take the risk of shirking at work. When the unemployment rate is low, high wage rates are necessary to motivate workers.

Because individuals can eventually migrate, this is not the end of the story. First, although actual wage and unemployment combinations will depend upon current demand shock variables, the average or expected wage needs to be higher in regions with low nonpecuniary attractions. This is because regions have to offer equal expected utilities. Second, a region with a relatively high level of unemployment benefit will have a relatively high wage curve (such as the bold curve, labeled II, in figure 3.6). The intuitive reason for this is that, in an area where the utility from being unemployed is relatively great, to ensure that there is no shirking the employer must pay better than in areas where the utility of the jobless is comparatively low. It is more expensive to motivate workers who have good outside options. Some regions thus have wage curves that lie vertically above those in other regions.

Individuals do not all move to the regions with the highest wage curves, nor to the regions with the greatest nonpecuniary advantages, because these kinds of regions are areas that more commonly have wage and unemployment outcomes in the lower right-hand segments of their own wage curves (that is, more recessions and worse recessions).

3.2.2 Other Differences across Regions

The previous section adapted an efficiency wage framework to allow for regions to differ in their levels of inherent attractiveness. Regional advantages took a very simple form and, like climate or scenery, for example, could be enjoyed by the employed and unemployed alike. Within the efficiency wage framework there are at least five ways in which real regions might differ. They might have (1) different nonpecuniary utility levels; (2) different unemployment benefit levels; (3) different required levels of effort at work ; (4) different shirking detection rates; and (5) different production functions. The previous section concentrated on numbers (1) and (2). It is worth expanding informally on some of the implications of cases (3) to (5).

A way in which regions (or industries) can differ is in the intensity of work demanded of employees. Working effort, e, may be intrinsically higher in some areas. This could be because of extremes of climate, or for some geographical reason, or because of congestion costs caused by the centralization of employers within large cities. A temperate climate, for example, might be most conducive to the supply of effort. A densely populated urban area, where employees face large costs of commuting to work, may find individuals less willing to hold a job, ceteris paribus, because of the effort required to get to work.

Consider variations in required effort. In this case a two-region economy must generate an equilibrium wage and unemployment distribution in which workers are compensated, either implicitly or explicitly, for working in the high-effort area. Think of a good region labelled G and a bad region labelled B. Within each of the two areas, as usual, a no-shirking condition must be satisfied.

Equilibrium requires:

$$w^g = e^g + b + \frac{e^g \delta}{(1 - \delta)[1 - \alpha(U^g)]} \qquad (3.2.21)$$

$$w^b = e^b + b + \frac{e^b \delta}{(1 - \delta)[1 - \alpha(U^b)]} \qquad (3.2.22)$$

The first of these equations states the wage necessary to ensure zero-shirking in the good region, in which effort, e^g, is low relative to that, e^b, required in the bad (high-effort) region. The second equation gives the equivalent no-shirking condition in that less attractive, high-effort region. There must also be a condition requiring that wage and unemployment

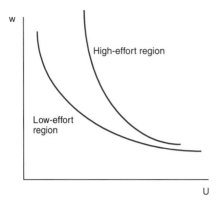

Figure 3.8
Regions that differ in required work-effort levels, e

levels in region G are sufficiently unattractive to counter-balance exactly
the low-effort advantage of living in region G.

The high-effort area, B, must have a no-shirking curve that lies everywhere above that for region G, where work is less taxing. They have
different gradients, however, because the derivatives of the no-shirking
wage equation are

$$\frac{\partial w}{\partial e} = 1 + \frac{\delta}{(1 - \delta)[1 - \alpha(U)]} > 0 \tag{3.2.23}$$

$$\frac{\partial^2 w}{\partial U \partial e} = \left(\frac{\delta}{1 - \delta}\right)[1 - \alpha(U)]^{-2}\alpha'(U) < 0 \tag{3.2.24}$$

The greater the effort level, therefore, the greater in absolute terms is the
responsiveness of pay to unemployment, so the steeper the slope in figure
3.8.

The case of varying shirking-detection rates is similar. Individuals who
choose to shirk (and so provide zero effort) have a chance of avoiding
detection. Their probability of successfully shirking, in this sense, is δ. Their
probability of being detected is then $1 - \delta$. If this detection rate varies by
region, the now-familiar kind of interregional analysis can be modified
again.

Differentiating the appropriate wage equation gives

$$\frac{\partial w}{\partial \delta} = \frac{e}{[1 - \alpha(U)](1 - \delta)^2} > 0 \tag{3.2.25}$$

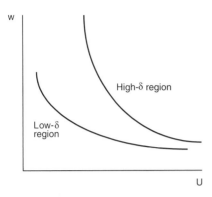

Figure 3.9
Regions that differ in shirking detection rates, $1 - \delta$

$$\frac{\partial^2 w}{\partial \delta \partial U} = \frac{e}{1 - \delta}[1 - \alpha(U)]^{-2}\alpha'(U) + \frac{e\delta}{(1 - \delta)^2}[1 - \alpha(U)]^{-2}\alpha'(U) \quad (3.2.26)$$

$$= \frac{e}{(1 - \delta)^2}[1 - \alpha(U)]^{-2}\alpha'(U) < 0 \quad (3.2.27)$$

so that a rise in δ results in a higher wage curve twisted more towards the vertical, as shown in figure 3.9.

3.2.3   The Demand Side

The previous models did not specify where demand shocks come from. It is reasonable to ask how this gap might be filled. The no-shirking condition provides one half of a model of a region's labor market (or, equivalently, one for the economy as a whole). To complete the framework, and so determine which wage/unemployment combination emerges in equilibrium, assumptions about technology and competition must be made.

Assume, for example, that two inputs are used to produce a single output. Let the inputs be labor, n, and another input, k. Assume k is traded on a world market at exogenously given price r. In practice this input could be viewed generally as machines, or imported raw materials, or even as a single specific input such as oil. All that is required is that it be essential to production.

Assume that output is generated through a constant returns to scale technology. The production function is

$$y = f(n, k), \quad (3.2.28)$$

where y is output and $f(..)$ is homogeneous of degree one. Perfect competition in the product market is assumed. Firms operate at the minimum point on their cost schedules. Define the minimum cost function

$$C(y, w, r) \equiv \min_{n,k} \{wn + rk | y = f(n, k)\} = yc(w, r), \qquad (3.2.29)$$

using the assumption of constant returns.[11]

Given perfect competition, profits must be eliminated in equilibrium. Hence the price of output, p, equals

$$p = c(w, r), \qquad (3.2.30)$$

as conventional. The unit minimum cost function $c(..)$ is homogeneous of degree one, so the above can be written simply as

$$1 = c(w/p, r/p). \qquad (3.2.31)$$

Taking the price of output as the numeraire, p can be set to unity without loss of generality. Therefore, laboring the point slightly, real prices in this economy are connected by the equation

$$1 = c(w, r), \qquad (3.2.32)$$

where the wage, w, and the price or rental rate of input k, r, can be thought of as in real units.

Equilibrium in this simple model of an economy is given by the simultaneous solution of (3.2.32) and a wage equation such as (3.2.2). Employers must be earning zero supernormal profits. The no-shirking condition must hold. Figure 3.10 sketches a picture of wage/unemployment equilibrium.[12] The w^*, U^* pair is determined by the intersection of the wage equation and the zero-profit equation.

The remainder of this section describes two ways to generate a full inter-regional equilibrium in which there is a wage curve. Each of the ways

---

11. Hamermesh's (1993) survey suggests that most microeconometric evidence is, in fact, reasonably consistent with a Cobb-Douglas function.

12. On a historical note, this kind of picture, derived in a slightly different way, was the core element in a series of lectures given annually by David Soskice at Oxford University during the late 1970s. This is the earliest source of which we know. Carlin and Soskice (1990) is a textbook account. An aggregate version of this kind of diagram, and variants on it, are developed in Layard (1986) and Clark and Layard (1989), and in the joint work of Richard Jackman, Richard Layard and Steve Nickell (such as Layard et al. 1991). See also the work of Assar Lindbeck and Edmund Phelps. Carruth et al. (1993) study oil price effects using a similar framework.

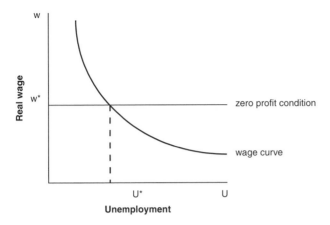

Figure 3.10
Equilibrium in a simple model

assumes a two-region economy. However, the ideas generalize to industries instead of regions, and to many sectors rather than two.

MODEL I   Consider an economy divided into region G and region B. Region G provides unemployment benefit b^g, while the other provides benefit b^b. Region G produces an internationally-traded good under constant returns to scale. This good is sold at a fixed price in the world market. Firms earn zero profit, as described by the condition

$$\bar{p} = c(w^g, r) \tag{3.2.33}$$

in which $c(..)$ is a unit minimum cost function, w^g is the wage paid in region G, and r is the rental price of capital.

Region B produces a different good, which is not internationally traded, and which is the country's only consumption good. Without loss of generality, its price can be set at unity. Assume that this good is not generated by a constant returns technology, but that the product market is perfectly competitive. The requirement of zero profit may then be written

$$y^b = C(y^b, w^b, r), \tag{3.2.34}$$

where y^b is the output of the good produced in region B, $C(\ldots)$ is a (total) minimum cost function, w^b is the wage in the region and hence this industry, and r is the rental price of k.

General equilibrium in the economy demands that five equations hold simultaneously. For simplicity, assume there are no demand shocks, so that all selling prices are known with certainty. The equilibrium conditions are then simply as follows

$$(w^g - e)\alpha(U^g) + b^g[1 - \alpha(U^g)]$$
$$= (w^b - e)\alpha(U^b) + b^b[1 - \alpha(U^b)] \quad \text{zero migration} \qquad (3.2.35)$$

$$w^g = e + b^g + \frac{e\delta}{(1 - \delta)[1 - \alpha(U^g)]} \quad \text{no-shirking in region } G \qquad (3.2.36)$$

$$w^b = e + b^b + \frac{e\delta}{(1 - \delta)[1 - \alpha(U^b)]} \quad \text{no-shirking in region } B \qquad (3.2.37)$$

$$\bar{p} = c(w^g, r) \quad \text{zero-profit in } G\text{'s good} \qquad (3.2.38)$$

$$y^b = C(y^b, w^b, r) \quad \text{zero-profit in } B\text{'s good.} \qquad (3.2.39)$$

These five equations determine the equilibrium values of five variables: real wages in region G, real wages in region B, unemployment in region G, unemployment in region B, and the level of output in region B. The variables are w^g, w^b, U^g, U^b, y^b. As a technical matter it is not possible to assume constant returns to scale in both regions; such an assumption would make the model overdetermined.

The real wage in region G is determined exogenously by the international going price p and the rental price of capital goods, r. The two no-shirking conditions then fix the equilibrium rate of unemployment in region G and the locus of feasible wage/unemployment combinations in region B. With w^g and U^g thus fixed, the requirement that expected utility be the same in each region implies a zero-migration locus defined by

$$(w^b - e)\alpha(U^b) + b^b[1 - \alpha(U^b)] = \text{constant}. \qquad (3.2.40)$$

This has gradient

$$\frac{dw^b}{dU^b} = -\frac{(w^b - e - b^b)\alpha'(U^b)}{\alpha(U^b)} > 0. \qquad (3.2.41)$$

The intersection of the zero-migration locus with the lower of the two no-shirking conditions—noting benefit superscripted b is below benefit superscripted g—determines the real wage and unemployment rate in region B. Output in that region, y^b, is determined implicity. This model is designed only to illustrate, as simply as possible, how the demand side can be filled in without changing the essence of the earlier ideas. In applied work the omission here of uncertainty would probably lead to difficulties; a richer structure would be needed.

Model II   A different model of interregional equilibrium can be constructed by building upon the earlier framework in which one region, G, had a nonpecuniary benefit. Label it slightly differently from before, by $\emptyset$. Assume that this amenity now measures a lack of congestion, determined by low population relative to the geographical area, of the region. Congestion is determined endogenously by population distribution.

In this case, assume that each of two regions produces under constant returns to scale. Region G produces a good at price

$$p = c(w^g, r) \tag{3.2.42}$$

and region B a different good at price

$$1 = \gamma(w^b, r), \tag{3.2.43}$$

where $c(..)$ and $\gamma(..)$ are unit minimum cost functions. Assume that both goods are traded on international markets at given prices. These assumptions fix the real wage in each of the two regions. As in the earlier section, there is a common no-shirking condition, or wage curve, in the regions. Equilibrium values of w^g, w^b, U^g and U^b emerge.

If, say, region B at first offers a more attractive level of expected utility than region G, individuals migrate into region B. This raises region G's value of $\emptyset$, or non-pecuniary benefit. Equilibrium requires that $\emptyset$ keep on increasing in region G until

$$(w^g - e + \emptyset)\alpha(U^g) + (b + \emptyset)[1 - \alpha(U^g)]$$

$$= (w^b - e)\alpha(U^b) + b[1 - \alpha(U^b)], \tag{3.2.44}$$

that is, until the zero migration condition is just satisfied.

Figure 3.11 depicts the type of interregional equilibrium. Real wages in each sector are determined by technology and the internationally-going prices of the regions' products. The unemployment rates take on those values that are just necessary, given the endogenous costs of congestion, to equate workers' expected utilities across regions. Again the omission of all uncertainty is made here only for pedagogic reasons.

3.2.4   Conclusions on an Efficiency Wage Explanation

In the class of efficiency wage models described in this section, unemployment acts as a discipline device that dissuades employees from shirking on the job. A high unemployment rate allows the firm to pay less in equi-

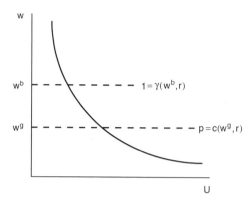

Figure 3.11
General equilibrium in model II

librium. There exists a negatively inclined locus linking pay and local unemployment.

The section shows how this idea can be incorporated into a model of interregional equilibrium. Its predictions are different from, and in some cases almost the opposite of, those in the tradition of Harris and Todaro (1970) and Hall (1970, 1972). One reason for the difference is that this literature has not distinguished as clearly as it could have done between, on the one hand, a positive regional correlation between expected pay and expected unemployment, and, on the other, a negative regional correlation between contemporaneous pay and unemployment.

Shapiro and Stiglitz (1984) outline a model in which there exists an aggregate no-shirking condition taking the form of a downward-sloping locus in wage/unemployment space. This chapter attempts to demonstrate how their central idea generalizes. A no-shirking condition must hold in each region; firms must be behaving optimally and making zero super-normal profit; each region must offer workers the same level of expected utility. Then neither employers nor individuals have an incentive to migrate. A number of versions of the basic framework have been sketched in the section. They allow for regions to differ, in turn, in their levels of nonpecuniary benefits, unemployment benefits, required working effort, shirking detection rates, and production functions.

This framework can generate a coherent model in which no simple Harris-Todaro relationship would ever be seen in raw data. Figure 3.7 captures the essence of the idea. In such a model, which should be thought of as an illustration rather than empirically general, all observed points lie on a single downward-sloping curve.

3.3   Bargaining and Competition: Wages, Profits, and Unemployment

Up to this point the emphasis has been on models in which firms can set their wage rates unilaterally. Yet many industrialized countries have large unionized sectors. Moreover, some economists have argued that even non-union labor markets may behave like markets where there is rent-sharing between firms and employees.[13] This suggests that to understand the link between pay and the local unemployment rate it may be useful to think within a bargaining framework. Here the key assumption is that "outside" unemployment weakens workers' bargaining power and thereby reduces the share of profits that those workers can appropriate.[14]

The textbook model of a competitive labor market implies that firms are wage-takers so that, for example, profitability will not affect the wage that they offer to homogeneous employees. This is the assumption of an infinitely elastic supply of labor. When firms bargain with their employees, however, a crucial issue is how much of any supernormal profits (so-called rents) can be appropriated by the workforce.

This section proves the following analytical results. First, in a bargaining model with rent-sharing, there is a positive partial correlation between wages and profit-per-employee, and a negative partial correlation between wages and unemployment. These are long-run correlations in the sense that they exist in steady-state equilibrium. Higher unemployment in the relevant local labor market means lower pay for the worker. Second, in a competitive model, given an upward-sloping labor supply curve, there is a positive short-run correlation between wages and profits. There may also be a positive correlation between wages and profit-per-employee: a sufficient condition for this is that the elasticity of labor demand be less than unity. There is no long-run relation between wages and profit variables. Third, in a labor contract model (with symmetric information) in which both workers and the firm are risk-averse, profits and wages are positively correlated. The elasticity of wages with respect to profits equals the ratio of the parties' relative risk-aversion parameters.

Three models of wage determination are now set out. One is a bargaining framework in which rents are divided between the firm and its

---

13. Pencavel (1991), for example, discusses this possibility. Closely related ideas are implicit in writings such as Slichter (1950), Mackay et al. (1971), Dickens and Katz (1987), Krueger and Summers (1988), Blanchflower et al. (1990), and Nickell and Wadhwani (1990).
14. This section draws upon joint work with Peter Sanfey. Further results are reported in Blanchflower et al. (1993) and in Sanfey's 1992 Yale Ph.D. dissertation.

employees; another is a competitive model in which the short run industry supply curve of labor slopes up; a third, which touches in a different way on a theme explored in an earlier section, is an optimal labor contract model under which risk-sharing occurs. If workers earn supernormal returns, it is not clear whether it is appropriate to require that a model include in it a zero-migration condition that ensures that everyone obtain the same going level of expected utility. For this reason, the bargaining model to be described below will look only at microeconomic issues, and leave open the question of how a full regional equilibrium would be defined.

The main proposition is the following:

PROPOSITION 3.1   Under union bargaining, the equilibrium wage is a decreasing function of unemployment in the outside labor market, and an increasing function of profit-per-employee.

Proof   Consider a bargaining model in which supernormal rents exist. Somehow they must be divided between workers and the employer. A useful and common assumption is that wages are determined as if by a Nash problem[15] in which η is the bargaining power of employees. Write this maximization problem as

$$\text{Maximize}\quad \eta \log\{[u(w) - u(\overline{w})]n\} + (1 - \eta)\log \pi \tag{3.3.1}$$

where $u(w)$ is the worker's utility from wage w, $\overline{w}$ is the wage available from temporary work in the event of a breakdown in bargaining, n is employment, and π is profits. The workers here are assumed to be represented by a so-called utilitarian trade union (Oswald, 1982) with risk-averse members.

This formulation relies on the assumption that in the event of bargaining delay the firm earns zero profit and the worker wage $\overline{w}$, and by the choice of units the variable n is also the probability of employment. Define profits as $f(n) - wn$, where f is a concave revenue function. The maximization's solution must be such that each side earn at least what is available as an outside option.

At an interior optimum, the following first-order conditions hold:

$$w: \frac{\eta u'(w)}{[u(w) - u(\overline{w})]n} - \frac{1 - \eta}{\pi} = 0 \tag{3.3.2}$$

$$n: \frac{\eta}{n} + \frac{(1 - \eta)[f'(n) - w]}{\pi} = 0 \tag{3.3.3}$$

---

15. The Nash approach can be justified axiomatically, as in Nash (1953), or strategically, as in Binmore et al. (1986).

Rewrite the first of these as

$$\frac{u(w) - u(\overline{w})}{u'(w)} = \left(\frac{\eta}{1 - \eta}\right)\frac{\pi}{n} \tag{3.3.4}$$

This can be simplified by using the first-order Taylor approximation

$$u(\overline{w}) \cong u(w) + (\overline{w} - w)u'(w) \tag{3.3.5}$$

to the more useful form

$$w \cong \overline{w} + \left(\frac{\eta}{1 - \eta}\right)\frac{\pi}{n}. \tag{3.3.6}$$

This equation shows that, to a first-order approximation, the equilibrium wage is determined by the outside wage available in the event of a temporary dispute in bargaining, the relative bargaining strength of the two sides, and the level of profit-per-employee.

Equation (3.3.6) is more general than might at first be apparent. Because it stems only from the first of the two first-order conditions, equation (3.3.6) is true independently of the exact nature of the employment function. In particular, given efficiency, it does not depend on whether employment is fixed along a labor demand curve—stemming from efficient bargaining under locally horizontal indifference curves as in the seniority or flat-indifference-curve model described in Oswald (1985, 1993)—or along an upward-sloping contract curve.[16]

A conventional assumption about the underlying determinants of $\overline{w}$, the outside temporary wage, is that it can be described by the function $c(w^0, b, U)$, where w^0 is the going wage in other sectors of the economy, b is the level of income when unemployed, and U is the unemployment rate among workers of the type employed by the firm. A natural interpretation of the algebra is that $\overline{w}$ is expected income and U determines the probability of receiving b rather than w^0. Written in full, therefore,

$$w \cong c(w^0, b, U) + \left(\frac{\eta}{1 - \eta}\right)\frac{\pi}{n} \tag{3.3.7}$$

In a regression equation for (3.3.7), estimated on longitudinal data, year

---

16. Equation 3.3.6 would not, however, be generated by the Layard et al. (1991) or Nickell and Wadhwani (1990) version of a labor demand model. That form of model, because it relies upon an unexplained inefficiency, would include one extra term for the elasticity of labor demand.

dummies are likely to capture w^0 and b, leaving unemployment U and profit-per-employee π/n as the key explanatory variables.[17]

At the other extreme from a bargaining model lies competitive theory. It is of interest to examine whether this, too, can imply a positive co-movement of wages and profitability.[18] Because the focus is the relationship between wages and profits, it is convenient to define a maximum profit function

$$\pi(\mu, w) = \max[\mu f(n) - wn] \tag{3.3.8}$$

where employment, n, is chosen to maximize the difference between revenue and labor costs, and $f(n)$ is a concave production function, μ is a demand shock (or output price) variable, and w is the wage. The function $\pi(\mu, w)$ is convex and homogenous of degree one in the prices μ and w. The later analysis assumes that the function is twice differentiable.

Assume that $\pi(\mu, w)$ represents the profit of the representative firm within an industry. By an appropriate choice of units, the long-run equilibrium level of profits can be set as $\pi(\mu, w) = 0$. This is the usual convention that profits be written net of some required return to the entrepreneur who runs the firm.

In this framework there is a labor demand curve defined by the derivative of the maximum profit function with respect to wages. Assume that there is also a labor supply function $l(w)$, which may be upward-sloping in the short-run, but which is horizontal in the long-run. This captures the competitive notion that, although in the long-run there should be free entry along a perfectly elastic labor supply curve, in the short-run there may be frictions that cause wages to be bid up by a demand shock.

It is not sufficient, for later purposes, to appeal to a conventional demand/supply picture, because profits cannot be read from such a diagram. But a simple algebraic argument is as follows. Equilibrium in this market is given by the equation

$$-\pi_w(\mu, w) = l(w) \tag{3.3.9}$$

where the function on the left is the demand curve for labor, and the function on the right is the supply curve of labor. The differential of equation (3.3.9) is

$$-\pi_{ww}\, dw - \pi_{w\mu}\, d\mu = l'(w)\, dw \tag{3.3.10}$$

---

17. If micro data are used w^0 could be a regional wage but it would in turn be a function of regional unemployment.
18. Hildreth and Oswald (1993) provide an analysis.

so that the relationship between demand shocks and wages is

$$\frac{dw}{d\mu} = -\frac{\pi_{w\mu}}{l'(w) + \pi_{ww}} \geq 0 \tag{3.3.11}$$

showing that wages rise in a boom.

Because the profit function is homogeneous of degree one, π can be written

$$\pi = \mu\pi_\mu + w\pi_w. \tag{3.3.12}$$

Differentiating this partially with respect to the wage:

$$\pi_w = \mu\pi_{\mu w} + w\pi_{ww} + \pi_w. \tag{3.3.13}$$

Cancelling terms and rearranging:

$$\frac{\pi_{ww}}{\pi_{w\mu}} = -\frac{\mu}{w} < 0. \tag{3.3.14}$$

To establish the reduced-form relationship between wages and profits, differentiate throughout the profit function $\pi(\mu, w)$ to give

$$\frac{d\pi}{dw} = \pi_\mu \frac{d\mu}{dw} + \pi_w \tag{3.3.15}$$

$$= -\pi_\mu[l'(w) + \pi_{ww}]/\pi_{w\mu} + \pi_w \tag{3.3.16}$$

$$= -\frac{\pi_\mu l'(w)}{\pi_{w\mu}} + \frac{\mu\pi_\mu}{w} + \pi_w \tag{3.3.17}$$

where equations (3.3.11) and (3.3.14) have been used to substitute terms. Note that $d\mu/dw$ is simply the inverse of the derivative of wages with respect to the exogenous demand shock.

The right hand side of equation (3.3.17) is non-negative. It is strictly positive if either supernormal profits are being made ($\pi > 0$), or the labor supply curve is strictly increasing. To check the former, note that, by homogeneity, $\pi > 0$ implies and is implied by

$$\frac{\mu\pi_\mu}{w} + \pi_w > 0. \tag{3.3.18}$$

The latter follows from $l'(w) > 0$, and the fact that $\pi(\mu, w)$ is increasing in the demand shock μ and has a negative cross-partial derivative. Equation (3.3.17) shows that wages and profits are positively correlated.

This suggests that an empirical inquiry into the role of unemployment in wage determination might have to include a profitability variable as an extra regressor. A natural question to ask is that of whether there is also, within the competitive framework, a positive correlation between profit-per-employee and the wage. Profit-per-employee is given by the ratio of profit to the wage-derivative of the profit function. Where n is employment, then,

$$\frac{\pi}{n} \equiv \frac{\pi}{-\pi_w} \tag{3.3.19}$$

so that

$$\frac{d}{dw}\left(\frac{\pi}{n}\right) = \frac{d}{dw}\left(\frac{\pi}{-\pi_w}\right). \tag{3.3.20}$$

Consider the derivative

$$\frac{d}{dw}(\pi_w) = \pi_{ww} + \pi_{w\mu}\frac{d\mu}{dw} \tag{3.3.21}$$

$$= -l'(w), \tag{3.3.22}$$

which uses equation (3.3.11) to cancel terms. Hence, the right hand-side of equation (3.3.20) can be written out in full, substituting from equations (3.3.12), (3.3.17) and (3.3.22), as

$$\frac{d}{dw}\left(-\frac{\pi}{\pi_w}\right) = -\frac{1}{\pi_w}\left[\frac{\mu\pi_\mu}{w} + \pi_w - \frac{\pi_\mu l'(w)}{\pi_{w\mu}} + \frac{\pi}{\pi_w}l'(w)\right] \tag{3.3.23}$$

$$= -\frac{1}{\pi_w}\left[\frac{\mu\pi_\mu}{w} + \pi_w - \frac{\pi_\mu l'(w)}{\pi_{w\mu}} + \frac{\mu\pi_\mu l'(w)}{\pi_w} + wl'(w)\right]. \tag{3.3.24}$$

By the earlier assumptions of an upward-sloping labor supply curve and non-negative profit:

$$\frac{\mu\pi_\mu}{w} + \pi_w \geq 0 \tag{3.3.25}$$

$$wl'(w) \geq 0. \tag{3.3.26}$$

Therefore, a sufficient condition for profit per capita and the wage to be positively correlated is:

$$-\frac{\pi_\mu l'(w)}{\pi_{w\mu}} + \frac{\mu\pi_\mu l'(w)}{\pi_w} \geq 0. \tag{3.3.27}$$

Using the definition of the elasticity of labor demand, combined with equation (3.3.13), the inequality in (3.3.27) is guaranteed to hold if the labor demand elasticty is below unity. Hence, a sufficient condition for the term in square brackets in equation (3.3.24) to be positive is that the elasticity of labor demand be less than unity.[19]

The final model to be considered is a generalization of the Baily (1974) and Azariadis (1975) optimal contract framework. In this the firm and workers are assumed to reach an implicit contract in which wages are set to provide efficient "insurance" against random demand shocks. Although the original articles assumed that firms are risk-neutral, and thus obtained the result that wages should be rigid, that assumption can be generalized to allow the firm to be averse to risk. The model then predicts a positive correlation between pay and profitability.

A labor contract model can be represented as the solution to the problem

$$\text{Maximize} \quad \int v(\pi) g(\mu) \, d\mu \tag{3.3.28}$$

subject to

$$\int [nu(w) + u(b)(1 - n)] g(\mu) \, d\mu \geq \bar{u} \tag{3.3.29}$$

$$\pi \equiv \mu f(n) - wn. \tag{3.3.30}$$

The solution is a wage function $w(\mu)$ defined on demand shocks. Implicit in the preceding formulation are the following assumptions. First, the firm's utility depends upon profits and can be represented by a concave function $v(\pi)$. Second, the worker receives utility $u(w)$ when employed and $u(b)$ when unemployed. Normalizing the size of the labor pool to unity, the probability of employment is n and of unemployment $1 - n$. Assume that there is no private unemployment insurance and that b is exogenously given. Although theoretically questionable, this is in line with U.K. and U.S. data.

Demand shocks here follow a probability density function $g(\mu)$. Firms must offer their employees the market level of expected utility.

---

19. A modified sufficient condition for a positive correlation between wages and profits-per-employee is that the elasticity of labor demand is less than the ratio of revenues to profits.

The key first-order conditions are

$$w(\mu): -v'(\pi) + \lambda u'(w) = 0 \tag{3.3.31}$$

$$n(\mu): v'(\pi)[\mu f'(n) - w] + \lambda[u(w) - u(b)] = 0, \tag{3.3.32}$$

where λ is a multiplier on the integral constraint (3.3.29) and is thus independent of μ. Equation (3.3.31) defines an implicit function linking profits and wages. Differentiating:

$$\frac{dw}{d\pi} = \frac{v''(\pi)}{\lambda u''(w)}, \tag{3.3.33}$$

which is strictly positive if both parties are strictly risk-averse, is undefined if workers are risk-neutral, and is zero if firms are risk-neutral. The latter is the case studied earlier.

Assume that workers' relative risk-aversion is r and the firm's relative risk-aversion is Ω. Then, combining (3.3.31) and (3.3.33),

$$\frac{dw}{d\pi}\frac{\pi}{w} = \frac{\Omega}{r}. \tag{3.3.34}$$

In words, the elasticity of wages with respect to profits is equal to the ratio of the firm's relative risk-aversion to the workers' relative risk-aversion. Here the firm and its employees choose to share the risk of demand fluctuations, so that wages and profits move together.

To summarize, the extreme competitive model, with instantaneous entry and exit of workers, implies that firms' wages will be unaffected by profit shocks. Intuition suggests that this result will disappear when frictions are introduced into the competitive framework, and the section formalizes that intuition. The testable characteristic of a competitive theory therefore becomes the hypothesis that long-run wage levels do not respond to profit movements. By contrast, there is a long-run relationship between pay and profits in either a rent-sharing model or a labor contract framework with risk-averse firms.

Under rent-sharing, a high level of unemployment in the local labor market can be expected to lead to low pay. This is because workers' power is depressed by poor outside opportunities. By its very nature this argument implies that the availability of rents—the size of the pie to be divided —matters. Hence a profitability variable of some kind might be expected to play a complementary role to unemployment in an empirically estimated wage equation.

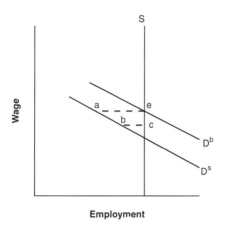

Figure 3.12
Why demand-and-supply theory does not produce a wage curve

3.4   Disequilibrium and Final Points

Some further points merit brief discussion. It might be thought, intuitively, that a downward-sloping relationship between pay and unemployment could emerge from conventional competitive theory if that approach were modified to allow for the possibility of sluggish adjustment of wage rates. This view is mistaken. It probably arises from the unconscious mixing up of the idea of low wages with that of falling wages. An account of the fallacy goes as follows.

Consider a demand-and-supply picture like figure 3.12 in which a demand curve shifts left from a position of boom demand. Total labor supply is assumed inelastic for clarity (nothing crucial rests upon this assumption). Lines D^b and D^s are, respectively, boom and slump demand curves. Equilibrium is initially at point e. After the drop in demand, a gap, given by segment ae in the diagram, opens up between the supply of people looking for jobs and the new level of labor demand by firms. Wages slowly start to fall from point a. Imagine that data are collected by the government just as a point like b in figure 3.12 is being reached. Unemployment is then given by the length of the line segment bc. Here, so the argument might go, there is low pay and fairly high unemployment. Thus the beginning of a wage curve is apparent, but the wage curve is just temporary and an illusion.

There are several criticisms of such logic. First, the argument rests upon a selective choice of points and time periods. There is no reason to choose to look at outcome *bc* rather than, say, outcome *ae*. The nature of the argument should work equally well at the *start* of the slump. But there the initial wage is high (at *ae*) at the same time as employment is low and unemployment is at its highest. Then the correlation between pay and joblessness is the reverse of that needed: it is positive. Second, a disequilibrium interpretation rests upon an assumed slowness of wage adjustment. It is presumably inapplicable, therefore, in the long-term: any observed empirical negative association between wages and unemployment cannot last. Although this is not intrinsically a problem, the evidence documented in later chapters suggests that there is a long-run wage curve. Third, at bottom there is a confusion at work here between levels and changes. The "disequilibrium" view in figure 3.12 is ultimately dependent on the textbook assumption that in a competitive market an excess supply will lead to a fall in the price of the good. Unemployment, therefore, should produce declining wages. But this is not the same as low wages. Although competitive disequilibrium logic may rationalize a Phillips curve—indeed that has been the traditional approach since Lipsey (1960)—it will not rationalize a curve linking the level of unemployment to the level of the wage.

The models in this chapter hold constant such factors as the underlying wealth or productivity of an economy. The idea that there is a negative relationship between pay and unemployment does not mean that high-wage countries have low unemployment rates, nor does it imply that secularly growing wages will be associated with slowing reducing levels of unemployment. The efficiency wage model, for example, makes it clear that richer countries have (vertically) higher no-shirking conditions because they will have higher *b* levels for the unemployed to live on.

Demand shocks play an important but varied role in the three different models of the chapter. They embellish the contract explanation, but do little more than that, because the curve is not produced by demand shocks per se. They are central to the efficiency wage approach, because it is shocks that trace out the no-shirking condition. They complement the bargaining framework, because profits should be an extra independent variable.

It might be thought that search models could generate an alternative theory of the wage curve. This remains an open question. Pissarides (1990), for example, argues analytically that wages are depressed by rises in unemployment. However, this is not for a reason intrinsic to search theory, but rather because, as in the previous section of this chapter, the assumption of Nash bargaining is made. Storer (1992) attempts to build a search-theoretic model of the wage curve. The slope of the crucial locus turns out to have an ambiguous sign.[20]

3.5 Conclusions

Contrary to the conventional wisdom of papers such as Harris and Todaro (1970), wages need not be positively related to the local unemployment rate. As this chapter has shown, there are at least three models in which the wage is a declining function of the local rate of joblessness. If a negative relationship were to be found in the data, therefore, there would be various ways to interpret that correlation. First, the relationship might be the equation of a contract curve. Second, it might be a no-shirking condition. Third, it might be a kind of bargaining-power locus.

These facts do not mean that the Harris-Todaro concept of compensating differentials across regions is inherently wrong or irrelevant. Migration generates heavy short-run costs; it is closer to an investment decision than to a consumption decision. Therefore migrants' choices are not likely to respond to transitory movements in economic conditions. More probably, something akin to expected values will determine migration flows, so that, by the theory of compensating differentials, it is the "permanent" values of pay and joblessness that will be positively related across regions in a long-run equilibrium. The Harris-Todaro concept can then sit comfortably alongside the existence of a negatively-sloped relationship between contemporaneous pay and joblessness, because permanent values can be positively related while movements around the mean are negatively related.[21] This simple point, which plays a continuing role in the chapters to come, has received little attention in the literature.

Three theories of a downward-sloping "wage curve" have been proposed in this chapter. It is now appropriate to ask whether they make distinctive predictions that could be checked empirically.

The idea that area wages and area unemployment might be (inversely) related by a contract curve is, on the face of it, an appealing one. Contract theory retains some of the logical coherence of competitive analysis and

---

20. Paul Evans, as a conference discussant of an early version of part of this book, showed that a standard search model has trouble generating the crucial negative slope.

21. Those who wonder about this might consider the case of hurricanes and average income. Regions hit by hurricanes suffer falls in income that year. Yet there may still be a Harris-Todaro effect ensuring that, on average, hurricane-prone places offer a compensating income differential. To check for this positive slope, a regression would have to be run on "permanent" values of the two variables. One run on actual values would tend to produce a negative slope, merely because hurricanes destroy crops and factories.

yet simultaneously allows a central role for unemployment, wage stickiness, and demand shocks. There are no supernormal rents to be had—on either side of the labor market—in the long run. The wage can be rigid. Such models have no unexplained inefficiencies and no unexploited gains from trade.

Yet the multi-region contract model developed in section 3.1 has features that some economists are likely to view as weaknesses. One is that it rests on the hypothesis that labor demand curves do not exist. Decades of labor economics textbooks could, of course, be incorrect; the wage/employment outcomes observed in real labor markets may be on upward-sloping contract curves and not, despite what students are taught, on labor demand curves. Nevertheless, there is comparatively little hard evidence to suggest that that is true. First, there is an immense econometric literature, surveyed recently by Hamermesh (1993), which documents the apparent existence of labor demand functions. Not all of this is conclusive. It would have to be admitted, for example, that some of the evidence is from highly aggregated time series studies, and that these are not only intrinsically open to doubt but also that at the economy-wide level a contract approach could be consistent with an apparent aggregate labor demand curve. Moreover, measurement error is a routine problem in this research area, where the "wage" is on many occasions defined by dividing a wage bill series by an employment series. Even so, not all studies suffer in these ways, and the weight and consistency of microeconometric findings recorded in Hamermesh (1993) is difficult to reconcile with a belief that there are no labor demand functions in the world. Second, although tests between labor demand curves and efficiency-locus contract curves have so far proved inconclusive,[22] the most recent evidence appears to be tilting toward the labor-demand approach. For example, Card (1990b), Nickell and Wadhwani (1991) and Abowd and Kramarz (1992) have better data than were available to most previous investigators and provide reasonably convincing support for the view that, consistent with marginal productivity theory, a firm's employment is depressed by high wages. Third, real collective bargaining appears to be rarely over the employment level but is routinely over pay. This asymmetry raises doubts about the existence of contractual arrangements that are predicated upon symmetry and which might be difficult to implement without the existence of some form of influence by

---

22. The small amount of literature offering econometric findings consistent with efficient contracts includes MaCurdy and Pencavel (1986), Abowd (1989), and Christofides and Oswald (1991).

workers over the total level of employment. A final way to question the contractual approach is to point out that wage-rigidity predictions arise only under restrictive conditions, that contract models that truly rely on no assumed inefficiencies collapse to a competitive framework, and that the theories' implications about overemployment could be deemed unattractive.[23] Some of the traditionally-cited benefits of the efficient contract approach may thus be illusory.

The contract models in section 3.2.1 have implications that can be checked empirically.

1. The driving force is a positive correlation between employment and the wage. Wage regressions using unemployment as an independent variable might be expected to perform more poorly than those that rely on employment per se.

2. The principal model, with risk-neutral employers, implies that wages are independent of demand shocks and that differences in regional wage levels stem from unchanging characteristics such as climatic variation across space. This implies that regressions that control for regional fixed effects (that is, include a set of regional dummy variables) should show little or no sign of a negative unemployment effect upon pay.

3. A negative association between pay and unemployment is not causal but rather reflects a partial correlation. This might be expected to show up as a lack of robustness in estimated coefficients and high sensitivity to different lists of included regressors.

4. Contract theory presumes that employer and employees perceive themselves to be in a lasting relationship where there is little likelihood of turnover. A traditional labor demand framework, by contrast, might be considered more plausible for low-skill workers with highly transitory jobs. This suggests that a contract model would predict a negative wage/unemployment correlation more strongly and more naturally in the well-paid primary sector than in poorly-paid secondary sector activities.

The case for an efficiency wage approach also has strengths and weaknesses. The model set out in section 3.2 generates with comparative ease a downward-sloping relationship between employee remuneration and local joblessness. This no-shirking equation is the result of the assumption that workers' effort levels are difficult to monitor. Thus employees have a chance of shirking without being caught. Their effort choices are made with

---

23. A discussion of such criticisms is available in Rosen (1985) and Manning (1990).

one eye on the outside labor market. Unemployment in the surrounding locale acts as a disincentive to laziness at work. When firms are surrounded by a high degree of joblessness, they can pay less well. The reason is that employees are then keen to work hard, and to retain their jobs, even if the pay is mediocre.

The approach's testable implications appear to include the following.

1. In sectors where the monitoring and supervision of effort levels is especially easy, the negative effect of unemployment upon pay should be small or even negligible.

2. In jobs where workers earn large rents (certain unionized or specialist posts, perhaps) the unemployment elasticity of pay might be expected to be small. The reason is that such jobs are inherently attractive to workers, so that variation in the outside unemployment rate ought to make little difference to their willingness to put in effort at work. Even if unemployment is low, therefore, these workers are unlikely to risk the consequences of shirking.

3. Because it is unemployment per se that creates the incentives, estimated wage equations should be better specified with unemployment, rather than employment, as a regressor.

A bargaining approach also suggests that higher unemployment will be associated with reduced wage settlements. The foundation here is the notion that it is relative power that decides the wage outcome and that workers' power declines as local joblessness grows. When it is hard to get another job, the wage settlement tends to be at a lower level. This approach leads to the following empirical predictions.

1. Where workers' power is negligible, firms should be pure wage-takers and the unemployment rate should then (at least through this mechanism) have no influence.

2. Wages will be higher where profitability-per-employee, ceteris paribus, is greater.

3. The unemployment elasticity of wages is likely to be lower the higher is profitability.

4. The level of unemployment should be a more effective regressor than the level of employment.

It is not possible, with normal data sets, to provide exact tests of all these different ideas and predictions. They are recorded here partly because in some instances they help later on in the book, partly for the theoretical record, and partly because one day with new sorts of statistical sources they may be testable.

This chapter develops models with characteristics and predictions that are different from those described in chapter 2. As with any effort to confront theoretical models with data, the predictions listed above are open to different emphasis. Some economists will think of other testable characteristics, or may doubt the accuracy and usefulness of those listed here. The preceding analysis is not meant to preclude alternative theories or interpretations. The chapter's aim is the more modest one of designing models that seem coherent, have testable implications, and might be capable of fitting the facts.

4

The U.S. Wage Curve I: Basics

The vision I would like you to carry away from this lecture sees economics as fundamentally an observational discipline.

Arnold Harberger (1993) Richard T. Ely Lecture to the American Economic Association

The models of the last chapter suggest that it may be wrong to predict, as Harris-Todaro (1970) models do, that in a cross-section across space the level of wages and the level of unemployment will be positively correlated. They raise the possibility that pay and unemployment are inversely related and that the competitive approach to labor market analysis is misguided. Moving from theoretical supposition to empirical test is then the next, and inherently more difficult, step.

In many other disciplines an underlying hypothesis can be scrutinized by the construction of a carefully designed experiment. The researcher creates an ossified laboratory world that allows him or her to trace out, against a background where nothing is altering, the consequences of a single change in the driving variable of interest. A good example is the medical experimenter who studies the impact of a chemical upon health. Randomly chosen groups of subjects are given doses of different amounts; their later health is recorded; at the end of the trial a statistical judgment is made about the effect of the chemical. The economist, however, can rarely use such methods. Experiments cannot usually be constructed. Despite common misconceptions, this does not mean that all experimental-style information is unavailable. Reality is full of natural experiments. Just as a medical statistician who cannot generate a laboratory experiment can go out and seek data where by chance people have been exposed to the chemical of interest, so the social scientist has, fortuitously or not, to hit upon data that inadvertently contain naturally experimental material.

This methodology is probably inherently less reliable than the one to which chemists are accustomed. Sorting out causality is likely to be difficult. The justification for it has to be that some topics are sufficiently important that we need to understand them even if the tools open to us are imperfect. Failing the existence of a U.S. president who is willing to run giant economics experiments in which, say, New Hampshire's unemployment rate is changed artificially to study scientifically the implications for pay, statistical patterns must somehow be discerned in the myriad facts of history. Fortunately this has been made less awesome a task by the recent creation by governments of randomly sampled surveys of individuals.

This chapter is an attempt to examine the influence of local unemployment upon—or more accurately the correlation with—the determination of wages in the United States. It uses two sources of information. The first is the General Social Surveys (GSS) of 1974 to 1988.[1] The second, which is nearly 150 times larger, is the March Current Population Surveys of 1964 to 1991, otherwise known as the Annual Demographic Files. In these data, joblessness and pay turn out to be inversely related. This spatial relationship is what the book calls the wage curve. There is also an "industry" wage curve.

The next two sections present evidence that a disaggregated measure of local unemployment, whether measured as an area or industry rate, enters negatively and significantly in U.S. earnings equations. The finding seems to be a robust one. It makes little difference whether the dependent variable is defined as annual, weekly, or hourly earnings. Moreover, however broadly or narrowly the regional and industry unemployment rates are measured, the results are approximately the same.

The analysis estimates pooled cross-section equations on micro data. The general form is a function ϕ given by

$$\ln w = \phi(x, U_i, U_r, r, i, t) \tag{4.1}$$

where x is a vector of individual or workplace characteristic variables, U_i is the unemployment rate in the relevant industry, U_r is the unemployment rate in the relevant region, r is a vector of regional dummies, i is a vector of industry dummies, t is a vector of year dummies, and $\ln w$ is the logarithm of the individual's wage or earnings. Willis (1986) is a standard reference on earnings equations, although it contains nothing about the role of unemployment.

---

1. The GSS has not been used a great deal by economists.

The earlier theoretical analysis of chapter 3 produced models of real wage determination. There are no regional price deflators for the U.S. regions, so regional and time dummies must be relied upon to play that role. The x variables are of a kind conventional in the literature on cross-section wage equations. In this sense, the equations begin from the standard microeconometric formulation. Their novelty is in the inclusion of local unemployment as a regressor.

It may be necessary to stress that this relationship is not Phillips's (1958) famous curve, which is a locus linking wage change to the rate of unemployment. It is, however, related to the curve of textbook fame. The chapters of this book will suggest that the Phillips curve is probably a misspecified aggregate wage curve. They estimate microeconometric wage equations in which lagged dependent variables are routinely close to zero. This is sufficient to reject Phillips's concept: it predicts (at least in its original form) that lagged pay should enter with a unit coefficient in an equation where the dependent variable is the level of pay. In tables such as 4.36 of this chapter, for example, where data are for the U.S. states from 1979 to 1987, the coefficient on the lagged logarithm of wages is estimated at 0.0 with a t-statistic of almost zero. Things are less clear intellectually, however, in cases where the lagged dependent variable is simply small. Table 4.30, for instance, shows that in an industry wage curve the lagged dependent variable has a coefficient of 0.1. Should this degree of autoregression count as evidence for a Phillips curve? Modern error-correction methods suggest that a natural generalization of the Phillips curve is to allow Phillips's wage change equation to have a level wage term on the right-hand side. The question, though, is that of how low the estimated coefficient on the lagged wage level term has to go before Phillips can reasonably be seen as more misleading than helpful. For example, a few of the more aggregated equations estimated later, such as in table 4.27, obtain a lagged dependent variable just below 0.3 with a well-defined t-statistic. This is the highest seen in the monograph, and it may not be coincidental that the largest number stems from the book's most highly aggregated regressions. In chapter 6, for Great Britain, the lagged dependent variable's coefficient is again literally zero. The view taken in this monograph is that the evidence suggests that it is probably time to jettison the Phillips curve.

What emerges from the data is evidence of a negative association between pay and unemployment. The extent of the nonlinearity is investigated by fitting different polynomial structures (in both regional and industry unemployment). In most cases these give similar results. As a check, in order to ensure that the curvature identified here is not being forced upon the data by the use of any particular functional form, the following specifications are fitted to both the regional and industry unemployment series.

1. The unemployment rate entered as a level.

2. The unemployment rate and its square.

3. The natural logarithm of the unemployment rate.

4. The logarithm of the unemployment rate and its cube.

5. The reciprocal of the unemployment rate.

6. A series of unrestricted estimates with a dummy variable for each one-point interval of the unemployment distribution.

7. A series of unrestricted estimates with a dummy variable for each 5% (that is, one twentieth of the axis) of the unemployment distribution.

Many experiments were done, and a selection is reported later.

In most cases these suggest a robust, negative, nonlinear relationship between unemployment and pay. It is not practicable—especially as there are many chapters on different countries to come—to keep repeating equations with a variety of nonlinear specifications. Principally for ease of interpretation and computation, number three is treated eventually in the book as the standard specification. This means that, because the dependent variable is a logarithm, a double log form is the dominant structure in the book's later analysis. Such a choice imposes a constant elasticity, of course, so has implications that are not insignificant.

4.1 The U.S. General Social Surveys, 1974–1988

With two exceptions, this series of surveys has been conducted annually since 1972. The exceptions are the years 1979 and 1981 when no survey was carried out. Details of the surveys are described in the appendix. The U.S. General Social Survey is a small annual sample of English-speaking persons aged eighteen years or over who live in noninstitutional arrangements (so those in prison, for example, are omitted). Between 1972 and 1988, there were 23,356 individuals in the sample, of whom 13,076, or 56%, were working at the time of interview. Earnings data are not reported prior to 1974, so the sample employed in the analysis is for the years 1974 to 1978, 1980, and 1982 to 1988. The usable sample is of 10,703 workers.

The dependent variable in the regressions is the natural logarithm of gross annual earnings. This variable is grouped and is open-ended at the top end. The mid-points of the wage bands were used in the regressions,

Table 4.1
Numbers of observations per year from the GSS

Year	Number of observations
1974	708
1975	730
1976	698
1977	718
1978	827
1980	775
1982	963
1983	854
1984	839
1985	863
1986	812
1987	1,068
1988	848
Total	10,703

and the top category was closed in a necessarily arbitrary fashion (experimentation suggested that the results were insensitive to the upper values chosen). The numbers of individual observations per year are listed in table 4.1.

Table 4.2 reports ten different earnings equations estimated using ordinary least squares. Each equation includes a set of personal controls such as experience, years of schooling, gender, marital status, union membership, race, and part-time, as well as a full set of year dummies. No regional or industry dummy variables are included at this stage. Moving across the ten columns of the table, various specifications of the unemployment terms are reported. As explained later in this chapter, the data for the unemployment variables are from standard outside sources and are mapped onto the data file at the level of the region and the industry. "Industry" unemployment is calculated by using jobless workers' previous industry affiliation. The GSS contains only a broad classification of geographical area. It does not, for example, record the exact state where the respondent lives. Consequently, the regional unemployment variable is defined in the analysis across nine large areas of the United States (New England, West South Central, and so on) for each of the thirteen years of the sample. This could, of course, cause problems, because the relevant unemployment rate in wage determination may be better captured by that in the worker's immediate narrow area.

Table 4.2
Log earnings equations with an unemployment regressor ("wage curves") for the United States: GSS 1974–1988

	(1)	(2)	(3)	(4)	(5)	(6)	(7)	(8)	(9)	(10)
Log regional U	.0120 (0.31)	−.4595 (2.72)								−.4643 (2.76)
(Log regional U)^3		.0429 (2.87)								.0440 (2.95)
Regional U			.0051 (0.93)	−.0525 (2.05)					−.0525 (2.05)	
(Regional U)^2				.0037 (2.31)					.0037 (2.35)	
Log industry U					−.1020 (5.87)	−.4186 (7.84)				−.4181 (7.83)
(Log industry U)^3						.0308 (6.27)				.0306 (6.23)
Industry U							−.0089 (3.59)	−.0597 (7.55)	−.0599 (7.58)	
(Industry U)^2								.0028 (6.77)	.0028 (6.77)	
Constant	7.5274	8.1198	7.5242	7.7305	7.7830	8.1304	7.6414	7.8510	8.0260	8.6990
$\bar{R}^2$	.4952	.4964	.4961	.4963	.4977	.4995	.4967	.4988	.4991	.4999
F	348.05	300.02	308.44	299.90	310.41	303.76	309.14	302.89	286.83	287.77

Source: General Social Surveys.
Notes: In all cases $N = 10,615$. All equations include controls for (1) experience and its square, (2) children, (3) gender, (4) three marital status dummies, (5) two race dummies, (6) union states, (7) past unemployment, (8) self-employment, (9) part-time, (10) supervisor, (11) probability of losing job dummy, (12) thirteen-year dummies, and (13) years of schooling.
The dependent variable is the log of annual earnings. U is the unemployment rate.
t-statistics are in parentheses.

One hundred seventeen separate regional unemployment observations are produced for the GSS sample. For industries, there is an average of 25 observations per year across thirteen years, thereby leading to 325 separate unemployment observations. As might be expected, there is greater variance in the latter series than the former. The range of the industry unemployment series is from 1.0% to 20.3%, compared to 3.1% and 12.5% for the regional series. The secondary source for these data is *Employment and Earnings* (various issues), although the primary source is the Current Population Survey used in the following section. Full details of how the variables are defined, as well as the means and standard deviations, are provided in the appendix.

The empirical analysis begins, inauspiciously, with column 1 of table 4.2. The logarithm of regional unemployment variable is entered (along with the personal controls and year dummies mentioned above) into a conventional form of earnings equation. A tiny, positive and insignificant coefficient on local unemployment is found. There is no support in the first column of Table 4.2 for an upward-sloping Harris-Todaro locus, nor any for a downward-sloping "wage curve."

This result probably conceals as much as it reveals, however, because beneath the surface there is a nonlinearity in the data. Although later sections of the book will move away from this somewhat, it is probably useful to start systematically.

The possibility of complicated nonlinearities has, in this sense, rarely been considered in empirical work on pay determination. However, both Carruth and Oswald (1987b) and Nickell (1987) find that, on British time-series data, the best wage equation is more complex than a log-linear function of unemployment. Nickell, for example, shows that the male wage equation reaches a minimum at 19% unemployment, which although high is not absurdly above the peak that unemployment reached in Britain. Carruth and Oswald (1987b) report wage equations in which the coefficients of both the natural logarithm of unemployment and its cube are statistically significant. In an earlier paper (Blanchflower and Oswald, 1990b) with a series of cross-section equations for the United Kingdom and the United States, evidence was found in favor of a number of nonlinear specifications in the unemployment rate.

The columns of table 4.2 gradually add nonlinear terms. Column 4 is representative: its quadratic form shows that there is a U-shaped relationship in wage/unemployment space. The addition (to column 1's specification) of the cube of the log of unemployment, in column 2, markedly improves the performance of the original equation. Both regional unemployment terms move to significance, with t-statistics over 2.7. Doing this is unattractive, of course, because it is hard to know what it means theoretically to add high powers of logs. But it seems to fit the data.

A similar picture emerges when the regional unemployment rate is included as a level (column 3) followed by a level and its square (column 4). In column 5 of table 4.2, the regional unemployment variable is replaced with an industry unemployment variable, which is significant with a coefficient of -0.1 and a t-statistic of nearly 6. This negative slope is noteworthy. The addition of the cubic term in column 6 again improves the performance of the equation, as it did with regional unemployment. Industry unemployment entered as a level is significant in column 7. A squared term and the unemployment rate are significant in column 8 (t-statistics of 6.8 and 7.6 respectively).

In column 9 of table 4.2 the level of regional unemployment and its square are included alongside equivalent quadratic terms in industry unemployment. All four are statistically significant. A preferred specification in this table is perhaps column 10, which has an adjusted R^2 of 0.50, and which includes the log and cube-of-log terms in both regional and industry unemployment. It seems from the table that the regional and industry wage curves are orthogonal to one another. A similar result is described in the next section for the CPS.

Figure 4.1 graphs the two wage curves obtained from column 10 of table 4.2. The dependent variable and both unemployment rates are set at their mean values, which allows the constant to be solved for in each equation. Various unemployment values are inserted into the two equations:

1. Industry wage curve $w = 9.8184 - .4181 \log U + .0306 (\log U)^3$

2. Regional wage curve $w = 9.8091 - .4643 \log U + .0440 (\log U)^3$

By construction, the two wage curves pass through the intersection of the means of the wage and unemployment series. The curves are plotted only over the range of unemployment rates that are present in the data (which explains the differences, within the Figures, in the lengths of the two curves). The two wage curves in figure 4.1 are of broadly similar shape. Both minimize at an unemployment rate of approximately 6%–8%. A substantial part of both wage curves also appears to slope upwards, which might, in principle, reflect Harris-Todaro forces, although such an interpretation would be highly speculative. The best that could be said about these slightly curious results is that they indicate there may be something of interest going on in the data.

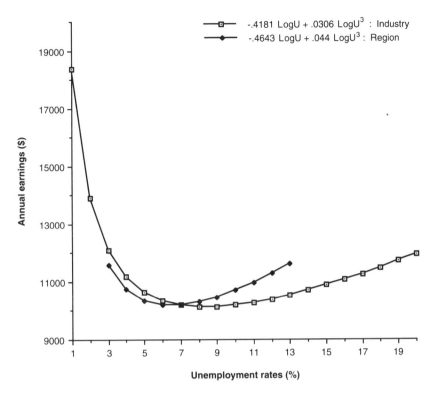

Figure 4.1
Industry and regional wage curves: 1974–1988

The theoretical analysis of the previous chapter suggests that terms may be missing from the equations of table 4.2 and figure 4.1. One possibility is that the upward-sloping section of the wage curve arises because of the existence of fixed region-specific and industry-specific forces. These are unchanging "permanent" factors. This hypothesis is explored in column 1 of table 4.3 by re-estimating the equation reported in column 10 of table 4.2 but including eight regional dummies. This has the effect of driving the two regional unemployment terms to insignificance. In column 2, the inclusion of thirty industry dummies has an equivalent effect on the industry unemployment terms. In columns 3 and 4, full sets of regional and industry dummies are included along with the various unemployment terms. On the basis of a series of F-tests, the performance of the equations reported in table 4.3 is better than that of the equations in table 4.2. The data support the hypothesis that these dummies should be included. The addition of the industry dummies has the effect of driving the industry unemployment

Table 4.3
Wage curve experiments for the United States: GSS 1974–1988

	(1)	(2)	(3)	(4)	(5) 1970s	(6) 1970s	(7) 1980s	(8) 1980s
Log regional U	−.3169	−.4522	−.0343	−.3726	−.0909	−.5735	−.1297	−.4485
	(1.72)	(2.71)	(0.67)	(2.05)	(0.44)	(0.99)	(1.37)	(1.99)
(Log regional U)³	.0256	.0418		.0308		.0417		.0299
	(1.59)	(2.82)		(1.93)		(0.88)		(1.57)
Log industry U	−.4351	−.1227	−.0061	−.1025	−.0531	−.1740	.0970	.0080
	(8.16)	(1.45)	(0.14)	(1.24)	(0.61)	(1.18)	(1.27)	(0.06)
(Log industry)³	.0321	.0101		.0086		.0117		.0072
	(6.53)	(1.53)		(1.36)		(0.99)		(0.87)
Regional dummies	8	—	8	8	8	8	8	8
Industry dummies	—	30	30	30	30	30	30	30
Constant	8.5801	8.3573	7.9419	8.4310	7.5771	8.3063	7.9293	8.3843
$\bar{R}^2$	.5012	.5106	.5129	.5131	.5106	.5105	.4755	.4756
N	10,615	10,615	10,615	10,615	3,647	3,647	6,992	6,992
F	243.34	171.37	163.37	158.90	63.35	61.36	100.03	97.06

Source: General Social Surveys.
Notes: All equations include controls for (1) experience and its square, (2) children, (3) gender, (4) three marital status dummies, (5) two race dummies, (6) union states, (7) past unemployment, (8) self-employment, (9) part-time, (10) supervisor, (11) probability of losing job dummy, (12) thirteen-year dummies, and (13) years of schooling.
The dependent variable is the log of annual earnings. U is the unemployment rate.
t-statistics are in parentheses.

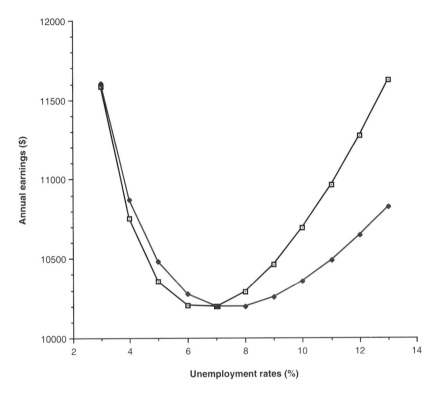

Figure 4.2
Regional wage curves: 1974–1988

terms to insignificance in both columns 3 and 4. However, in column 4 of table 4.3, both of the regional unemployment terms (the log and its cube) have *t*-statistics of approximately two. Regional dummies are included here. Similar specifications to those estimated in columns 3 and 4 are then given in columns 5 and 6 for the 1970s and in columns 7 and 8 for the 1980s. For these time periods the unemployment terms also have relatively low levels of significance. In figure 4.2 the regional wage curve shown in figure 4.1 is redrawn alongside the new one obtained from column 4 of table 4.3 (the one based on controls for the regional fixed effects). The two curves are similar, although it appears that the addition of regional dummies has the effect of flattening somewhat the right-hand side of the wage curve. This result is confirmed in the next section using the CPS.

No strong conclusions, but a number of empirical puzzles, emerge from this analysis of the General Social Surveys. Economists expecting an upward-sloping relationship between pay and local unemployment apparently find nothing in the data to support their view. There is weak evidence of a downward-sloping wage curve in both industry and region space, and fairly strong support for the idea, strange though it seems, of complicated nonlinearities. These conclusions are not highly robust to the inclusion of industry and regional dummies, so to make further progress requires a more comprehensive data set.

4.2   The Current Population Surveys, 1964–1991

The Current Population Survey (CPS) is the source of the official U.S. government statistics on employment and unemployment. The survey has been conducted monthly for over forty years. A stratified cluster sample of about 56,500 households is interviewed each month, randomly selected on the basis of area-of-residence to represent the nation as a whole, individual states, and specified areas. Each household is interviewed once a month for four consecutive months in one year, and again for the corresponding time period a year later. The March CPS, also known as the Annual Demographic File, contains basic monthly demographic and labor force data, plus additional data on work experience, income, noncash benefits, and migration. The files record information on each respondent's labor market status during the survey week—usually the third week in March—as well as retrospective data on labor market activity during the previous calendar year. The annual-earnings question is deliberately asked in the month of March because it is hoped that individuals will be especially knowledgeable of their income at this time of the year (since income tax returns are done in April). The retrospective data include answers to questions about annual earnings and weeks of employment and unemployment. They also include answers to questions about the industry and occupation of the longest job held during the year. Earnings in the CPS are meant to reflect all wages, salary, tips, and bonuses. Virtually all of what follows is based on retrospective data.

For estimation, each March CPS household file was first spread into distinct individual files. A subfile was selected for each year of the CPS. It consisted of those individuals who were employed in the previous year and who reported a wage. Following the approach taken in Katz and Murphy (1992), the sample includes individuals with imputed earnings. In contrast to Katz and Murphy, no correction is made for the fact that the imputation procedures changed between the 1975 and 1976 March CPS surveys. However, the later regressions include year dummies in all equations.

No adjustment is made to the earnings of workers whose data were top-coded (that is, assigned an upper limit) or to the earnings of those individuals who did not report their earnings to the CPS and who were assigned values via the so-called hot-deck procedure (for a description and analysis of such procedures, see Lillard et al., 1986). Experimentation suggested that the econometric results are not sensitive to these exclusion criteria. After omitting the self-employed and those working without pay, the separate files for each of the years 1964 to 1991 were pooled. This leads to a data file with more than 1.7 million observations. Each observation is a full-time or part-time worker. The exact annual numbers of observations used in the estimation are listed in table 4.4. The majority of the empirical work in this section uses 1964 to 1988 files. Shortly before com-

Table 4.4
Numbers of observations per year from the CPS

Year	Number of observations
1964	26,247
1965	26,501
1966	56,852
1967	36,710
1968	54,610
1969	62,213
1970	60,848
1971	61,594
1972	58,966
1973	58,110
1974	51,105
1975	51,219
1976	42,959
1977	70,448
1978	69,565
1979	70,324
1980	83,220
1981	82,864
1982	73,769
1983	71,661
1984	72,091
1985	73,932
1986	72,840
1987	72,520
1988	72,925
1989	57,315
1990	57,731
1991	69,475

pletion of this book, however, CPS surveys for the years 1989 to 1991 became available, and brief later results are given in this chapter. The remaining sections of this chapter report CPS earnings equations in which unemployment appears as a right-hand-side regressor. Section 4.2.1 offers evidence of both regional and industry wage curves, mostly for the whole twenty-five year period, 1963 to 1987, and occasionally for the 1963 to 1990 period. The reason that the first period is not 1964 to 1988 is because respondents in the CPS report their earnings for the previous year.

Subsample estimates are given for the 1960s, 1970s, and 1980s. Various experiments are done to try to discover the most appropriate linear or nonlinear specification for the wage curve. On grounds of computational simplicity and ease of exposition, the final conclusion is that the simple log formulation is the best choice. Experiments are done with various specifications of both the dependent variable and the regional unemployment rate. This turns out to have little effect on the results.

It is important, of course, to be sure that these methods are not "forcing" wage curves onto the data, as some commentators have claimed (Paldam, 1990). In section 4.2.2 a series of unrestricted estimates using dummy variables instead of nonlinear unemployment terms is reported. This elementary type of nonparametric approach also produces evidence of downward-sloping wage curves. Section 4.2.3 presents a series of disaggregated estimates of wage curves. These examine the unemployment elasticity of pay for different groups of individuals. The disaggregations are by both personal characteristics such as gender, age and race, and by workplace characteristics such as industry and sector. Section 4.3 contains conclusions.

4.2.1   U.S. Wage Curves from the CPS, 1963–1990

Because of changes in the Industrial Classification over the period in question, 1963 to 1990, it was possible only to distinguish 46 consistent and continuous industry groupings for which unemployment rates could be defined. Analogously, because of changes in the way regions are defined in the 1968 to 1975 CPS, it is possible to identify only 21 continuous regional areas over the twenty-five year period. Regional dummies for these are incorporated in subsequent regressions. Identities of the areas are listed in the appendix. For the 1964 to 1967 and 1976 to 1990 CPSs, unemployment rates can be mapped in at the state level.

The unemployment and earnings data used in the subsequent regressions relate to the respondent's labor market behavior in the year preceding the date of interview. When an earnings equation is estimated with, for example, the March 1987 CPS, regional unemployment and industry unemployment rates for 1986 are used. This matches 1986 earnings to 1986 unemployment rates. In what follows, years relate to the year preceding the survey rather than to the date of the survey.

The dependent variable in the regressions is the log of annual earnings in the year prior to interview. Weekly or hourly earnings are used by Juhn et al. (1991), Murphy and Welch (1992), Katz and Murphy (1992), and Katz and Krueger (1992), for example. The annual variable was chosen here with an eye on the need for a long period of years. It is possible to derive a consistent annual pay series for each of the years of the CPS from 1964 to 1988. For a number of the years, hours (weeks) are only reported as bands, even where actual hours (weeks) are reported; in some years they relate to the previous week and in others to the preceding year. This is why the analysis does not use, say, hourly earnings. The possible sensitivity of wage curves to changes in the definition of the dependent variable is considered later in the section.

Table 4.5 sets out the first CPS results. It reports estimates of log annual earnings equations for the sample of approximately 1.7 million individuals. These equations are comparable to those reported in table 4.3, which used the GSS. They include full sets of year, regional and industry dummies, and a vector of personal controls. The controls include experience, years of schooling, race, gender, marital status, and a part-time dummy. One difference from the earlier section is that the dependent variable here is continuous (not grouped and open-ended as in the case of the GSS). Definitions, means, and standard deviations for variables are given in the appendix. An early version of this kind of equation is presented in Blanchflower and Oswald (1993), which is a reply to the idea of Sessions (1993) that the wage curve is U-shaped. As argued in Blanchflower and Oswald (1990b), a U-shape should probably be distrusted because the right-hand tail typically lies outside the observed data.

Apart from being estimated on a longer time period, and larger data file, the main difference between the specifications in tables 4.3 and those in table 4.5 is that the regional unemployment variable in table 4.5 is measured at a more disaggregated level.

In column 1 of table 4.5, the log of regional unemployment and the log of industry unemployment are entered as regressors. They have negative coefficients with t-statistics of around twenty five and thirty five, respectively. These large t-statistics may overstate the true level of significance, if there are common group errors, but that is checked in a later section. Both unemployment coefficients are -0.1.[2] To explore the possible non-

---

2. The complete equation presented in column 1 of table 4.5 is reported in the appendix.

Table 4.5
The U.S. wage curve

	(1) 1963–1987	(2) 1963–1987	(3) 1963–1987	(4) 1963–1987	(5) 1963–1990
Log industry U	−.1093 (35.19)	−.0252 (4.11)	−.0252 (4.09)		
(Log industry U)^3		−.0094 (15.84)	−.0094 (15.87)		
Log regional U	−.0987 (24.83)	−0.885 (7.73)	−.0981 (25.48)	−.1020 (26.49)	−.1034 (25.88)
(Log regional U)^3		−.0010 (0.89)			
Year dummies	24	24	24	24	27
Regional dummies	20	20	20	20	20
Constant	5.9391 (444.36)	5.8428 (312.59)	5.8542 (427.77)	5.7160 (485.63)	5.0853 (456.52)
$\bar{R}^2$	.5757	.5757	.5757	.5753	.5105
F	20,606.930	20,410.72	20,612.80	20,783.84	17,863.88
N	1,534,093	1,534,093	1,534,093	1,534,093	1,730,175

Source: Current Population Survey—March tapes.
Notes: All equations include full sets of year dummies, industry dummies (43), plus controls for (1) experience and its square, (2) years of schooling, (3) four marital status dummies, (4) two race dummies, (5) private sector dummy, (6) a gender dummy, and (7) a part-time dummy. All unemployment rates, U, and the dependent variable (annual earnings) are in natural logarithms.
t-statistics are in parentheses.

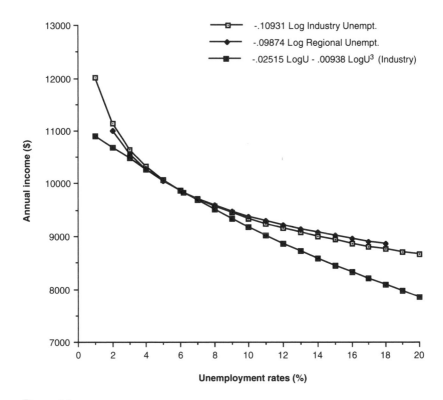

Figure 4.3
U.S. wage curves: 1963–1987

linearity of these wage curves, column 2 of table 4.5 adds two additional (log) cubic terms in regional and industry unemployment. The cube of the log of industry unemployment is significant at conventional levels, but the regional one is not. The specification in column 2 does not improve the adjusted R^2. Column 3 of table 4.5 excludes the cube of the log of regional unemployment. All three of the unemployment terms are significant. In column 4 of the table the coefficient of the regional unemployment variable alone is estimated. It is essentially the same as that in column 1 where industry unemployment was included. Thus, as noted with the GSS, these two measures of outside unemployment appear to be orthogonal to one another. Finally, column 4's equation is repeated in column 5 of table 4.5 for the longer sample 1963 to 1990. The answer is again an unemployment elasticity of -0.1.

What shape are the wage curves in table 4.5? The coefficients of the regional and industry unemployment variables are used to construct the curves graphed in figure 4.3. In addition, the estimated coefficients of

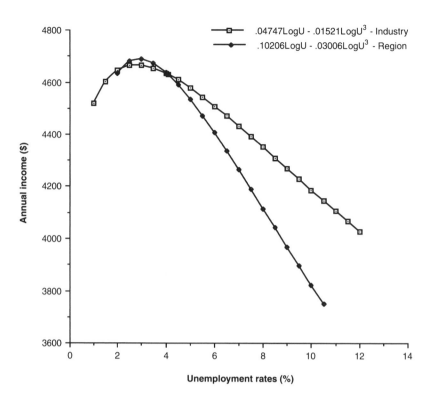

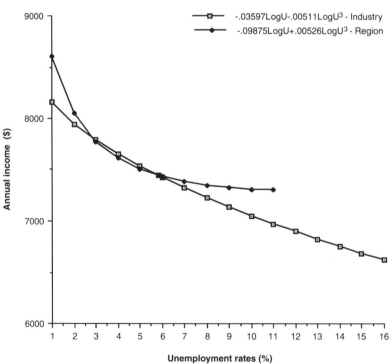

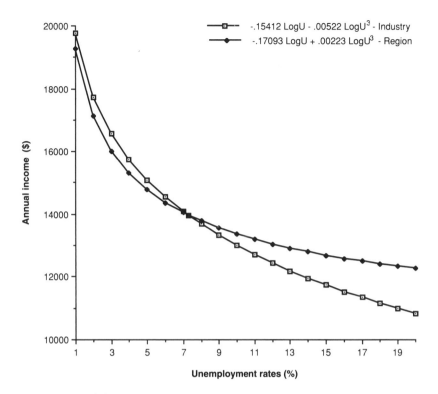

Figure 4.4 (top left)
U.S. wage curves: 1960s

Figure 4.5 (bottom left)
U.S. wage curves: 1970s

Figure 4.6 (above)
U.S. wage curves: 1980s

the log and the cube of the log of industry unemployment are applied to derive a third curve. It is similar, but slightly more linear. Employing the method described in section 4.1 to construct the graphs, by construction they pass through the intersection of the means of the wage and unemployment series. The two wage curves obtained from column 1 are virtually identical, and slope down from left to right. The negative sign on the cubic term in industry unemployment generates slightly less curvature than the single log formulations. Unlike the wage curves obtained from the GSS, there is no evidence of an upward-sloping portion to the curves.

Table 4.5 paints a distinctive and, relative to conventional wisdom, startling picture. There seems to be a well-defined downward-sloping curve

Table 4.6
The U.S. wage curve: Subsamples and "permanent" unemployment

	(1) 1963–1968	(2) 1969–1978	(3) 1979–1987	(4) 1979–1987
Log industry U	.0475 (2.654)	−.0360 (3.23)	−.1541 (11.15)	−.1431 (10.31)
(Log industry U)^3	−.0152 (4.77)	−.0051 (4.16)	−.0052 (4.69)	−.0079 (7.07)
Log regional U	.1021 (2.33)	−.0988 (4.26)	−.1709 (9.04)	−.0566 (3.21)
(Log regional U)^3	−.0301 (4.55)	.0053 (2.19)	−.0022 (1.33)	−.0130 (8.39)
Log permanent U				.2888 (33.20)
Year dummies	5 21	9 21	8 21	8
Constant	5.1915 (95.17)	7.0868 (206.27)	7.5892 (223.48)	6.5505 (198.68)
$\bar{R}^2$	.5441	.5676	.5363	.5319
F	23,739.84	8,776.99	9,088.71	11,634.05
N	263,133	595,138	675,822	675,822

Source: Current Population Surveys—March tapes.
Notes: All equations include full sets of year dummies, industry dummies (43), plus controls for (1) experience and its square, (2) years of schooling, (3) four marital status dummies, (4) two race dummies, (5) private sector dummy, (6) a gender dummy, and (7) a part-time dummy. All unemployment rates, U, and the dependent variable (annual earnings) are in natural logarithms. Permanent unemployment is the average state unemployment, 1963 to 1988. t-statistics are in parentheses.

linking pay and local unemployment in the United States. Over the period from the beginning of the 1960s to the end of the 1980s, a doubling of either the industry or regional unemployment rate is estimated to be associated with a 10% decline in annual earnings. In other words, there is a downward-sloping wage curve, and the unemployment elasticity of pay is approximately −0.1.

It is natural to ask how stable these findings are across subsample time periods, and whether there is any way to obtain a positively sloped unemployment effect. Table 4.6 re-estimates equation 2 of table 4.5. It does so for the periods 1963 to 1968, 1969 to 1978, and 1979 to 1987, respectively.[3] In what follows, these are referred to as the 1960s, 1970s, and

---

3. The coefficients on the personal control variables as well as the industry and region dummies for each of the three time periods are reported in the appendix.

1980s respectively. There is continuing evidence of a wage curve in both industry and regional space.

The wage curves for the three periods are plotted in figures 4.4, 4.5, and 4.6 respectively. In the case of the 1960s the log terms are both positive while the cubes are negative. As can be seen from figure 4.4, both 1960s wage curves appear to slope upward at low levels of unemployment. This is not robust and may be an artifact of the small number of unemployment observations at the low end. The vast majority of the sample is found in the downward-sloping portion of the curves. For the 1970s (figure 4.5) and 1980s (figure 4.6), both regional and industry wage curves slope down across the complete range of data points.

The theory developed in chapter 3 draws a dividing line, conceptually, between a downward-sloping curve linking current unemployment to current pay and an upward-sloping relationship linking (loosely) expected unemployment to expected pay. The data, it seems, favor a distinction of this sort. Column 4 of table 4.6 re-estimates the equation in column 3 for the 1980s but replaces the regional dummies with the average unemployment rate between 1960 and 1988 for each state. This long-run average is denoted the "permanent" unemployment rate. It enters positively. The purpose here is to separate out the underlying effects of unemployment arising because of structural differences across states (for example, the general attractiveness of the area as a place to live) from the more transitory components.

The average unemployment rates in each state over the period 1960 to 1987 that are used in the regressions are summarized in table 4.7. Graphs of the unemployment time-series in each state for the period 1960 to 1992 are provided at the end of this chapter as figures 4.35 to 4.85. Aggregate unemployment in the United States was roughly the same at the beginning of the period (5.4%) as it was at the end (6.1%). It fell to a low of 3.4% in 1969 compared to a high of 9.5% in 1982 and 1983, and averaged 6% with a variance of 2.67 percentage points. State by state there are substantial differences in both the level and variability of unemployment. For example, Alaska and West Virginia had the highest rates recorded (9.48% and 9.25% respectively) while Nebraska and South Dakota had the lowest (3.66% and 3.79% respectively). With the notable exceptions of Alaska and Washington D.C., states with the highest average unemployment had the highest variance.

In areas where the permanent (or long-run) unemployment rate is high, workers are paid a positive compensating differential. Table 4.6 reveals that the permanent unemployment variable enters positively and significantly

Table 4.7
Average state unemployment rates, 1960–1987

	Mean	Variance		Mean	Variance
Alabama	7.21	9.24	Montana	6.27	1.41
Alaska	9.48	1.01	Nebraska	3.66	1.00
Arizona	5.92	4.64	Nevada	6.63	2.46
Arkansas	6.59	3.59	New Hampshire	4.19	2.77
California	6.98	2.39	New Jersey	6.43	3.01
Colorado	4.91	2.18	New Mexico	6.87	2.65
Connnecticut	5.61	3.09	New York	6.35	3.34
Delaware	5.62	4.51	North Carolina	5.28	2.70
District of Columbia	5.50	10.09	North Dakota	4.84	0.73
Florida	5.57	4.26	Ohio	6.46	6.88
Georgia	5.44	2.47	Oklahoma	5.16	2.32
Hawaii	5.41	3.40	Oregon	6.89	4.77
Idaho	6.25	2.54	Pennsylvania	6.69	5.13
Illinois	5.91	6.05	Rhode Island	6.35	3.74
Indiana	6.09	6.40	South Carolina	6.05	3.13
Iowa	4.34	3.80	South Dakota	3.79	0.64
Kansas	4.18	0.98	Tennessee	6.15	5.50
Kentucky	6.48	5.05	Texas	5.13	2.73
Louisiana	7.47	5.67	Utah	5.76	1.20
Maine	6.28	3.17	Vermont	5.76	2.21
Maryland	5.06	2.16	Virginia	4.48	1.83
Massachusetts	5.86	3.35	Washington	7.61	4.34
Michigan	8.09	10.09	West Virginia	9.25	11.14
Minnesota	4.96	1.65	Wisconsin	5.35	4.04
Mississippi	6.95	6.78	Wyoming	4.61	1.18
Missouri	5.38	3.13	United States	6.02	2.67

(with a t-statistic of over 30). The coefficient of approximately 0.3 implies that a doubling of an area's permanent unemployment would be associated with a rise of nearly a third in the area's wage. Although the inclusion of this variable improves the performance of the regional unemployment variables, it worsens the overall performance of the equation—notably the cubed variable—compared with when the regional dummies are included. It does not seem to be unreasonable, then, to revert to the use of regional dummies to control for region-specific fixed effects. This is what is done in the remainder of the chapter, and in a sense in the remainder of the book.

As explained in chapter 2, a number of authors have argued that wages and some measure of area unemployment are positively correlated in the

Table 4.8
The U.S. wage curve without regional dummies

	(1) 1963–1968	(2) 1969–1978	(3) 1979–1987	(4) 1963–1987
Log industry U	−.0158	−.0786	−.2123	−.0899
	(1.39)	(15,45)	(34.64)	(28.82)
Log regional U	.0133	.1066	−.0696	−.0021
	(1.44)	(20.46)	(15.69)	(0.65)
Regional dummies	No	No	No	No
Industry dummies	Yes	Yes	Yes	Yes
Year dummies	Yes	Yes	Yes	Yes
Constant	5.9851	6.7400	7.5579	6.3116
	(195.64)	(333.98)	(368.43)	(462.62)
$\bar{R}^2$	.5398	.5649	.5326	.5748
F	5,061.45	11,708.25	12,034.70	25,604.57
N	263,133	595,138	675,822	1,534,093

Source: Current Population Surveys—March tapes.
Notes: All equations include full sets of year dummies and industry dummies (43), plus controls for (1) experience and its square, (2) years of schooling, (3) four marital status dummies, (4) two race dummies, (5) private sector dummy, (6) a gender dummy, and (7) a part-time dummy. All unemployment rates, U, and the dependent variable (annual earnings) are in natural logarithms.
t-statistics are in parentheses.

United States (including Hall, 1970, 1972; Topel, 1986; Reza, 1978; Marston, 1985; Adams, 1985). It is perhaps worth noting in passing that, largely unnoticed, Freeman (1982) found that this pattern did not hold for youths, whose unemployment rate was similar between high-wage and low-wage metropolitan areas, and whose ratio of employed workers to the population was lower in low-wage areas, possibly because the federal minimum wage reduced youth employment most in those areas.

It is possible to make sense of this difference between early findings and those given here. In table 4.8, which does not include regional dummies, the logarithm of regional unemployment has a coefficient of $+0.11$ for the 1970s subsample (column 2). There is no significant effect in the 1960s, however, although there is evidence of a strongly significant negative coefficient of -0.07 (t-statistic $= 15.7$) for the 1980s. Over the whole sample period, the regional unemployment variable entered in log form is insignificantly different from zero (column 4). It appears from this that the omission of regional dummies biases upwards the coefficient on unemployment.

Table 4.9 suggests that table 4.8 uses the wrong specification. In table 4.9, a complete set of twenty-one regional dummies is included. On the

Table 4.9
The U.S. wage curve with regional dummies

	(1) 1963–1968	(2) 1969–1978	(3) 1979–1987	(4) 1979–1987
Log industry U	−.0190	−.0981	−.2122	−.2141
	(1.68)	(19.33)	(34.75)	(35.12)
Log regional U	−.0779	−.0453	−.1475	−.1396
	(5.25)	(5.84)	(24.84)	(18.40)
Regional dummies	21	21	21	50
Industry dummies	Yes	Yes	Yes	Yes
Year dummies	Yes	Yes	Yes	Yes
Constant	5.3697	6.61677	7.6273	7.8417
	(132.39)	(296.55)	(351.22)	(336.23)
$\bar{R}^2$	.5440	.5650	.5363	.5381
F	3,877.01	9,096.36	9,304.54	6,906.47
N	263,133	595,138	675,822	675,822

Source: Current Population Surveys—March tapes.
Notes: All equations include full sets of year dummies and industry dummies (43), plus controls for (1) experience and its square, (2) years of schooling, (3) four marital status dummies, (4) two race dummies, (5) private sector dummy, (6) a gender dummy, and (7) a part-time dummy. All unemployment rates, U, and the dependent variable (annual earnings) are in natural logarithms.
t-statistics are in parentheses.

basis of F-tests, their inclusion improves the overall performance of these equations. For each period, the coefficient on the regional unemployment term in the columns of table 4.9 is negative and statistically significantly different from zero. As demonstrated earlier for the entire period, the log regional unemployment term is significant with a coefficient of −0.099 (column 1, table 4.5). The coefficient is also negative across each of the three decades. The coefficient on the regional unemployment variable for the 1980s is the largest (−0.15), in absolute terms, while that for the 1970s is the smallest (−0.05).

For the 1980s, the state in which the individual lived at the time of interview is reported in the CPS interviews. Consequently, it is possible to check the extent to which the need to rely on only twenty-one area dummies limits earlier estimates. The final column, 4, of table 4.9 re-estimates with regional unemployment rates as an independent variable, but replaces the twenty-one regional dummies with fifty state dummies. The results of column 4 are similar to those in column 3 of table 4.9. It is apparent that including a larger number of regional dummy variables has little effect on the estimated regional unemployment coefficient.

Table 4.10
Further CPS experiments, 1963–1987

	(1)	(2)	(3)
Industry U	−.0181	−.0152	
	(38.87)	(12.83)	
(Industry U)^2		−.0001	
		(2.76)	
Regional U	−.0138	−.0238	
	(23.72)	(11.83)	
(Regional U)^2		.0006	
		(5.18)	
1/(Industry U)			.3432
			(26.27)
1/(Regional U)			.4268
			(21.52)
Year dummies	24	24	24
Regional dummies	21	21	21
Constant	5.7767	5.79974	5.42090
	(576.54)	(455.086)	(566.310)
$\bar{R}^2$	.57532	.57533	.57506
F	20,783.79	20,377.014	20,761.128
N	1,534,093	1,534,093	1,534,093

Source: Current Population Surveys—March tapes.
Notes: All equations include full sets of year dummies and industry dummies (43), plus controls for (1) experience and its square, (2) years of schooling, (3) four marital status dummies, (4) two race dummies, (5) private sector dummy, (6) a gender dummy, and (7) a part-time dummy. The dependent variable (annual earnings) is in natural logarithms. U is the level of unemployment.
t-statistics are in parentheses.

Table 4.10 reports three further experiments to try to determine the appropriate specification of the unemployment terms. In column 1, levels of unemployment are included alone, while squared terms are added in column 2. Finally, column 3 includes the reciprocals of the industry and regional unemployment rates. None of these specifications dominates the ones reported in earlier tables that include log unemployment terms at the industry or regional levels. Estimated wage curves obtained using these specifications are similar to those reported earlier and consequently are not presented.

Table 4.11 explores the stability of the estimates of the wage curve to additional variations in the way in which the regional unemployment variable is measured and the way the dependent variable is defined. This table makes use of data from a single year, namely, the 1987 annual merged CPS

Table 4.11
Wage equations on a 1987 CPS Subsample

	Log U	(Log U)^3	U	U^2
1. Hourly earnings—Degrees of freedom = 54623				
a			−.0133	
			(16.8)	
b			−.0363	.0016
			(13.16)	(8.69)
c	−.0900			
	(19.15)			
d	−.1860	.0108		
	(11.82)	(6.37)		
e		−.0083		
		(16.34)		
2. Weekly earnings (i)—Degrees of freedom = 54623				
a			−.0136	
			(14.5)	
b			−.038	.0017
			(11.69)	(7.83)
c	−.0904			
	(16.60)			
d	−.1882	.0110		
	(10.15)	(5.42)		
e		−.0085		
		(14.20)		
3. Weekly earnings (ii)—Degrees of freedom = 99855				
a			−.0134	
			(17.5)	
b			−.0331	.0015
			(13.3)	(8.48)
c	−.0864			
	(19.90)			
d	−.1732	.0103		
	(12.04)	(6.35)		
e		−.0084		
		(17.04)		
f			−.029	.0007
			(8.60)	(3.66)
g	−.112			
	(15.26)			
h	−.102	−.001		
	(5.18)	(0.53)		

Table 4.11 (cont.)

Equations 1–3e include the following variables:

1. Race	5. Hourly paid	9. Schooling (years)
2. Marital status (3)	6. Regional dummies (3)	10. Union status
3. Full-time/part-time	7. Public sector	11. Occupation dummies (14)
4. Children	8. Age + Age^2	12. Industry dummies (47)

Notes: Equations 3f–h include fifty state dummy variables. The unemployment rate, U, is defined at the level of the MSA/CMSA/PMSA.

Source: 1987 Current Population Survey–Annual Merged File.
t-statistics are in parentheses.

file. It measures the unemployment rate at a much lower level of aggregation than previously done in the analysis. In this file, following Freeman (1990b), it is feasible to identify three relatively narrow groupings: (1) metropolitan statistical areas (MSAs), (2) primary metropolitan statistical areas (PMSAs), and (3) consolidated metropolitan statistical areas (CMSAs). These three types of areas are the most disaggregated measures of geographic location available in the Current Population Survey and thus of the local labor market in which a person resides. In 1987 the CPS identified 202 such areas. Rates of unemployment for these areas based on the full year's survey are published by the Bureau of Labor Statistics in each year's May *Employment and Earnings* and in various editions of *Geographic Profile of Employment and Unemployment*.[4] Freeman (1990b) estimates earnings equations using the same 1987 CPS data but for young men and finds a significant negative impact from the unemployment rate. The effect is greatest for young black men. In the same paper, Freeman documents a negative effect of area unemployment in an earnings equation for young men using data from the 1983 to 1987 National Longitudinal Survey of Youth. Once again the responsiveness of wages is larger for young blacks than for young whites.

Rows 1a to 1e of table 4.11 are from regression equations for 1987. They give coefficients on the unemployment variables in an hourly earnings equation. Rows 2a–e provide results for the same sample as above but where the dependent variable is defined as weekly earnings. Only half of the sample reported the number of hours worked, so columns 3a–3e re-estimate the same equation but on a sample nearly twice the size of that

4. We are grateful to Richard Freeman for help in obtaining these unemployment data and for providing his computer programs for the 1987 Annual Merged CPS file.

Table 4.12
Unrestricted wage curves, 1963–1987

	(1) 1963–1987	(2) 1963–1968	(3) 1969–1978	(4) 1979–1987
Regional unemployment (%)				
3–4	−.0002 (0.05)	−.0058 (0.65)	.0050 (0.94)	.0021 (0.12)
4–5	−.0301 (6.17)	−.0234 (2.61)	−.0078 (1.74)	−.0672 (4.04)
5–6	−.0329 (6.25)	−.0000 (0.02)	−.0137 (2.98)	−.0740 (4.51)
6–7	−.0501 (9.12)	−.0110 (0.86)	−.0186 (3.95)	−.0932 (5.69)
7–8	−.0839 (14.51)	−.0625 (2.76)	−.0278 (4.95)	−.1276 (7.76)
8–9	−.0999 (16.65)	−.0095 (0.17)	−.0307 (4.23)	−.1535 (9.26)
9–10	−.0888 (13.71)	−.3148 (2.39)	−.0172 (2.18)	−.1484 (8.87)
10–11	−.0797 (10.67)	−.2336 (3.58)	−.0490 (4.90)	−.1275 (7.31)
11–12	−.0955 (11.47)	n/a	.1281 (7.31)	−.1745 (9.78)
12–13	−.1078 (10.43)	n/a	n/a	−.1617 (8.61)
13–14	−.1617 (9.04)	n/a	n/a	−.2213 (9.35)
14–15	−.1040 (5.81)	n/a	n/a	−.1637 (6.83)
15–16	−.1899 (10.27)	n/a	n/a	−.2283 (9.42)
16–17	n/a	n/a	n/a	n/a
17 +	−.2915 (7.93)	n/a	n/a	−.3563 (8.94)
Industry unemployment (%)				
3–4	−.0442 (12.32)	−.0204 (2.22)	−.0055 (1.20)	−.0435 (5.39)
4–5	−.0541 (14.57)	−.0059 (0.62)	−.0056 (1.05)	−.1290 (13.63)
5–6	−.0758 (17.48)	−.0358 (3.08)	.0009 (0.16)	−.1914 (18.54)
6–7	−.1029 (24.18)	−.0461 (3.08)	−.0564 (11.23)	−.1457 (14.19)
7–8	−.0879 (18.83)	−.0993 (4.90)	−.0106 (1.90)	−.2136 (21.19)

Table 4.12 (cont.)

	(1) 1963–1987	(2) 1963–1968	(3) 1969–1978	(4) 1979–1987
8–9	−.1222 (23.23)	−.2441 (7.67)	−.0836 (11.83)	−.2587 (23.84)
9–10	−.1047 (18.37)	−.1257 (5.20)	−.0323 (4.16)	−.2823 (23.84)
10–11	−.1812 (28.96)	n/a	−.0678 (6.43)	−.3474 (29.81)
11–12	−.1703 (22.19)	−.1096 (3.22)	−.1733 (12.21)	−.3498 (26.23)
12–13	−.2459 (24.59)	n/a	−.1442 (8.14)	−.4754 (30.20)
13–14	−.2038 (22.15)	n/a	.0612 (2.09)	−.3896 (26.65)
14–15	−.3218 (29.37)	n/a	n/a	−.4607 (28.70)
15–16	−.2336 (20.61)	n/a	−.1525 (8.24)	−.3726 (21.23)
16–17	−.4411 (19.11)	n/a	n/a	−.7589 (28.80)
17+	−.3370 (30.54)	n/a	n/a	−.4857 (30.10)
Regional dummies	21	21	21	21
Year dummies	24	24	24	24
Industry dummies	46	46	46	46
$\bar{R}^2$	.5755	.5416	.5653	.5352
F	16,384.0	3,274.85	7,440.35	7,083.59
N	1,535,006	263,202	595,167	676,637

Source: Current Population Surveys—March tapes.
Notes: All equations include full sets of year dummies, industry dummies (43), plus controls for (1) experience and its square, (2) years of schooling, (3) four marital status dummies, (4) two race dummies, (5) private sector dummy, (6) a gender dummy, and (7) a part-time dummy. All unemployment rates, U, and the dependent variable (annual earnings) are in natural logarithms.
t-statistics are in parentheses.

reported in part 2 of the table. Finally, rows 3f–h include a full set of state dummies. This includes all those individuals in part 2 of table 4.11 and an additional 45,232 individuals who did not report their hours of work. In all cases there seems to be evidence of a wage curve. The unemployment elasticity of pay is once again approximately −0.1. The inclusion of a set of state dummies has the effect of reducing the significance of the cube of the log of regional unemployment although the log term remains significant. This is equivalent to the result reported in column 3 of table 4.6 and suggests that redefining the dependent variable as usual hourly or weekly earnings, or changing the level of the regional unemployment variable down to CMSA, has comparatively little effect.

4.2.2 Unrestricted Estimates of the U.S. Wage Curve

In an attempt to ensure that the wage curves described above are not being forced onto these data by the use of particular functional forms, this section estimates unrestricted specifications. The first results are in table 4.12. Dummy variables are entered for each percentage point of both the regional and industry unemployment distributions. Of the 95 unemployment coefficients reported in the table, only two are significantly positive, while 80 are significant and negative, with the remainder insignificant. Column 1 of table 4.12 contains full sets of regional, industry and year dummies and a vector of personal controls, and twenty-nine unemployment dummies, all but one of which are significant and negative. As the amount of unemployment increases, it appears that the absolute size of the coefficient also increases. This is true for both regional and industry unemployment. Figure 4.7 graphs the antilog of the coefficients obtained in the first part of column 1 (whether or not they are individually significant) against the midpoint of the relevant unemployment interval. The coefficient is anti-logged because the dependent variable itself is in natural logs.

Figure 4.7 offers a nonparametric way of looking for a local-unemployment effect upon U.S. wages. The specifications appear to confirm the view that there is a wage curve, that is, a downward sloping function in wage/regional-unemployment space. A similar result is obtained in figure 4.8, which plots unrestricted industry estimates. In columns 2 to 4 of table 4.12, comparable equations are given separately for the 1960s, 1970s, and 1980s. As unemployment was relatively low in the 1960s, column 2 reports eight coefficients each in both regional and industry unemployment space. In the case of the eight regional unemployment dummies, only four are negative and significant. None is positive and significant. In the case of the industry

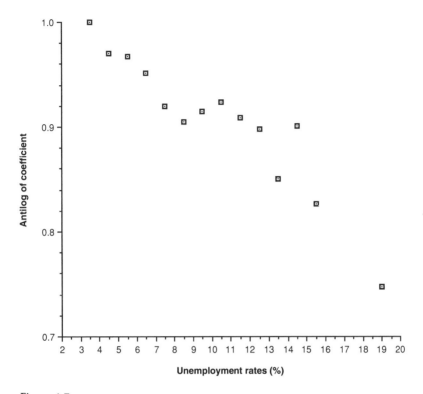

Figure 4.7
Regional unrestricted wage curve: 1963–1987

dummies, seven are negative and significant. Figures 4.9 and 4.10 plot these coefficients: there is little or no evidence of a downward-sloping relationship between wages and regional unemployment. However, there is some evidence of a negatively-sloped wage curve in the 1960s in the case of industry unemployment.

Column 3 of table 4.12 provides unrestricted estimates of wage curves for the 1970s. There is a greater range of unemployment rates in the 1970s than in the 1960s, so there are twenty-one separate coefficients to discuss. Of these, thirteen are significantly negative (*t*-statistics > 2) and two significantly positive, with the remainder insignificant. Figures 4.11 and 4.12 plot the anti-logs of all of the coefficients of the regional and industry unemployment dummies, respectively, whether or not they achieved significance. There is some evidence here of downward-sloping wage curves, although in both figures there is a single outlier at relatively high levels of unemployment. Finally, column 4 of table 4.12 has unrestricted estimates

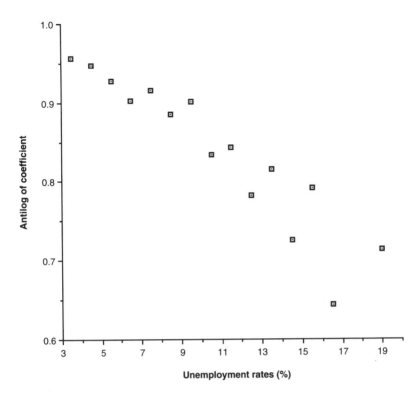

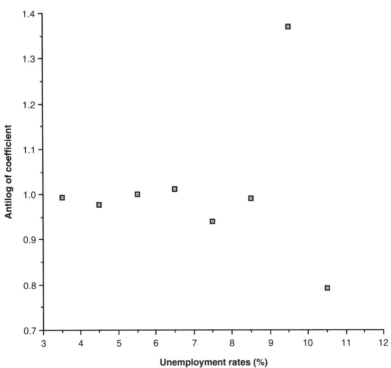

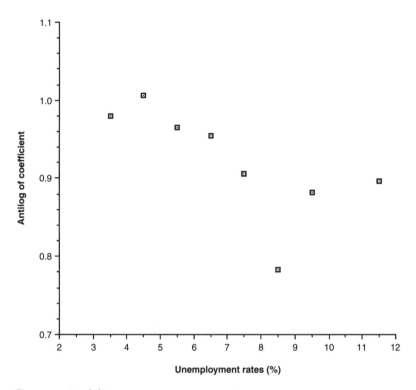

Figure 4.8 (top left)
Industry unrestricted wage curve: 1963–1987

Figure 4.9 (bottom left)
Regional unrestricted wage curve: 1963–1968

Figure 4.10 (above)
Industry unrestricted wage curve: 1963–1968

for the 1980s. There is strong evidence, in this period, for downward-sloping wage curves. Of the twenty-nine coefficients that are reported, all but one are significantly negative. Figures 4.13 and 4.14 plot the anti-logs of the coefficients. In both regional and industry space there is fairly clear evidence of downward-sloping wage curves in the U.S. labor market in the 1980s.

Using this methodology—including a dummy variable for each point of the unemployment distribution—makes it less easy to ascertain the precise shape of the wage curve. This is principally because of the different weights that have to be allocated to each of the data points. Such considerations are particularly important in the 1960s and 1970s, where there are found to be

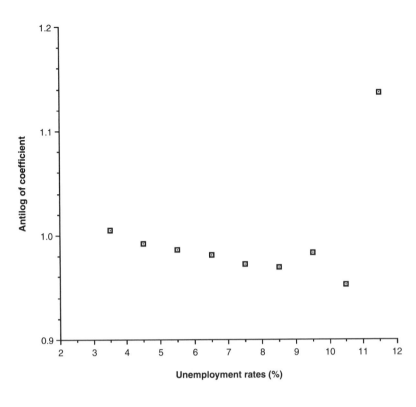

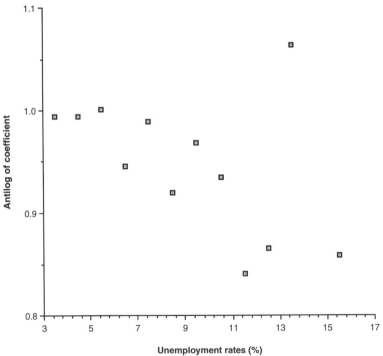

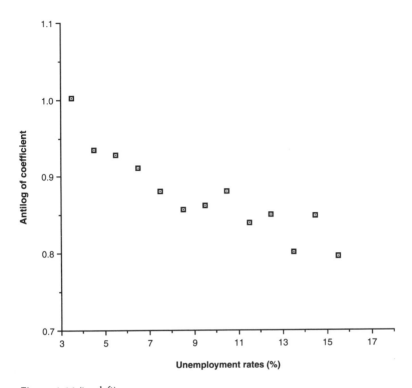

Figure 4.11 (top left)
Regional unrestricted wage curve: 1969–1978

Figure 4.12 (bottom left)
Industry unrestricted wage curve: 1969–1978

Figure 4.13 (above)
Regional unrestricted wage curve: 1979–1987

a number of significant outlier observations. For example, the second coefficient on industry unemployment in column 1 of table 4.12 (−0.0541) relates to 294,188 cases while the final one (−0.3370) relates to only 684 individuals. One possible way to overcome this difficulty is to ensure that each of the data points carries approximately the same weight. This can be done by adjusting the intervals over which each of the points are defined.

The unemployment distributions were divided into twenty segments. Each piece comprises approximately 5 percent of the total unemployment distribution. A dummy variable was then allocated to each, and the earnings equation was re-estimated.

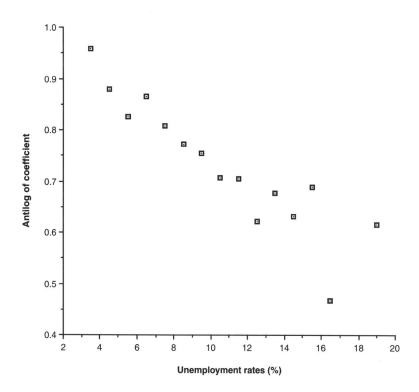

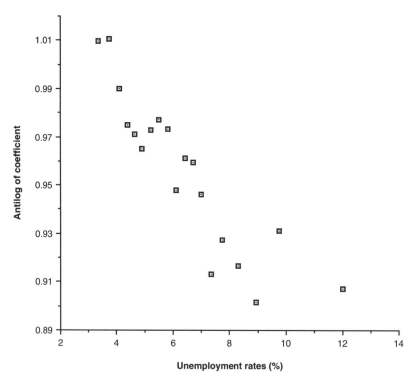

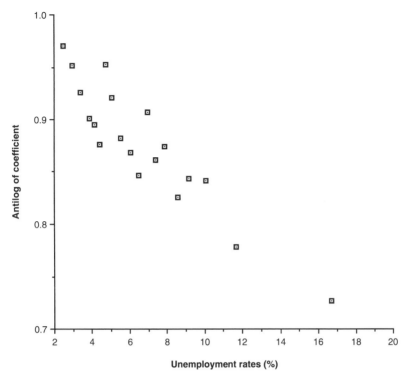

Figure 4.14 (top left)
Industry unrestricted wage curve: 1979–1987

Figure 4.15 (bottom left)
Unrestricted regional wage curve: 1963–1987 (5% sample)

Figure 4.16 (above)
Unrestricted industry wage curve: 1963–1987 (5% sample)

The results of performing this exercise on the entire sample for the period 1964 to 1988 are shown in table 4.13. Of the 38 unemployment variables reported in the table, all but one are significantly different from zero—though two are positive—at conventional levels of significance. There is some evidence that the higher is the unemployment rate the larger is the coefficient. Figure 4.15 plots the antilog of each of the coefficients on the regional unemployment variables against the mid-point unemployment rate. Figure 4.16 performs a similar exercise using industry unemployment data. By the nature of the test, each graph has nineteen observations (twenty observations, less one for the base). In both cases—region and industry —there is evidence from figures 4.15 and 4.16 of a downward-sloping

Table 4.13
5% disaggregations: 1963−1987

Industry unemployment (%)	
2.3−2.7	−.0306
	(6.07)
2.8−3.1	−.04936
	(9.38)
3.2−3.6	−.0767
	(13.87)
3.7−4.0	−.1044
	(18.09)
4.1−4.2	−.1110
	(18.89)
4.3−4.5	−.1322
	(2.136)
4.6−4.8	−.0483
	(7.39)
4.9−5.2	−.0823
	(13.91)
5.3−5.7	−.1254
	(20.35)
5.8−6.3	−.1412
	(23.73)
6.4−6.6	−.1668
	(25.71)
6.7−7.2	−.0982
	(15.35)
7.3−7.5	−.1489
	(23.40)
7.6−8.1	−.1342
	(20.54)
8.2−8.7	−.1920
	(27.45)
8.8−9.5	−.1705
	(24.02)
9.6−10.5	−.1721
	(24.48)
10.6−12.7	−.2502
	(34.38)
13.1 +	−.3198
	(38.08)
Regional unemployment (%)	
3.2−3.5	.00974
	(2.01)
3.6−3.9	.0105
	(2.05)

Table 4.13 (cont.)

4.0–4.2	−.0099
	(1.93)
4.3–4.5	−.0254
	(5.17)
4.6–4.7	−.0292
	(4.87)
4.8–5.0	−.0356
	(6.90)
5.1–5.3	−.0274
	(4.91)
5.4–5.6	−.0230
	(4.17)
5.7–5.9	−.0270
	(4.96)
6.0–6.2	−.0537
	(9.70)
6.3–6.5	−.0395
	(6.69)
6.6–6.8	−.0414
	(6.80)
6.9–7.1	−.0551
	(9.69)
7.2–7.5	−.0909
	(15.07)
7.6–7.9	−.0756
	(12.65)
8.0–8.6	−.0871
	(15.08)
8.7–9.2	−.1036
	(17.06)
9.3–10.2	−.0711
	(11.10)
10.3 +	−.0972
	(15.34)
Regional dummies	21
Year dummies	24
Industry dummies	46
$\overline{R}^2$	.5756
F	15,535.659
N	1,535,006

Notes: Equation includes the full set of controls reported in table 4.5.
t-statistics are in parentheses.

Table 4.14
5% disaggregations: 1963–1968

Industry unemployment (%)	
1.9–2.1	−.0120
	(0.83)
2.2–2.3	−.0172
	(1.02)
2.4–2.5	−.0767
	(1.50)
2.6	.0050
	(0.31)
2.7	−.0153
	(0.95)
2.8–3.4	−.0329
	(1.78)
3.5–3.8	−.0477
	(2.52)
3.9	−.0523
	(2.38)
4.0	−.0097
	(0.52)
4.2–4.3	.0006
	(0.02)
4.4–4.5	−.0686
	(3.72)
4.7–4.8	.0376
	(1.99)
4.9	.0262
	(1.52)
5.0–5.5	−.0482
	(2.39)
5.7–5.9	−.0978
	(4.69)
6.0–6.4	−.0754
	(3.43)
6.5–7.1	−.1067
	(4.29)
7.3–11.9	−.1897
	(6.69)
Regional unemployment (%)	
2.8	.0087
	(0.62)
2.9–3.0	−.0170
	(1.28)
3.1	−.0034
	(0.24)

Table 4.14 (cont.)

3.2	−.0235
	(1.93)
3.3	.0209
	(1.25)
3.4−3.5	−.0172
	(1.37)
3.6−3.7	−.0057
	(0.42)
3.8	−.0209
	(1.45)
3.9	−.0248
	(1.75)
4.0−4.1	−.0011
	(0.08)
4.2	−.0363
	(2.79)
4.3−4.4	−.0098
	(0.70)
4.5	−.0311
	(1.92)
4.6−4.7	−.0242
	(1.74)
4.8	−.0252
	(1.63)
4.9−5.0	−.0380
	(2.54)
5.1−5.4	−.0538
	(3.46)
5.5−5.9	−.0643
	(3.98)
6.0−10.3	−.0924
	(5.53)
Regional dummies	21
Industry dummies	46
Year dummies	24
$\bar{R}^2$	.5444
F	2,711.65
N	263,202

Notes: Equation includes the full set of controls reported in table 4.5.
t-statistics are in parentheses.

Table 4.15
5% disaggregations: 1969–1978

Industry unemployment (%)	
2.2–2.8	−.0166
	(2.09)
2.9–3.1	−.0264
	(2.85)
3.2–3.5	−.0428
	(4.52)
3.7–4.0	−.0994
	(9.98)
4.1–4.3	−.0596
	(5.90)
4.4–4.7	−.0418
	(3.98)
4.8–5.1	−.0579
	(5.09)
5.2–5.3	−.0389
	(3.67)
5.4–5.9	−.0767
	(6.89)
6.0–6.3	−.1228
	(12.28)
6.4	−.1052
	(8.63)
6.6–6.8	−.1801
	(15.73)
6.9–7.2	−.0333
	(2.94)
7.3–7.5	−.0931
	(7.91)
7.6–8.0	−.1188
	(10.31)
8.1–8.8	−.1910
	(16.19)
8.9–9.6	−.0929
	(7.58)
9.7–11.1	−.1805
	(13.25)
11.1 +	−.2162
	(13.91)
Regional unemployment (%)	
3.1–3.6	−.0269
	(3.28)
3.7–4.0	−.0078
	(0.87)

Table 4.15 (cont.)

4.1–4.2	−.0152
	(1.38)
4.3–4.4	−.0195
	(2.22)
4.5–4.6	−.0276
	(2.83)
4.7–4.8	−.0234
	(2.33)
4.9–5.0	−.0586
	(5.63)
5.1–5.3	−.0340
	(3.30)
5.4–5.6	−.0200
	(1.99)
5.7	−.0440
	(4.21)
5.8–6.0	−.0677
	(6.03)
6.1–6.4	−.0580
	(5.76)
6.5–6.7	−.0323
	(3.00)
6.8–7.0	−.0334
	(3.05)
7.1–7.2	−.0502
	(4.33)
7.3–7.8	−.0733
	(6.33)
7.9–8.7	−.0813
	(6.78)
8.8–9.5	−.0642
	(5.32)
9.6+	−.0375
	(2.95)
Regional dummies	21
Year dummies	24
Industry dummies	46
$\bar{R}^2$	.5656
F	6,406.00
N	595,167

Notes: Equation includes the full set of controls reported in table 4.5.
t-statistics are in parentheses.

Table 4.16
5% disaggregations: 1979–1987

Industry unemployment (%)	
3.0–3.5	−.0366
	(4.21)
3.6–3.9	−.0564
	(5.88)
4.0–4.1	−.1422
	(13.43)
4.2–4.4	−.1061
	(9.55)
4.5–4.6	−.1270
	(10.87)
4.7–5.3	−.1746
	(15.81)
5.4–5.8	−.1794
	(15.22)
5.9–6.4	−.1512
	(13.29)
6.5–7.2	−.1755
	(15.92)
7.3–7.4	−.2114
	(17.68)
7.5–8.0	−.2271
	(21.26)
8.1–8.3	−.2596
	(21.40)
8.5–8.6	−.2871
	(23.01)
8.7–9.2	−.2479
	(20.26)
9.3–10.1	−.2811
	(23.01)
10.2–10.7	−.3801
	(29.73)
10.8–11.5	−.3490
	(26.54)
11.6–13.6	−.4121
	(29.90)
13.7 +	−.4885
	(33.00)
Regional unemployment (%)	
4.0–4.7	−.0746
	(9.84)
4.8–5.0	−.0657
	(8.10)

Table 4.16 (cont.)

5.1–5.4	− .0894
	(11.61)
5.5–5.7	− .0666
	(8.60)
5.8–6.0	− .0804
	(9.78)
6.1–6.2	− .1076
	(12.62)
6.3–6.5	− .0803
	(9.80)
6.6–6.8	− .1075
	(12.87)
6.9–7.0	− .1151
	(14.16)
7.1–7.3	− .1272
	(15.48)
7.4–7.6	− .1526
	(17.85)
7.7–7.9	− .1148
	(13.93)
8.0–8.2	− .1535
	(18.19)
8.3–8.5	− .1359
	(14.92)
8.6–8.9	− .1787
	(21.80)
9.0–9.5	− .1570
	(18.20)
9.6–10.1	− .1387
	(15.58)
10.2–11.4	− .1580
	(16.51)
11.5 +	− .1899
	(20.18)
Regional dummies	21
Year dummies	24
Industry dummies	46
$\overline{R}^2$	.5352
F	6,539.14
N	675,822

Notes: Equation includes the full set of controls reported in table 4.5.
t-statistics are in parentheses.

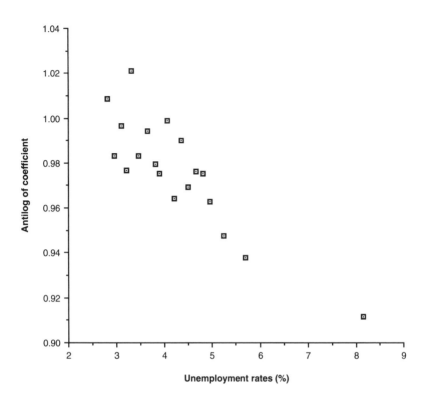

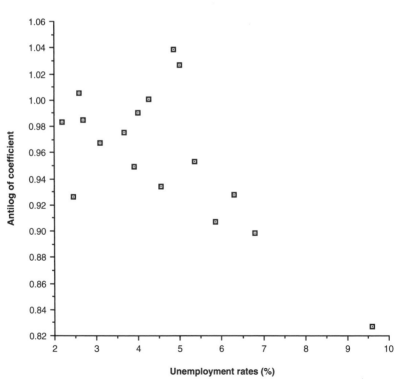

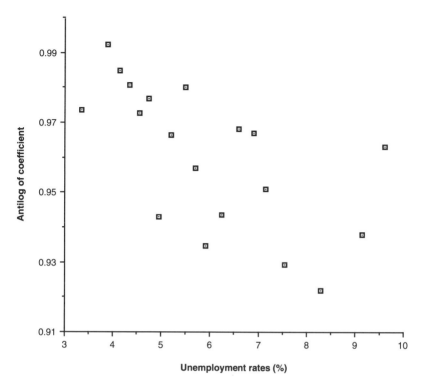

Antilog of coefficient

Unemployment rates (%)

Figure 4.17 (top left)
Unrestricted regional wage curve: 1963–1968 (5% sample)

Figure 4.18 (bottom left)
Unrestricted industry wage curve: 1963–1968 (5% sample)

Figure 4.19 (above)
Unrestricted regional wage curve: 1969–1978 (5% sample)

relationship between wages and unemployment. Although these new scatter plots are qualitatively different from those reported earlier in figures 4.7 and 4.8, they appear to confirm the earlier judgment of a negative relationship between wages and local joblessness over the period 1963 to 1987.

Tables 4.14, 4.15 and 4.16 report unrestricted regression results for the 1960s, 1970s, and 1980s. Both the regional and industry unemployment distributions are again split into 5 percent sections. Figures 4.17 to 4.22 plot the antilogs of these coefficients against the midpoint of the range or against the actual value where a single unemployment rate is indicated. Thus for each year there are thirty-eight different unemployment dummy

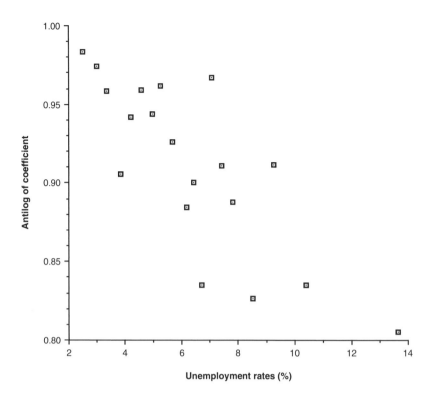

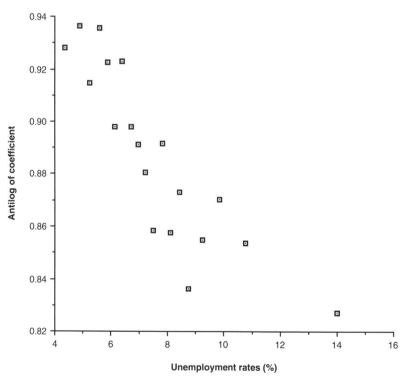

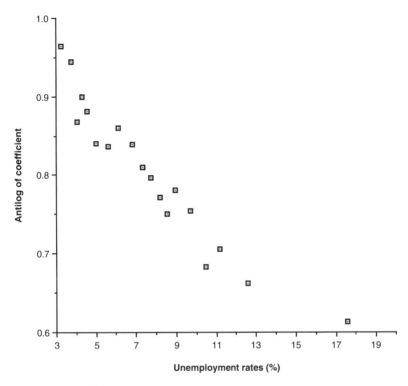

Figure 4.20 (top left)
Unrestricted industry wage curve: 1969–1978 (5% sample)

Figure 4.21 (bottom left)
Unrestricted regional wage curve: 1979–1987 (5% sample)

Figure 4.22 (above)
Unrestricted industry wage curve: 1979–1987 (5% sample)

variables. The unemployment dummy variables work best in the 1970s and 1980s. In table 4.14, which displays disaggregations for the 1960s, less than half of the coefficients are significantly negative, while the vast majority are significant in the 1970s and 1980s. In all three decades there are signs of a negative wage/unemployment relationship. In figure 4.19 there is some evidence for an upward-sloping portion of the wage curve in the 1970s, where regional unemployment is approximately 8.5% or higher. Just over 10% of individuals are located in this range. There is no evidence for a U-shape in figure 4.20 using industry unemployment. Figures 4.21 and 4.22, which display wage curves for the 1980s, do not show any clear flattening of the wage curves.

4.2.3 Disaggregated Wage Curves

An obvious next step in the analysis of the wage curve is to explore the extent to which the estimates of the unemployment elasticities of pay presented above vary according to different characteristics of the individuals in the sample. For each subsample, a separate regression is estimated, which includes the set of controls included in earlier tables. Regional and industry unemployment are entered expressed as natural logarithms.

In what follows the total sample is divided into two (or more) subgroups according to a certain characteristic, such as gender, and equations of the following form are then estimated:

$$\ln w_i = \lambda_0 + \lambda_1 X_i' + \varepsilon_i \qquad i = 1, 2 \ldots N_1 \qquad\qquad (4.2.3.1)$$

$$\ln w_i = \gamma_0 + \gamma_1 X_i' + \vartheta_i \qquad i = 1, 2 \ldots N_2 \qquad\qquad (4.2.3.2)$$

where X_i' is a vector of explanatory variables and ε_i and ϑ_i are error terms assumed normally distributed. Regressions (4.2.3.1) and (4.2.3.2) present the following four possibilities:

1. $\lambda_0 = \gamma_0$ and $\lambda_1 = \gamma_1$; that is, the regressions are not significantly different,

2. $\lambda_0 \neq \gamma_0$ but $\lambda_1 = \gamma_1$; the two regressions differ only in their intercepts,

3. $\lambda_0 = \gamma_0$ but $\lambda_1 \neq \gamma_1$; the two regressions have the same intercepts but different slopes,

4. $\lambda_0 \neq \gamma_0$ and $\lambda_1 \neq \gamma_1$; the two regressions are significantly different from each other.

Individual regressions can be run and techniques such as a Chow test then used to test the preceding possibilities. Alternatively, these possibilities can be tested by pooling N_1 and N_2 observations and estimating the following regression, assuming that ε and ϑ in (4.2.3.1) and (4.2.3.2) have the same properties, especially common variance:

$$\ln w_i = \alpha_0 + \alpha_1 D_i + \beta_1 X_i' + \beta_2 (D_i X_i') + \mu_i \qquad\qquad (4.2.3.3)$$

where $D_i = 1$ if the individual was in category N_1

where $D_i = 0$ if the individual was in category N_2.

To see the implications of model (4.2.3.3), and assuming $E(\mu_i) = 0$,

$$E(W_i|D_i = 0, X_i') = \alpha_0 + \beta_1 X_i' \tag{4.2.3.4}$$

$$E(W_i|D_i = 1, X_i') = (\alpha_0 + \alpha_1) + (\beta_1 + \beta_2)X_i', \tag{4.2.3.5}$$

which are the mean wage functions for sectors N_1 and N_2 respectively. Gujarati (1970b) has shown that (4.2.3.4) and (4.2.3.5) are the same as (4.2.3.1) and (4.2.3.2) with $\lambda_0 = \alpha_0, \lambda_1 = \beta_1, \gamma_0 = (\alpha_0 + \alpha_1)$ and $\gamma_1 = (\beta_1 + \beta_2)$. Therefore, estimating (4.2.3.3) is equivalent to estimating the two separate wage equations (4.2.3.1) and (4.2.3.2).

One possibility is that pay is more flexible (that is, the unemployment elasticity of pay larger in absolute terms), the weaker the 'bargaining power' of that group. Thus it might be expected that the effects of unemployment upon pay would be greatest for those with the least education, the young, those working in non-union workplaces, and in sectors that are highly cyclical in nature.

Table 4.17 reports estimates of equations (4.2.3.1) and (4.2.3.2) disaggregated according to a series of individual and workplace characteristics. The logs of the industry and regional unemployment rates are incorporated as indicators of the state of the outside labor market. The equations also include the sets of control variables used in earlier tables, together with full sets of industry and regional dummies, to capture fixed effects. Details of variables' definitions are provided in the appendix.

For purposes of comparison, the first row of table 4.17 presents the equation that was reported in column 1 of table 4.5 for the entire sample period. The estimated unemployment elasticity of pay is -0.1 in both regional and industry space. Male pay is nearly twice as responsive to regional unemployment than is female pay (rows 2 and 3). The gender groups seem to react equally, however, to changes in industrial unemployment. Perhaps surprisingly, there is little difference between the coefficients on the unemployment rate between full-time and part-time workers (rows 4 and 5) or between whites, non-whites, and blacks (rows 6, 7, and 8). However, evidence is found in support of the above hypothesis with respect to years of schooling (rows 9–11) and age (rows 12–16). The effect of unemployment seems to be greater in absolute terms for the least educated and the youngest workers. This is consistent with the results of Katz and Krueger (1991b). They examined earnings in a sample of fast-food restaurants in Texas in 1989 and 1990 in an attempt to examine the effects of changes in the minimum wage. They suggest that the starting wage, which applies to the least-skilled (usually young) workers, is significantly lower the higher is the city unemployment rate.

Table 4.17
Disaggregated unemployment elasticities of pay: 1963–1987

	Industry unempt.	Regional unempt.	$\bar{R}^2$	N	F
1. All	−.109 (35.19)	−.098 (25.66)	.5757	1,534,093	20,606.93
2. Males	−.098 (25.87)	−.119 (26.12)	.6047	844,743	13,055.84
3. Females	−.107 (21.48)	−.064 (10.48)	.5067	689,350	7,153.71
4. Part-time	−.095 (8.78)	−.116 (9.54)	.2926	258,408	1,080.63
5. Full-time	−.114 (37.59)	−.082 (21.81)	.5036	1,275,685	13,072.90
6. Blacks	−.112 (11.37)	−.110 (8.00)	.5808	144,201	2,019.14
7. Other nonwhites	−.082 (3.44)	−.100 (3.92)	.5224	31,964	354.09
8. Whites	−.109 (33.18)	−.093 (23.00)	.5779	1,357,928	18,777.12
9. ≤11 yrs. school	−.111 (16.09)	−.155 (18.59)	.6163	403,045	6,409.86
10. 12 yrs. school	−.128 (26.38)	−.108 (18.47)	.5204	580,305	6,297.74
11. ≥13 yrs. school	−.057 (12.17)	−.064 (10.89)	.5417	550,742	6,446.40
12. ≤25 yrs.	−.133 (19.81)	−.192 (24.39)	.5651	433,907	5,582.43
13. 26–35 yrs.	−.092 (16.56)	−.081 (11.80)	.4903	368,762	3,512.75
14. 36–50 yrs.	−.096 (19.60)	−.065 (10.56)	.5508	417,649	5,071.81
15. 51–65 yrs.	−.088 (13.87)	−.063 (7.73)	.5192	273,194	2,921.94
16. 66+ yrs.	−.067 (2.59)	−.007 (0.23)	.3287	40,576	197.70

Notes: Equation includes the full set of controls reported in table 4.5.
t-statistics are in parentheses.

Further disaggregations appear in table 4.18. It is based on the 1987 annual merged CPS file, using a more disaggregated measure of area unemployment. The sample is that presented in section 3 of table 4.11, with unemployment measured at the level of the CMSA, MSA, or PMSA. There is no included variable for the degree of industry unemployment, although there are forty-seven industry dummies (see footnotes to table 4.11 for further details). The first column presents the coefficient on the log of area unemployment; the second column adds a set of regional dummies at a higher level of aggregation. Columns 3 and 4 repeat the exercise but with the level and the square of unemployment. Finally, columns 5 and 6 do the same but with a log and a cube-of-the-log specification. Row 1 of the table duplicates the results in lines 3c–3h of table 4.11.

It is useful to concentrate on the results in column 2 of table 4.18. There is little or no indication of a difference in the effects of unemployment across gender or race or union status. However, the unemployment elasticity of pay is greater for the less educated, for the young, and for those employed in the service sector. Their wages, in other words, are in a sense more flexible.

Katz and Krueger (1991a) use data from the full year Outgoing Rotation Group files of the 1979 and 1988 CPS to compare the way in which pay in the public and private sectors responds to local labor market conditions. They estimate a series of log hourly earnings equations for private, state, local, and federal workers on a standard set of controls and a full set of regional dummies. The private sector equations include two-digit industry dummies. The state dummy variable coefficients obtained from each of these equations, for 1979 and 1988, are then plotted against the state unemployment rate for that year. Their results are summarized in figures 4.23 to 4.28.[5] The authors find that upward-sloping wage curves are apparent for all three sectors in 1979 (figures 4.23 to 4.25), while downward-sloping wage curves are present for the private sector and for state and local government and federal government workers in 1988 (figures 4.26 to 4.28). When Katz and Krueger control for state fixed effects by plotting the *changes* in the state wage coefficients by sector against the changes in state unemployment rates between 1979 and 1988 (figures 4.29 to 4.31), they find, first, strong negative responses of private sector and state and local government wages to changes in state unemployment rates, and, second, virtually no response of federal wages to state labor markets. More

---

5. We are grateful to Larry Katz for providing us with these data.

Table 4.18
Disaggregated unemployment elasticities of pay: 1987 CPS

	(1) Log U no region	(2) Log U + region	(3) U no region	(3) U² no region	(4) U + region	(4) U² + region
1. All	−.086 (19.9)	−.112 (15.26)	−.033 (13.3)	.0015 (8.48)	−.029 (8.60)	.0007 (3.66)
2. Male	−.092 (15.83)	−.121 (12.77)	−.035 (10.32)	.0015 (6.52)	−.032 (7.29)	.0009 (3.30)
3. Female	−.083 (13.09)	−.106 (10.07)	−.032 (8.57)	.001 (5.35)	−.027 (5.50)	.0006 (2.20)
4. 16−24	−.109 (10.36)	−.120 (7.00)	−.037 (6.42)	.001 (3.72)	−.033 (4.25)	.001 (2.02)
5. 25−44	−.070 (7.33)	−.105 (6.76)	−.024 (4.19)	.001 (2.41)	−.023 (3.12)	.0004 (0.88)
6. 45−64	−.072 (7.82)	−.106 (7.14)	−.024 (4.36)	.001 (2.45)	−.023 (3.19)	.0004 (0.82)
7. White	−.004 (17.58)	−.111 (14.62)	−.031 (11.64)	.0013 (7.35)	−.028 (8.09)	.0007 (3.36)
8. Black	−.109 (9.79)	−.098 (4.57)	−.059 (7.29)	.003 (5.37)	−.041 (3.60)	.002 (2.48)
9. High schl.	−.091 (16.45)	−.131 (13.56)	−.033 (10.49)	.0014 (6.52)	−.074 (7.58)	.0009 (3.33)
10. College	−.089 (9.96)	−.079 (7.52)	−.045 (8.42)	.0024 (6.34)	−.023 (4.63)	.0007 (2.29)
11. Union	−.071 (8.05)	−.108 (8.33)	−.039 (6.64)	.0021 (4.94)	−.045 (6.11)	.002 (4.13)
12. Nonunion	−.086 (17.46)	−.107 (13.18)	−.031 (10.93)	.0012 (6.59)	−.024 (6.45)	.0004 (2.08)
13. Manufact.	−.066 (7.40)	−.075 (5.57)	−.053 (9.81)	.0033 (8.76)	−.044 (6.48)	.002 (5.43)
14. Services	−.089 (16.4)	−.121 (13.3)	−.029 (9.20)	.0011 (4.96)	−.027 (2.05)	.0005 (2.05)

Table 4.18 (cont.)

	(5) Log U	(5) Log U^3	(6) Log U	(6) Log U^3
	no region		+ region	
1. All	−.173	.0103	−.102	−.001
	(12.0)	(6.35)	(5.18)	(0.53)
2. Male	−.186	.0108	−.113	−.0008
	(9.62)	(5.09)	(4.07)	(0.29)
3. Female	−.154	.008	−.062	−.0047
	(7.26)	(3.48)	(2.01)	(1.50)
4. 16–24	−.170	.0068	−.088	−.003
	(5.00)	(1.87)	(1.77)	(.070)
5. 25–44	−.137	.008	−.072	−.003
	(4.29)	(2.19)	(1.57)	(0.75)
6. 45–64	−.136	.0075	−.073	−.004
	(4.44)	(2.20)	(1.66)	(0.79)
7. White	−.161	.009	−.077	−.004
	(10.43)	(5.27)	(3.49)	(1.61)
8. Black	−.313	.024	−.211	.013
	(7.29)	(4.93)	(3.07)	(1.73)
9. High schl.	−.168	.0087	−.106	−.003
	(9.15)	(4.42)	(3.70)	(0.93)
10. College	−.236	.017	−.082	.0003
	(7.86)	(5.14)	(2.65)	(0.09)
11. Union	−.151	.009	−.174	.007
	(5.03)	(2.78)	(4.38)	(1.77)
12. Nonunion	−.159	.008	−.069	−.004
	(9.80)	(4.75)	(3.13)	(1.79)
13. Manufact.	−.279	.0249	−.205	.014
	(9.76)	(7.83)	(5.17)	(3.48)
14. Services	−.137	.0055	−.056	−.007
	(7.51)	(2.73)	(2.08)	(2.59)

Source: 1987 Annual Merged File, 1987 CPS.
Notes: Sample size = 99,940.
"No region" means without regional dummies.
t-statistics are in parentheses.

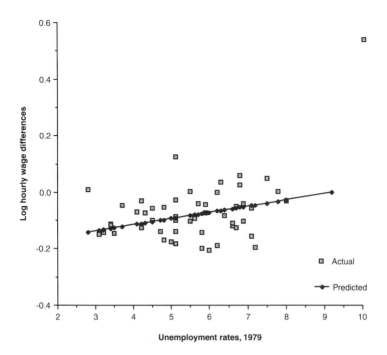

Figure 4.23
Private sector state hourly wage differences, 1979

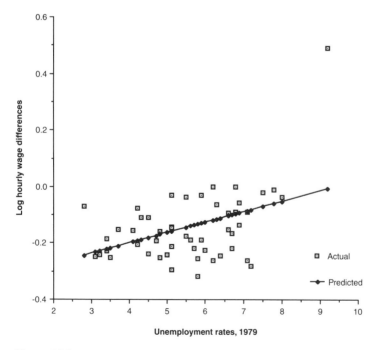

Figure 4.24
State and local government hourly wage differences, 1979

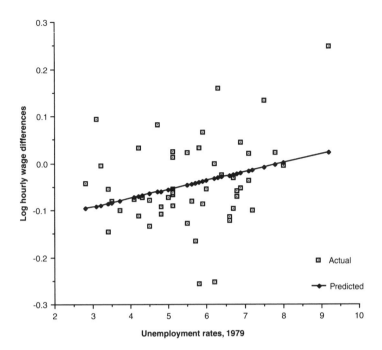

Figure 4.25
Federal government hourly wage differences, 1979

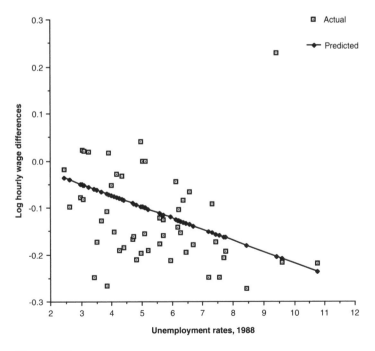

Figure 4.26
Private sector hourly wage differences, 1988

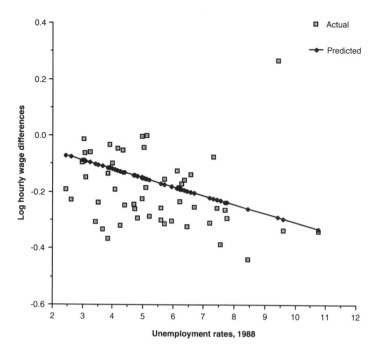

Figure 4.27
State and local government hourly wage differences, 1988

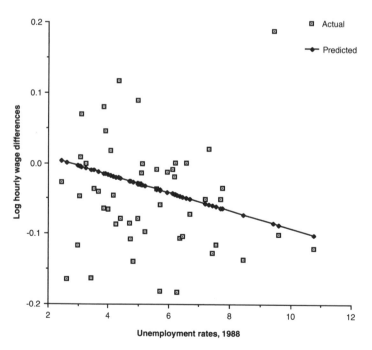

Figure 4.28
Federal government hourly wage differences, 1988

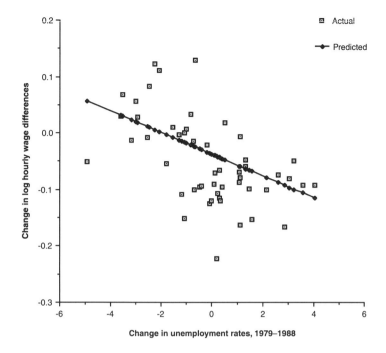

Figure 4.29
Private sector changes in state wage differences: 1979–1988

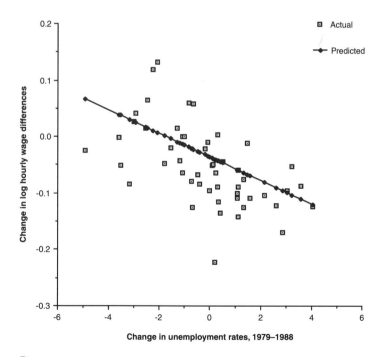

Figure 4.30
State and local government changes in state wage differences: 1979–1988

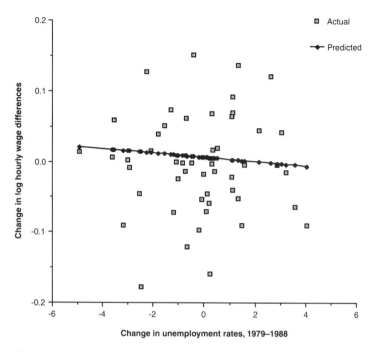

Figure 4.31
Federal government changes in state wage differences: 1979–1988

formally, the authors' findings are as follows (where w is wage and U unemployment, and standard errors are given):

Private sector: $\Delta \text{wage} = -.038 - .019^* \Delta U, \quad R^2 = 0.32$
                            $(.007) \quad (.004)$

State and local: $\Delta \text{wage} = -.036 - .021^* \Delta U, \quad R^2 = 0.39$
                            $(.007) \quad (.004)$

Federal: $\Delta \text{wage} = .006 - .003^* \Delta U, \quad R^2 = 0.01.$
                            $(.008) \quad (.004)$

The following two equations, estimated on the book's 1963 to 1987 CPS sample, successfully replicate the results found by Katz and Krueger.

	Industry unempt.	Regional unempt.	Adjusted R^2	N	F
1. Private sector	$-.138$	$-.100$	.5778	1,262,754	17,453.83
	(38.24)	(23.54)			
2. Public sector	$-.024$	$-.047$	.5615	271,339	3,583.35
	(3.26)	(5.70)			

Table 4.19
Union and nonunion wage curves: 1983–1988

	(1) All	(2) Union	(3) Nonunion
Log industry U	−.2090	−.0532	−.2337
	(14.58)	(1.89)	(14.27)
Log regional U	−.1142	−.0697	−.1193
	(5.05)	(1.54)	(4.67)
Union	.1928	n/a	n/a
	(26.23)		
Constant	8.0838	8.5704	8.0903
	(114.87)	(60.13)	(101.63)
$\bar{R}^2$	.5332	.3760	.5311
F	875.19	86.41	715.02
DF	86,379	15,765	70,502
N	86,493	15,878	70,615

Source: Current Population Surveys—March tapes.
Notes: All equations include full sets of year, state (50) and industry variables (43) plus controls for (1) experience and its square, (2) years of schooling, (3) four marital status variables, (4) two race variables, (5) private sector, (6) gender, and (7) part-time status. All unemployment rates, U, and the dependent variable (annual earnings) are in natural logarithms. t-statistics are in parentheses.

Private sector pay appears to be much more responsive to changes in unemployment than is the case for public sector pay. This is true for industry and regional unemployment. The unemployment elasticity of pay in the private sector is between −0.10 and −0.14; that in the public sector is between −0.02 and −0.05. This makes intuitive sense because the public sector is more centralized in the way it decides pay.

Further experiments are in tables 4.19 to 4.22. Union wage curves are flatter than those in the nonunion sector, and public sector pay is again relatively unresponsive to local unemployment. For the 1983–1988 period for which data are available, table 4.19 shows that the regional unemployment elasticity is estimated at −0.11 in column 1. Splitting by union-status, however, produces the result that the pay of those in U.S. trade unions is half as flexible to unemployment as the pay of nonunion individuals. These findings are in columns 2 and 3 of table 4.19. The estimated union elasticity is −0.07 (poorly defined). That in the non-union sector is −0.12. More detailed results are set out in table 4.20. The pay of unionized public sector workers is the least responsive. For this group, as column 5 of table 4.20 reveals, the unemployment elasticity of wages is −0.059. In the private sector subsample, shown in table 4.21, cubic terms work only

Table 4.20
Union and nonunion wage curves: 1982–1987

	Private sector			Public sector		
	All (1)	Union (2)	Nonunion (3)	All (4)	Union (5)	Nonunion (6)
Log industry U	−.2223 (14.45)	−.0702 (2.18)	−.2473 (14.33)	−.0343 (0.59)	+.0547 (0.63)	−.0654 (0.86)
Log regional U	−.1216 (4.69)	−.0761 (1.25)	−.1254 (4.42)	−.0880 (1.99)	−.0592 (0.90)	−.0976 (1.67)
Union	.1937 (21.36)	n/a	n/a	.1936 (15.81)	n/a	n/a
Constant	8.1717 (104.47)	8.7123 (49.70)	8.1753 (94.97)	7.6849 (33.07)	8.2095 (22.33)	7.5634 (25.38)
$\bar{R}^2$	.5275	.3800	.5268	.5561	.3937	.5646
F	708.13	57.91	609.07	197.87	39.71	134.81
DF	70,192	10,103	59,979	16,085	5,568	10,422
N	70,304	10,214	60,090	16,189	5,664	10,531

Source: Current Population Surveys—March tapes.
Notes: All equations include full sets of year, state (50) and industry variables (43) plus controls for (1) experience and its square, (2) years of schooling, (3) four marital status variables, (4) two race variables, (5) private sector, and (6) part-time status. All unemployment rates, U, and the dependent variable (annual earnings) are in natural logarithms.
t-statistics are in parentheses.

Table 4.21
Private-sector wage curves: 1982–1987

	Union (1)	Nonunion (2)
Log industry U	−.0858	−.2311
	(1.29)	(5.48)
(Log industry U)^3	.00095	−.0016
	(0.19)	(0.44)
Log regional U	−.2300	−.4479
	(1.86)	(6.83)
(Log regional U)^3	.0139	.0301
	(1.43)	(5.45)
Constant	8.9238	8.5480
	(39.01)	(73.50)
$\bar{R}^2$	.3800	.5270
F	56.89	598.74
DF	10,101	59,977
N	10,214	56,090

Source: Current Population Surveys—March tapes.
Base: Private sector workers only.
Notes: All equations include full sets of year, state (50) and industry variables (43) plus controls for (1) experience and its square, (2) years of schooling, (3) four marital status variables, (4) two race variables, (5) private sector, and (6) part-time status. All unemployment rates, U, and the dependent variable (annual earnings) are in natural logarithms.
t-statistics are in parentheses.

at the regional level and for nonunion employees. It might be guessed that the remuneration of public sector workers would depend more on local unemployment when the employer is the state than when it is the federal government. This is confirmed in table 4.22. Federal employees have pay levels that are unaffected by the local rate of unemployment (column 1 of table 4.22), whereas other public sector men and women have a regional unemployment elasticity of pay like that in the private sector.

Does the unemployment elasticity of pay change over time? Table 4.23 reverts to the main 1964 to 1988 CPS file.[6] It splits the sample period into seven time periods, and reports a series of coefficients on regional and industry unemployment variables. In all cases, the industry unemployment term is significantly negative. In absolute size the coefficients are generally larger at the end of the time period than at the beginning. The coefficients on the regional terms are different; five are significantly negative, one on

6. These are the calendar years 1963 to 1987, hence the tables' labeling.

Table 4.22
Public-sector wage curves: 1982–1987

	(1) Federal	(2) Local	(3) State
Log industry U	+.0008	−.0743	−.2337
	(0.01)	(0.59)	(14.27)
Log regional U	+.0438	−.1428	−.1193
	(0.47)	(1.92)	(4.67)
Union	.1016	.2688	.2032
	(3.65)	(12.95)	(9.69)
Constant	7.1510	8.2609	8.4782
	(15.50)	(16.40)	(20.59)
$\bar{R}^2$	.5332	.3760	.5710
F	875.19	86.41	80.76
DF	3,603	5,706	5,540
N	3,703	5,801	5,635

Source: Current Population Surveys—March tapes.
Notes: All equations include full sets of year, state (50) and industry variables (43) plus controls for (1) experience and its square, (2) years of schooling, (3) four marital status variables, (4) two race variables, (5) private sector, (6) gender, and (7) part-time status. All unemployment rates, U, and the dependent variable (annual earnings) are in natural logarithms.
t-statistics are in parentheses.

Table 4.23
Unemployment elasticities of pay in different subperiods

	Industry unempt.	Regional unempt.	$\bar{R}^2$	N	F
1. 1963–1966	−.04083	−.05396	.5389	146,310	2,312.03
	(2.14)	(2.72)			
2. 1967–1970	−.04700	−.15574	.5955	239,265	4,403.92
	(4.70)	(9.21)			
3. 1971–1974	−.06291	.04318	.5294	219,400	3,248.64
	(3.79)	(1.93)			
4. 1975–1978	−.10315	.00785	.5672	253,296	4,369.37
	(13.80)	(0.68)			
5. 1979–1982	−.34710	−.07360	.5260	311,514	4609.29
	(43.67)	(7.47)			
6. 1983–1985	−.10899	−.15025	.5390	218,863	3,324.76
	(5.39)	(11.11)			
7. 1986–1987	−.45807	−.18348	.5328	145,445	2,183.00
	(9.36)	(11.05)			

Notes: Equation includes the full set of controls reported in table 4.5.
All unemployment rates and the dependent variable (annual earnings) are in natural logarithms.
t-statistics are in parentheses.

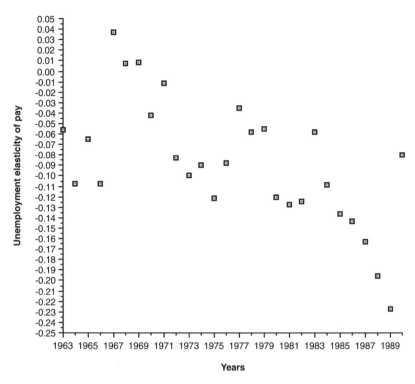

Figure 4.32
Unemployment elasticity of pay: Regional wage curves 1963–1990

the border of significantly positive, and one zero. The latter two occur in the 1970s. Perhaps the most surprising result is the coefficient of + 0.04 for 1971 to 1974, the period of the first oil price shock. Its positivity is a puzzle, and may reflect an identification problem.

In order to examine further the extent to which the unemployment elasticity of pay varies through time, a further check was performed. This used the complete set of CPS data from 1963 to 1990. Interaction terms between the local unemployment rate and the year dummies were included, along with the (log of the) unemployment rate itself. Figure 4.32 plots the relevant estimate for each year obtained by summing the effect from the unemployment variable itself and that from the relevant interaction term. There is evidence of a downward trend, which is considered again in Section 4.2.4.

Table 4.24 divides the sample according to the industry in which the individual is employed. In all but one case, automobiles, the coefficient on

Table 4.24
Regional unemployment elasticities of pay by industry

	Regional unempt.	$\overline{R}^2$	N	F
United States	−.0987 (24.83)	.5757	1,534,093	20,606.93
Agriculture	−.3603 (10.96)	.5334	39,743	798.08
Mining	−.0980 (3.33)	.4410	17,383	245.94
Construction	−.2443 (15.66)	.4561	83,513	1,229.65
Lumber & wood	−.1603 (3.78)	.4842	11,930	197.50
Furniture	−.0634 (1.29)	.5119	4,367	102.75
Stone, clay & glass	−.0229 (0.68)	.4896	11,617	196.45
Primary metals	−.0228 (0.88)	.5051	18,554	339.17
Fabricated metals	−.0830 (3.51)	.5020	26,162	463.66
Machinery excl. electrical	−.1310 (7.53)	.5250	37,938	736.65
Electrical machinery	−.0724 (3.67)	.5473	33,943	733.83
Automobiles	+.0718 (2.38)	.5268	16,248	329.81
Aircraft	−.0178 (0.68)	.5441	20,115	422.16
Misc. manufacturing	−.0790 (1.98)	.5893	9,707	249.66
Food	−.1237 (5.02)	.5137	34,028	63,131
Tobacco and photographic	−.1109 (2.91)	.4710	14,926	247.15
Textiles	.0023 (0.60)	.4730	16,114	254.69
Apparel	−.01923 (0.60)	.3839	23,960	267.60
Paper	−.0790 (1.98)	.5893	9,707	249.66
Printing	−.1115 (3.44)	.6483	22,024	781.83
Chemicals	−.0386 (1.59)	.5534	19,741	430.21
Petroleum	−.05308 (1.16)	.6222	7,123	210.76
Rubber	−.0507 (1.29)	.4997	9,669	186.71

Table 4.24 (cont.)

	Regional unempt.	$\bar{R}^2$	N	F
Leather	−.1218 (1.94)	.3985	4,727	62.31
Transport	−.0857 (5.11)	.4716	58,439	915.93
Communications	−.0296 (1.29)	.5913	21,874	556.16
Utilities and sanitary	−.0430 (1.99)	.5702	24,822	578.65
Wholesale trade	−.0988 (5.84)	.5436	72,465	1,515.02
Retail trade	−.0805 (7.66)	.4705	245,461	3,827.20
Banking	−.0631 (2.99)	.5919	35,820	928.69
Insurance and real estate	−.1081 (4.62)	.4675	43,406	669.49
Private household services	−.2099 (6.31)	.4749	39,744	631.66
Business services	−.1698 (5.98)	.5142	37,444	696.36
Repair services	−.1459 (3.84)	.4876	15,327	261.47
Personal serv./excl. priv.	−.0745 (2.70)	.4460	38,587	555.79
Entertainment	−.0361 (1.02)	.5130	23,867	442.04
Hospitals	−.0092 (0.56)	.5215	57,226	1,095.26
Health excl. hospitals	−.0481 (2.37)	.4831	50,370	826.93
Education	−.0271 (2.11)	.5729	124,443	2,981.52
Social services	−.0449 (0.91)	.4816	10,521	218.22
Other professional servs.	−.0656 (3.00)	.5061	53,260	958.47
Forestry and fishing	.0608 (0.30)	.5306	1,026	30.71
Public administration	−.0637 (4.21)	.5371	81,732	1,725.04

Notes: Equation includes the full set of controls reported in table 4.5, excluding industry dummies.

All unemployment rates, U, and the dependent variable (annual earnings) are in natural logarithms.

t-statistics are in parentheses.

Table 4.25
Industry unemployment elasticities by region

	Industry unempt.	$\bar{R}^2$	N	F
United States	−.1093 (35.19)	.5757	1,534,093	20,606.93
New England	−.1256 (9.85)	.5672	96,240	1,597.64
Connecticut	−.1011 (3.78)	.5836	18,864	339.89
New York	−.0748 (6.76)	.5479	111,079	1,705.25
New Jersey	−.0702 (4.23)	.5778	52,539	911.35
Pennsylvania	−.0812 (6.11)	.5836	74,781	1,327.86
Ohio	−.1052 (7.51)	.5971	70,098	1,315.90
Indiana	−.1083 (5.42)	.5887	33,246	603.25
Illinois	−.0701 (5.02)	.5790	71,290	1,242.04
Michigan/Wisconsin	−.0794 (6.25)	.6093	86,117	1,722.74
Min/Miss/Iowa/ND/SD/Neb/Kan	−.1209 (10.87)	.5884	125,787	2,306.61
Del/Mary/Virg/W.Virg	−.1114 (9.13)	.6120	95,005	1,922.13
Washington, D.C.	−.0433 (1.21)	.5889	10,998	202.94
N & S. Carolina/Georgia	−.1389 (10.38)	.5921	91,517	1,682.78
Florida	−.0811 (4.69)	.5356	51,455	753.76
Kentucky/Tennessee	−.1461 (7.63)	.5670	42,313	713.17
Alabama/Mississippi	−.1460 (7.17)	.5979	38,502	734.95
Arkansas/Louisiana/Oklahoma	−.1267 (7.89)	.5740	59,287	1,012.32
Texas	−.1031 (7.56)	.5737	79,515	1,373.06
Mon/Ariz/Id/Wy/Col/NM/Ut/NV	−.1240 (10.52)	.5637	116,286	1,926.95
California	−.0697 (6.70)	.5604	140,567	2,297.97
Washington/Oregon/Alas/Haw	−.1089 (7.23)	.5788	74,626	1,299.02

Table 4.25 (cont.)

Notes: Equation includes the full set of controls reported in table 4.5, excluding region dummies.
All unemployment rates, U, and the dependent variable (annual earnings) are in natural logarithms.
t-statistics are in parentheses.

the regional unemployment rate is negative or zero. In approximately two-thirds of examples it is statistically significantly different from zero. In four sectors—agriculture, construction, private household services, and business services—pay is apparently particularly responsive to movements in the unemployment rate. The effect is most pronounced in agriculture. For automobiles, which is the sector where some national bargaining takes place and three-year union contracts are common, pay appears to be positively correlated with current unemployment.

Disaggregation by geographical area is also of interest, so table 4.25 splits the sample according to the region in which individuals live. In each of the twenty-one areas (see the appendix), the industry unemployment rate is included. In every geographical area the coefficients on that variable are negative, and in all but one case—the nation's capital—they are significantly different from zero. In contrast, however, to the results in table 4.24, there is relatively little difference in the nature of the estimated wage curves across regions. The largest unemployment elasticity of pay, in absolute terms, is approximately -0.15 for Kentucky/Tennessee and the smallest -0.04 in the District of Columbia.

4.2.4 Correcting for Regional, Industry, and State Averages

The previous sections combine microeconomic data with highly aggregated unemployment rates as regressors. Because area unemployment rates relate to groups that may have common components in their residuals, the standard errors in the regressions estimated above are likely to be biased downwards (see Moulton, 1986, 1987, 1990). In other words, the earlier *t*-statistics on unemployment may be biased upwards. This section corrects for this, and shows that the key results stand.

Intuitively the problem arises because area (and industry) differences reflect a relatively small number of independent observations—fifty in a single U.S. cross-section of states, for example—rather than the huge number of observations that the regression program uses to calculate the standard error. The degree of bias depends on the correlation of disturbances

Table 4.26
The wage curve on region cell means with nonlinearities: 1963–1987

	(1)	(2)	(3)
Log regional U	−.0274	−.0481	−.0224
	(2.78)	(5.56)	(1.04)
(Log regional U)^3			−.0027
			(1.31)
Regional dummies	–	20	20
	5.6722	6.6106	6.5770
Constant	(25.10)	(29.38)	(29.07)
$\bar{R}^2$	.9956	.9974	.9975
F	1,488.83	2,045.06	2,028.22
DF	445	424	423

Source: Current Population Surveys—March tapes.
Notes: All equations include full sets of year (25) and industry variables (43), plus controls for (1) experience and its square, (2) years of schooling, (3) four marital status variables, (4) two race variables, (5) private sector, (6) gender, (7) part-time, and (8) industry unemployment. All unemployment rates and the dependent variable (annual earnings) are in natural logarithms. Unemployment rates, U, relate to regions.
All variables, including the dependent variable, are measured as the mean of all observations in a year/region cell.
t-statistics are in parentheses.

within areas (industries) and the number of persons in each area (industry). A discussion is provided by Kloek (1981), Greenwald (1983), and Moulton (1986, 1987, 1990). The procedure used here to resolve the difficulty is to re-estimate the regressions with cell means as observations. The first step is to construct three separate data matrices (1) by year and by region, (2), by year and by industry for the whole sample period of 1963 to 1987, and (3) by year and by state for the period 1979 to 1987. The average values of the dependent variable and of the independent variables, in each cell of the relevant matrix, is calculated. In the case of the industry matrix this involves over two billion separate calculations. These constructed cell-averages are then taken as the units of observation in the regressions. This methodology allows the generation of a series of lagged values of the dependent and independent variables.

a. Regional Averages   The first stage was to produce a matrix of observations defined across the twenty five years of the CPS and the twenty one regions used previously. Each newly aggregated variable is constructed at the first-stage of the procedure as the mean value of the variable for all individuals in one of 525 cells (25 years*21 regions).

Table 4.27
Using region cell means with lagged unemployment

	(1)	(2)	(3)	(4)	(5)
Log U_t	−.0469	−.0297			−.0258
	(5.81)	(2.87)			(2.53)
Log U_{t-1}		−.0281	−.0475	−.0228	−.0070
		(2.63)	(5.69)	(2.27)	(0.59)
Log U_{t-2}				−.0411	−.0397
				(3.86)	(3.75)
Log w_{t-1}	.2876	.2748	.2726	.2489	.2515
	(8.96)	(8.52)	(8.38)	(7.57)	(7.69)
Constant	4.9314	5.0349	5.1093	5.4948	5.4342
	(16.38)	(16.70)	(16.86)	(17.08)	(16.97)
$\bar{R}^2$	.9978	.9978	.9978	.9978	.9978
F	2,288.66	2,299.44	2,281.41	2,173.63	2,182.92
DF	403	402	403	382	381

Source: Current Population Surveys—March tapes.
Notes: All equations include full sets of year, region and industry variables (43), plus controls for (1) experience and its square, (2) years of schooling, (3) four marital status variables, (4) two race variables, (5) private sector, (6) gender, and (7) part-time. All unemployment rates, U, the dependent variable (annual earnings) and its lag are in natural logarithms.
Unemployment rates relate to regions.
All variables, including the dependent variable, are measured as the mean of all observations in a year/region cell.
t-statistics are in parentheses.

Column 1 of table 4.26 reports the results of estimating an earnings equation using these aggregated data (including the standard set of control variables). The dependent variable is the log of the average annual wage in each cell, and the unemployment variable is the log of the unemployment rate. Without regional dummies, the (log of the) regional unemployment rate has a coefficient of −0.027 and a t-statistic of 2.8. The inclusion of a full set of dummies makes the coefficient better defined and raises the estimate of the unemployment elasticity to −0.05. There is little support statistically for the inclusion of nonlinear unemployment terms (column 3). Adjusting for the group bias reduces the coefficient on unemployment by approximately one half compared with that obtained from the micro regression (see column 1 of table 4.5), while the standard error more than doubles (from 0.00398 to 0.00865). Freeman (1990b) uses a comparable procedure to adjust for such biases in estimating earnings equations for young people on the 1983 and 1987 CPS Annual Merged Files. He finds little evidence of bias in the least squares calculations using the micro-data.

Table 4.28
Using region cell means with further lags

	(1)	(2)	(3)	(4)	(5)
Log U_t		−.0483	−.0289		
		(5.98)	(2.85)		
Log U_{t-1}	−.0351		−.0103	−.0275	
	(3.37)		(0.86)	(2.70)	
Log U_{t-2}	−.0371		−.0339	−.0362	−.0551
	(3.34)		(3.18)	(3.36)	(6.33)
Log w_{t-1}		.2103	.1951	.1985	.2532
		(5.46)	(5.13)	(5.17)	(7.67)
Log w_{t-2}	.1806	.1174	.0975	.0866	
	(5.93)	(3.40)	(2.82)	(2.50)	
Constant	5.8837	4.7524	5.0183	6.0432	6.2305
	(20.64)	(15.24)	(16.06)	(16.95)	(17.76)
$\bar{R}^2$	.9977	.9978	.9979	.9978	.9978
F	2,072.70	2,166.74	2,209.90	2,190.65	2,171.82
DF	382	382	380	381	383

Source: Current Population Surveys—March tapes.
Notes: All equations include full sets of year, region and industry variables (43), plus controls for (1) experience and its square, (2) years of schooling, (3) four marital status variables, (4) two race variables, (5) private sector, (6) gender, and (7) part-time. All unemployment rates, U, the dependent variable (annual earnings) and its lags are in natural logarithms.
Unemployment rates relate to regions.
All variables, including the dependent variable, are measured as the mean of all observations in a year/region cell.
t-statistics are in parentheses.

Table 4.27 includes a lagged dependent variable,[7] which is statistically significant with a coefficient around 0.3. In table 4.28 a second lag on earnings is included, which also enters positively and significantly. It seems to make little difference whether unemployment is included contemporaneously or as a lag. There is nothing to choose statistically between the various formulations of the wage curve.

Table 4.27 is, inadvertently, a loose test of one of the famous ideas in economics. If Phillips (1958) was right, and the textbook Phillips curve taught to undergraduates is correct, the lagged dependent variable in table 4.27 should be close to unity. Yet, as all the columns show, it is below 0.3. At the best, then, wages are simply autoregressive and only a weak version of Phillips's hypothesis is true.

---

7. Nickell (1981) shows that in short panels this needs to be instrumented. Because the bias is a function of $1/T$ and there are 25 years here it can probably be neglected. Instrumenting the lagged dependent variable made a negligible difference.

Table 4.29
Using region cell means: Nonlinearities on subsamples

	(1)	(2)	(3)	(4)
	1963–1973		1974–1987	
Log U_t	−.0312	.0675	−.0658	−.1220
	(1.61)	(1.67)	(6.49)	(3.96)
$(\text{Log } U_t)^3$		−.0144		.0053
		(2.76)		(1.93)
Constant	7.0939	7.0279	8.9863	8.4667
	(13.73)	(13.95)	(24.42)	(23.09)
$\bar{R}^2$	.9894	.9899	.9955	.9955
F	230.61	240.13	787.83	788.44
DF	124	123	226	225

Source: Current Population Surveys—March tapes.
Notes: All equations include full sets of year, region and industry variables (43), plus controls for (1) experience and its square, (2) years of schooling, (3) four marital status variables, (4) two race variables, (5) private sector, (6) gender, (7) part-time status, and (8) industry unemployment and a lagged dependent variable. All unemployment rates and the dependent variable (annual earnings) are in natural logarithms.
Unemployment rates relate to regions.
All variables, including the dependent variable, are measured as the mean of all observations in a year/region cell.
t-statistics are in parentheses.

The sample is split into two time periods in table 4.29. They are before and after the first OPEC oil shock, that is, 1963–1973 and 1974–1987. The unemployment elasticity of pay is twice as large in the second period as in the first (−0.066 and −0.031 respectively). In both periods the cubic term is significant or nearly so. Despite the fact that the signs on the log and the cubic terms are reversed for the two periods, the two curves are downward sloping over the majority of the range of data points.

b. Industry Averages   A similar exercise is performed in table 4.30, but for industry rather than regional unemployment. In this case there are forty-three industries across twenty-five years, giving a new data file with cell averages of 1,075 cases. There are three specifications, one without industry dummies, one with them, and one with a cubic unemployment term. The industry unemployment term enters with a coefficient of −0.027 in column 1 without industry dummies; it falls to −0.011 but is insignificant in column 2 in the presence of a full set of industry dummies ($t = 1.41$). As in table 4.5, which used the micro-data, there turns out to be some evidence to support the inclusion of higher order terms in industry unemployment (columns 3 and 4 of table 4.30).

Table 4.30
Industry wage curves on cell means: 1963–1987

	(1)	(2)	(3)	(4)
Log industry U	−.0263	−.0172	.0431	.0507
	(3.21)	(1.41)	(2.68)	(3.21)
(Log industry U)^3			−.0056	−.0060
			(4.23)	(4.67)
Log w_{t-1}				.1133
				(8.76)
Industry dummies	—	41	41	41
Constant	6.0079	5.0190	4.9239	4.1972
	(26.79)	(22.64)	(22.30)	(18.11)
$\bar{R}^2$	.9833	.9893	.9893	.9927
F	1,019.67	1,260.57	1,271.42	1,307.88
DF	945	904	903	860
N	1,004	1,004	1,004	961

Source: Current Population Surveys—March tapes.
Notes: All equations include full sets of year and region variables (20), plus controls for (1) experience and its square, (2) years of schooling, (3) four marital status variables, (4) two race variables, (5) private sector, (6) gender, and (7) part-time status. All unemployment rates, U, the dependent variable (annual earnings) and its lag are in natural logarithms.
Unemployment rates relate to industries.
All variables, including the dependent variable, are measured as the mean of all observations in a year/industry cell.
t-statistics are in parentheses.

Table 4.30 suggests even less support for Phillips (1958). The lagged dependent wage variable is now 0.1. Some might call this a version of the Phillips curve, but that seems an unnatural thing to do.

In table 4.31 the lagged dependent variable is significant, as it was in table 4.27, which used the regional data. In contrast, little support is adduced for the inclusion of any lagged unemployment terms. A similar picture emerges from table 4.32, which includes a second lag on earnings that, as in table 4.28, is significant. The coefficients on the lagged dependent variables are a good deal smaller when aggregating across industries than when doing so across regions.

Table 4.33 present a series of specifications that include higher-order industry unemployment terms measured both contemporaneously and lagged. In all cases a one-year lag on the dependent variable is also included. In column 1, the two unemployment rates measured in levels are significant. Experimentation, with relatively limited success, produced a series of specifications involving both the unemployment rate and higher

Table 4.31
Lags in an industry wage curve: 1963–1987

	(1)	(2)	(3)	(4)	(5)
Log U_t	−.0149	−.0141			−.0124
	(2.03)	(1.86)			(1.75)
Log U_{t-1}		−.0010	−.0036	.0009	.0031
		(1.45)	(0.60)	(0.16)	(0.52)
Log U_{t-2}				−.0036	−.0027
				(0.64)	(0.47)
Log w_{t-1}	.1131	.1133	.1135	.1064	.1061
	(8.64)	(8.60)	(8.60)	(8.77)	(8.75)
Constant	4.2993	4.3819	4.2672	4.3290	4.5736
	(18.42)	(18.64)	(18.12)	(19.98)	(20.36)
$\bar{R}^2$	.9925	.9925	.9925	.9944	.9944
F	1,289.72	1,260.52	1,269.57	1,423.14	1,412.57
DF	861	848	849	798	797
N	961	949	949	898	898

Source: Current Population Surveys—March tapes.
Notes: All equations include full sets of year, region and industry variables (41), plus controls for (1) experience and its square, (2) years of schooling, (3) four marital status variables, (4) two race variables, (5) private sector, (6) gender, and (7) part-time status. All unemployment rates, U, the dependent variable (annual earnings) and its lag are in natural logarithms. Unemployment rates relate to industries.
All variables, including the dependent variable, are measured as the mean of all observations in a year/industry cell.
t-statistics are in parentheses.

order terms, in both levels and logs. Column 5 of table 4.33 documents a result where higher-order lagged terms were significant. It is not possible to distinguish statistically between this specification and that in column 1. In table 4.34, however, which reverts to cell means for regions, there is a little support for the inclusion of both the log of unemployment lagged twice and its cube. In the earlier period the preferred specification includes the contemporaneous, rather than lagged, measures of the same variables.

c.   *State Averages*   This section discusses the results from estimating a series of earnings equations aggregated across the fifty U.S. states and the District of Columbia for the period 1979 to 1987.[8] There are 459 observations. Although the results reported here are disaggregated across states

---

8. Although the details are not explained, page 315 of Layard et al. (1991) records an equation for the United States in which unemployment is negative and the lagged dependent variable equals 0.68.

Table 4.32
More lags in an industry wage curve

	(1)	(2)	(3)	(4)	(5)
Log U_t		−.0118	−.0111		
		(1.77)	(1.57)		
Log U_{t-1}	.0009		.0024	.0005	
	(0.16)		(0.41)	(0.08)	
Log U_{t-2}	−.0036		−.0018	−.0026	−.0030
	(0.57)		(0.31)	(0.46)	(0.55)
Log w_{t-1}	.1064	.0938	.0948	.0949	.1060
	(8.77)	(7.67)	(7.64)	(7.64)	(8.81)
Log w_{t-2}		.0434	.0442	.0452	
		(3.65)	(3.67)	(3.75)	
Constant	6.0902	5.1687	4.2769	4.1059	5.3781
	(26.34)	(22.18)	(18.44)	(18.41)	(23.83)
$\bar{R}^2$	.9944	.9945	.9907	.9945	.9944
F	1,423.14	1,486.86	952.46	1,432.11	1,456.58
DF	798	821	796	797	810
N	898	921	898	898	909

Source: Current Population Surveys—March tapes.
Notes: All equations include full sets of year, region and industry variables (41), plus controls for (1) experience and its square, (2) years of schooling, (3) four marital status variables, (4) two race variables, (5) private sector, (6) gender, and (7) part-time status. All unemployment rates, U, the dependent variable (annual earnings) and its lags are in natural logarithms. Unemployment rates relate to industries.
All variables, including the dependent variable, are measured as the mean of all observations in a year/industry cell.
t-statistics are in parentheses.

rather than regions, and are for a shorter period than when the disaggregation was across regions in section a, the qualitative results are similar. As can be seen from table 4.35, the log of the state unemployment rate is significant when a full set of state dummies is included. The unemployment elasticity of pay is here estimated at −0.073 compared with −0.048 in table 4.28. The coefficient is consistent with the conclusion that the unemployment elasticity of pay for the period is approximately −0.1. More complicated dynamic specifications are set out in tables 4.36 (lagged unemployment terms are statistically significant) and 4.37, but without altering the substance of the results.

Last, figures 4.33 and 4.34 plot measures, period by period, of the estimated unemployment elasticity of pay. These are obtained once again by interacting the regional log unemployment variable with year dummies. All the underlying equations control for regional and industry fixed effects,

Table 4.33
Testing for nonlinearities: Industry wage curves, 1963–1987

	(1)	(2)	(3)	(4)	(5)	(6)
U_t	−.0044		−.0047			
	(2.85)		(2.95)			
$(U_t)^2$	.00006		.00006			
	(2.24)		(2.32)			
U_{t-1}		.0004	.0013			
		(0.31)	(0.96)			
$(U_{t-1})^2$		−.00002	−.00003			
		(0.90)	(1.45)			
Log U_t				.0213		.0084
				(1.44)		(0.53)
$(\text{Log } U_t)^3$				−.0023		−.0017
				(2.53)		(1.79)
Log U_{t-1}					.0331	.0333
					(3.14)	(2.96)
$(\text{Log } U_{t-1})^3$					−.0022	−.0021
					(3.25)	(3.12)
Log w_{t-1}	.0812	.0809	.0818	.0801	.0811	.0806
	(5.42)	(5.35)	(5.41)	(5.34)	(5.39)	(5.35)
Constant	5.8537	5.0153	5.0568	5.7932	5.0203	5.0327
	(25.47)	(22.58)	(22.76)	(25.06)	(22.72)	(27.63)
$\bar{R}^2$	.9895	.9893	.9895	.9895	.9895	.9896
F	914.04	901.29	886.19	913.23	910.58	892.95
DF	887	887	874	887	887	874

Source: Current Population Surveys—March tapes.
Notes: All equations include full sets of year, region (20) and industry variables (43), plus controls for (1) experience and its square, (2) years of schooling, (3) four marital status variables, (4) two race variables, (5) private sector, (6) gender, and (7) part-time status. The dependent variable (annual earnings) and its lags are in natural logarithms.
All variables, including the dependent variable, are measured as the mean of all observations in a year/region cell.
t-statistics are in parentheses.

Table 4.34
Further nonlinearities with region cell means

	(1) 1963–73	(2) 1963–73	(3) 1963–73	(4) 1974–87	(5) 1974–87	(6) 1974–87
U_t	.0152 (1.41)			−.0018 (1.40)		
U_t^2	−.0019 (1.98)			.00002 (0.81)		
Log U_t		.0638 (1.91)			.0080 (0.50)	
(Log U_t)^3		−.0118 (2.43)			−.0012 (1.31)	
Log U_{t-2}			−.0104 (0.78)			.0247 (1.89)
(Log U_{t-2})^3			.0057 (1.83)			−.0015 (2.06)
Log w_{t-1}	.2510 (6.12)	.2486 (6.07)	.2767 (7.63)	.0125 (0.95)	.0121 (0.92)	.0121 (0.91)
Constant	3.5229 (8.71)	3.3691 (8.49)	3.6540 (9.85)	5.8548 (32.38)	5.7351 (31.65)	5.1189 (29.06)
$\overline{R}^2$	.9861	.9862	.9909	.9915	.9915	.9914
F	305.26	305.71	419.39	782.00	782.22	777.50
DF	282	282	240	528	528	528

Source: Current Population Surveys—March tapes.
Notes: All equations include full sets of year, region (20) and industry variables (43), plus controls for (1) experience and its square, (2) years of schooling, (3) four marital status variables, (4) two race variables, (5) private sector, (6) gender, (7) part-time status, and (8) industry unemployment. All unemployment rates, U, the dependent variable (annual earnings) and its lag are in natural logarithms.
Unemployment rates relate to regions.
All variables, including the dependent variable, are measured as the mean of all observations in a year/region cell.
t-statistics are in parentheses.

and necessarily include an interaction term between the unemployment variable and the year, as explained earlier. There is evidence both of an autocorrelated pattern and, intriguingly, a long-term downward trend. A whole set of unanswered questions is thrown up by these pictures and more research is going to be needed to get to the bottom of them.

By table 4.36, with data on fifty American states by nine years, the lagged dependent variable has a coefficient of zero with a t-statistic that is also essentially zero. The Phillips curve has disappeared.

As final background information, figures 4.35 to 4.85 provide graphs of U.S. unemployment by state over time. They do not exhibit the uniformity

Table 4.35
Wage curves using state cell means: 1979–1987

	(1)	(2)	(3)
Log U_t	−.0100	−.0730	−.1462
	(0.74)	(7.32)	(5.88)
$(\text{Log } U_t)^3$			.0070
			(3.21)
State dummies	—	50	50
Constant	6.9651	7.5761	7.6692
	(20.56)	(26.28)	(27.47)
$\bar{R}^2$	.9375	.9829	.9833
F	110.32	232.41	236.73
DF	390	340	339

Current Population Surveys—March tapes.
Notes: All equations include full sets of year and industry variables (43), plus controls for (1) experience and its square, (2) years of schooling, (3) four marital status variables, (4) two race variables, (5) private sector, (6) gender, and (7) part-time status. All unemployment rates, U, and the dependent variable (annual earnings) are in natural logarithms.
Unemployment rates relate to states.
All variables, including the dependent variable, are measured as the mean of all observations in a year/state cell.
t-statistics are in parentheses.

common, as will be seen in chapter 5, in some other countries. In other words, the United States appears to have distinct regional business cycles, and not merely a single national cycle.

4.3   Conclusions

This chapter studies pay determination in the United States. The data are from the Current Population Surveys of 1964 to 1991 and the General Social Surveys of 1974 to 1988. The first of these is the principal source: it provides a random sample of roughly 1.7 million U.S. employees. The second gives a smaller sample of approximately 11,000 Americans. As might be expected, the econometric results are more clear-cut using the CPS data set.

Few economists would have predicted the findings. They appear to challenge orthodox thinking in labor economics, macroeconomics, and regional economics. The econometric evidence described in the chapter raises doubts, for example, about the idea, commonly associated with work by Harris and Todaro (1970) and Hall (1970, 1972), that wages and unemployment are positively correlated across space. Instead there is fairly unambig-

Table 4.36
State wage curves with lagged unemployment: 1979–1987

	(1)	(2)	(3)	(4)	(5)	(6)
Log U_t	−.0877	−.0658	−.0511			−.0653
	(7.26)	(4.28)	(3.92)			(4.28)
Log U_{t-1}		−.0330	−.0337	−.0715	−.0546	−.0169
		(2.29)	(2.58)	(6.18)	(3.65)	(1.00)
Log U_{t-2}					−.0264	−.0255
					(1.78)	(1.77)
Log w_{t-1}	.0086	.0024		−.0049	−.0054	.0018
	(0.46)	(0.13)		(0.25)	(0.29)	(0.11)
Constant	7.8094	8.1929	7.6393	8.0009	8.2983	5.4342
	(22.11)	(22.11)	(26.63)	(21.93)	(22.03)	(16.97)
$\bar{R}^2$	.9797	.9800	.9831	.9788	.9789	.9801
F	171.76	172.82	234.78	164.22	164.60	173.21
DF	285	284	340	286	285	284

Source: Current Population Surveys—March tapes.
Notes: All equations include full sets of year dummies, state dummies (50), industry dummies (43), plus controls for (1) experience and its square, (2) years of schooling, (3) four marital status dummies, (4) two race dummies, (5) private sector dummy, (6) gender dummy, and (7) part-time dummy. All unemployment rates, the dependent variable (annual earnings) and its lag are in natural logarithms.
All variables, including the dependent variable, are measured as the mean of all observations in a year/state cell.
t-statistics are in parentheses.

uous evidence of a downward-sloping locus: high unemployment goes with low pay. The United States apparently has a wage curve. The unemployment elasticity of pay is approximately −0.1. This means, to put things in more straightforward terms, that a hypothetical doubling of unemployment would be associated with a fall in workers' remuneration of approximately 10% (that is, by one tenth from the original wage level). This is to be understood as a ceteris paribus change, holding other things, including macro variables, constant.

A representative earnings equation is that in column 1 of table 4.5. Here the dependent variable is the logarithm of annual earnings and there are slightly more than one and a half million observations. The equation includes control variables for individuals' work experience, years of schooling, marital status, race, a dummy for whether working in the private sector, and a part-time work dummy. It also includes a full set of twenty-four year dummies, of twenty-one regional dummies, and of forty-three industry dummies. The coefficient on the log of regional unemployment is

Table 4.37
Further lags in a state wage curve: 1979–1987

	(1)	(2)	(3)	(4)	(5)
Log U_t		−.0916	−.0660		
		(6.67)	(3.78)		
Log U_{t-1}	−.0602		−.0274	−.0275	
	(3.37)		(1.37)	(2.70)	
Log U_{t-2}	−.0341		−.0275	−.0292	−.0610
	(1.96)		(1.31)	(1.65)	(5.21)
Log w_{t-1}		−.0001	−.0109	−.0213	.0004
		(0.02)	(0.45)	(0.84)	(0.00)
Log w_{t-2}	−.0082	.0056	.0104	.0151	
	(0.04)	(0.20)	(0.36)	(0.50)	
Constant	8.4799	7.7971	7.9634	8.0135	7.8505
	(19.53)	(18.72)	(19.35)	(19.21)	(21.76)
$\bar{R}^2$	.9744	.9758	.9762	.9749	.9780
F	118.68	124.09	124.87	118.96	159.10
DF	235	231	229	230	286

Source: Current Populaton Surveys—March tapes.
Notes: All equations include full sets of year, state (50) and industry variables (43), plus controls for (1) experience and its square, (2) years of schooling, (3) four marital status variables, (4) two race variables, (5) private sector, (6) gender, and (7) part-time status. All unemployment rates, the dependent variable (annual earnings) and its lag are in natural logarithms.
All variables, including the dependent variable, are measured as the mean of all observations in a year/state cell.
t-statistics are in parentheses.

−0.10 and that on the log of industry unemployment is −0.11. The t-statistics on these coefficients are large. They may be inflated, following Moulton (1986) and others, by common group errors (intuitively, because there are approximately five hundred unemployment observations but 3,000 times as many observations on earnings). A table such as 4.27 corrects for this. It uses regional averages—so-called cell means—for all variables. The tenor of the results is unchanged. The long-run regional unemployment elasticity of pay is estimated, as in column 2 of table 4.27, for example, at approximately −0.08. It is well-determined.[9]

These conclusions rest upon estimation using nominal annual earnings as the dependent variable. A natural objection is that a true real-wage-per-hour variable would be preferable. Although most of the force of the point that there is no price deflator is eliminated by the fact that regional and

9. This is obtained, of course, by solving the difference equation for its steady-state values. The number comes from $(0.0297 + 0.0281)/(1 − 0.2748) = 0.08$ approx.

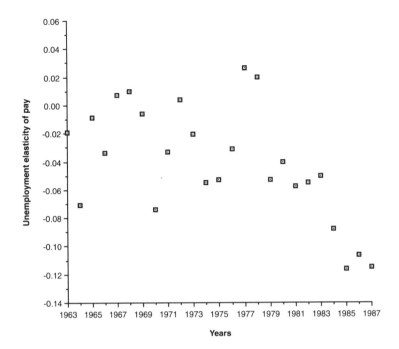

Figure 4.33
Unemployment elasticity of pay: 1963–1987 (regional cell means)

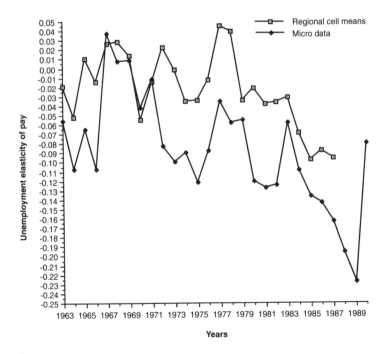

Figure 4.34
Time series of the unemployment elasticity of pay: 1963–1990

time dummies are in the equations, there is no perfectly convincing reply to the criticism. Nevertheless, later chapters show that the key result goes through in many countries with dependent variables closer to the theoretical ideal. Moreover, table 4.11, using the 1987 CPS, suggests that the U.S. CMSA regional unemployment elasticity of pay is −0.09 in an hourly earnings equation. This has fifty state dummies, which ought to pick up most of the variation in consumer prices across space. The lack of a regional price deflator is presumably irrelevant when estimating a wage curve with industry unemployment as the regressor. Encouragingly, it does not seem to matter whether the dependent variable is defined as annual earnings or an hourly wage.

Conventional macroeconomics seems to be at threat from these results. They are consistent with the view that it is wrong to believe in a Phillips curve. This chapter's industry wage curves, for example, obtain a lagged dependent variable, within a logarithmic earnings equation, of 0.1. Even in the most aggregated case, that of the CPS with twenty-one large regions, the coefficient on the lagged dependent wage variable is below 0.3. Using data for the fifty U.S. states over the period from 1979 to 1987, the estimate of the lagged dependent variable is zero. This microeconometric analysis of U.S. pay levels seems to suggest that Phillips-style regressions, run on aggregated data, may be misleading.

It might appear from the tables in this chapter that Harris and Todaro's (1970) idea of compensating differentials across space is also dead. Such a view would not be accurate. As the theoretical models in chapter 3 make clear, permanent values of pay and unemployment can be positively correlated while, with many shocks hitting the regions of the economy, movements in these two are negatively related. Column 4 of table 4.6, in which permanent unemployment—by region again—enters positively, is consistent with such a theory. The wage curve, for which there is evidence in the data, is not incompatible with the idea of long-run compensating regional differentials. The mistake in the empirical literature has been to omit controls for regional fixed effects.

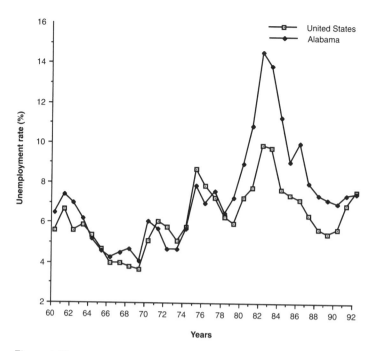

Figure 4.35
Alabama unemployment rates: 1960–1992

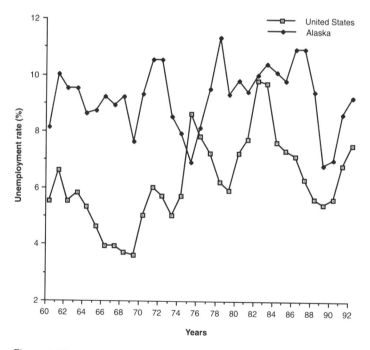

Figure 4.36
Alaska unemployment rates: 1960–1992

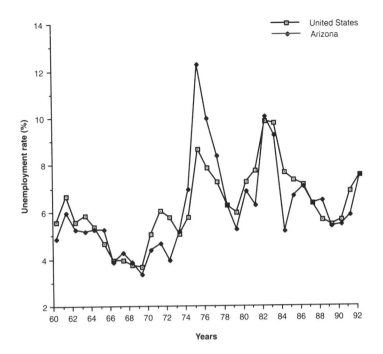

Figure 4.37
Arizona unemployment rates: 1960–1992

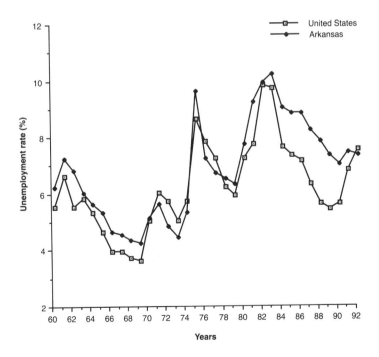

Figure 4.38
Arkansas unemployment rates: 1960–1992

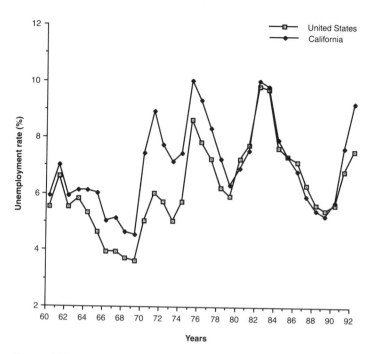

Figure 4.39
California unemployment rates: 1960–1992

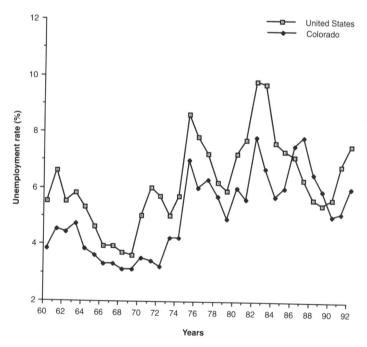

Figure 4.40
Colorado unemployment rates: 1960–1992

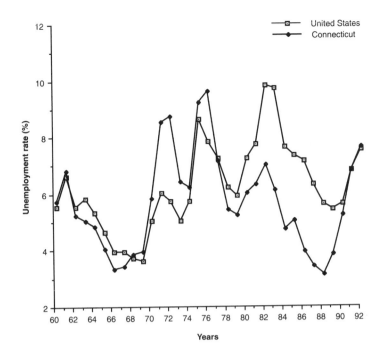

Figure 4.41
Connecticut unemployment rates: 1960–1992

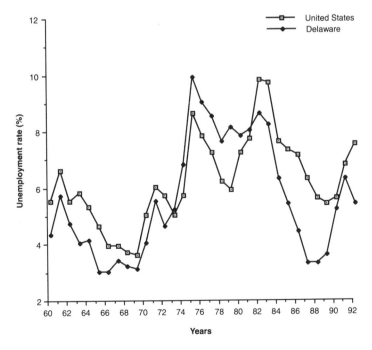

Figure 4.42
Delaware unemployment rates: 1960–1992

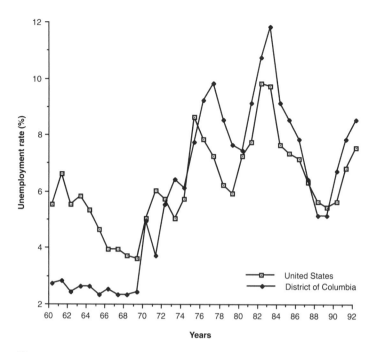

Figure 4.43
District of Columbia unemployment rates: 1960–1992

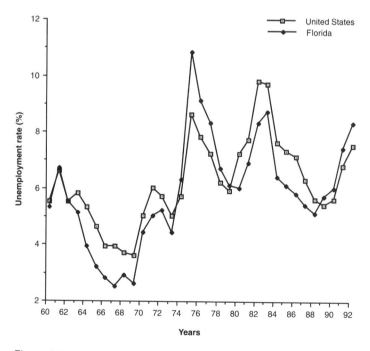

Figure 4.44
Florida unemployment rates: 1960–1992

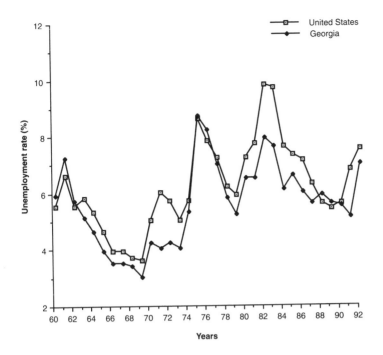

Figure 4.45
Georgia unemployment rates: 1960–1992

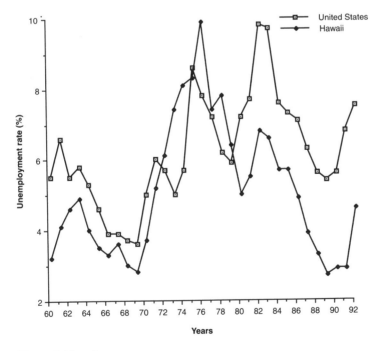

Figure 4.46
Hawaii unemployment rates: 1960–1992

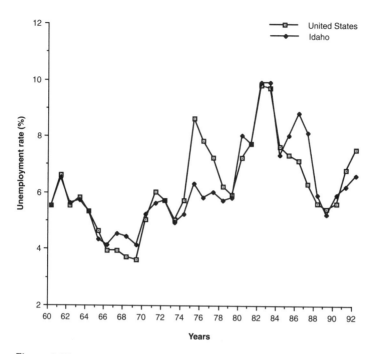

Figure 4.47
Idaho unemployment rates: 1960–1992

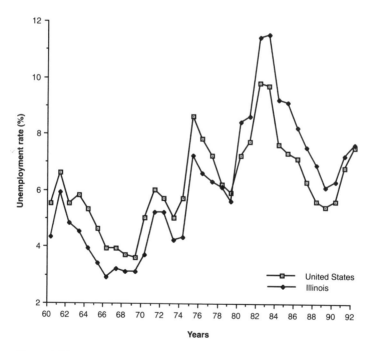

Figure 4.48
Illinois unemployment rates: 1960–1992

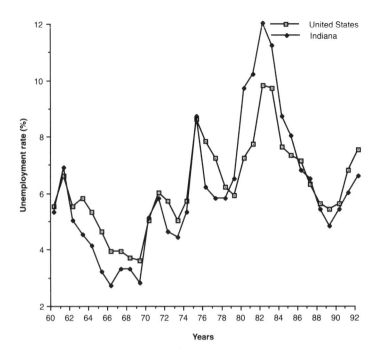

Figure 4.49
Indiana unemployment rates: 1960–1992

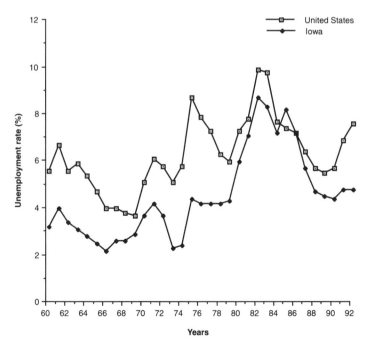

Figure 4.50
Iowa unemployment rates: 1960–1992

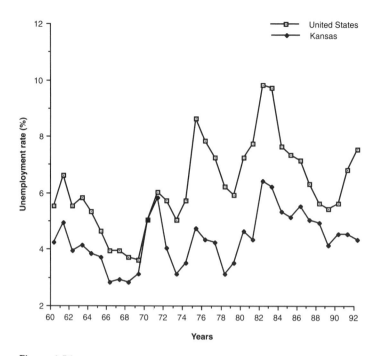

Figure 4.51
Kansas unemployment rates: 1960–1992

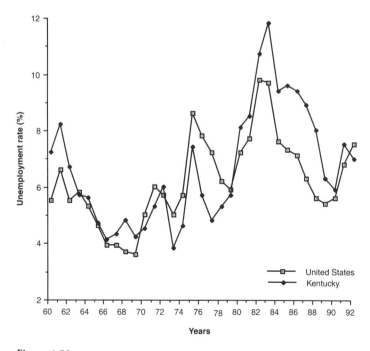

Figure 4.52
Kentucky unemployment rates: 1960–1992

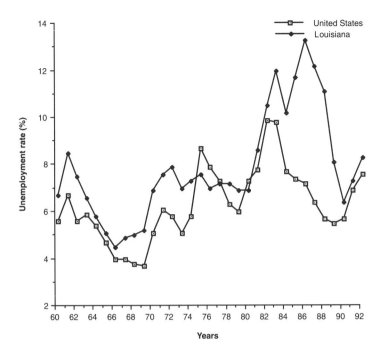

Figure 4.53
Louisiana unemployment rates: 1960–1992

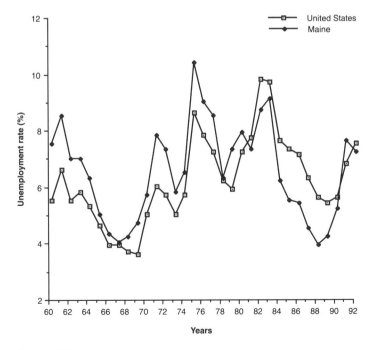

Figure 4.54
Maine unemployment rates: 1960–1992

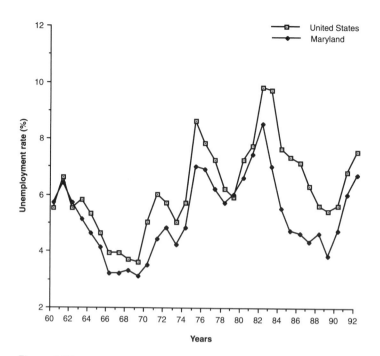

Figure 4.55
Maryland unemployment rates: 1960–1992

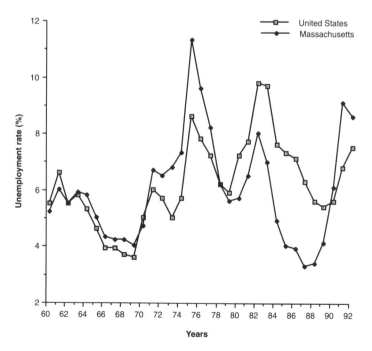

Figure 4.56
Massachusetts unemployment rates: 1960–1992

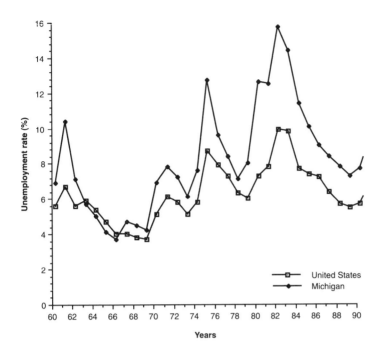

Figure 4.57
Michigan unemployment rates: 1960–1992

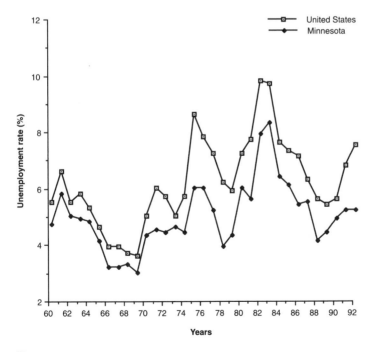

Figure 4.58
Minnesota unemployment rates: 1960–1992

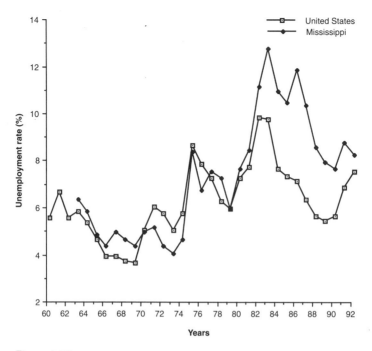

Figure 4.59
Mississippi unemployment rates: 1963–1992

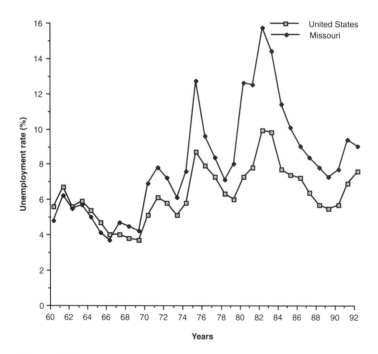

Figure 4.60
Missouri unemployment rates: 1960–1992

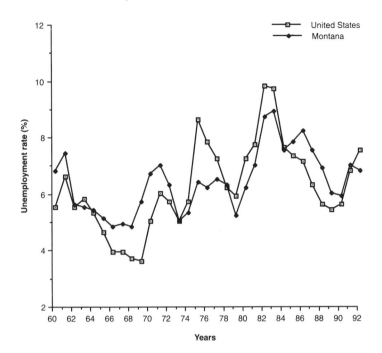

Figure 4.61
Montana unemployment rates: 1960–1992

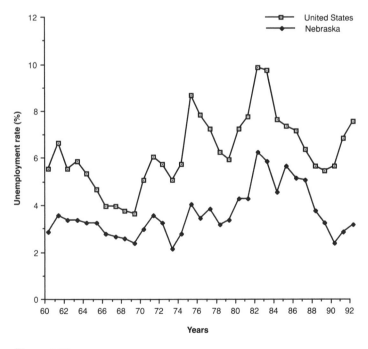

Figure 4.62
Nebraska unemployment rates: 1960–1992

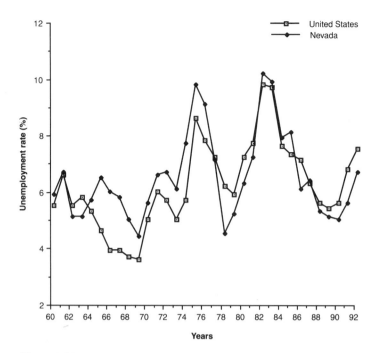

Figure 4.63
Nevada unemployment rates: 1960–1992

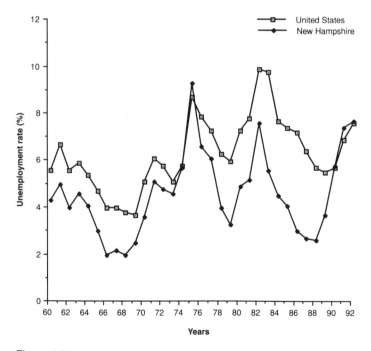

Figure 4.64
New Hampshire unemployment rates: 1960–1992

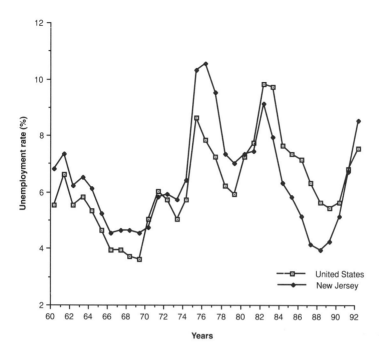

Figure 4.65
New Jersey unemployment rates: 1960–1992

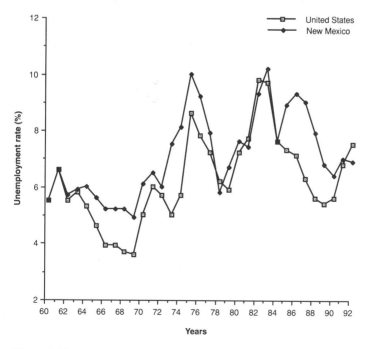

Figure 4.66
New Mexico unemployment rates: 1960–1992

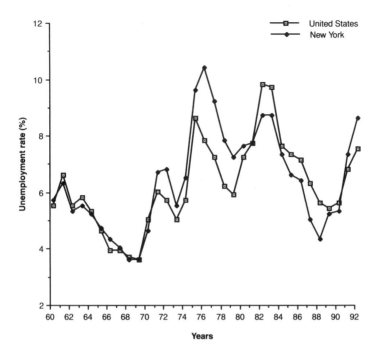

Figure 4.67
New York unemployment rates: 1960–1992

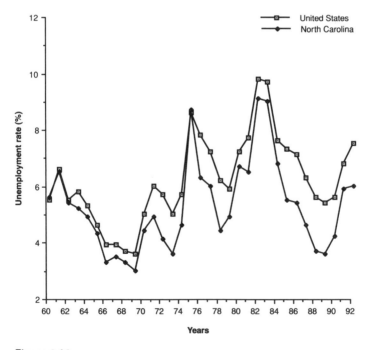

Figure 4.68
North Carolina unemployment rates: 1960–1992

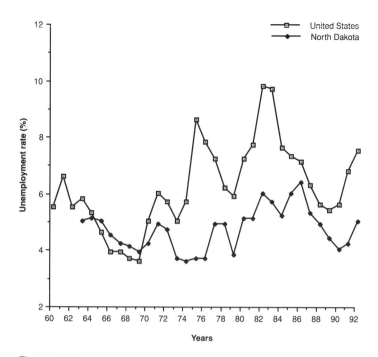

Figure 4.69
North Dakota unemployment rates: 1963–1992

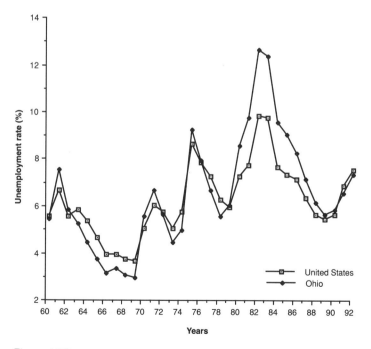

Figure 4.70
Ohio unemployment rates: 1960–1992

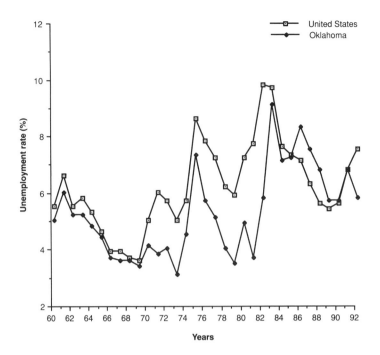

Figure 4.71
Oklahoma unemployment rates: 1960–1992

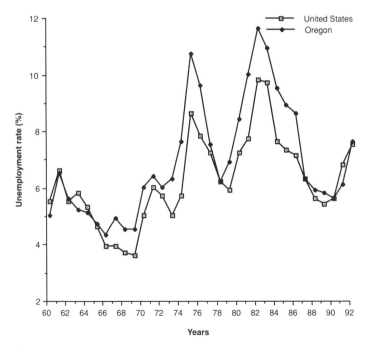

Figure 4.72
Oregon unemployment rates: 1960–1992

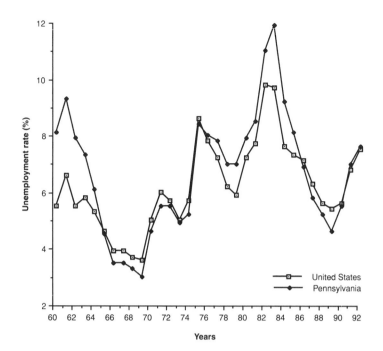

Figure 4.73
Pennsylvania unemployment rates: 1960–1992

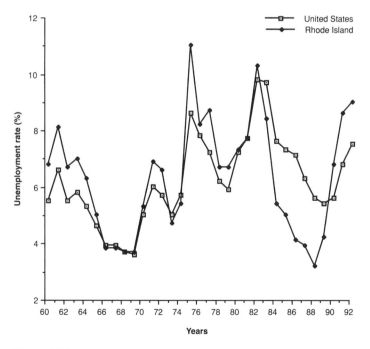

Figure 4.74
Rhode Island unemployment rates: 1960–1992

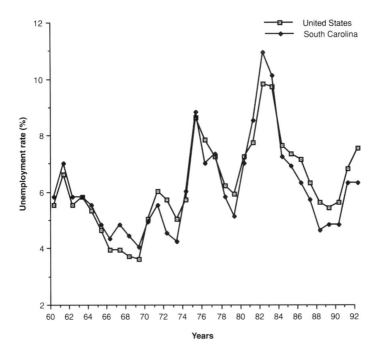

Figure 4.75
South Carolina unemployment rates: 1960–1992

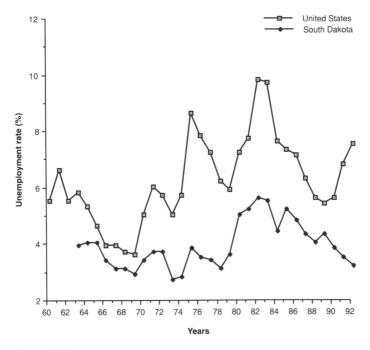

Figure 4.76
South Dakota unemployment rates: 1963–1992

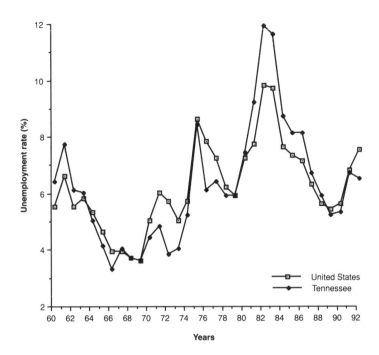

Figure 4.77
Tennessee unemployment rates: 1960–1992

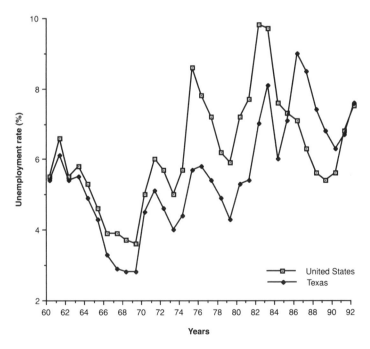

Figure 4.78
Texas unemployment rates: 1960–1992

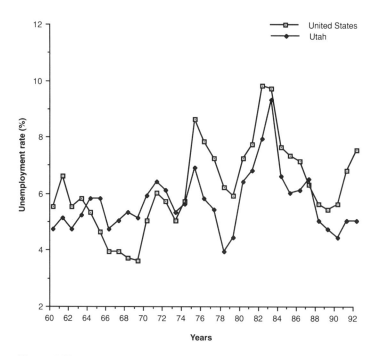

Figure 4.79
Utah unemployment rates: 1960–1992

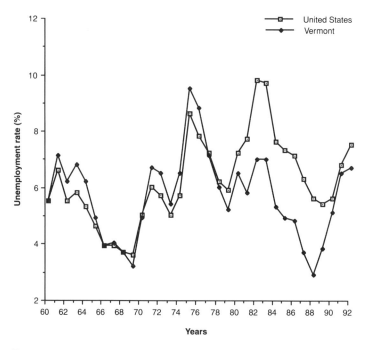

Figure 4.80
Vermont unemployment rates: 1960–1992

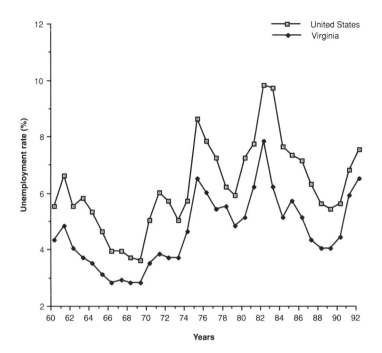

Figure 4.81
Virginia unemployment rates: 1960–1992

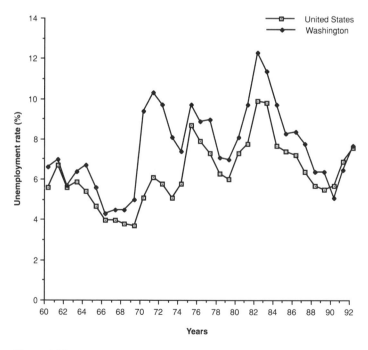

Figure 4.82
Washington unemployment rates: 1960–1992

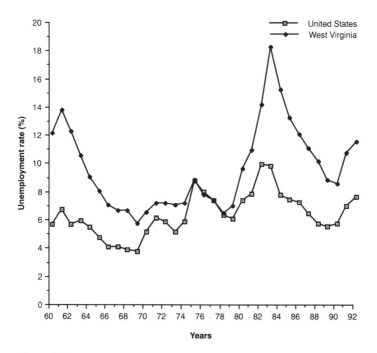

Figure 4.83
West Virginia unemployment rates: 1960–1992

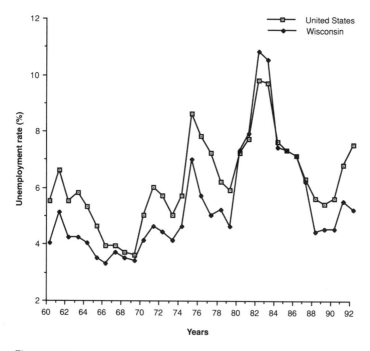

Figure 4.84
Wisconsin unemployment rates: 1960–1992

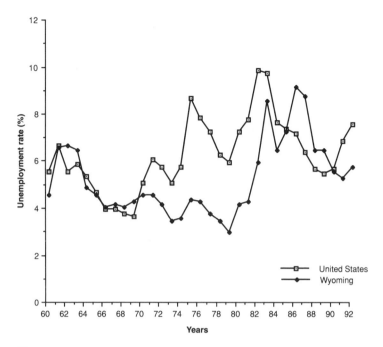

Figure 4.85
Wyoming unemployment rates: 1960–1992

5

The U.S. Wage Curve II:
Further Tests

Inspiration is most likely to come through the stimulus provided by the patterns, puzzles and anomalies revealed by the systematic gathering of data, particularly when the prime need is to break our existing habits of thought.

Ronald Coase, Nobel Prize Lecture (1991)

Although it draws upon an unusually rich source of data, chapter 4 leaves a number of questions unanswered. This chapter subjects the evidence for a U.S. wage curve to closer scrutiny. Three main issues are confronted. They concern the correct interpretation of the pattern found in the data, the problem of simultaneity bias, and the chance that there are omitted variables.

Is it possible that the wage curve is just a conventional, but misspecified, labor supply curve? Some economists are likely to argue that nothing mysterious or novel is going on in these data, that a normal inverted labor supply curve to the region or industry is merely being captured inadvertently. According to this interpretation, workers' desired supply is mismeasured, in chapter 4's regression equations, by the use of an unemployment rate as the independent variable. The wage curve is, in other words, a statistical chimera. The appropriate course of action is then to switch to a more accurate variable for aggregate labor supply such as the participation rate. This view, which threatens the core idea in the book, needs to be evaluated.[1]

Second, the regression equations in the last chapter use ordinary least squares methods. This ignores the fact that wages and unemployment are presumably simultaneously determined—as in the models of chapter 3—

---

1. It might be that wage curve evidence would be of some use even if it were just estimating a neoclassical labor supply function.

within a system of equations. If unemployment is a positively sloped function of the wage, the use of OLS biases upward the coefficient on unemployment in a wage equation. This will make it harder to obtain a negative coefficient, which is one way to respond to critics concerned about endogeneity. Nevertheless, if simultaneity bias exists, the estimates in the previous chapter are flawed, and perhaps seriously so.

Third, the bargaining model in chapter 3 derives a downward-sloping wage curve in a framework where workers and firms share economic rents. As the equations of the model make clear (see back to 3.3.7, for example), a properly specified wage equation should in this case include as an independent variable a measure of rents per employee, such as profit-per-capita. This is missing from the analysis. Hence the previous chapter's estimates might be biased by the omission of some additional regressor of this kind.

5.1 Testing Whether the Wage Curve Is a Labor Supply Curve, and Other Checks

Some checks are described in this subsection. A labor force participation rate is included in wage equations; year dummies are replaced with the national unemployment rate and the aggregate consumer price level; the effect of a variable measuring the employment to population ratio is examined.

To test for the possibility that the wage curve is simply a labor supply curve, table 5.1 includes the labor force participation rate—the so-called activity rate—as a regressor in earnings equations. The sample is restricted to the period from 1979 to 1987, so that U.S. state data can be used. Both the participation rate and the unemployment rate for each of the fifty states (plus the District of Columbia) are mapped into the CPS data set. In column 1 of table 5.1 the log of industry unemployment and the log of regional unemployment both have negative coefficients with large t-statistics. These are slightly different estimates from those reported in column 5 of table 4.9, because there is a slightly smaller CPS sample for whom activity rates are available. Column 1 forms the standard against which later columns are judged. In column 2 the state unemployment variable is replaced with the log of the state participation rate. This regional variable, which captures a kind of total labor supply, enters with a coefficient of 0.3 and a t-statistic over 5. Column 2's result is what would be expected if the idea of a distinctive form of wage curve, as something different from textbook competitive labor supply, were mistaken. The concept of a wage curve is then

Table 5.1
The U.S. wage curve: Experiments, 1979--1987

	(1)	(2)	(3)	(4)
Log Industry U	−.2361	−.2386	−.2373	−.2360
	(38.67)	(39.09)	(38.68)	(38.66)
Log State U	−.1354		−.0006	−.1325
	(17.77)		(0.11)	(17.14)
Log State Participation rate		.3117	.8364	.1342
		(5.15)	(30.93)	(2.19)
State dummies	50	50	---	50
Industry dummies	Yes	Yes	Yes	Yes
Year dummies	Yes	Yes	Yes	Yes
Constant	7.4293	5.9014	3.5520	6.8650
	(345.49)	(23.35)	(30.42)	(26.52)
$\bar{R}^2$	.5381	.5366	.5318	.5368
F	36,906.47	6,845.54	11,855.34	6,781.04
DF	667,876	667,876	667,925	667,875

Source: Current Population Surveys---March tapes.
Notes: All equations include full sets of year dummies (8) and industry dummies (43), plus controls for (1) experience and its square, (2) years of schooling, (3) four marital status dummies, (4) two race dummies, (5) private sector dummy, and (6) part-time dummy. All unemployment rates, the participation rate and the dependent variable (annual earnings) are in natural logarithms.
All variables are at the state level.
t-statistics are in parentheses.

in jeopardy. This line of criticism appears to stand up well to further scrutiny, as demonstrated in column 3 of table 5.1. When the participation variable is included along with the log regional unemployment term,[2] the regional participation variable is highly significant, with a coefficient of 0.84, and the unemployment term is insignificant and quantitatively tiny.

Column 4 of table 5.1 suggests that this is an illusion caused, once more, by a failure to control for unchanging regional characteristics. Once a set of state dummies is included, the unemployment term becomes statistically significant again. The coefficient on unemployment returns to its column 1 value, namely, −0.13. The coefficient on the participation variable also falls considerably, to 0.13. Although the rate of labor force participation is still a statistically significant variable, unemployment has a more robust statistical role in U.S. earnings equations of the type studied in this chapter.

2. Because it mixes two different ways of thinking, the logical status of the specification in columns 3 and 4 is unclear. It should be thought of only as an encompassing experiment.

The message from table 5.1 seems to be that log unemployment is not playing the role of a mismeasured labor participation variable. In this sense, the wage curve does not appear to be a labor supply function. Two objections can reasonably be raised against this argument. One is that the estimation with the participation rate fails to control for its endogeneity, so that this may be at the heart of the variable's poor performance. A correction for this is done later, however, and without effect. The second is that the employment to population ratio, rather than the labor force participation rate, may be a truer measure of labor supply. This view suffers from the weakness that it treats unemployed workers as not being willing to supply their labor, or somehow not part of a region's total labor supply curve, but it will also be analyzed in the chapter.

Table 5.2 summarizes the results from three experiments where year dummies are replaced by the (log of) the national unemployment rate. Because of the upward trend in nominal wages over the period, the (log of) the implicit price deflator is also included in these specifications. Column 1

Table 5.2
The U.S. wage curve with national unemployment: 1963–1987

	(1)	(2)	(3)
Log Regional U		−.0037	−.0944
		(1.16)	(24.84)
Log Industry U		−.1070	−.1064
		(34.80)	(34.68)
Log implicit price deflator*	1.0511	1.0433	1.0508
	(358.30)	(357.57)	(358.36)
Log national unemployment	−.1466	−.0465	+.0535
	(32.95)	(7.58)	(8.18)
Regional dummies	20	—	20
Constant	2.1468	2.1702	2.1704
	(197.17)	(222.42)	(198.59)
$\bar{R}^2$	.5744	.5720	.5750
F	26,908.81	35,344.11	26,271.09
DF	1,534,928	1,534,034	1,534,013

Source: Current Population Surveys—March tapes; *Economic Report of the President*, 1991, Table B.3, p. 298 col. 1.
Notes: All equations include full sets of year dummies (24), industry dummies (43) and region dummies (20), plus controls for (1) experience and its square, (2) years of schooling, (3) four marital status dummies, (4) two race dummies, (5) private sector dummy, (6) part-time dummy, and (7) industry unemployment. All unemployment rates, the wage variable (annual earnings) and the annual price index are in natural logarithms.
t-statistics are in parentheses.

incorporates both of the new variables. As in Bils (1985), real earnings are procyclical. National unemployment, in column 1, has an elasticity of approximately −0.15. However, in column 2, where regional and industry unemployment rates are added to the specification, and regional dummies are omitted, the coefficient on the national unemployment rate falls from −0.15 to −0.05. The coefficient on the industry unemployment rate is essentially unchanged from those reported in table 4.3, in which year dummies were included. Controlling for region-specific fixed effects, in column 3 of table 5.2, by again including a full set of regional dummies, produces a coefficient of +0.05 on the national unemployment rate with a *t*-statistic of over 8. Regional unemployment here has an elasticity of −0.09. Sanfey (1991) also obtains a positive coefficient on the (lagged) national unemployment rate when estimating industry-level earnings equations for the United States.[3] With two-digit industry data for the period from 1948 to 1984, he finds a coefficient of around +0.14. It is difficult to know how to interpret this; it is possible that it is due to the omission of a variable for real-wage growth. The conclusion from column 3 of table 5.2 is that regional unemployment has more explanatory power than national unemployment, which is perhaps what would be expected if the concept of a regional wage curve is correct.

Tables 5.3 to 5.5, which use state cell means, provide more evidence on the issue of whether the wage curve might be proxying a standard labor supply equation. It is evident that strings of lagged participation rates contribute little. In a variety of settings unemployment continues to be statistically significant. Its size is stable across these specifications. Switching to an employment-to-population ratio (here ER), as in table 5.5, leaves the negative unemployment effect unaffected. The significance of ER disappears—in columns 2, 4, and 5—once unemployment is introduced.

There is one other, and quite separate, reason to doubt the idea that the wage curve correlation is a strangely written sectoral labor supply function. If it were, disaggregated wage curve equations should exhibit the properties expected of the labor supply curves of different groups in the economy. It is natural to believe, for example, that the supply curve (across space) of young workers is likely to be far more elastic than the supply of older people. The latter have less time left in their lives to reap the benefits of the migration investment decision, and more ties, of all kinds, than the young. The old have a steep supply curve to a region: small quantity

---

3. Brian Bell has pointed out to us that the positivity of national unemployment might be because the relative (regional/national) rate matters.

Table 5.3
The participation rate in the state wage curve: 1979–1987

	(1)	(2)	(3)	(4)	(5)	(6)
Log P_t	.1802	.1801	.0016	.0012	.0008	.0004
	(2.69)	(2.42)	(2.26)	(1.11)	(0.71)	(0.29)
Log P_{t-1}					.0003	.0003
					(0.71)	(0.23)
Lot P_{t-2}						.0007
						(0.55)
Log U_t			−.0690	−.0839	−.0647	−.0671
			(6.73)	(6.67)	(4.16)	(3.82)
Log U_{t-1}					−.0303	−.0216
					(2.05)	(1.08)
Log U_{t-2}						−.0282
						(1.63)
Log w_{t-1}		.0011		.0050	−.0003	
		(0.06)		(0.27)	(0.07)	
Constant	6.7143	6.9645	7.4112	6.9960	7.7967	7.8569
	(15.88)	(14.50)	(24.66)	(14.78)	(21.22)	(20.44)
$\bar{R}^2$	.9805	.9763	.9828	.9795	.9787	.9752
F	202.19	146.47	227.52	168.13	166.58	120.04
DF	337	283	336	282	280	233

Source: Current Population Surveys—March tapes.
Notes: All equations include full sets of year (8), state (50) and industry variables (43), plus controls for (1) experience and its square, (2) years of schooling, (3) four marital status variables, (4) two race variables, (5) private sector, and (6) part-time status. All unemployment rates U, participation rates P, and the dependent variable (annual earnings) w are in natural logarithms. All variables are at the state level.
All variables, including the dependent variable, are measured as the mean of all observations in a year/state cell.
t-statistics are in parentheses.

movements are associated with large wage movements. This implies, turning it round, that small movements in pay should, for the highly mobile young workers, be associated with relatively large changes along the quantity axis. A labor supply interpretation of the wage curve asserts that it is a neoclassical supply equation. Then the wage curve of young people, assuming that these are the most mobile, should be relatively flat. It is flatness that corresponds to a high labor supply elasticity.

This prediction is rejected by the data. Chapter 4's table 4.17 reveals that the young have the steepest wage curve, that is, the largest unemployment elasticity. Those under twenty-five have an unemployment elasticity near −0.2. Once again, a labor-supply interpretation fails.

Table 5.4
The state wage curve with more lags on participation: 1979–1987

	(1)	(2)	(3)	(4)	(5)
Log P_t					.0009
					(0.84)
Log P_{t-1}	.0740	.1112	.0156	.0333	.0003
	(0.95)	(1.24)	(0.16)	(0.45)	(0.24)
Log P_{t-2}		−.0058	−.0326		
		(0.07)	(0.34)		
Log P_{t-3}			−.0624		
			(0.68)		
Log U_t					−.0623
					(4.02)
Log U_{t-1}				−.0693	−.0312
				(5.89)	(2.12)
Constant	7.4652	7.4164	8.2813	7.8891	7.8385
	(16.39)	(11.65)	(9.95)	(18.42)	(24.19)
$\bar{R}^2$	.9757	.9704	.9694	.9782	.9793
F	145.17	103.67	85.73	161.02	166.83
DF	288	237	186	287	285

Source: Current Population Surveys—March tapes.
Notes: All equations include full sets of year, state (50) and industry variables (43), plus controls for (1) experience and its square, (2) years of schooling, (3) four marital status variables, (4) two race variables, (5) private sector, and (6) part-time status. All unemployment rates U, participation P and the dependent variables (annual earnings) w are in natural logarithms. All variables are at the state level.
All variables, including the dependent variable, are measured as the mean of all observations in a year/state cell.
t-statistics are in parentheses.

A number of recent econometric studies have found evidence of significant and positive effects of firms' profitability on pay (see, for example, Blanchflower et al., 1990; Carruth and Oswald 1989; Christofides and Oswald 1992; Denny and Machin 1991; Dickens and Katz 1987; Hildreth and Oswald 1993; Katz and Summers 1989; and Sanfey 1991). The consensus from these papers is that industry wage differentials cannot be explained fully by compensating differentials or by differences in skills.[4] The next section takes up this issue.

---

4. Further papers providing rent-sharing evidence include Allen (1992), Beckerman and Jenkinson (1990), Blanchflower and Oswald (1988), Carruth and Oswald (1987b), Carruth et al. (1986), Gregory et al. (1985, 1986, 1987), Groshen (1991), Holmlund and Zetterberg (1991), Krueger and Summers (1987), Lester (1952), Nickell and Wadhwani (1990), Nickell and Kong (1992), Rowlatt (1987), Sanfey (1993), and Wulfsberg (1993).

Table 5.5
Earnings equations with an employment regressor: 1979–1987

	(1)	(2)	(3)	(4)	(5)
Log U_t		−.0672		−.0484	−.0658
		(5.95)		(3.55)	(4.05)
Log U_{t-1}				−.0333	−.0322
				(2.46)	(2.19)
ER_t	.0035	.0010	.0033	.0005	.00001
	(3.93)	(1.00)	(3.41)	(0.51)	(0.01)
Log w_{t-1}			.0005		.0026
			(0.03)		(0.14)
Constant	7.2073	7.4487	7.4730	7.5394	7.8595
	(22.92)	(24.64)	(19.48)	(24.94)	(21.46)
$\bar{R}^2$	.9809	.9827	.9768	.9829	.9797
F	207.08	225.98	149.46	227.97	168.27
DF	337	336	282	335	281

Source: Current Population Surveys—March tapes.
Note: All equations include full sets of year (8), state (50) and industry variables (43), plus controls for (1) experience and its square, (2) years of schooling, (3) four marital status variables, (4) two race variables, (5) private sector dummy, and (6) part-time. All unemployment rates U and the dependent variable (annual earnings) w are in natural logarithms. All variables are at the state level.
All variables, including the dependent variable, are measured as the mean of all observations in a year/state cell.
ER_t is defined as the employment/population* 100.
t-statistics are in parentheses.

5.2 Profits and Unemployment in an Industry Wage Curve

This section examines empirically the predictions of the theoretical models in section 3.3 of chapter 3.[5] It studies the implications of a bargaining framework. The analysis draws upon data on a CPS subsample of approximately 400,000 workers in U.S. manufacturing industry. These data are from the March tapes of the Current Population Survey (CPS), and cover the years 1964 to 1985.[6] To avoid the aggregation problems identified by Moulton (1986), which result in the standard errors in these kinds of microequations being artificially small, and to exploit the availability of industrial profit statistics, the data are converted into a panel of cell means. This

---

5. This section draws on joint work with Peter Sanfey and we thank him for permission to use the material.
6. The earnings data are taken from the 1965 to 1986 Current Population Surveys. The use of an unbalanced panel was necessitated by coding differences across the years in the industry variables.

Table 5.6
Profits and per capita profits for U.S. manufacturing: 1958 to 1985 (in 1972 dollars)

	π $million	π/n $thousands
SIC20. Food and Kindred Products	426.04	17.85
SIC22. Textile Mill Products	127.23	5.05
SIC23. Apparel and Other Textile Products	164.09	4.38
SIC24. Lumber and Wood Products	186.26	4.91
SIC25. Furniture and Fixtures	176.39	5.75
SIC26. Paper and Allied Products	355.47	9.18
SIC27. Printing and Publishing	550.39	7.61
SIC28. Chemical and Allied Products	719.07	21.91
SIC29. Petroleum and Coal Products	892.59	22.95
SIC30. Rubber and Miscellaneous Plastics	802.18	7.34
SIC31. Leather and Leather Products	106.25	4.24
SIC32. Stone, Clay and Glass Products	193.62	8.31
SIC33. Primary Metals	312.53	8.76
SIC34. Fabricated Metals	307.35	7.82
SIC35. Machinery except Electrical	383.35	8.51
SIC36. Electric and Electronic Equipment	357.16	8.81
SIC371. Motor Vehicles and Equipment	2,357.52	9.70
SIC37. Other Transportation Equipment (excl. SIC371)	556.94	6.83
SIC39. Miscellaneous Manufacturing	143.20	7.40

Note: The estimation uses unweighted data. Dickens (1990) shows that it is misleading to weight because individual error terms are likely to be correlated due to group-specific error components.

satisfies Moulton's condition that the level of aggregation be the same on both sides of the regression equation.

The reported regressions use an unbalanced panel of 19 industries by 22 years, giving 394 observations in all. Details of the industries covered are outlined in Table 5.6. The dependent variable and all of the independent variables with the exception of the year dummies are the calculated year/industry cell means from the underlying CPS data. The industry unemployment and profit data were merged from external sources and are as follows (further explanation is in Sanfey, 1992).

The profit variable (equivalent to Sanfey's variable Profit3c) is:

$$\pi = \frac{\text{value added} - \text{payroll}}{\text{CPI}} - \text{real depreciation}$$

$$- \text{(real interest rate*real capital stock)}.$$

A description is provided in Gray (1989) and Sanfey (1992: appendix 2, and 1993). The sample here is restricted to individuals employed in manu-

Table 5.7
Earnings equations with profit-per-employee: U.S. manufacturing, 1964–1985

	(1)	(2)	(3)	(4)	(5)
Log U_t		−.0716	−.0159	−.0239	−.0306
		(3.86)	(1.61)	(2.79)	(2.47)
$(\pi/n)_t$	.0060	.0060	−.0014	.0022	.0022
	(6.25)	(6.27)	(2.40)	(2.33)	(2.34)
w_{t-1}	.8217	.7896	.1396	.0654	.0672
	(34.71)	(31.97)	(5.95)	(2.73)	(2.83)
Year dummies	Yes	Yes	Yes	Yes	Yes
Personal controls	No	No	Yes	Yes	Yes
Fixed effects	No	No	No	Yes	No
Random effects	No	No	No	No	Yes
$\bar{R}^2$		.9559	.9576	.9905	.9946	.9864
Log likelihood	132.26	140.052	434.18	545.41	n/a
Autocorrelation $e(i,t)$	n/a	n/a	n/a	.3218	.0009
Lagrange multiplier test	n/a	n/a	n/a	n/a	343.85
Hausman test	n/a	n/a	n/a	n/a	2.6916
N	394	394	394	394	394

Source: Current Population Surveys—March tapes.
Note: Personal control variables are averages across industry/year cells and are as follow: (1) experience, (2) years of schooling, (3) four marital status variables, (4) two race variables, (5) private sector variable, (6) part-time status variable, (7) percent female, and (8) a constant. All unemployment rates U and the dependent variable w (annual earnings) are in natural logarithms. Profit-per-employee, π/n, is not logged. These are industry-level variables.
All variables, including the dependent variable, are measured as the mean of the observations in a year/industry cell.
t-statistics are in parentheses.

facturing for the period 1963 to 1985. Average real profits and per-capita real profits for the longer period 1958 to 1985 are available at the four-digit level for each of these years in 1972 dollars (deflator = CPI). The profit data were aggregated up to the two-digit level for each year, and then mapped onto the two-digit CPS data files. The mean levels of total profits and per capita profits, for the longer period 1958 to 1985, are given in Table 5.6 in 1972 dollars. The first column is for π and the second column for π/n.

An application of the rent-sharing bargaining model is estimated in table 5.7. This is a version of a theoretical equation like that of 3.3.7 in chapter 3:

$$w \cong c(w^0, b, U) + \left(\frac{\phi}{1-\phi}\right)\frac{\pi}{n} \qquad (5.2.1)$$

where the estimation on industry cell means, and the absence of industry unemployment benefit data, requires that the outside wage be substituted out leaving a regression of earnings on year and regional dummies, industry unemployment and industry profit-per-employee. Table 5.7 includes a set of individual control variables. These are measured by industry/year cell and as usual include average years of experience (the square was not significant), average number of years of schooling, percentage female, a set of variables distinguishing marital status and racial mix, the proportion of individuals employed in the private sector, the proportion part-time, and a set of year dummies.

Profits are, of course, determined endogenously. In estimating a wage equation such as 5.2.1, therefore, it is necessary to bear in mind the simultaneity between profitability and pay. If a demand shock μ were observable to the econometrician, there would, in principle, be no difficulty. Because μ does not enter the wage equation except through its influence upon the profit measure π/n, it would be a suitable instrument for profit-per-employee in a wage equation.

In reality, there is not information on the exogenous shocks causing the changes in product prices, so this route cannot be exploited. The chapter has to rely instead upon information about timing. If lagged profits can be taken as predetermined, the wage equation may be identified. This amounts to the idea that causality might be captured by demonstrating that, in the test undertaken here, lagged movements in profits feed through into later changes in workers' remuneration.

Table 5.7 takes as its dependent variable the logarithm of workers' income, by calendar year, in each manufacturing industry. The dependent variable is entered in nominal terms; the price level, and other aggregate effects, are subsumed into the year dummies. The first three columns are estimated by ordinary least squares; the fourth is estimated by a one-way fixed effects model; the fifth column is estimated using a one-way random effects panel estimator.[7] The models are of the general form

$$y_{it} = \mu_i + \beta' x_{it} + \varepsilon_{it} \tag{5.2.2}$$

where $E[\varepsilon_{it}] = 0$ and $\mathrm{Var}[\varepsilon_{it}] = \sigma_\varepsilon^2$. In the fixed effects model μ_i is a separate constant term for each unit. This model may be written

$$y_{it} = \alpha_1 d_{1it} + \alpha_2 d_{2it} + \cdots + \beta' x_{it} + \varepsilon_{it} \tag{5.2.3}$$

$$= \alpha_i + \beta' x_{it} + \varepsilon_{it} \tag{5.2.4}$$

---

7. A two-way random effects estimator was rejected against both the fixed effects and one-way random effects models.

where the α_i's are industry-specific constants and the dj's are dummy variables which are 1 only when $j = 1$. In the random effects model (REM) μ_i is an industry specific disturbance. This model is

$$y_{it} = \alpha + \beta' \mathbf{x}_{it} + \varepsilon_{it} + \mu_i \tag{5.2.5}$$

where $E[u_i] = 0$, $\mathrm{Var}[u_i] = \sigma_u^2$, $\mathrm{Cov}[\varepsilon_{it}, u_i] = 0$. All disturbances have variance

$$\mathrm{Var}[\varepsilon_{it} + u_i] = \sigma^2 = \sigma_\varepsilon^2 + \sigma_u^2 \tag{5.2.6}$$

but for a given i, the disturbances are correlated,

$$\mathrm{Corr}[\varepsilon_{it} + u_i, \varepsilon_{is} + u_i] = \rho = \sigma_u^2 / \sigma^2. \tag{5.2.7}$$

The variance components are first estimated with LIMDEP using the residuals from an OLS regression. Then feasible GLS estimates are computed using the estimated variances (Greene, 1990: chapter 16; Hsiao, 1986: chapter 6).

Each of the earnings equations in table 5.7 includes explanatory variables for profits-per-employee, industry unemployment, and lagged earnings. The last of these is a conventional lagged dependent variable. Unemployment is entered at the industry-level and as a logarithm. In column 1 of table 5.7, lagged earnings and current profitability are included in an OLS regression along with a set of twenty-one year dummies. In column 2, the industry unemployment rate is added, followed by a series of worker-characteristics variables in column 3. Column 4 includes the group fixed effects, and column 5 is the random effects model. Both Hausman's Chi-square and the Breusch-Pagan Lagrange multiplier statistics provide tests between the specifications and favor the random effects model. In what follows all estimation uses the random effects model.

The lagged dependent variable, which is also in log form, falls in size from around 0.8 in the first two columns of table 5.7 to only 0.14 in column 3, and then to below 0.07 in columns 4 and 5. Because of the smallness of the estimated coefficient on the lagged dependent variable, the long-run elasticities are only (approximately) one tenth larger than the short-run elasticities. Unemployment in the industry does enter negatively. The long-run unemployment elasticity, however, is no larger than -0.03, which suggests that a ceteris paribus doubling of an industry's unemployment rate would be associated with a three per cent drop in earnings. This is one of the smallest unemployment coefficients estimated in this book. The negativity of the unemployment rate conforms to the prediction of the

rent-sharing bargaining model and appears to be robust across many specifications.[8] If there is any simultaneity bias, it should act to make the coefficient smaller in absolute terms (that is, closer to a positive value).

Profit-per-employee is denoted by the symbol π/n. When entered contemporaneously in the full specifications of columns 4 and 5 of table 5.7,
profit-per-employee has a coefficient of 0.0022 with a t-statistic of approximately 2.3. The variable π/n is not entered as a log (because it takes the
occasional negative value). To convert to an elasticity in this semi-log
equation, therefore, it is necessary to multiply by the mean of the independent variable. The mean of π/n over the period is approximately 10 (the
units are thousands of dollars) so the short-run profit elasticity of earnings
is approximately 0.02, and the long-run elasticity is approximately 0.025.
This estimate almost certainly understates the likely true effect, because of
simultaneity, but illustrates the flavor of the results.

Although later tables discuss variants on these conclusions, table 5.7
conveys the main ideas. Wages are positively correlated with profitability
per employee, and negatively correlated with the unemployment rate in
the relevant industry. Although this result comes through in an OLS specification without any controls, such as column 2 of table 5.7, the parameter
estimates generated in that way appear to be too large. The favored specification, the random effects model of column 5, has a smaller coefficient
on lagged wages, and the coefficients on unemployment and profits-per-
employee are less than half those in the simple OLS specification of column
2.

It is not easy to see how these estimates could be compatible with the
competitive labor market framework. The main possibility appears that
temporary frictions could induce a short-term positive correlation between
profits and pay. Perhaps the only other route would be to argue that the
wage equation is a misspecified inverted labor demand curve. With a Cobb-
Douglas production function, for example, profit maximization can generate a positive association between w and π/n. To investigate these issues it
is useful to examine the autoregressive structure of profits within wage
equations.

Columns 1, 2, and 3 of table 5.8 keep current profit-per-employee as a
regressor, and add respectively profit-per-employee lagged one year, two
years, and three years. These maintain the random effects specification. In
each case the contemporaneous profit variable is statistically weak while

---

8. MacLeod and Malcomson (1993) produce this kind of rent-sharing result in a nonunion
model.

Table 5.8
Earnings equations with lagged profit-per-employee: 1964–1985

	(1)	(2)	(3)	(4)	(5)	(6)	(7)
Log U_t	−.0258	−.0269	−.0336	−.0257	−.0322	−.0289	−.0272
	(2.11)	(3.13)	(2.75)	(3.06)	(2.65)	(3.47)	(3.25)
Log $(\pi/n)_t$	−.0012	.0006	.0010				
	(0.73)	(0.54)	(1.01)				
Log $(\pi/n)_{t-1}$	.0042			.0032			.0032
	(2.61)			(3.44)			(1.97)
Log $(\pi/n)_{t-2}$		.0028			.0035		−.0035
		(2.39)			(3.51)		(1.51)
Log $(\pi/n)_{t-3}$			.0036			.0039	.0049
			(3.62)			(4.21)	(2.97)
Log w_{t-1}	.0624	.0594	.0531	.0627	.0592	.0535	.0541
	(2.64)	(2.50)	(2.25)	(2.66)	(2.49)	(2.26)	(2.29)
$\bar{R}^2$	.9862	.9860	.9854	.9862	.9861	.9858	.9855
Autocorrelation $e(i,t)$	.0009	.0008	.0008	.0009	.0009	.0009	.0009
Lagrange multiplier test	348.34	334.31	339.26	345.18	333.15	337.80	338.88
Hausman test	2.7838	2.9063	3.1050	2.7982	2.8898	2.9887	3.1069
N	394	394	394	394	394	394	394

Source: Current Population Surveys March tapes.

Notes: All equations include full sets of year dummies (21), plus controls for (1) experience and its square, (2) years of schooling, (3) four marital status variables, (4) two race variables, (5) private sector variable, (6) part-time status variable, (7) percent female, and (8) a constant. All unemployment rates U and the dependent variable w (annual earnings) are in natural logarithms. Profit-per-employee, π/n, is not logged. These are industry-level variables within manufacturing.

All variables, including the dependent variable, are measured as the mean of the observations in a year/industry cell.

t-statistics are in parentheses.

the lagged value is fairly precisely estimated. The sum of the profit coefficients is approximately 0.003 in each of the equations 1 and 2 in table 5.8. In column 3 it is 0.0046. Hence a central estimate of the long-run elasticity of pay with respect to profit-per-employee is approximately 0.04.

Columns 4 through 6 of table 5.8 conduct the further experiment of removing the current profit variable. The results are similar to those in columns 1 and 2. The large coefficient on profitability three years ago seems to be noteworthy; it is larger and more exactly estimated than the more recent profit variables. At the mean, the long-run unemployment elasticity of profits-per-employee in column 6 is again approximately 0.04. In column 7 of table 5.8, all three lags are included, with the first and third positive and significant. The long-run coefficient on π/n is now approximately 0.005. The significance of lagged profit levels back to $t - 3$ is difficult to square with the idea that the wage equation might mistakenly be identifying an inverted labor demand relationship.

Are these effects large? Profitability might, in principle, have an effect that is well-defined statistically but that is quantitatively minor. Although this would not wholly eliminate the interest of the finding, it would reduce its practical importance. At first glance the parameter estimates on profitability look small, taking a representative coefficient value to be approximately 0.004. The true size of the effect, however, is not. The reason is that profitability is one of the most volatile series studied by economists. The mean of profit-per-employee, π/n, in this data set is approximately 10.24. Its standard deviation is 6.64. A natural calculation is to examine the consequences of a movement in profit-per-employee from one standard deviation below the mean to one standard deviation above. This is a change in π/n from 3.60 to 16.88, or, in other words, slightly over a four-fold movement in profitability. Using the central parameter estimate of table 5.8, such a two-standard-deviation rise in profit-per-employee is associated with an increase in the level of pay by a little over 8%. Given that the chapter's methods control for fixed effects, it may be appropriate to think of this as the wage difference for identical workers between two sectors with different profitability. For a variable such as pay—one famous for its supposed uniformity and inflexibility—this effect seems to be fairly large. It suggests that, using Richard Lester's (1952) early terminology, the range of wages may be close to 16%.

It might be thought that this aggregate calculation puts too much weight on inherent industry differences. However, a similar picture emerges over time within industries. The minimum single value of π/n, which occurs in the primary metals sector in 1983, is -0.33. Profit-per-employee in that sector was 16.41 in 1980; it fell to 7.15 in 1982; and it rose from its negative 1983 value to reach 4.5 by 1985. The data thus suggest that large movements, such as a quadrupling of profitability, are not uncommon in this sector. At the other end of the spectrum, the maximum value taken by π/n in the data is in the petroleum industry in 1980. It is 44.91. By contrast, the 1985 figure for profit-per-employee in petroleum is 15.07. Three- or four-fold movements of profits are, again, not unusual. These kinds of fluctuations, when combined with an elasticity of 0.04, once more suggest reasonably large effects from profits on to pay. Of course, some industries are more stable. The food sector, for example, sees π/n vary over the years of the data set from 15.29 to 22.33. Nevertheless, an examination of the twenty-two-by-nineteen matrix of data points on industry profits suggests that major fluctuations in profits are commonplace. This is consistent with common observation. Adjusting the data by the CPI makes no difference to this conclusion.

Some experimentation was done to check robustness. Allowing for more complex autoregressive equations, using other lagged profit-per-employee terms, left the conclusions unchanged. The sum of the profit coefficients was reliably close to 0.004, so that the long-run elasticity remained at approximately 0.04.

Total industry profits, π, are used as an independent variable in table 5.9. It can be seen that statistically this is nearly as well-defined as per-capita profit (table 5.7), and that the direction of the effects is the same. The first three columns of the table omit personal control variables, and the final three include them. There is little to choose between the results obtained using the fixed effects or the random effects model (columns 5 and 6 respectively). As found in table 5.7, however, the REM model is preferred statistically on the basis of the Breusch-Pagan and Hausman tests.

Experiments (not reported) showed that even within a sub-sample of industries with low levels of pay, there appears to be evidence of rent-sharing in U.S. wage determination. These results are consistent with those reported recently in Hildreth and Oswald (1993) and Sanfey (1993), and with Holmlund and Zetterberg's (1991) conclusions.

5.3   Instrumenting the Local Unemployment Rate

Unemployment does not merely affect pay, it might be thought, but is itself likely to be a function of pay. To assess this possibility, a variety of instrumented wage equations are described next.

Table 5.9
Earnings equations with total profits as a regressor: 1964--1985 (π = gross profits * 10^4)

	(1)	(2)	(3)	(4)	(5)	(6)
Log U_t			-.0217		-.0215	-.0213
			(1.57)		(2.53)	(2.52)
Log π_t	.5670	.5525	.5025	.4623	.4172	.4202
	(5.16)	(3.12)	(2.80)	(4.26)	(3.82)	(3.93)
Log w_{t-1}	.8401	.2619	.2557	.0683	.0645	.0655
	(35.83)	(7.06)	(6.94)	(2.88)	(2.73)	(2.80)
Personal controls	No	No	No	Yes	Yes	Yes
Fixed effects	No	Yes	Yes	Yes	Yes	No
Random effects	No	No	No	No	No	Yes
$\bar{R}^2$	.9545	.9843	.9844	.9946	.9947	.9886
Autocorrelation $e(i,t)$						.0009
Lagrange multiplier test						349.48
Hausman test						2.3168
N	394	394	394	394	394	394

Source: Current Population Surveys---March tapes.
Notes: All equations include full sets of year dummies (21), plus controls for (1) experience and its square, (2) years of schooling, (3) four marital status variables, (4) two race variables, (5) private sector variable, (6) part-time status variable, (7) percent female, and (8) a constant. All unemployment rates U and the dependent variable w (annual earnings) are in natural logarithms. Profit, π, is not logged. These are industry-level variables within manufacturing. All variables, including the dependent variable, are measured as the mean of the observations in a year/industry cell. t-statistics are in parentheses.

Table 5.10
U.S. regional unemployment equations: 1963–1987

	(1)	(2)	(3)	(4)	(5)
Log U_{t-1}	.6178	.6209	.6150	.5742	.5948
	(15.04)	(15.12)	(12.23)	(11.36)	(11.69)
Log U_{t-2}			.0540	.0496	.0756
			(1.02)	(0.92)	(1.40)
Log w_t	−.5351	−.6767	.1002	−.7173	
	(2.45)	(2.87)	(0.61)	(2.92)	
Log w_{t-1}		.2601			−.1186
		(1.56)			(0.62)
Log w_{t-2}				.4492	.3760
				(2.95)	(2.17)
Constant	2.5655	.9475	−2.3518	.4294	−.30862
	(1.24)	(0.51)	(1.46)	(0.22)	(1.89)
$\bar{R}^2$	.9192	.9194	.9174	.9198	.9181
F	58.184	57.836	54.090	55.735	54.489
DF	403	402	382	381	381

Source: Current Population Surveys—March tapes.
Notes: All equations include full sets of year dummies, region dummies, industry dummies (43), plus controls for (1) experience and its square, (2) years of schooling, (3) four marital status dummies, (4) two race dummies, (5) private sector dummy, and (6) part-time dummy. Lagged unemployment rates and the dependent variable (region unemployment) are in natural logarithms. The wage variable, w, is annual earnings.
All variables, including the dependent variable, are measured as the mean of all observations in a year/region cell.
t-statistics are in parentheses.

To set the scene, and for reference, simple autoregressive unemployment, participation, and employment equations are summarized in tables 5.10, 5.11, and 5.12. Perhaps the most interesting fact to emerge from these is that lagged wage levels—more precisely, annual earnings levels—have some explanatory power in these kinds of U.S. state-level quantity equations. In the unemployment equations of table 5.10, for example, wages lagged sufficiently far back enter positively. This could be interpreted as weak signs of a neoclassical demand curve for labor. The fact that current wages are negative indicates that the wage curve correlation can be seen even in this case in which unemployment is the dependent variable in a highly autoregressive structure.

Consider table 5.13 in which only OLS estimates are reported for U.S. states from 1979 to 1987. Once regional dummies are included, the unemployment elasticity of wages is very slightly below −0.1 in absolute terms. To correct for simultaneity, table 5.14 moves to instrumental vari-

Table 5.11
U.S. participation equations: 1979–1987

	(1)	(2)	(3)	(4)	(5)	(6)
Log P_{t-1}	.1158		.0787	.0690	.0794	
	(1.88)		(1.17)	(1.00)	(1.15)	
Log P_{t-2}		−.1918	−.1945	−.1797	−.1809	−.1866
		(3.01)	(3.07)	(2.79)	(2.80)	(2.91)
Log w_t				.0838		
				(1.69)		
Log w_{t-1}				.0502	.0507	.0386
				(2.52)	(2.53)	(2.39)
Log w_{t-2}				−.0256	−.0263	
				(1.10)	(1.12)	
Constant	3.8633	5.4368	4.0773	4.0893	4.7720	4.9670
	(10.53)	(13.93)	(6.86)	(6.53)	(9.37)	(11.73)
$\bar{R}^2$	.8460	.8601	.8622	.8634	.8623	.8620
F	20.74	20.44	20.44	19.85	19.84	20.35
DF	288	238	236	226	227	233

Source: Current Population Surveys—March tapes.
Notes: All equations include full sets of year dummies, region dummies, industry dummies (43), plus controls for (1) experience and its square, (2) years of schooling, (3) four marital status dummies, (4) two race dummies, (5) private sector dummy, and (6) part-time dummy. Lagged participation rates and the dependent variable (participation) are in natural logarithms. The wage variable, w, is annual earnings.
All variables, including the dependent variable, are measured as the mean of all observations in a year/state cell.
t-statistics are in parentheses.

able estimates (IV columns 1 to 5). The dependent variable in these equations is, as before, the annual earnings of those workers sampled in the CPS measured as the state mean by each year. The control variables— experience, schooling, and the others listed at the foot of table 5.14—are also calculated as state averages. A convincing correction for the endogeneity of the area unemployment rate requires plausible instruments, namely, a set of variables that can be omitted from the wage equation but have a role in the determination of the regional rate of joblessness. There is no well-established literature upon which to draw, though Bartik (1991) and Blanchard and Katz (1992) make original contributions, so this section's approach is to check the influence of a number of different instrumental variables. The instruments used for regional unemployment are in turn: (1) two lags on unemployment, (2) average daily rainfall and hours of sunshine, (3) military spending and a lag on unemployment, (4) an industry-mix (or composition) variable and a lag on unemployment, and (5) the full set of all

Table 5.12
U.S. employment equation: 1979–1987

	(1)	(2)	(3)	(4)	(5)
Log E_{t-1}	.6994	.6641	.7026	.6684	.6646
	(13.69)	(12.64)	(13.71)	(12.63)	(12.46)
Log E_{t-2}	−.1109	−.0915	−.1106	−.0915	−.0830
	(2.42)	(1.99)	(2.41)	(1.98)	(1.77)
Log w_t		.1045		.0984	.0916
		(2.47)		(2.29)	(2.10)
Log w_{t-1}			.0104	.0106	.0195
			(0.76)	(0.78)	(1.15)
Log w_{t-2}					−.0153
					(0.78)
Constant	3.6812	1.3667	2.3093	1.6047	1.2967
	(9.79)	(3.16)	(6.78)	(3.52)	(2.76)
$\bar{R}^2$	.9997	.9997	.9997	.9997	.9997
F	9,945.05	10,065.95	9,788.32	9,877.27	9,637.69
DF	240	239	235	234	229

Source: Current Population Surveys—March tapes.
Notes: All equations include full sets of year dummies, region dummies, industry dummies (43), plus controls for (1) experience and its square, (2) years of schooling, (3) four marital status dummies, (4) two race dummies, (5) private sector dummy, and (6) part-time dummy. Lagged employment levels and the dependent variable (state employment) are in natural logarithms. The wage variable, w, is annual earnings.
All variables, including the dependent variable, are measured as the mean of all observations in a year/state cell.
t-statistics are in parentheses.

of these. Everything here is defined at the state level over eight years so there are approximately 400 observations. The weather variables are taken from U.S. government data. The miltary spending and industry mix variables[9] are adapted from Blanchard and Katz (1992) and Bartik (1991).

It is apparent from table 5.14 that the coefficient on unemployment is affected rather little by the different ways of instrumenting. Moving from left to right, the unemployment coefficients from the five specifications are −0.11, −0.10, −0.11, −0.10, and −0.10. These specifications omit the lagged dependent variable because it had a tiny and statistically insignificant coefficient (this can be guessed, for example, by inspecting table 5.13). As might be expected, if labor demand is depressed by high pay levels, the unemployment coefficients in the instrumented table 5.14 are a little larger in absolute terms than those in the OLS equations. The unemployment

---

9. Larry Katz generously provided his data on these variables.

Table 5.13
Log earnings OLS equations: 1979–1987

	(1) OLS	(2) OLS	(3) OLS	(4) OLS	(5) OLS	(6) OLS
Log U_t	−.0338	−.0036	−.0130	−.0156	−.0953	−.0738
	(1.93)	(0.23)	(0.92)	(0.98)	(7.96)	(7.42)
Log w_{t-1}	.6208	.2900	—	.1443	−.0044	—
	(15.16)	(8.80)		(4.97)	(0.23)	
Personal controls	No	No	Yes	Yes	Yes	Yes
Industry dummies	No	Yes	Yes	Yes	Yes	Yes
Region fixed effects	No	No	No	No	Yes	Yes
$\bar{R}^2$	.6966	.8748	.9331	.9212	.9784	.9818
F	102.53	56.60	102.89	76.06	162.26	219.69
DF	389	348	391	336	286	341

Source: Current Population Surveys—March tapes, 1980–1988.
Notes: All equations include full sets of year dummies (8). Personal controls are the following (1) experience and its square, (2) years of schooling, (3) four marital status dummies, (4) two race dummies, (5) private sector dummy, and (6) part-time dummy and a constant. The unemployment rate U and the wage w_t and w_{t-1} (annual earnings) are in natural logarithms. These are measured at the state level.
All variables, including the dependent variable, are measured as the mean of all observations in a year/state cell.
t-statistics are in parentheses.

elasticity is now estimated at approximately −0.10 to −0.11, rather than the OLS estimates of −0.07 to −0.09.

Further corrections for simultaneity, this time by instrumenting the regional participation rate (P), are in table 5.15. Its coefficient is always positive and sometimes statistically different from zero; it is unstable across specifications. A representative result is that in column 7 of table 5.15 in which participation has a coefficient of approximately 0.56 with a t-statistic of just below 2. The instability of the participation rate P is a worrying feature of the equations. Although it might be unwise, because of the possibility of Type II errors, to conclude that the region's participation rate has no role to play, these results seem to confirm that participation, as a variable in a wage equation, is distinctly weaker statistically than is unemployment. Tables 5.16 and 5.17 are in the same spirit. Each of the seven columns in table 5.16 has the log of state unemployment entering with a well-determined coefficient of between −0.07 and −0.11. The

Table 5.14
Log earnings equations with various ways of instrumenting unemployment: 1979–1987

	(1) IV	(2) IV	(3) IV	(4) IV	(5) IV
Log U_t	−.1135	−.1042	−.1081	−.1037	−.1009
	(7.42)	(6.43)	(7.08)	(7.35)	(6.77)
$\bar{R}^2$	.9810	.9811	.9812	.9814	.9812
F	209.9	205.89	212.25	214.00	207.19
DF	341	324	341	341	341

Source: Current Population Surveys—March tapes, 1980–1988.
Notes: All equations include full sets of year dummies (8), region dummies (50), industry dummies (42), plus controls for (1) experience and its square, (2) years of schooling, (3) four marital status dummies, (4) two race dummies, (5) private sector dummy, and (6) part-time dummy and a constant. The unemployment rate U and the wage variable w are in natural logarithms. These are measured at the state level.
The instruments on unemployment are as follows: column 1—one and two year lags on unemployment; column 2—average state daily rainfall and hours of sunshine and a one year lag on unemployment; column 3—military spending by state and a one year lag on unemployment; column 4—industry mix by state and a one year lag on unemployment; column 5—all of these.
All variables, including the dependent variable, are measured as the mean of all observations in a year/state cell.
t-statistics are in parentheses.

estimate of approximately −0.1 is not sensitive to the inclusion of the terms labeled E/Pop and $(E + U)$/Pop, which are respectively the state employment to population ratio and the state participation rate. None of these terms is significant at the 5% level; this applies whether or not the variables are instrumented. On its own, E/Pop is significant, as table 5.17 shows, but the fact that this variable becomes so weak when unemployment is included (table 5.16) suggests that it is a mismeasured proxy for the unemployment rate rather than the other way around. Again there is extreme variation in the coefficients across different specifications in table 5.17. When coupled with the evidence of table 5.16, where unemployment dominates, it is not obvious that employment-to-population is a convincing regressor. IV estimation does not alter chapter 4's arguments.

Finally, table 5.18 dispenses with instruments and relies instead upon the idea that lagged unemployment may be a predetermined variable. Such an approach can be criticized on the grounds that unemployment is inherently autoregressive, but is worth exploring. Table 5.18 sets out permutations of lags on the state unemployment level (U_{t-1}, U_{t-2}, U_{t-3}), where these are all still measured as logarithms. Columns 1 to 3 reveal that the coefficient on local unemployment is −0.075 regardless of whether the independent

Table 5.15
Log earnings equations with an instrumented participation rate as a regressor: 1979–1987

	(1) OLS	(2) OLS	(3) IV	(4) IV	(5) IV	(6) IV	(7) IV
Log P_t	.1501	.1827	.1850	.7937	.6490	1.0254	.5558
	(2.16)	(2.35)	(0.65)	(1.46)	(1.08)	(2.00)	(1.87)
Log w_{t-1}		−.0134					
		(0.64)					
$\bar{R}^2$	.9790	.9741	.9672	.9688	.9706	.9630	.9670
F	188.11	133.76	80.67	110.93	120.04	96.25	92.80
DF	337	283	187	275	289	289	228

Source: Current Population Surveys March tapes, 1980–1988.
Notes: All equations include full sets of year dummies (8), region dummies (50), industry dummies (42), plus controls for (1) experience and its square, (2) years of schooling, (3) four marital status dummies, (4) two race dummies, (5) private sector dummy, and (6) part-time dummy and a constant. The participation rate P and wage variables w and w_{t-1} are in natural logarithms. These are measured at the state level.
The instruments on unemployment are as follows: column 3 one two year lags on the activity rate; column 4 average daily rainfall and hours of sunshine and a one year lag on the activity rate; column 5 military spending and a one year lag on the activity rate; column 6 industry mix and a one year lag on the activity rate; column 7 all of these.
All variables, including the dependent variable, are measured as the mean of all observations in a year/state cell.
t-statistics are in parentheses.

Table 5.16
Log earnings equations testing a mixture of regressors: 1979–1987

	(1) OLS	(2) OLS	(3) OLS	(4) IV	(5) IV	(6) IV	(7) IV
Log U_t	−.0701	−.0709	−.0802	−.0997	−.1011	−.1003	−.1132
	(6.25)	(6.90)	(6.17)	(6.34)	(6.89)	(6.04)	(6.92)
Log $(E/Pop)_t$	.0330		−.1696	.0272		.0145	
	(0.57)		(1.18)	(0.47)		(0.11)	
$[(E+U)/Pop]_t$		.0751	.2527		.0315	.0164	.3767
		(1.14)	(1.53)		(0.64)	(0.11)	(0.79)
$\bar{R}^2$	.9815	.9816	.9816	.9816	.9816	.9815	.9777
F	212.00	212.62	211.00	212.59	212.59	210.11	157.43
DF	336	336	335	336	336	335	287

Source: Current Population Surveys March tapes, 1980–1988.

Notes: All equations include full sets of year dummies (8), region dummies (50), industry dummies (42), plus controls for (1) experience and its square, (2) years of schooling, (3) four marital status dummies, (4) two race dummies, (5) private sector dummy, and (6) part-time dummy and a constant. The unemployment rate U, employment: population ratio E/POP, and unemployment rate U and the wage variable w are in natural logarithms. These are measured at the state level.

In columns 4–6 the instruments on unemployment are a one year lag on unemployment, military spending and industry mix. In column 7 $(E+U)/P_t$ is also instrumented using a one year lag on the participation rate, military spending and industry mix. The results are the same when E/P_t is instrumented. All variables, including the dependent variable, are measured as the mean of all observations in a year/state cell.

t-statistics are in parentheses.

Table 5.17
Log earnings equations with instrumented employment/population rate as a regressor: 1979–1987

	(1) OLS	(2) OLS	(3) IV	(4) IV	(5) IV	(6) IV	(7) IV
Log $(E/Pop)_t$	.4056	.3690	.6981	3.7653	2.9924	3.4311	.8662
	(4.83)	(5.08)	(2.21)	(13.12)	(13.22)	(12.65)	(4.32)
w_{t-1}		.0537	−.0123	−.0315	−.0112	−.0117	−.0379
		(2.20)	(0.54)	(1.46)	(0.54)	(0.55)	(1.66)
$\bar{R}^2$	.9612	.9719	.9789	.9742	.9738	.9729	.9711
F	77.23	89.64	93.97	94.47	120.04	131.03	101.04
DF	340	285	221	273	289	398	211

Source: Current Population Surveys—March tapes, 1980–1988.
Notes: All equations include full sets of year dummies (8), region dummies (50), industry dummies (42), plus controls for (1) experience and its square, (2) years of schooling, (3) four marital status dummies, (4) two race dummies, (5) private sector dummy, and (6) part-time dummy and a constant. The employment/population rate E/Pop and the wage variable w are in natural logarithms. These are measured at the state level. The instruments are as follows: column 3—one and two year lags on the employment/population rate; column 4—average daily rainfall and hours of sunshine and a one year lag on the employment/population rate; column 5—military spending and a one year lag on the employment/population rate; column 6—industry mix and a one-year lag on the employment/population rate; column 7—all of these.
All variables, including the dependent variable, are measured as the mean of all observations in a year/state cell.
t-statistics are in parentheses.

Table 5.18
Further log earnings equations with lagged unemployment: 1979–1987

	(1)	(2)	(3)	(4)	(5)	(6)	(7)	(8)
Log w_{t-1}	−.0736				−.0189	−.0118	−.0164	−.0225
	(7.16)				(0.98)	(0.59)	(0.82)	(1.18)
Log U_{t-1}				−.0450	−.0849			−.0690
				(3.48)	(7.31)			(4.62)
Log U_{t-2}		−.0765		−.0166		−.0686		.0029
		(7.19)		(1.04)		(5.61)		(0.17)
Log U_{t-3}			−.0741	−.0450			−.0703	−.0426
			(7.17)	(3.41)			(5.80)	(2.90)
Constant	7.8064	7.7808	7.7943	7.8963	8.8041	8.3686	8.6156	8.8711
	(28.45)	(28.42)	(28.43)	(29.62)	(24.40)	(23.44)	(23.34)	(24.89)
$\bar{R}^2$	.9817	.9817	.9817	.9828	.9778	.9763	.9764	.9784
F	217.59	217.81	217.68	227.77	157.51	147.18	148.18	159.47
DF	341	341	341	339	286	286	286	284
N	454	454	454	454	399	399	399	399

Source: Current Population Surveys—March tapes.
Notes: All equations include full sets of year dummies, region dummies, industry dummies (43), plus controls for (1) experience and its square, (2) years of schooling, (3) four marital status dummies, (4) two race dummies, (5) private sector dummy, and (6) part-time dummy. All unemployment rates and the dependent wage variable (annual earnings) are in natural logarithms. These are measured at the state level.
All variables, including the dependent variable, are measured as the mean of all observations in a year/state cell.
t-statistics are in parentheses.

variable is lagged once, twice or three times. A full autoregressive equation is reported in column 8, where the first and third lags on unemployment are negative and significant at the five per cent level, and the lagged level of unemployment two years earlier has a negligible effect. The eight specifications in table 5.18 each generate a long-run unemployment elasticity of pay of approximately -0.1. This robustness is another indication that simultaneity bias, caused by the endogeneity of unemployment in a wage equation, seems not to be a difficulty.

The lagged dependent variable continues to have a coefficient of zero. There is no hint of a Phillips-style relationship between wage inflation and the level of unemployment.

Finally, the wage curve is not an illusion caused by some composition effect. It is not that people's incomes drop when they lose their jobs, nor because in a recession there is downward-bumping to junior posts, nor because hours decline in a recession, nor because low-paid workers are forced to stay in depressed areas because mobility costs are prohibitive. The wage curve finding is robust to the removal from the CPS sample of all people with an unemployment spell in the period (results not reported). It holds, as the next chapter will demonstrate, for a cross-section of plant wage levels and not just for individuals' income levels.

5.4   Conclusions

The checks described in this chapter support the hypothesis that the U.S. labor market is characterized by a negatively sloped relationship between pay and local unemployment. This "wage curve" does not appear to be a labor supply curve; the previous chapter's estimates seem to be unaffected by allowing for simultaneity between wages and joblessness; the introduction of profitability variables into wage equations does not remove the wage curve's pattern from the data.

As its initial step, the chapter examines the idea that the wage curve is just a conventional kind of neoclassical labor supply function. This is done by first calculating, for each area, the participation rate (the proportion of the population who want to work) and the employment to population rate (the proportion of the population who have jobs). These are used as proxy measures of labor supply by region. They are entered as regressors in U.S. earnings equations. If the wage curve is a statistical mirage—an illusion caused by incorrect measurement of the underlying true labor supply variable—the participation rate and the employment to population rate should out-perform the regional unemployment variable. By contrast, if a noncompetitive theory of the wage curve is the true interpretation of the data, these two labor supply measures should be out-performed by the local unemployment rate. This seems a suitable test.

As results like column 4 of table 5.1 reveal, the significance and size of the unemployment variable in a wage equation is almost untouched by the inclusion of the participation rate as a regressor. This is the opposite of what would be predicted by the hypothesis that chapter 4's U.S. wage curve is a mismeasured labor supply curve. The wage curve is apparently not a textbook ghost in disguise. Tables 5.3 and 5.4, which experiment with complex lag structures for the participation rate, fare no better. Participation, P, is consistently weak. The employment to population rate appears to do even worse: table 5.5 shows its insignificance next to a statistically robust unemployment effect.

There is another argument. The wage elasticity of the supply of young people to a region is presumably higher than for older (intrinsically less mobile) individuals. If the wage curve is really a labor supply function, therefore, it should be flatter for young people than for the old. In other words, small wage movements of the young should be associated with big quantity movements in the employment of young workers. This prediction is apparently rejected by the data. It is the young—see back to table 4.17—who have the steepest wage curves. This pattern, moreover, will shortly be seen to hold in other countries.

It is possible, of course, that the tables generated here are either somehow wrong or are forced to use labor supply data that contain so much measurement error that the unemployment rate has more true labor supply information. Although the CPS is possibly the most carefully constructed micro data survey in the world, these kinds of criticisms can always be made, and are probably never wholly false. Nevertheless, if clung to sufficiently tenaciously, such opinions lead the believer inevitably to push aside this, and any other, rejection of the conventional neoclassical theory of the labor market. That position may be the correct one. However, it is then sustained by faith rather than by science, and by predisposition rather than by evidence.

A straightforward objection to the previous chapter is that its equations are estimated by ordinary least squares and the probability is that simultaneity is important in practice. This is an attractive argument theoretically, and probably embodies a useful principle for evaluating empirical work in economics. Yet the experiments of the chapter seem to indicate that simultaneity bias is of minor importance in this particular case. The instrumenting done here—see, for example, table 5.14 in which five different methods are used—reinforces the last chapter's conclusion that in the United States the local unemployment elasticity of pay is approximately -0.1. Why OLS does so well is not entirely clear. A possible explanation is that unemployment within a region in year X is so close to a predetermined variable that instrumenting U_X makes no appreciable difference.

The final major check in this chapter—smaller ones can be found in tables such as 5.2—concerns the role of rent-sharing variables. Consistent with the bargaining approach of chapter 3, a variable for profit-per-employee seems to enter significantly and positively in U.S. earnings equations. In all cases there continues to be a significant and negative unemployment effect. However, estimated on cell means for U.S. manufacturing, as in a table like 5.8, the industry unemployment elasticity of pay is below the level of -0.1 that otherwise dominates the data throughout this monograph. This avenue warrants further analysis with other data. Nevertheless, a well-determined wage curve exists even in the chapter's least favorable case.

6   Britain's Wage Curve

Good empirical evidence tells its story regardless of the precise way in which it is analyzed. In large part, it is its simplicity that is persuasive.

Lawrence Summers (1991)

It has been traditional in empirical economic research for investigators to concentrate in depth upon a single country. Although such an approach has advantages—for example, it may make it easier for the economist to be knowledgeable about the institutional background to a problem—its weaknesses are apparent. Patterns found in one nation may be special to that setting. Estimated coefficients may not be deep ones about economic structures, as an analyst would be prone to hope. They may instead reflect mundane problems in measurement that are in turn the product of some peculiarity of data collection, or of data definition, or of national idiosyncrasy. They may be chance results, generated unconsciously by data-mining, that would not stand up to experimentation. They may be, worse, the outcome of one's own or a research assistant's errors. The prevalence of one-country studies is something that the current generation of economists has grown up with, and so has come to view as natural. This style of research, however, is probably not the calculated product of researchers' long experience with real numbers or of leisurely unconstrained choice. It seems more likely that its parochialism is an inheritance from a time when data were so difficult to obtain about one's own country that there was little time or energy left to hunt through mysterious dusty library volumes in which the language itself might be different and the source-books' footnotes and subheadings impossible to comprehend in a way that would convincingly dispel the fear of seminar disgrace.

Despite tradition, the ability to establish an empirical finding across many nations has intuitive and scientific appeal. The commonsense checks

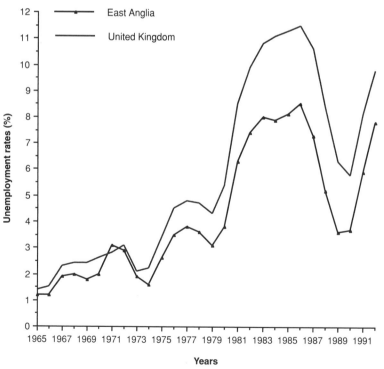

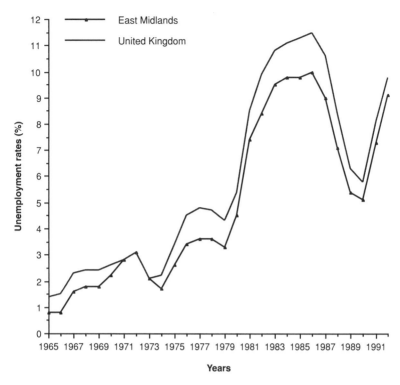

Figure 6.1 (top left)
U.K. and U.S. unemployment rates: 1965–1992

Figure 6.2 (bottom left)
Unemployment in East Anglia: 1965–1992

Figure 6.3 (above)
Unemployment in the East Midlands: 1965–1992

that it offers are obvious. The availability of consistent kinds of international data is starting to make multi-country analysis an attainable target rather than an ideal.

This chapter estimates British wage curves. Using four micro data series, it includes unemployment rates by geographical area—at the level of the travel-to-work area (TTWA), the county, and the standard region—in a series of wage and earnings equations. For Britain it is not possible, with recent data, to include industry unemployment rates because they are no longer published by the British government.[1]

---

1. Lee and Pesaran (1993), however, find evidence for a kind of wage curve, with an elasticity close to -0.2, using constructed industry data.

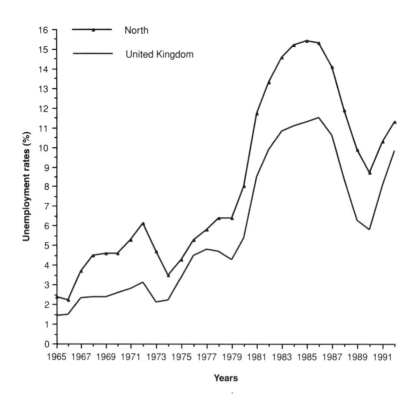

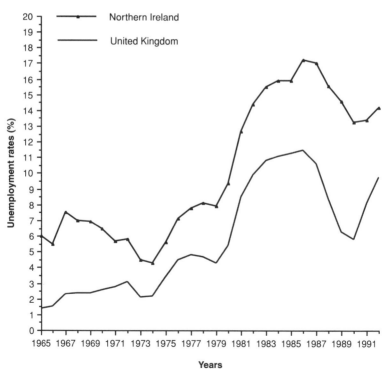

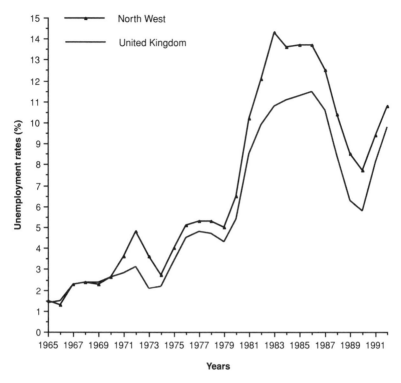

Figure 6.4 (top left)
Unemployment in the North: 1965–1992

Figure 6.5 (bottom left)
Unemployment in Northern Ireland: 1965–1992

Figure 6.6 (above)
Unemployment in the North West: 1965–1992

Between 1965 and 1990, unemployment in the United Kingdom rose from 1.4% to 5.8%. It reached a high of 11.5% in 1986. By contrast, the U.S. unemployment rate over the same period rose from 4.4% to 5.5%, peaking at 9.5% in 1982 and 1983 (see figure 6.1). The most dramatic increase in unemployment in the United Kingdom occurred between 1979 and 1981 when unemployment virtually doubled. In 1979 there were 1.3 million registered unemployed compared with approximately 2.5 million in 1981. For the years up to 1982, the U.K. unemployment rate was consistently below that of the United States. Subsequently, the U.K. rate has been the higher of the two, although the rates began converging at the end of the 1980s.

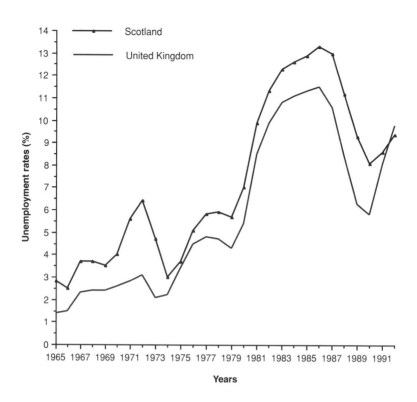

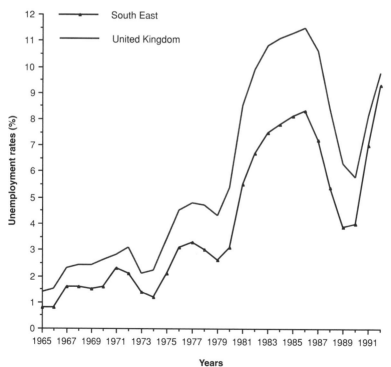

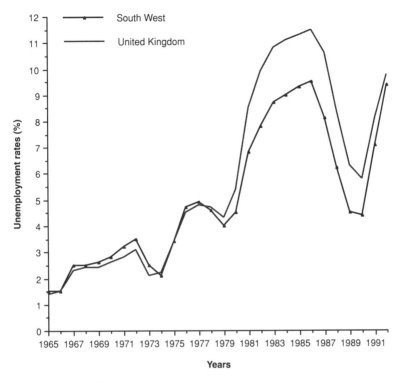

Figure 6.7 (top left)
Unemployment in Scotland: 1965–1992

Figure 6.8 (bottom left)
Unemployment in the South East: 1965–1992

Figure 6.9 (above)
Unemployment in the South West: 1965–1992

Figures 6.2 to 6.12 trace the path of regional unemployment rates over the period 1965 to 1987 for each of the eleven standard regions. There are large differences in the average levels of unemployment across regions. Unemployment rates in the prosperous South East average 3.7% over the period of interest. This compares with 9.9% for Northern Ireland, 7% for Wales and 7.1% for Scotland. In all of these years, unemployment in the South East was below the national average while unemployment in Northern Ireland, Wales, and Scotland was above the average. The areas with concentrations of heavy manufacturing industry, such as the West Midlands and the North and North West of England, were hit especially hard by the oil-shock recession of 1979 to 1981. Somewhat in contrast to the state unemployment rates reported in chapter 4 for the United States, it is

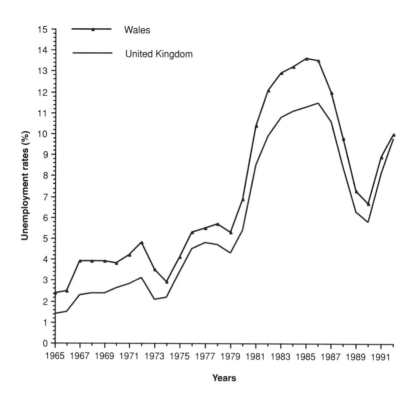

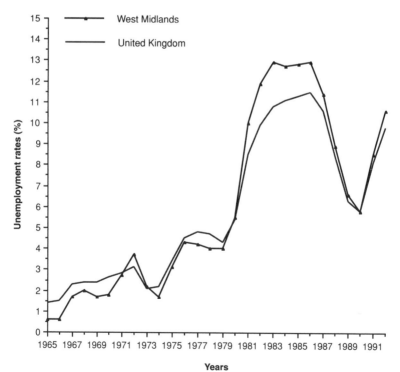

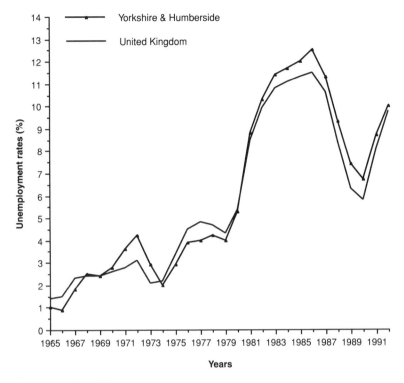

Yorkshire & Humberside

United Kingdom

Figure 6.10 (top left)
Unemployment in Wales: 1965–1992

Figure 6.11 (bottom left)
Unemployment in the West Midlands: 1965–1992

Figure 6.12 (above)
Unemployment in Yorkshire and Humberside: 1965–1992

striking how closely all the U.K. regions track the path of the national unemployment series. Individual regional cycles seem less important than in the United States.

The empirical work uses the following microeconomic data sets.

1. The *Workplace Industrial Relations Surveys of 1980, 1984, and 1990* (WIRS1, WIRS2, and WIRS3), which provide information on approximately 1,500 British establishments in each of the three years. These are different cross-sections in different years.

2. The *National Child Development Study of 1981* (NCDS), which provides information on approximately 6,000 twenty-three-year-old employees from a single birth cohort.

3. The *British Social Attitude Surveys* of 1983 to 1989 (BSA) which, after pooling the separate cross-sections, give information on approximately 7,000 employees.

4. The *General Household Surveys* (GHS) of 1973 to 1990, which when pooled offer a representative sample of approximately 175,000 employees.

5. The *Family Expenditure Surveys* (FES) of 1980 to 1986, which when pooled provide information on nearly 26,000 male workers. The econometric work using the FES is due to Blackaby et al. (1991).

For WIRS1, WIRS2, and NCDS, county unemployment rates across sixty-five counties were mapped onto the data sets. For the BSA and GHS data series, regional unemployment rates across eleven regions in each year were used. For WIRS3, unemployment rates were allocated at the more disaggregated level of the local labor market area (LLMA) and the travel-to-work area (TTWA). There are 322 TTWAs and 280 LLMAs. They are derived by government statisticians from a study of commuting flows data in the Census of Population. There tend to be more TTWAs than LLMAs in rural areas and vice versa in metropolitan areas (see Champion et al. 1987; Green et. al. 1991). The unemployment variables used are total unemployment rates.

These data sets are considered in turn. The final section of the chapter undertakes experiments using different measures of the degree of slack in the outside labor market.

6.1   The Workplace Industrial Relations Surveys of 1980, 1984, and 1990

Table 6.1 reports wage equations using a collection of approximately 1,700 randomly sampled establishments. These data are from WIRS1.[2] The dependent variable in each case is the gross weekly pay of the "typical" employee. It is defined for skill categories. The wage data are grouped and open-ended. When there was no single typical worker, managers gave multiple answers. The analysis allocates mid-points to the wage bands. Stewart's (1987) alternative method gave similar results to Blanchflower (1984), as reported in Blanchflower (1986). The open ends were closed off in an inevitably ad hoc way. Sensitivity tests suggested that the results described here are stable to changes in the values allotted to the end categories. This is to be expected given the small numbers of observations

---

2. The background specification follows Blanchflower (1984) and Blanchflower et al. (1990).

Table 6.1
The British wage curve using WIRS: 1980

a) Manual workers	(1) Semi-skilled	(2)	(3) Skilled	(4)
Log U_r	−.0827	−.1091	−.0531	−.0342
	(4.35)	(3.14)	(3.26)	(1.14)
Regional dummies	No	Yes	No	Yes
Constant	4.1432	4.1693	4.4883	4.4472
	(90.96)	(65.64)	(106.25)	(77.98)
$\bar{R}^2$	.4929	.4965	.3966	.4018
F	26.68	23.17	16.41	14.39
DF	1,449	1,439	1,269	1,269

b) Nonmanuals	(1) Clericals	(2)	(3) Middle managers	(4)
Log U_r	−.0403	.0198	−.0578	−.0612
	(2.59)	(0.69)	(2.86)	(1.65)
Regional dummies	No	Yes	No	Yes
Constant	4.3663	4.2257	4.9766	4.9422
	(106.25)	(82.20)	(105.98)	(73.72)
$\bar{R}^2$	.2394	.2599	.2733	.2848
F	10.61	10.09	12.04	10.91
DF	1,653	1,643	1,588	1,578

Source: Workplace Industrial Relations Survey, 1980.
Notes: All equations include the following controls: (1) 37 industry dummies, (2) total employment and its square, (3) percent part-time in the workforce, (4) percent blue-collar, (5) percent skilled, (6) foreign-owned dummy, (7) shiftworking dummy, (8) percent female blue collar workers in total workforce, (9) three workplace performance dummies, (10) four age of plant dummies, (11) private sector dummy, (12) union recognition dummy, (13) pre-entry closed shop dummy, and (14) post-entry closed shop dummy. The dependent variable (gross weekly pay of a typical worker) and unemployment rates are in natural logarithms. t-statistics are in parentheses.

in the end groupings. Other features of the survey design are explained in the appendix.

The equations in table 6.1 include a vector of control variables identifying workplace, workforce, and industry characteristics. A workplace has to employ one or more of the particular category of workers to be included in the sample and to have no missing values for the control variables. Survey responses come from the manager in charge of personnel and industrial relations matters. The specifications are based on those first reported in Blanchflower (1984), which used some of the same data. In that paper, significant union relative wage effects for British semi-skilled manual workers, of approximately 10%, were reported. There were no significant union effects on the pay of skilled manual employees. In a subsequent paper Stewart (1987) showed that semi-skilled and skilled workers in pre-entry closed shops enjoyed an extra wage premium of around 8%. It is only recently that data on the location of WIRS plant has become available. This information remained confidential for a number of years, to ensure that individual workplaces could not be identified. The estimated union effects reported in the earlier papers are unaffected by the inclusion of the new locational variables—the local unemployment rate and regional dummies.

Column 1 of table 6.1, for semi-skilled workers' wages, includes a set of industry, workforce, and workplace control variables, and also the natural logarithm of the relevant county unemployment rate. There are sixty-five counties, so sixty-five unemployment observations. Column 3 duplicates this specification for skilled manual workers. For both skill groups the coefficient on the unemployment variable is significantly negative. In the case of semi-skilled manuals, the unemployment elasticity of pay is esti-mated at −0.08, compared with −0.05 for those who are skilled. The first cut at British data suggests, therefore, that the spatial correlation between remuneration and joblessness is not positive, as some Harris-Todaro inter-pretations might predict, but negative. The unemployment elasticity looks reminiscent of that found in chapters 4 and 5 for the United States.

One possible concern here, as usual, is that the significance of the unem-ployment variable may be driven by area-specific fixed effects. Perhaps Wales has many low-paid agricultural workers who, by the nature of the countryside and their seasonal, agricultural occupation, are unemployed a lot, and somehow this is not being controlled for adequately. Or it could be that the omission of regional price deflators is at fault. As there is only one year of observations, it is not possible to include a full set of county dummies at the same time as county unemployment is a regressor. There is, however, a potentially useful half-way step that can be taken.

The specifications on the right-hand side of table 6.1 include ten regional dummy variables. These are at a higher level of aggregation, necessarily, than the county observations on unemployment. The inclusion of the re-gional dummies actually increases the absolute size of the coefficient on the log unemployment term, very slightly, from −0.08 to −0.10 in the case of the semi-skilled group. For the other groups of workers, the inclusion of the dummies drives the unemployment term to insignificance.

Table 6.2 reports broadly comparable earnings equations using data from the second Workplace Industrial Relations Survey, which took place in 1984. The unit of observation is again the establishment. The respondent

Table 6.2
Wage curves using WIRS: 1984

a) Manuals	(1) Unskilled	(2)	(3) Semi-skilled	(4)	(5) Skilled	(6)
Log U_t	−.1354	−.0914	−.0652	−.0030	−.1190	.0080
	(3.58)	(1.53)	(2.14)	(0.06)	(4.55)	(0.20)
Reg. dummies	No	Yes	No	Yes	No	Yes
Constant	4.3852	4.2267	4.6053	4.4205	4.9938	4.6474
	(49.07)	(35.13)	(37.52)	(27.35)	(59.28)	(43.03)
$\overline{R}^2$	.5366	.5509	.5011	.5136	.4966	.5244
F	19.00	17.87	13.76	12.87	14.94	14.79
DF	1,120	1,110	901	891	1,011	1,001

b) Nonmanuals	(1) Clericals	(2)	(3) Foremen/supervisors	(4)
Log U_t	−.0537	.0086	−.0738	.0293
	(3.22)	(0.33)	(2.53)	(0.63)
Reg. dummies	No	Yes	No	Yes
Constant	4.5766	4.4102	5.2774	4.9931
	(94.12)	(66.94)	(94.12)	(42.75)
$\overline{R}^2$	.3081	.3357	.3425	.3692
F	9.63	9.60	10.43	10.30
DF	1,323	1,313	1,231	1,221

Source: Workplace Industrial Relations Survey, 1984.
Notes: All equations include the following controls: (1) 50 industry dummies, (2) total employment and its square, (3) percent part-time, (4) percent blue-collar, (5) one-year employment change at plant, (6) foreign-owned dummy, (7) shiftworking dummy, (8) majority male dummy, (9) five workplace performance dummies, (10) four age of plant dummies, (11) private sector dummy, (12) nationalised industry dummy, (13) profit sharing dummy, (14) single plant firm dummy, (15) union recognition dummy, (16) pre-entry closed shop dummy, and (17) post-entry closed shop dummy. The dependent variable (gross weekly pay of a worker) and unemployment rates are in natural logarithms.
t-statistics are in parentheses.

is defined in the same way, namely, as the manager in charge of personnel and industrial relations. Other statistical procedures are as in table 6.1. Unemployment is at the level of the county. There are notable differences between the first two WIRS surveys. First, in 1984 a question on the earnings of foremen and supervisors replaced one about middle managers, and a new category—unskilled manuals—was added. Second, the precise wording of the earnings question changed between 1980 and 1984. In 1980 the manager was asked for the gross weekly pay of a typical worker in a particular category. In 1984 the manager was asked to identify whether the majority of workers in five skill groups (unskilled, semi-skilled, and skilled manual workers, clerical/secretarial/administrative, and supervisors/ foremen/forewomen) were men or women. This is the "majority male" variable in the regressions. Respondents were requested to report the gross earnings, inclusive of any bonus or overtime, of a typical man (woman) depending upon whichever sex was in the majority. With a couple of minor differences, the control variables used in table 6.2 are the same as those employed in Blanchflower et al. (1990). Definitions of the variables and their means, the distribution of county unemployment rates, and the results of the full equation estimated in column 2 of table 6.2 are reported in the appendix.

There is some evidence in table 6.2 of a negative effect from the county unemployment rate upon the pay levels earned by individuals in the county. The magnitude of the effect ranges from −0.14 in the case of unskilled manuals to −0.05 for clerical workers, administrative staff, and secretaries. However, the inclusion of the set of ten aggregated regional dummies drives the coefficient on county unemployment close to zero and to statistical insignificance. Table 6.2 offers a little British evidence for a wage curve, but it is not compelling.

Table 6.3 sets out a number of log annual earnings equations using establishment data from the third Workplace Industrial Relations Survey of 1990. The earnings questions in this survey differ from those in the earlier surveys as they were only asked where there were at least five workers of the particular type at the workplace. In part A of table 6.3 the log of the Travel to Work Area unemployment rate is included; in part B the log of the Local Labor Market Area rate is used. The results in the two sections are similar. Significant negative unemployment effects are observed for unskilled and skilled manuals, and for clericals. The effect is greatest for unskilled manuals. Due to confidentiality requirements imposed by the sponsors of the data, it is not possible in this case to identify regions.[3] Hence the equations have no controls for (even highly-aggregated) region-specific fixed effects.

These surveys of establishments reveal signs in support of the hypothesis that there is a downward-sloping wage curve in the United Kingdom. Nevertheless, in every case except one, the inclusion of a set of regional dummies drives down the unemployment rate, usually to insignificance.

---

3. This is because the data set comes with an attached unemployment rate but no separate code for the area's identity. Although detective work might manage to identify some of the regions, it would be impossible to do so fully, because there are so many areas with similar rates. It would also violate the sponsors' intentions.

Table 6.3
The British wage curve with WIRS: 1990

	(1) Unskilled manual	(2) Semi-skilled manual	(3) Skilled manual	(4) Clerical	(5) Foremen/ supervisors
Part A—Travel to work area					
Log U_t	−.0916	−.0230	−.0325	−.0434	−.0048
	(3.93)	(1.22)	(2.13)	(3.49)	(0.30)
Constant	8.7031	9.1996	9.4951	9.3715	9.6989
	(92.36)	(151.55)	(198.5)	(182.46)	(153.49)
$\bar{R}^2$	.5466	.5090	.4411	.3154	.4433
F	20.92	14.68	12.50	10.42	12.58
DF	1,040	829	923	1,342	921
N	1,108	898	992	1,412	990
Part B—Local labor market area					
Log U_t	−.0981	−.0249	−.0327	−.0295	−.0048
	(4.00)	(1.23)	(2.04)	(2.23)	(0.30)
Constant	8.7329	9.2057	9.5000	9.3571	9.6841
	(90.40)	(146.73)	(192.35)	(177.97)	(150.29)
$\bar{R}^2$	.5469	.5090	.4408	.3117	.4425
F	20.94	14.68	12.49	10.26	12.55
DF	1,040	829	923	1,342	921
N	1,108	898	992	1,412	990

Source: Workplace Industrial Relations Survey, 1990.
Notes: all equations include the following controls: (1) fifty industry dummies, (2) two union dummies, (3) nine status of organization dummies, (4) percent manual, (5) percent female, (6) percent part-time, (7) establishment size and its square, and (8) majority male dummy. The dependent variable is the log of weekly pay. The unemployment rate is in natural logarithms. t-statistics are in parentheses.

6.2   The National Child Development Study, 1981

This section studies the wages of young people. Table 6.4 lists earnings equations that draw upon data from one of the world's few randomly selected birth cohorts. The National Child Development Study (NCDS) is a longitudinal survey of all individuals born in the UK between the 3rd and the 9th March 1958. This is some 18,500 births. In total the respondents have been sampled five times—at birth, and at ages seven, eleven, sixteen, and twenty-three.[4] There were also medical check-ups and a series of IQ, maths and reading tests, and interviews with parents and teachers.

---

4. At the time of writing, a new sweep, NCDS 5, is about to become available.

Table 6.4
The U.K. wage curve for NCDS twenty-three year olds in 1981

	(1)	(2)
Log U_r	−.1671	−.0644
	(11.75)	(2.66)
Regional dummies	No	Yes
Constant	4.5876	4.5047
	(82.92)	(67.76)
$\bar{R}^2$	.5223	.5337
F	66.72	63.85
DF	6,265	6,255

Source: National Child Development Study, 1958–1981.
Notes: All equations include the following controls: (1) 63 industry dummies, (2) three marital status dummies, (3) promotion prospects dummy, (4) two security of employment dummies, (5) expect to be with same employer in one year dummy, (6) shiftworking dummy, (7) gender dummy, (8) part-time dummy, (9) union membership dummy, (10) disabled dummy, (11) migration dummy, (12) four size of workplace dummies, (13) limited company dummy, (14) single independent plant dummy, (15) fifteen highest qualifications dummies, (16) tenure in current job, (17) children dummy, (18) number of jobs since leaving school, (19) ever been out of the labor force dummy, (20) ever been unemployed dummy, (21) maths and reading scores taken when respondent was 7, 11, and 16, (22) problems with literacy dummy, and (23) problems with numeracy dummy.
The dependent variable (gross weekly pay) and unemployment rate are in natural logarithms. U is measured at the county level.
t-statistics are in parentheses.

The equations estimated here use earnings data when the respondents were age twenty-three in 1981. By that time the vast majority of respondents (98%) had left full-time schooling and had entered the labor force. (see Elias and Blanchflower, 1987, 1989; Blanchflower and Oswald, 1990b). The survey design is described in the appendix. The data have also been used for the study of labor market behavior by Robertson and Symons (1990), Micklewright (1989), and Connolly et al. (1992).

This section's equations are comparable to those in Blanchflower and Oswald (1990b: table 3, p. 226), with the exception that two additional controls derived from earlier sweeps of the survey are now included. These are composite ability scores obtained from a series of maths and reading tests taken by the respondents at ages seven, eleven, and sixteen. In addition, the (insignificant) long-term unemployment terms that were included in the earlier paper are omitted. In the NCDS survey the respondent reported to the nearest £ their own gross weekly pay before deductions for tax and National Insurance including any overtime, bonus, commission and

Table 6.5
U.K. wage curve on BSA data: 1983–1987 and 1989

	(1)	(2)
Log U$_r$	−.1519	−.1232
	(8.71)	(5.33)
Year dummies	5	5
Industry dummies	Yes	Yes
Regional dummies	No	Yes
Constant	7.2058	7.1966
	(86.57)	(81.04)
$\overline{R}^2$	.6568	.6607
F	181.77	164.25

Source: British Social Attitudes Survey Series.
Notes: In all cases there are 7,462 observations. Unless stated otherwise the following control variables were included: (1) 60 industry dummies, (2) eleven regional dummies, (3) three marital status dummies, (4) nonmanual dummy, (5) supervisor dummy, (6) two union dummies, (7) gender dummy, (8) experience and its square, (9) years of schooling, (10) whether-employment-is-expected-to-rise-at-the-workplace dummy, and (11) unemployed-in-previous-five-years dummy.
The dependent variable is the log of gross annual earnings.
t-statistics are in parentheses.

tips on the last occasion they were paid. Unlike the WIRS establishment-level surveys, where the earnings variable is grouped, this variable is continuous. Equation 1 of table 6.4 is a now-standard specification and has the county unemployment rate in logs. Moving from column 1 to column 2, the inclusion of a set of 10 regional dummies reduces the unemployment coefficient from −0.17 to −0.06. It remains significant (t-statistic = 2.7). In contrast to the earlier equations reported in this chapter, a cubic unemployment term is significant, but that term is omitted for simplicity.

6.3 The British Social Attitudes Surveys, 1983 to 1989

None of the data sets used so far in this chapter have been pooled cross-sections of adult workers, so they are not easy to compare to the U.S. chapter. Tables 6.5 and 6.6 begin to remedy this. They estimate wage curves using individual data from the British Social Attitudes Survey series of 1983–87 and 1989 (there was no survey in 1988). The dependent variable is gross annual earnings before deductions of income tax and national insurance. Once again the wage data are grouped and open-ended, in this case into thirteen categories. The method described previously in

Table 6.6
5% disaggregations: 1983–1987 and 1989

(%)	
4.1–4.8	−.0263
	(0.44)
4.8–6.8	−.0297
	(0.62)
7.5	−.1219
	(2.69)
7.6–8.4	−.1727
	(4.14)
8.5	−.1123
	(2.54)
8.6	−.1517
	(2.76)
8.7	−.1128
	(2.40)
8.8–9.1	−.1965
	(3.89)
9.4–9.5	−.1187
	(1.83)
9.6–10.1	−.1211
	(1.83)
10.2–11.7	−.1434
	(2.77)
11.9–12.7	−.1433
	(2.77)
13.0–13.1	−.1999
	(3.10)
13.4	−.1300
	(2.40)
13.7–13.8	−.2087
	(4.26)
14.0–14.2	−.1722
	(5.46)
14.3–14.6	−.1710
	(3.11)
14.7–14.8	−.2294
	(3.33)
14.9+	−.1637
	(2.39)
Constant	7.0925
	(88.83)
$\bar{R}^2$	.6611
DF	7,354
F	137.01

Table 6.6 (cont.)

Source: British Social Attitudes Survey Series.

Notes: In all cases there are 7,462 observations. The following control variables were included: (1) sixty industry dummies, (2) eleven regional dummies, (3) three marital status dummies, (4) nonmanual dummy, (5) supervisor dummy, (6) two union dummies, (7) gender dummy, (8) experience and its square, (9) years of schooling, (10) whether employment is expected to rise at the workplace dummy, and (11) unemployed in previous five years dummy.

The dependent variable is the log of gross annual earnings.

t-statistics are in parentheses.

the case of WIRS1, WIRS2, and WIRS3 was again used to create wage data. The unemployment rate is mapped in at the level of the region, of which there are eleven here, including Greater London, for the years up to 1987. In 1989 an additional survey was undertaken in Northern Ireland and so in that year there is an additional regional observation. All equations include a set of workplace and personal controls as well as a set of two-digit industry and year dummies.[5] This BSA data file has the advantage that it is possible, for the first time in this chapter, to include a full set of controls for area-specific fixed effects, namely, to have regional dummies at the same level of aggregation as the unemployment variable. Interestingly enough, this has relatively little effect on the size and the statistical significance of the estimate of the regional unemployment elasticity of pay. In column 1 of table 6.5, for example, the log of unemployment has a coefficient of -0.15 and a t-statistic of nearly 9. The inclusion of 11 regional dummies reduces the coefficient, but only slightly. It falls to -0.12 with a t-statistic over 5.

To explore the shape of these wage curves, unrestricted specifications, as for the United States, are estimated. In order to ensure that each data point carries approximately the same weight, the unemployment distribution is divided into 5% sections. Then 19 dummy variables—one for each part of the unemployment axis—are entered into an earnings equation that has the same vector of independent variables as in table 6.5. This also includes one dummy for each region. The results are in table 6.6. In each case the unemployment coefficient is negative, and in fifteen cases out of nineteen it is significantly different from zero. In another two cases the t-statistics are over 1.8. The antilogs of these coefficients are plotted against the unemployment rate in figure 6.13. The two (insignificant) data points at relatively low levels of unemployment are outliers and for clarity are omitted in figure 6.14.

---

5. The specifications used here are similar to those reported in Blanchflower (1991).

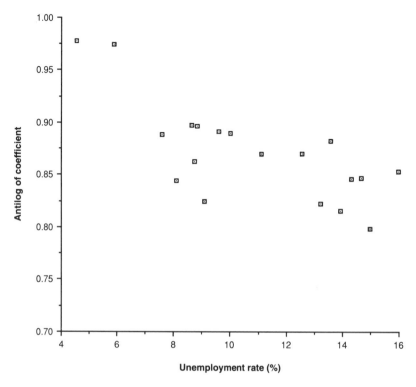

Figure 6.13
Unrestricted U.K. wage curve: 1983–1989 (5% sample)

There seems to be evidence, from these BSA data, for a downward-sloping wage curve. A further step was to fit a second-order polynomial to the data points, of the form

$$w = 1.0826 - .0347U + .00108U^2.$$

This equation fits the data points reasonably well ($R^2 = 0.71$). Over the range of unemployment rates available here (3.3% to 16.6%), it appears that the wage curve flattens out at fairly high levels of unemployment (i.e. $\geq 13\%$).

It is natural to try to compare the unemployment elasticities of pay of different workers' groups with those estimated for the United States. Table 6.7 reports unemployment elasticities for disaggregated wage curves. Once again the dependent variable is the log of annual earnings. The table gives the coefficient on the log of the unemployment rate obtained when estimating separate pay equations for each relevant subgroup. Manual work-

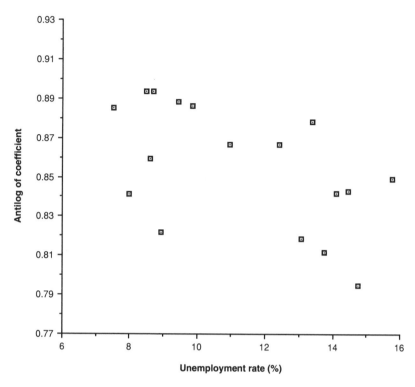

Figure 6.14
Unrestricted U.K. wage curve: 1983–1989 (5% sample), two outliers omitted

ers, nonunion workers, those working in small plants, the youngest, least schooled, and least experienced individuals—all these people have a relatively high unemployment elasticity of pay in absolute terms. The coefficient on the log unemployment term in these cases has a coefficient around −0.2, which implies that a doubling of the unemployment rate reduces the pay of these workers by around 20%. Yet the pay of union workers and those with at least thirteen years of schooling is not sensitive to the local unemployment rate. In contrast to the evidence presented in chapter 4 in this book, for the United States, the estimated unemployment elasticities of pay are apparently not significantly different from each other, at least in these data, in the public or private sectors. There are no significant differences between the estimates for manufacturing and services.

Differences in the unemployment elasticities across groups reported in table 6.7 might be an illusion. They could arise because of differences in the number of hours worked per week across the cycle rather than because of

Table 6.7
Unemployment elasticities from disaggregated weekly wage curves: United Kingdom, 1983–1989

	Coefficient	t-statistic	N
All workers	−.1232	5.33	7,462
Union member	−.0140	0.40	4,260
Nonmember	−.1881	5.91	3,202
Union recognition	.1017	0.77	3,899
Non-union plant	−1677	5.70	3,563
Male	−.2161	7.82	4,220
Female	−.0404	0.87	3,242
< 10 employees	−.1533	2.72	1,622*
10–25 employees	−.1762	3.47	1,520*
25–99 employees	−.0820	1.81	1,474*
100–499 employees	−.1291	2.11	1,037*
≥ 500 employees	−.1533	2.72	1,622*
Private sector	−.1562	5.20	4,595*
Public sector	−.1378	2.90	2,076*
Manufacturing	−.0851	1.77	1,875
Services	−1344	4.98	5,586
Age < 25 yrs.	−.2125	4.17	1,171
Age ≥ 25 but < 50 yrs.	−.1227	4.23	4,593
Age ≥ 50 yrs.	−.0979	1.86	1,698
Experience < 10 yrs.	−.2122	4.69	1,497
Experience 10–29 years	−.1138	3.50	3,593
Experience ≥ 30 yrs.	−.1061	2.37	2,372
≤ 10 years schooling	−.1668	4.09	3,040
11 or 12 years schooling	−.1533	4.29	2,296
≥ 13 years schooling	−.0080	0.16	1,331
Degree or higher degree	.0072	0.15	1,546
Nonmanual	−.0778	2.17	4,090
Professionals & managers	−.0821	1.51	1,433
Intermediate non-manual	.0114	0.18	1,135
Junior non-manual	−.0890	1.39	1,522
Manual	−.2238	5.85	3,296
Skilled manual	−.2454	5.32	1,730
Semi- and unskilled manual	−.1627	2.61	1,566

Source: British Social Attitudes Survey Series, 1983–1989.
Notes: * Estimates are for the years 1984–1987 and 1989—size of workplace and sector were not reported in 1983.
The dependent variable is the log of annual earnings. The (regional) unemployment variable is measured as a natural logarithm. Controls, including a full set of region dummies, are as in table 6.6.
t-statistics are in parentheses.

hourly wage movements. For example, in manufacturing, average hours per week in the sample are 41.1 compared with 36.3 in services. In order to allow for differences in the numbers of hours worked, the equations are re-estimated for most of the disaggregations reported in table 6.7. The dependent variable is the log of hourly earnings—calculated as annual earnings/(normal hours worked per week * 50). Hours of work are unavailable in the 1983 and 1984 surveys, so this time the sample for estimation is restricted to the years 1985 to 1987 and 1989. The outcome is contained in table 6.8. A few of the finer disaggregations reported in table 6.7 are omitted because of small sample sizes.

In the first row of table 6.8 the unemployment elasticity of pay is calculated using the same dependent variable (the log of weekly earnings) as in table 6.7, but for the restricted number of years. Reassuringly, the estimate here (− 0.1279) is insignificantly different from that in the first row of table 6.7 (− 0.1232). Thus little of substance is lost when the earlier two years of data are left out. When the dependent variable is altered to the log of hourly earnings, the estimated unemployment elasticity does change somewhat. It falls from − 0.12 to − 0.07, and remains significantly different from zero (t-statistic = 3.05). There does appear, therefore, to be some flexibility in hours worked as unemployment changes, but the adjustment is insufficiently large to remove the unemployment effect on pay. The elasticity continues to be approximately − 0.1. Adjusting for hours-worked changes very few of the substantive conclusions. As in table 6.7 the earnings of nonunion workers, the young and the least experienced are especially flexible. However, no significant difference in the estimated elasticities between manuals and nonmanuals, or by years of schooling, emerges from this data set.

Rødseth (1990), having listened to early British evidence, rightly questioned whether Britain's wage curve was really likely to be the same as across the regions of the United States. The general findings and disaggregated unemployment elasticities are interesting, indeed surprising, because they mirror so closely what was generated for the United States. Later chapters find similar patterns.

6.4   The General Household Surveys, 1973 to 1990

This section considers a more comprehensive data set. It is probably the closest that it is possible to come, for an analysis of Britain's labor market, to an equivalent of the pooled CPS data that are employed in the U.S. chapters.

Table 6.8
Unemployment elasticities from disaggregated hourly wage curves: United Kingdom, 1985–1989

	Coefficient	t-statistic	N
All workers—weekly pay	−.1279	4.68	5,892
All workers—hourly pay	−.0725	3.05	5,161
Union member	.0114	0.29	2,383
Nonmember	−.1242	3.74	2,779
Union recognition	.0782	0.55	2,909
Non-union plant	−.1335	4.42	2,253
Male	−.1461	4.81	2,778
Female	.0105	0.29	2,384
< 10 employees	−.0573	0.79	875
10–25 employees	−.0440	0.76	826
25–99 employees	−.1096	5.94	1,297
100–499 employees	−.0487	1.04	1,264
≥ 500 employees	−.0686	1.12	900
Private sector	−.1174	3.74	3,383
Public sector	−.1098	2.76	1,779
Manufacturing	−.0697	1.53	1,342
Services	−.0778	2.78	3,820
Age < 25 yrs.	−.1481	2.86	859
Age ≥ 25 but < 50 yrs.	−.0676	2.26	3,178
Age ≥ 50 yrs.	−.0586	1.01	1,029
Experience < 10 yrs.	−.1429	3.04	1,102
Experience 10–29 years	−.0485	1.42	2,357
Experience ≥ 30 yrs.	−.0685	1.39	1,469
≤ 10 years schooling	−.0482	1.13	1,979
11 or 12 years schooling	−.0873	2.48	2,033
≥ 13 years schooling	−.0535	1.06	1,149
Nonmanual	−.0854	2.70	2,910
Manual	−.0561	1.55	2,183

Source: British Social Attitudes Survey Series, 1985–1989.
Notes: *Estimates are for the years 1985–1987 and 1989—numbers of hours worked per week were not reported in 1983 or 1984.
The dependent variable is the log of hourly earnings.
The (regional) unemployment variable is measured as a natural logarithm. Controls, including a full set of region dummies, are as in table 6.6.
t-statistics are in parentheses.

Up to this point all of the estimated wage curves for the United Kingdom reported in the chapter have been for the 1980s. The availability of the General Household Survey series means that it is feasible to derive a broadly consistent series of estimates for the United Kingdom through both the 1970s and 1980s. There were changes in the design of the survey over time. These included alterations in the wording and coding of many of the questions, and in both the occupational and industry classifications.[6] Unfortunately it is not possible to obtain a consistent series on hours of work for the full period. Consequently the results are set out in two parts. Part A reports estimates of wage curves for the years 1973 to 1977, which are the years in which hourly earnings are available. These equations use information both on weekly earnings and hourly earnings, and so allow a comparison of the two different ways of defining the dependent variable. Part B provide estimates for the whole period, 1973 to 1990, with weekly earnings data. Part C has a description of some results from other authors who have used these same data to estimate wage equations.

Part A: The Subsample, 1973 to 1977

This analysis is limited to a data file of slightly over 60,000 individuals who were employees at the date of interview and who reported their gross weekly earnings, including wages, salary, tips, bonus, and commission for the preceding twelve months. Interviews were spread roughly evenly across the twelve months of the year. Therefore the regression equations include eleven month-dummies and four year-dummies, plus industry, occupation, region, and qualification dummies, and a set of personal controls. As in the case of the British Social Attitudes Survey, unemployment rates were mapped in at the level of the standard region for the year of the interview.

Table 6.9 lists four equations. The first two columns provide the results of estimating a weekly earnings equation for the five years between 1973 and 1977. In column 1 the log of the unemployment rate has a coefficient of -0.07 with a t-statistic of over 10. The addition of a set of regional dummies in column 2 raises the size of the coefficient by approximately 2 percentage points to -0.09. The coefficient remains significant with a t-statistic of just under 5. In both columns, therefore, the unemployment elasticity of pay is slightly below -0.1 in absolute value. The data do not support the inclusion of higher order unemployment terms, such as the

---

6. For further details, see Schmitt (1994) and the appendix.

Table 6.9
Alternative dependent variables using a GHS subsample: Great Britain, 1973–1977

	(1)	(2)	(3)	(4)
	Weekly earnings		Hourly earnings	
Log U_t	−.0704	−.0895	−.0796	−.0876
	(10.47)	(4.83)	(12.72)	(5.08)
Regional dummies	No	Yes	No	Yes
Constant	2.8902	2.9221	−.7634	−.7430
	(74.01)	(63.04)	(20.79)	(17.10)
$\bar{R}^2$	.5984	.6011	.4345	.4382
DF	60,486	60,476	60,186	60,176
F	1,158.21	1,038.12	594.73	535.12

Source: General Household Survey Series.
Notes: In all cases there are 60,565 observations. Unless stated otherwise the following control variables were included: (1) twenty-four industry dummies, (2) ten regional dummies, (3) five marital status dummies, (4) seventeen qualification dummies, (5) eighteen occupation dummies, (6) four year dummies, (7) gender dummy, (8) experience and its square, (9) part-time dummy, and (10) eleven month dummies. U is the regional unemployment rate.
t-statistics are in parentheses.

cube of the logarithm, so these are omitted. There is little to choose statistically between a specification with the log of unemployment and one with the level of unemployment. For ease of exposition the table reports only results with the log of the unemployment rate.

In columns 3 and 4 of table 6.9, the dependent variable is redefined as hourly earnings, that is, as total earnings in the previous year divided by (usual weeks * usual weekly hours). It is encouraging to find that the estimated unemployment elasticities of pay are virtually identical in the two halves of the tables. For example, in each of columns 2 and 4 of table 6.9 the estimated unemployment elasticity of pay is −0.09.

Disaggregated estimates of the unemployment elasticity of pay, even for this limited span of years, are also of interest. These are derived in the usual way, by estimating separate equations for each subgroup. Only the coefficient on the log of the unemployment rate, its t-statistic, and the number of observations are recorded in table 6.10. Perhaps the most notable thing about this table is the similarity of the different groups' estimates of the unemployment elasticity of pay. This differs somewhat from the BSA results (though the later full GHS sample rectifies the discrepancy). This result is replicated in table 6.11, using a dependent variable of log hourly earnings.

Table 6.10
Unemployment elasticities for different groups: GHS subsample, 1973–1977

	Coefficient	t-statistic	N
All workers	−.0895	4.83	60,565
Male	−.0763	3.26	35,210
Female	−.1213	4.19	25,355
Manual	−.0899	3.67	28,907
skilled manual	−.0794	2.31	13,653
Semi-skilled manual	−.0536	1.24	9,065
Unskilled manual	−.0938	1.28	4,050
Foreman—manual	−.1333	1.62	2,228
Nonmanual	−.0971	3.44	30,404
Managers	−.0089	0.11	4,877
Professionals & artists	−.0643	1.13	6,824
Junior/foremen nonmanual	−.0899	2.44	14,965
Personal service	−.1917	2.22	3,739
Manufacturing	−.1203	4.02	20,574
Services	−.0810	3.10	33,642
Agriculture and mining	−.0731	0.68	1,967
Construction	−.1126	1.80	4,108
Age <25 yrs.	−.1275	3.25	11,234
Age ≥25 but <50 yrs.	−.0630	2.52	32,460
Age ≥50 yrs.	−.1005	2.81	16,871
Experience <10 yrs.	−.1371	3.64	12,392
Experience 10–29 years	−.0500	1.70	24,341
Experience ≥30 yrs.	−.0971	3.32	23,832
No qualifications	−.0959	4.54	32,683
Left school <15	−.0729	2.51	20,971
Left school at 15	−.1375	4.65	20,362
Left school at 16	−.0009	0.02	11,015
Left school ≥17	−.0930	1.55	8,217
Attended college	−.0538	0.98	8,224

Source: General Household Survey Series, 1973–1977.
Note: The dependent variable is the log of weekly earnings.

Table 6.11
Unemployment elasticities of hourly pay for different groups: GHS Subsample, 1973–1977

	Coefficient	t-statistic	N
All workers	−.0876	55.08	60,265
Male	−.0906	3.86	35,029
Female	−.0955	3.94	25,236
Manual	−.0721	3.09	28,903
Skilled manual	−.0801	2.33	13,612
Semi-skilled manual	−.0257	0.62	9,031
Unskilled manual	−.0844	1.43	4,039
Foreman—manual	−.1166	1.38	2,221
Nonmanual	−.1068	4.16	30,226
Managers	−.0497	0.61	4,835
Professionals & artists	−.0631	1.23	6,770
Junior/foremen nonmanual	−.1073	3.15	14,913
Personal service	−.1820	2.71	3,708
Manufacturing	−.1282	4.39	20,515
Services	−.0797	3.41	33,435
Agriculture and mining	−.0543	0.52	1,967
Construction	−.0694	1.09	4,094
Age <25 yrs.	−.1113	2.91	11,192
Age ≥25 but <50 yrs.	−.0578	2.50	32,294
Age ≥50 yrs.	−.1174	3.59	16,779
Experience <10 yrs.	−.1187	3.26	12,345
Experience 10–29 years	−.0533	1.97	24,209
Experience ≥30 yrs.	−.1003	3.73	23,711
No qualifications	−.0906	4.88	32,557
Left school <15	−.0933	3.53	20,888
Left school at 15	−.1285	4.63	20,284
Left school at 16	−.0003	0.01	10,949
Left school ≥17	−.1005	1.82	8,144

Source: General Household Survey Series, 1973–1977.
Note: The dependent variable is the log of hourly earnings.

Table 6.12
5% disaggregations, 1973–1977

(%)	
1.4–1.7	−.0144
	(1.10)
1.8–1.9	−.0470
	(2.41)
2.0	−.0225
	(2.69)
2.1–2.2	−.0333
	(1.86)
2.5–2.8	−.0467
	(3.17)
2.9	−.0850
	(3.37)
3.0	−.0703
	(3.92)
3.3	−.0429
	(3.32)
3.4	−.0932
	(3.71)
3.5	−.0696
	(4.52)
3.6–3.7	−.0722
	(4.96)
3.9–4.0	−.0449
	(2.89)
4.1–4.3	−.0623
	(3.45)
4.4–4.5	−.0494
	(3.04)
4.7–5.1	−.0854
	(6.12)
5.6	−.0624
	(2.70)
5.7	−.0803
	(4.21)
Constant	2.8609
	(73.59)
$\overline{R}^2$	.6049
DF	63,860
F	942.44

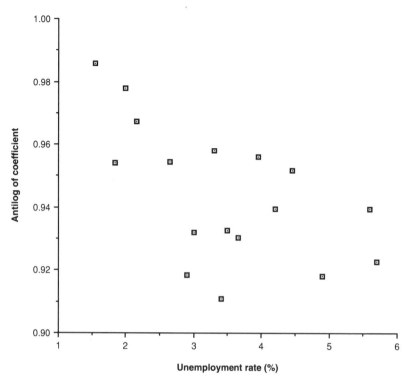

Figure 6.15
Unrestricted British wage curve: 1973–1977 (5% sample)

The final step is to check the effects of allowing an unrestricted specification. Table 6.12 adopts the practice outlined before, that of splitting the sample into approximately 5% portions, or as close to that as the unemployment distribution will allow. Dummy variables are allocated to each of the portions. Each dummy variable then has approximately the same weight.

In all but two cases the coefficients on these unemployment dummies are significantly negative. Figure 6.15 plots the points against the antilog of the coefficients (the dependent variable is in natural logs). Once again it seems that there is evidence of a downward-sloping wage curve. Figure 6.16 fits a second-order polynomial to the data points. It takes the form

$$w = 1.035 - .045U + .0048U^2 \qquad (R^2 = 0.47).$$

There is some flattening of the wage curve, according to figure 6.16, at unemployment levels above 4.5% during the mid-1970s.

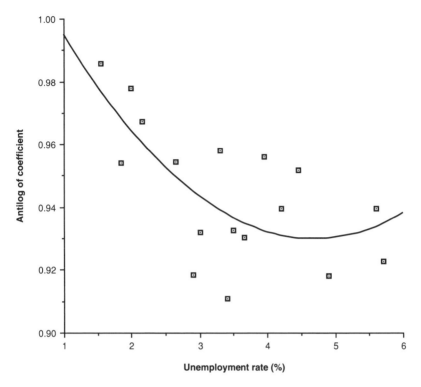

Figure 6.16
Fitted British wage curve: 1973–1977 (5% sample)

Part B: The Full GHS Sample, 1973 to 1990

Weekly wage curves can be estimated over the entire period from 1973 to 1990. The dependent variable is the log of weekly earnings. As outlined above, for the years 1973 to 1977 respondents were asked to report their earnings over the preceding twelve months and the number of weeks worked. In each survey after 1977 the following questions were asked of employees: (1) On what date were you last paid a wage or a salary?; (2) How long a period did your last wage/salary cover?; and (3) What was your gross pay last time before any deductions were made? These questions are used to construct the dependent variable, which is log weekly earnings. To control for the change in the nature of the earnings question in 1978 and onwards, the regressions include a series of eleven interaction terms. These are the interaction of the regional dummy variables with a dummy variable set to one if the data were taken from a survey prior to 1978 (to zero otherwise).

Table 6.13
Sample size of GHS, 1973–1990

Year	Sample size	Employees with wage data
1973	21,516	12,255
1974	19,884	11,434
1975	21,887	12,644
1976	21,653	12,061
1977	21,319	12,023
1978	21,165	11,802
1979	20,417	11,451
1980	21,087	11,597
1981	21,641	11,145
1982	18,339	9,137
1983	17,760	8,451
1984	16,947	7,966
1985	17,386	8,449
1986	17,704	8,763
1987	18,087	9,085
1988	13,058	6,524
1989	17,195	8,946
1990	4,356	2,213
Total	331,401	175,946

For the years 1973 to 1986 the GHS was held in every month of the calendar year. Since 1987 the survey has been conducted during the financial year April to March; hence the 1987 and subsequent surveys contain nine monthly interviews in 1987 and three in 1988. Consequently, the regressions include both month and year-of-interview dummies, as well as controls for gender, race, years of schooling, experience and its square, marital status, part-time, highest qualifications and industry.[7] The total sample size is just over a third of a million, of which there are 175,946 employees with wage data. This means that on average there are approximately 10,000 observations per year (each observation being an employee). However, as can be in table 6.13, sample sizes were reduced from 1982 onwards. This was apparently part of a series of cost-cutting measures in statistical collection by the U.K. government. The small sample size in 1990 is due to the fact that information is only available from January to March.

---

7. For other work using these wage data, and their implications for earnings inequality, see Katz et al. (1994).

Table 6.14
British wage curves from the GHS: 1973–1990

	(1) 1973–80	(2) 1973–80	(3) 1981–90	(4) 1981–90	(5) 1973–90	(6) 1973–90
Log U_t	−.0896	−.0697	−.1619	−.0927	−.1283	−.0822
	(18.05)	(4.41)	(22.91)	(2.79)	(24.64)	(6.23)
Reg. dummies	No	Yes	No	Yes	No	Yes
Constant	1.9049	2.8946	3.4217	3.3408	2.7832	2.7543
	(84.72)	(90.46)	(104.70)	(51.19)	(141.24)	(91.86)
$\bar{R}^2$	.7029	.7076	.6654	.6720	.7633	.7665
DF	96,352	96,332	79,108	79,098	175,495	175,485
F	4,387.04	3,240.78	2,916.73	2,534.60	7,862.87	7,028.98
N	96,405	96,405	79,163	79,163	175,568	175,568

Source: General Household Survey Series.
Notes: Unless stated otherwise the following control variables were included: (1) ten industry dummies, (2) four marital status dummies, (3) fifteen highest qualification dummies, (4) seventeen dummies, (5) gender dummy, (6) experience and its square, (7) part-time dummy, (8) eleven month of interview dummies, (9) race dummy, and (10) eleven region dummies interacted with dummy for years up to 1977.
The dependent variable is the natural log of gross weekly earnings. U_t is the regional unemployment rate.
t-statistics are in parentheses.

Is this U.K. wage curve stable across subperiods? Table 6.14 suggests that it is. The table contains results from estimating a log earnings equation for the periods 1973 to 1980, 1981 to 1990, and for the entire period 1973 to 1990. In each case, results are given with and without controls for regional fixed effects. The addition of the region dummies reduces slightly the size of the coefficient on the log of the unemployment rate. The unemployment elasticity of pay estimated using these micro-data is a little larger in the later of the two periods (-0.09 and -0.07 respectively) and is approximately -0.08 overall. The robustness across two such different periods of time seems remarkable.

Disaggregated wage curve estimates are described in table 6.15. These control for region-specific fixed effects. The pay of blacks, construction workers, the young, and the least experienced all seem to be unusually flexible in the face of changes in the unemployment rate. The unemployment elasticity of pay of black workers, for example, is -0.23, which is more than twice the figure for the full sample. Coefficients are not reported for the other control variables in this table. As these kinds of pooled GHS regression results are not available elsewhere, however, table 6.16 reports a limited selection of coefficients. In table 6.16 there are estimates for males, females, and blacks. Being married raises male earnings but reduces female earnings, confirming earlier GHS work by Greenhalgh (1980). The rate of return to an additional year of schooling is higher for men than it is for women, whereas the return to a college qualification (e.g., degree, HND, or a teaching diploma) is higher for women. Black men appear to earn nearly 15% less, ceteris paribus, than white men; black females do not appear to earn less than white females, ceteris paribus. Men's experience earnings profiles are steeper than females. Both male and female earnings maximize after approximately thirty years of experience. Apprenticeships appear to convey substantial benefits to men but none for women (corroborating findings from Blanchflower and Lynch, 1994, using National Child Development Survey data).

Table 6.17 reports on the now-familiar kind of unrestricted specification. The distribution of unemployment rates is split into 5% segments of approximately equal size to create nineteen separate dummy variables. Once again all the standard control variables discussed above are included, as well as a full set of region dummies. Eighteen of the nineteen dummies are significant and all are negative. As the unemployment rate rises, the size of the coefficient tends to fall. In figure 6.17 the antilogs of the coefficients are plotted against the mid-point of the range of unemployment rates reported

Table 6.15
Unemployment elasticities of pay from disaggregated British wage curves: 1973–1990

	Coefficient	t-statistic	N
All workers	−.0822	6.23	175,568
Male	−.0935	6.41	96,260
Female	−.0742	3.28	79,308
Black	−.2291	3.09	5,304
White	−.0809	6.00	170,265
Part-time	−.0462	1.06	34,945
Full-time	−.0888	7.17	140,623
Agriculture	−.0713	0.63	3,106
Energy and water	−.0097	0.14	4,220
Extraction	−.0709	1.45	7,899
Metal goods, engineering etc.	−.0554	2.10	24,489
Other manufacturing	−.1073	3.21	21,494
Construction	−.1497	3.59	10,696
Distribution	−.0206	0.55	26,295
Transport & communication	.0000	0.00	11,399
Banking, finance, insurance	−.1277	2.27	11,899
Other services	−.0918	3.32	54,074
Manufacturing	−.0863	4.51	53,881
Services	−.0728	3.82	103,665
Age <25 yrs.	−.1329	5.09	34,115
Age ≥25 but <50 yrs.	−.0677	3.78	97,629
Age ≥50 yrs.	−.0698	2.68	43,815
Experience <10 yrs.	−.1164	4.86	42,927
Experience 10–29 years	−.0564	2.66	73,557
Experience ≥30 yrs.	−.0764	3.51	59,084
No qualifications	−.0651	3.53	79,070
O-Levels etc.	−.1155	4.93	57,902
A-Levels	−.0003	0.01	12,998
College	−.0531	1.33	25,598

Source: General Household Survey Series, 1973–1989.
Notes: The dependent variable is the log of weekly earnings. The same controls were used as reported in table 6.14 plus ten region dummies.
t-statistics are in parentheses.

Table 6.16
Some coefficients from Log earnings equations: full GHS sample, 1973–1990

	Males	Females	Blacks
Log regional unemployment	−.0935 (6.4)	−.0742 (3.3)	−.2290 (3.1)
Higher degree	.6396 (50.7)	.8940 (25.5)	.5806 (10.1)
1st degree, university diploma	.5380 (86.9)	.7943 (61.7)	.6227 (19.9)
Teaching qualification	.5510 (42.0)	.9305 (71.8)	.8771 (11.3)
HNC, HND, technical certificate	.3353 (61.5)	.5142 (28.8)	.3032 (8.9)
Nursing qualification	.2068 (9.0)	.5246 (45.8)	.4115 (13.2)
GCE "A" level, ONC, OND.	.2284 (45.6)	.3116 (28.3)	.2547 (9.9)
GCE "O" level-5 or more	.1804 (38.1)	.2104 (25.1)	.1753 (7.0)
GCE "O" 1–4, with clerical qualifications	.1739 (5.9)	.1945 (18.4)	.3273 (6.7)
GCE "O" 1–4, no clerical qualifications	.1053 (18.0)	.1259 (13.9)	.1021 (3.5)
Clerical & commerical qualifications	.1178 (6.3)	.1291 (16.6)	.1327 (3.6)
CSE	.0326 (4.1)	.0764 (6.0)	.0940 (3.0)
Apprenticeship	.0695 (14.5)	.0023 (0.1)	.1237 (2.2)
Any foreign qualifications	.1757 (13.7)	.1760 (8.3)	.1298 (6.4)
Other qualifications	.1127 (13.6)	.0967 (6.6)	.1358 (2.8)
Years of schooling	.0396 (29.1)	.0292 (12.1)	.0067 (2.3)
Black	−.1452 (19.5)	−.0186 (1.5)	
Married	.1959 (49.1)	−.0687 (10.7)	.1186 (6.7)
Separated	.1181 (10.1)	−.0815 (5.8)	.1173 (2.8)
Divorced	.0949 (8.8)	−.0793 (6.4)	.0333 (0.8)
Widowed	−.0213 (3.2)	−.0561 (6.3)	−.0245 (0.9)
Part-time	−.8322 (103.8)	−.9358 (209.0)	−.8580 (40.8)
Male			.3407 (24.7)
Experience	.0489 (122.0)	.0336 (54.5)	.0324 (17.3)
Experience^2* 10^3	.8507 (115.3)	.5825 (48.8)	.5862 (15.0)
$\bar{R}^2$	.7589	.6953	.7435
N	96,260	79,308	5,304

Notes: All equations also include eleven month dummies, ten region dummies, seventeen year dummies, nine industry dummies, eleven pre-1978* region interactions and a constant. *t*-statistics are in parentheses.
The dependent variable is the log of weekly earnings.

Table 6.17
5% disaggregations: 1973–1990

(%)	
1.9–2.5	−.0120
	(1.38)
2.7–3.0	−.0469
	(4.08)
3.3–3.4	−.0511
	(3.99)
3.5–3.8	−.0598
	(4.50)
3.9–4.1	−.0547
	(3.66)
4.2–4.4	−.0664
	(4.16)
4.5–4.7	−.0816
	(5.08)
4.9–5.4	−.0575
	(3.21)
5.6–5.8	−.0977
	(4.90)
5.9–6.6	−.0965
	(4.61)
6.8–7.4	−.1224
	(5.73)
7.5–7.9	−.1344
	(5.90)
8.0–8.5	−.1336
	(5.40)
8.6–9.2	−.1428
	(5.69)
9.3–10.2	−.1585
	(5.95)
10.3–11.7	−.1744
	(6.10)
11.8–12.8	−.1877
	(6.14)
13.0–13.5	−.2015
	(6.24)
≥ 13.6	−.2185
	(6.33)
$\bar{R}^2$	.7665
DF	175,467
F	5,765.26
N	175,568

Source: General Household Survey Series, 1973–1989.
Notes: Dependent variable is the log of weekly earnings.
t-statistics are in parentheses.

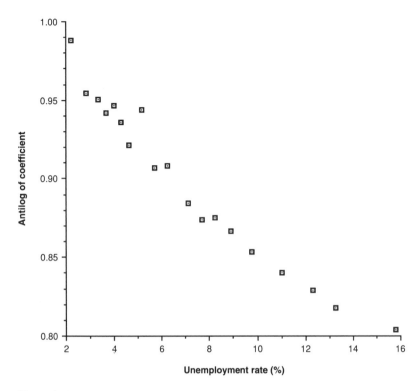

Figure 6.17
Unrestricted British wage curve: 1973–1990 (5% sample)

in table 6.17. In figure 6.18 a second-order polynomial of the following form seems to fit the data ($R^2 = 0.979$):

$$w = 1.0263 - .02344U + .00059U^2.$$

Part C: Other Work

As explained in chapter 2, Blackaby and Manning (1990c) use data from the 1975 and 1982 General Household Surveys to study wage determination. Blackaby and Manning conclude that they produce findings contrary to a result reported in Blanchflower and Oswald (1990b). Their arguments are developed further in Blackaby and Hunt (1992). Both the earlier paper and the analysis mentioned here fail to find compelling evidence for the interesting Layard and Nickell (1986) claim that the long term unemployed exert little or no downward pressure on the wage rate. Blackaby and

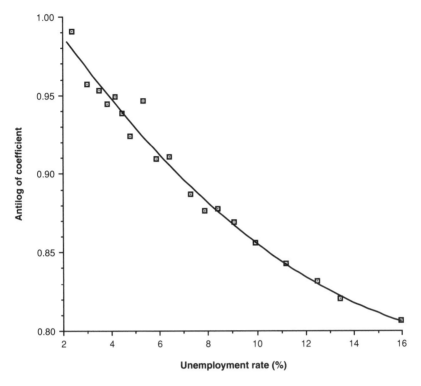

Figure 6.18
Fitted British wage curve: 1973–1990 (5% sample)

Manning suggest that their 1982 GHS regression results support an analog of Layard and Nickell's argument "that the existence of long-term unemployment reduces the overall negative impact of unemployment on (regional) earnings" (Layard and Nickell, 1986:524).

A shortage of degrees of freedom makes the Blackaby and Manning conclusion open to some question. The authors' critique of the earlier Blanchflower and Oswald finding rests upon a regression with ten data points on unemployment and four independent variables (plus a constant). The authors have unemployment observations only at the level of the ten standard regions but enter, as regressors in an earnings equation, two regional unemployment variables, a regional long-term unemployment variable, and a regional price variable. They conclude that the long-term unemployment variable enters statistically significantly. Although the authors may turn out to be correct when better data become available, a regression with what are effectively ten observations and four independent variables does not allow confident conclusions about a causal chain. Blackaby and Manning do, however, report evidence consistent with wage curves for 1975 and 1982. Using the 1975 GHS they estimate the following equation, which also includes a full set of standard controls, for male workers:

$$\ln w = \text{constant} - 0.068 \ln U + 0.615 \ln P: \text{Adjusted } R^2 = .6674$$
$$\quad\quad\quad\quad\quad\quad (3.79) \quad\quad\quad (7.57)$$

where U is the regional unemployment rate and P is a regional price index, w is annual earnings and t-statistics are in parentheses. Similarly, for 1982 the equivalent results are

$$\ln w = \text{constant} - 0.055 \ln U + .791 \ln P: \text{Adjusted } R^2 = .4624.$$
$$\quad\quad\quad\quad\quad\quad (1.93) \quad\quad\quad (7.25)$$

The finding that high unemployment significantly reduces pay using the 1982 sample is further confirmed in Blackaby and Murphy (1991). The paper attempts to identify the factors that influence the industry-regional wage structure. The authors first estimate an individual-level hourly earnings equation on a sample of 6,805 individuals. They then use this equation to construct industry and regional earnings free from the human capital characteristics of the sample. This generates a data file of 100 observations (ten regions by ten industries). The second stage of the exercise consists of regressing the newly constructed earnings measure on a vector of controls including the regional unemployment rate. The log of regional unemployment enters this equation (where wages are purged of their industry and region-specific fixed effects) with a coefficient of -0.13 and a t-statistic of over 2.5. Once these fixed effects are controlled for, Blackaby and Murphy produce the result that the long-term unemployment variable is insignificant.

A paper by Jackman and Savouri (1991) also studies the forces acting upon regions' wage levels. It uses aggregated data from the British New Earnings Survey for the period 1974 to 1989. This provides the authors with 150 observations—ten regions by fifteen years. Equations are first estimated on the whole sample. The dependent variable is the average level of earnings in a region measured relative to the national average, and the key independent variable is in most equations the rate of unemployment relative to the national average. The full sample appears to lead to a lagged dependent variable with a coefficient of 0.9, and an implied long-run unemployment elasticity of pay of -0.22 (Jackman and Savouri, 1991:48, table

2). These numbers are much higher than in this monograph. It might be argued that they are biased by the study's use of aggregates across heterogeneous people and the lack of controls for individual characteristics. Results that are consistent with such a view emerge when separate equations are estimated in the paper for groups of more homogeneous types of people, such as men and women, manual workers and nonmanual workers, and employees in the manufacturing sector and the non-manufacturing sector. The value on the lagged dependent variable is halved. The authors conclude that only the pay of manual workers is affected by the prevailing level of unemployment in the region. This chapter's results differ (as in tables such as 6.10), although, as shown in Blanchflower and Oswald (1990a), there is some evidence, especially from the British Social Attitude Survey, that manual workers' pay is more responsive than that of nonmanuals. Like Blanchflower et al. (1990), Jackman and Savouri find that a double-logarithmic form, namely, a specification in which both pay and regional unemployment are entered as logs, works well. Much of this book is in agreement with that, and it may be that the authors are right implicitly to criticize Blanchflower and Oswald (1990b) for using more highly non-linear terms (although their table 16 test appears to use as a regressor the level of unemployment rather than its value relative to the national mean). Moreover, the Jackman and Savouri study concludes that in the full equation for manual male employees "the implied long-run unemployment elasticity of wages is ... about -0.13" (p. 11), which is certainly similar to numbers discussed in this book.

Because it uses regional aggregates rather than microeconomic data, the Jackman and Savouri study cannot control properly for the characteristics of workers. This is a weakness and may be why the study finds a large coefficient, of around 0.5, on the lagged dependent wage variable. The paper does, however, allow for regional fixed effects with dummies, and for year effects by estimating the equations on regional variables expressed relative to national figures. Moreover, the authors experiment with the inclusion of regional variables for the proportion of long-term unemployment, cost-of-living, house prices, house prices multiplied by the proportion of owner-occupation, and the proportion of houses state-owned and rented from the local authority. These do not affect the key findings about unemployment, and generate the interesting fact that house prices are an important determinant of pay. The impact of long-term unemployment in Jackman and Savouri's (1991) equations is almost always positive but usually has a t-statistic of unity or a little over.

Table 6.18
U.K. wage curve (FES), males: 1980–1986

	(1)	(2)	(3)	(4)	(5)
U	−.0122	−.0380	−.0040	−.0047	−.0038
	(19.06)	(9.23)	(4.80)	(1.74)	(4.29)
U^2		.0009			
		(6.33)			
Price index			0.5947	.4295	0.3979
			(14.95)	(3.24)	(9.15)
Region dummies	No	No	No	10	3
Constant	0.193	0.3323	−2.6013	−1.8158	−1.7234
	(6.52)	(9.02)	(13.74)	(3.00)	(8.41)
$\bar{R}^2$	.4382	.4391	.4431	.4460	.4461
SEE	.3460	.3457	.3445	.3436	.3435
SSR	3,056.07	3,051.28	3,029.56	3,012.35	3,012.94

Source: Blackaby et al. (1991).
Notes: All equations use 25,653 observations. Controls include experience and its square, years of schooling, marital status, eighty-three month dummies, seven occupation dummies, and twenty-three industry dummies.
The dependent variable is the log of the normal hourly wage rate deflated by the monthly RPI. U is the regional level of unemployment.
t-statistics are in parentheses.

6.5   The Family Expenditure Survey Series, 1980–1986

In an interesting paper Blackaby, Bladen-Hovell, and Symons (1991) estimate a series of real hourly wage equations for males aged between sixteen
and sixty-five using the Family Expenditure Survey. Because interviews in
the FES are conducted every month, the authors are able to deflate the
wage rate by the monthly Retail Price Index and to include month dummies as well as industry, occupational and personal variables in their vector
of controls. Quarterly regional unemployment rates and a regional cost of
living variable—entered as the proportional deviation from the national
mean—are mapped onto the data file. The reason for using quarterly
unemployment data is because data on the duration of unemployment are
only available by region on a quarterly basis. The authors' main results are
presented in tables 6.18 and 6.19.

In column 1 of table 6.18, the level of unemployment—not in logarithmic form—is included (mean = 14.061) without any controls for
region-specific fixed effects. This gives an unemployment elasticity of pay
of approximately −0.17. The inclusion of the square of unemployment

Table 6.19
U.K. wage curve (FES), males: 1980–1986

	(1)	(2)	(3)	(4)
Log U	−.1034	−.0435	−.0687	
	(5.45)	(2.03)	(1.51)	
Log U^3			.0026	
			(1.16)	
U				−.0140
				(3.15)
U^2				.0006
				(3.38)
Price index	.6033	.3917		
	(14.22)	(8.43)		
Long-term U	.2841	−.0443		−.0202
	(2.94)	(0.41)		(3.28)
Region	No	3	3	3
Constant	−2.5456	−1.6253	0.2251	.1837
	(11.93)	(3.44)	(2.89)	(4.79)
$\bar{R}^2$	.4433	.4460	.4443	.4445
SEE	.3444	.3436	.3441	.3440
SSR	3,028.4	3,013.17	3,022.36	3,021.08

Source: Blackaby et al. (1991).
Notes: All equations use 25,653 observations. Controls include experience and its square, years of schooling, marital status, eighty-three month dummies, seven occupation dummies, and twenty-three industry dummies.
Long-term U is defined as the unemployment rate of those unemployed for at least 52 weeks/total unemployment.
The dependent variable is the log of the normal hourly wage rate deflated by the monthly RPI.
t-statistics are in parentheses.

improves the performance of the equation in column 2. The function minimizes at an unemployment rate of 21%, which is outside the range of unemployment observations in the data file. In column 3 both the level of unemployment and the regional price terms are significantly different from zero. Column 4 adds ten regional dummies to control for region-specific fixed effects, but the t-statistic on the unemployment term falls to below 1.8. However, on the basis of F-tests, Blackaby et al. (1991) consolidated the ten regional dummies into four separate groups ($F_{(7,\infty)} = 0.61$, which is easily accepted against a critical value of 2.01) and then included three regional dummies in column 5 of the table. Once again the unemployment variable reaches significance. At the mean level of unemployment, the unemployment elasticity of pay is estimated at −0.054.

In table 6.19 the logarithm of the unemployment rate is entered and has a coefficient of -0.10. However, the addition of the three regional dummies cuts the coefficient in half (though its significance remains). In column 2 the unemployment rate is included with the regional price term and a long term unemployment variable which is insignificantly different from zero. From these data it seems appropriate to conclude that the distinction between the long-term and the short-term unemployed is not relevant in the wage determination process. Blackaby et al. take a different view, however, and conclude that the duration of unemployment cannot be dismissed as a significant influence in wage determination. The difficulty with this argument is that it rests crucially on the specifications without fixed effects. The authors draw their inferences because "to the extent that regional dummies act as catch-all variables which do not allow the economic cause of the regional variation to be clearly identified, our prior would be to exclude regional fixed effects and concentrate upon the results obtained from incorporating the regional specific factors that are available" (Blackaby et al., 1991). In five of the six equations in the Blackaby et al. (1991) paper where long-term unemployment is included along with the regional dummies the variable is insignificant, and in one case, which is reported in column 4 of table 6.19, the variable has the wrong sign. The best statistical specification reported in the paper is that in column 5 of table 6.18 which includes the level of unemployment and a regional price term.

To conclude, there seems to be fairly strong evidence, from FES data, in support of a negatively sloped wage curve.[8] The unemployment elasticity of pay for the period 1980 to 1986 for males is estimated at up to -0.05. Those who believe that regional wage equations need to control for regional fixed effects are unlikely to be convinced by these results that wage determination depends upon the proportion of long-term unemployed in a region. More work, however, remains to be done before this debate can be settled.

6.6 Cell Means and Experiments

This section explores alternative specifications of the wage curve. These are similar to the experiments undertaken in chapter 4 for the United

---

8. New FES findings, as this book went to press, include Lanot and Walker (1993), Meghir and Whitehouse (1992), and Oswald and Walker (1993). Some of the earliest evidence was reported in unpublished work by Symons and Walker (1988).

Table 6.20
The British wage curve on GHS data using cell means: 1973–1990

	(1)	(2)	(3)	(4)	(5)	(6)
Log U_t	−.0385	−.1015	−.0192	−.0819	−.1215	
	(1.61)	(3.65)	(0.77)	(2.54)	(2.44)	
Log U_{t-1}					+.0487	−.0380
					(1.04)	(1.23)
Log w_{t-1}			.2382	.0615	.0707	.0745
			(3.45)	(0.89)	(1.01)	(1.04)
Reg. dummies	No	Yes	No	Yes	Yes	Yes
Constant	6.2407	5.8528	5.1973	5.6442	5.6326	5.4350
	(7.03)	(6.59)	(5.26)	(5.58)	(5.57)	(5.27)
$\bar{R}^2$	.9972	.9980	.9969	.9976	.9976	.9975
F	989.69	1,234.08	839.76	946.40	935.66	904.55
DF	126	116	115	105	104	105
N	198	198	187	187	187	187

Source: General Household Survey Series.
Notes: The following control variables were included, all of which were cell means: (1) ten industry variables, (2) four marital status variables, (3) fifteen qualification variables, (4) seventeen year dummies, (5) gender, (6) experience and its square, (7) part-time, (8) eleven month-of-interview variables, (9) race variable, (10) eleven region dummies interacted with dummy for years up to 1977.
The dependent variable is the natural log of gross earnings in the relevant year/region cell.
Log U_t is the natural log of the regional unemployment rate.
t-statistics are in parentheses.

States. First, U.K. wage curves are estimated using data aggregated into cell means. Second, by using these aggregated data it is possible to examine whether lagged unemployment terms are preferred statistically to contemporaneous terms. Finally, the chapter makes use of an alternative measure of the degree of slack existing in the outside labor market—the labor market participation or activity rate—to determine whether the wage curve is really a kind of misspecified labor supply curve.

Table 6.20 makes use of data from each year of the GHS from 1973 to 1990 aggregated across the eleven standard regions in Britain (including London). This gives a grand total of 198 year/region cells (eighteen years by eleven regions). Column 1 of the table includes the log of the current year unemployment rate without controls for regions' fixed effects. It has a coefficient of −0.04 and is insignificantly different from zero. The addition of the region dummies in column 2 results in a coefficient of −0.1 and a t-statistic of 3.7. The analysis can find no support statistically for the inclusion of a lagged dependent variable or a lag on the unemployment rate (once region dummies are included, columns 4–6).

These results have one striking implication. They could be interpreted as suggesting that the famous Phillips curve is an illusion. Just as for the United States, there is little sign of autoregression in wage equations. After controlling for fixed effects, table 6.20, for example, finds literally none. The coefficient on the log of the wage last period has a coefficient of 0.07 with a t-statistic of unity. Macroeconomists, it appears, may be unwise to work with aggregated wage data. The apparent autoregression in macro pay levels may be the result of aggregation error or measurement error or specification error or all three.

Experiments with specifications are in table 6.21. These include the participation (or activity) rate and use GHS data files to generate aggregate

Table 6.21
Checking participation-rate effects using cell means: 1973--1990

	(1)	(2)	(3)	(4)	(5)	(6)
Log U_t					−.0824	−.1209
					(2.54)	(2.42)
Log U_{t-1}						+.0475
						(1.01)
Log P_t	−.2117	−.2013	−.1349	−.0707	−.0900	−.0746
	(1.02)	(1.01)	(0.65)	(0.34)	(0.44)	(0.36)
Log w_{t-1}			.2474	.0957	.0635	.0721
			(3.56)	(1.36)	(1.91)	(1.02)
Reg. dummies	No	Yes	No	Yes	Yes	Yes
Constant	6.5628	6.0869	5.4261	5.6576	6.0135	5.9756
	(6.97)	(6.13)	(5.36)	(5.14)	(5.55)	(5.52)
$\bar{R}^2$	.9972	.9978	.9969	.9974	.9976	.9976
F	977.59	1,116.36	838.47	892.65	927.66	916.67
DF	126	116	115	105	104	105
N	198	198	187	187	187	187

Source: General Household Survey Series.
Notes: The following control variables were including, all of which were cell means: (1) ten industry variables, (2) four marital status variables, (3) fifteen qualification variables, (4) seventeen year dummies, (5) gender, (6) experience and its square, (7) part-time, (8) eleven month-of-interview variables, (9) race variable, and (10) eleven region dummies interacted with dummy for years up to 1977.
The dependent variable is the natural log of gross earnings in the relevant year/region cell. Log U is the natural log of the regional unemployment rate. Log P is the natural log of the regional participation rate.
t-statistics are in parentheses.

participation rates by region. The participation rate, whether measured as a level or as a log, is always insignificantly different from zero. In fact it has the wrong sign, in contrast to the earlier findings in chapter 4 for the United States. There is no sign, it seems, that the British wage curve is a misspecified labor supply curve.

Table 6.20 provides some corroboration of the key idea. Its estimate of an unemployment elasticity of pay of either −0.08 or −0.10 (choosing columns 2 or 4), obtained in the presence of a full set of area-specific fixed effects, is similar to those estimates in the first part of this chapter, and to those reported earlier for the United States using the CPS.

In passing, this number is similar to the time-series estimates of the unemployment elasticity of pay for the United Kingdom of Layard and Nickell (1986), Carruth and Oswald (1987b, 1989), and Newell and Symons (1985), and the estimates of Nickell and Wadhwani (1990)[9] and Blackaby and Manning (1990a), Blackaby, et al. (1991), the industry-level estimates of Blackaby and Murphy (1991), and the regional-level estimates of Jackman and Savouri (1991). Consistent with the suggestion of Oswald (1986b:190), the unemployment elasticity of real wages in the United Kingdom appears to be fairly close to −0.1, and probably in a rough band of zero to −0.15.

6.7   Some Final Checks on GHS

Some experiments were also done with data on regional prices and measures of long-term unemployment. David Blackaby kindly supplied a series of data that he obtained from a commercial company, Regional Rewards, that collects and sells information about the changing cost-of-living in different geographical areas within Great Britain. This source provides information about consumer prices (the series denoted RPI in tables 6.22 and 6.23) and about a required income or cost-of-living-including-housing index (denoted RPIH in table 6.23).[10] The U.K. Department of Employment also supplied a series of theirs on the proportion, by region from 1974 to 1990, of long-term unemployment in the total unemployment figures. In tables 6.22 and 6.23 this long-term unemployment percentage variable is denoted LTU. It is the percentage of people in a region who have been

---

9. Nickell and Wadhwani (1990) has only eight aggregate time-series observations on unemployment, so is not a powerful test for unemployment effects upon pay.

10. Some early results on the role of house prices are in Blanchflower and Oswald (1989a). Interest in this topic in the United Kingdom stems partly from the original work of Bover et al. (1989).

Table 6.22
Checking wage curves with long-term unemployment and prices: 1974–1990

	(1)	(2)	(3)	(4)
Log U_t	−.0793	−.0660	−.0438	−.0870
	(2.43)	(2.02)	(1.41)	(2.63)
Log RPI_t		.9883		
		(2.23)		
Log $RPIH_t$			.3956	
			(4.48)	
LTU_t				.1811
				(1.24)
w_{t-1}	.0660	.0385	−.0568	.0705
	(0.94)	(0.55)	(0.81)	(1.01)
Regional dummies	Yes	Yes	Yes	Yes
$\bar{R}^2$	.9977	.9977	.9979	.9976
F	929.48	953.41	1,086.76	923.02
DF	104	103	103	103
N	187	187	187	187

Source: General Household Survey Series.
Notes: The following control variables were included, all of which were cell means: (1) ten industry variables, (2) four marital status variables, (3) fifteen qualification variables, (4) sixteen year dummies, (5) gender, (6) experience and its square, (7) part-time, (8) eleven month-of-interview variables, (9) race variable, and (10) eleven region dummies interacted with dummy for years up to 1977 plus a constant.
U = Regional unemployment rate.
RPI = Retail price (consumers expenditure less housing).
RPIH = Retail prices (consumers expenditure including housing).
LTU = % of the unemployed continuously unemployed for over 52 weeks in the region (Source: Department of Employment).
The dependent variable is the natural log of gross earnings in the relevant year/region cell.
t-statistics are in parentheses.

unemployed continuously for more than a year *divided by* the total number of individuals unemployed in the region.

The region price index works better than one could reasonably hope. In table 6.22 it enters[11] a nominal GHS wage equation—year dummies are still included—with a coefficient of 0.988. Theory would predict 1.00. The unemployment coefficient moves from −0.079 to −0.066 and is still well-defined. In other words, the wage curve is almost unchanged by this control for regional prices. It could, of course, be argued that prices are endogenous, but the drift of these results probably does not lead one to believe that there is anything wrong with the claims made in this book.

---

11. Tables 6.22 and 6.23 have to use a fractionally shorter time period.

Table 6.23
More checks, United Kingdom: 1974–1990

	(1)	(2)	(3)	(4)
Log U_t	−.0736	−.0479	−.0567	−.0655
	(2.22)	(1.50)	(1.86)	(2.02)
Log RPI_t	.9701			
	(2.19)			
Log $RPIH_t$		.3867		
		(4.29)		
Log $RPIH_{t-1}$			.4320	.4242
			(4.51)	(4.41)
LTU_t	.1701	.0758		.1311
	(1.19)	(0.55)		(0.97)
w_{t-1}	.0432	−.0521	−.0713	−.0655
	(0.62)	(0.74)	(1.00)	(0.92)
Regional dummies	Yes	Yes	Yes	Yes
$\bar{R}^2$	.9977	.9979	.9979	.9979
F	945.77	1,066.58	1,080.06	1,075.30
DF	102	102	103	102
N	187	187	187	187

Source: General Household Survey Series.
Notes: The following control variables were included, all of which were cell means: (1) ten industry variables, (2) four marital status variables, (3) fifteen qualification variables, (4) seventeen year dummies, (5) gender, (6) experience and its square, (7) part-time, (8) eleven month-of-interview variables, (9) race variable, and (10) eleven region dummies interacted with dummy for years up to 1977 plus a constant.
U = Regional unemployment rate.
RPI = Retail price (consumers expenditure less housing).
RPIH = Retail prices (consumers expenditure including housing).
LTU = % of the unemployed continuously unemployed for over 52 weeks in the region (Source: Department of Employment).
The dependent variable is the natural log of gross earnings in the relevant year/region cell.
t-statistics are in parentheses.

Column 3 introduces the housing-inclusive index. It enters with a coefficient of 0.39. This is far short of a plausible coefficient for a price index in an otherwise nominal wage equation, so it might be thought that there is some problem with the measurement of the variable. Unemployment drops in coefficient to −0.04, but is now not as well-defined (the t-statistic is 1.4). It is possible that this indicates an important flaw in the statistical argument for a wage curve's existence. An alternative view is that RPIH is simply not a terribly reliable variable, but is collinear with regional wages. Simultaneity between wages and house prices may be a problem that future work will need to address.

A test of the role of long-term unemployment is contained in an equation such as 4 in table 6.22. It is not possible at conventional confidence levels to reject the null of zero for LTU's coefficient. This is the strongest result that we could find; still weaker effects are documented in table 6.23. The Layard-Nickell case could be correct, but is at best unproven. The LTU variable here has a coefficient of approximately 0.2 and a t-statistic of 1.2. Type II errors could be at work. The size of the effect seems similar to the one suggested in the work of Layard and Nickell (1987). A definitive test will require better data than in this panel of ten regions by seventeen years.

6.8 Conclusions

The patterns in the data for Great Britain look like those described in the previous chapter for the United States. Both countries, it seems, have a wage curve in which the unemployment elasticity of pay is approximately -0.1. This statement, in fact, does not do true justice to the results. The countries' coefficients appear to be remarkably similar. The most reliable estimate of the unemployment elasticity for the country on the western edge of the Atlantic Ocean is close to -0.10. That for the nation on the Atlantic's eastern shore is close to -0.08. This similarity between pooled CPS estimates for the United States and pooled GHS estimates for the United Kingdom is such that an econometrician who was presented with an anonymous data set would have difficulty telling which country was represented.

It could be, of course, that this congruence is the result of either fluke or error. The difficulty with such an interpretation, however, is that it fails to explain the uniformity across a range of different samples from the United Kingdom. Four series have been used here. They are the General Household Surveys of 1973 to 1990, the Workplace Industrial Relations Surveys of 1980 to 1990, the British Social Attitudes Surveys of 1983 to 1989, and the National Child Development Study of 1981. The sample sizes vary. They cover, respectively, approximately 175,000 individuals, 4,500 plants, 7,500 individuals, and 6,500 individuals. More important, the data sets provide a variety of differently sized regions, in reasonable number, over very different periods.[12] Corroborative results from the Family Expenditure Survey, derived by others, have also been summarized.

---

12. As this book was being completed, we were fortunate to see early results by Paul Gregg and Steve Machin (1993) indicating that, in pooled GHS data, there appears to be a kind of negatively sloped function linking pay to the unemployment rate in the workers' relevant educational group.

The chapter has failed to find much statistical support for long-term unemployment variables or for high-order nonlinearities in unemployment. A simple log form for regional unemployment seems to work reasonably well. Although more studies are needed, this tentatively suggests that Blanchflower and Oswald (1990b) were right to argue that long-term unemployment effects are weak and that the upward-slope in a U-shape should not be taken seriously, and possibly wrong to think of the unemployment elasticity as changing along the curve. Nevertheless, the possibility of Type II errors is a real one. Much remains to be done before these issues can be considered settled.

As in the case of chapters 4 and 5, the data suggest that Phillips's 1958 curve may be a result of aggregation error and misspecification. Tables such as 6.20 show that, after controlling for regional fixed effects, the lagged dependent variable in a wage-level equation has a coefficient of zero. This implies that two generations of macroeconomics textbooks may be wrong, and perhaps that the next generation of classroom texts will have to introduce students to a wage equation derived not from macro-economic time-series statistics but from microeconomic data.

These different random samples paint a uniform picture. Wages are low, other things constant, in areas where unemployment is high. This is not for reasons of composition: it is not because the North has fewer people who are highly educated, nor because the South East is full of white collar staff in head offices. Instead there appears to be some sort of genuine statistical link between joblessness and pay.

7   Wage Curves in Other European Countries

A full and complete microeoconomic foundation to wage adjustment with the power of the auction-model may never be forthcoming. If that is so, we may have to look to regularities ...

Charles Schultze (1984) Presidential Address to the American Economic Association

Great Britain and the United States share a common language, a similar culture, and some of the same institutions. To show that the wage curve is a deep economic phenomenon would require that its presence be uncovered in many other kinds of nations. This is the issue tackled in the next two chapters. The analysis begins with seven European countries. The chapter uses micro-data drawn from the International Social Survey Program series of 1985 to 1991.[1] It estimates earnings equations for Austria, Italy, Netherlands, the Federal Republic of Germany, Ireland, Norway, and Switzerland. Although, by the standard of the last two chapters, the data files are comparatively small, in all seven countries there is evidence of downward-sloping wage curves.[2]

The International Social Survey Program (ISSP) is a voluntary collaborative grouping of study teams crossing twenty-one countries. Each undertakes to run an annual self-completion survey containing an agreed set of

---

1. There is now a large literature using aggregate time-series data to study European wages and unemployment. See, for example, Nickell and Andrews (1983), Bruno and Sachs (1985), Newell and Symons (1985), the papers in the special 1986 issue of *Economica*, Beckerman and Jenkinson (1986), the papers in Calmfors (1990) including Andersen and Risager (1990) and Pissarides and Moghadam (1990), Calmfors and Nymoen (1990), Nickell (1990), Dreze and Bean (1990, 1991), Jackman, Layard and Pissarides (1990), Layard et al. (1991), Phelps (1993, 1994), and Bean (1994).
2. Earlier work using some of these data is in Blanchflower and Oswald (1989b, 1990b) and Blanchflower and Freeman (1992, 1993).

questions asked of a probability-based nationwide sample of adults. Some topics change from year to year by agreement, with replication every five years or so. The aim of the research teams is to build internationally comparable data sets. At the time of writing the following countries are members of the group: the United Kingdom, the United States, the Federal Republic of Germany, Italy, Australia, Austria, the Netherlands, Hungary, Ireland, Norway, the Philippines, Israel, Poland, Bulgaria, the Czech Republic, Japan, New Zealand, Russia, Canada, Sweden, and Slovenia.[3] The first surveys, with a special component on civil liberties, were conducted in 1985 in the United Kingdom, the United States, Germany, Italy, Australia, and Austria. Subsequent surveys had modules on social networks (1986), social inequality (1987), family and changing sex roles (1988), work orientation (1989), the role of government (1990), and religion (1991). The number of responses by country by year that are currently publicly available are reported in table 7.1.

Apart from the common modules conducted in each country, the various data files contain information on a range of personal, workplace, and region characteristics. For technical reasons this chapter is restricted to seven of these thirteen countries. In six of these seven there are pooled data from more than one year of surveys. In the case of Switzerland, only one year of suitable data (1988) is available.

The ISSP surveys are subsets of the General Social Survey series in the United States, the West German Allegemaine Bevoelkerungsumfrage der Sozialwissenschaften (ALLBUS) and the British Social Attitudes Survey series. The first and last of these three surveys have been examined in earlier chapters of this book. Further details of the ISSP surveys are given in Davis and Jowell (1989), Blanchflower and Freeman (1992, 1993), and Blanchflower and Oswald (1989b). An interesting discussion of different social attitudes across the countries, produced by using the ISSP data files, is contained in a set of book chapters by Taylor-Gooby on the role of the state, Smith on inequality and welfare, Finch on kinship and friendship, and Harding on the changing family, all in Jowell et al. (1989). A brief description of how the surveys have been conducted, along with variables' definitions, sample means, and representative earnings equations, are in the appendix.

---

3. Although Switzerland is not one of the countries participating in the ISSP, a team at the Soziologisches Institut der Universität Zurich has replicated the 1987 module, and kindly provided us with the data.

Table 7.1
Number of survey responses by country

	1985	1986	1987	1988	1989	1990	1991	Total
Australia	1,528	1,250	1,574		2,398			6,750
Austria	987	1,027	972	972	1,997			5,955
East Germany						1,028	1,486	2,514
Great Britain	1,530	1,416	1,212	1,307	1,297	1,197	1,257	9,216
S. Ireland				1,005	972	1,005	1,005	3,987
Hungary		1,747	2,606	1,737	1,000	977	1,000	9,067
Israel	1,580				1,133	991	991	3,115
Italy		1,033	1,027	1,027	1,028	983	983	7,661
Netherlands			1,638	1,737	1,690		1,635	6,700
New Zealand							1,070	1,070
N. Ireland					780	772	838	2,390
Norway					1,848	1,517	1,506	4,871
Philippines							1,200	1,200
Poland			3,943				1,063	5,006
Slovenia							2,080	2,080
Switzerland			987					987
United States	677	1,470	1,564	1,414	1,453	1,217	1,359	9,154
F.R. of Germany	1,048	2,809	1,397	2,994	1,575	2,812	1,346	13,981
Total	7,350	10,752	16,920	12,194	14,773	14,897	18,819	95,704

7.1   Background

The next seven subsections of the chapter examine in turn the evidence on wage curves for the Federal Republic of Germany, Austria, Italy, the Netherlands, Ireland, Switzerland, and Norway. The others could not be studied. For purposes of comparison, summary information is given here for the other countries in this book for which wage curves are derived: Australia, Canada, Korea, the United Kingdom, and the United States.

As can be seen from Table 7.2, these seven countries divide by size into three distinct groups. Austria, Switzerland, Norway, and Ireland are small; all have populations little bigger than that of New York City. The Netherlands is somewhat larger with nearly fifteen million inhabitants. Italy and Germany are medium-sized, with approximately the same population as the United Kingdom, namely, around sixty million people. In all of these countries there was real GDP growth over the period from 1985 to 1992. It was marked in the case of Ireland, where GDP increased by 31% while

Table 7.2
Country characteristics

	1991 population (millions)	Δ GDP (%)	1985–1992 Δ consumer prices (%)
Australia	17.34	21	52.6
Austria	7.88	21	19.7
Canada	27.03	18	33.4
Federal Republic of Germany	64.12	22	15.2
Ireland	3.52	31	25.1
Italy	57.05	18	47.4
Korea	43.27	85	51.7
Netherlands	15.07	22	11.7
Norway	4.26	13	43.3
Switzerland	6.79	14	24.7
United Kingdom	57.65	14	46.4
United States	252.69	16	30.4

Sources: Column 1: *OECD Economic Surveys, 1991/1992*
Yearbook of Labour Statistics, ILO, 1992.
Columns 2 & 3: *International Financial Statistics*, IMF, 1992.

consumer prices rose by 25.1%. There are considerable differences between the countries in both their activity and unionization rates. Table 7.3 reveals large variation in activity rates across these countries, partly through differences in the rate of female participation. For example, in 1987 two thirds of Canadians were in the labor force, compared with a half in the United States and two fifths in South Korea. Italy has a particularly low female participation rate.

In 1986–1987 over 60% of workers were unionized in Austria. The figure for the Netherlands was 35%. It was only 17% in the United States and 12% in South Korea. The time path of union density rates between 1950 and 1985 is presented in figure 7.1. There has been some tendency for union density to decline in the 1980s: this has been especially marked in the United States and to a lesser extent in the United Kingdom, the Netherlands, and Italy. The decline in density in the United Kingdom is especially marked when measured as a percentage of the labor force. This is associated statistically with the rise in unemployment after 1980. In contrast, union density went up in the 1980s in West Germany, Switzerland, Ireland, and Austria. Density remained roughly constant, at a high level, in Norway over the same period.

Table 7.3
Labor market characteristics

	Participation rate 1991 (% of population that are active)			Unionization rate 1991 (% of employed)
	Total	Male	Female	
Australia	63.8	75.6	52.2	55
Austria*	45.8	56.5	36.0	60
Canada*	67.0	75.9	58.4	30
Germany*	49.6	60.8	39.2	43
Ireland**	50.9	71.4	30.9	60
Italy*	42.0	54.3	30.3	15
South Korea	60.6	74.7	47.4	12
Netherlands	67.6	80.3	54.5	25
Norway	68.0	75.0	62.0	60
Switzerland	52.4	65.6	39.5	29
United Kingdom	62.1	73.1	52.0	38
United States	63.6	72.2	55.6	17

Source: *Yearbook of Labour Statistics*, ILO, 1992; *The Current Industrial Relations Scene in Canada, 1992* by P. Kumar, M. L. Coates, and D. Arrowsmith, Queens University, Canada; Blanchflower and Freeman (1992); and *Statistical Yearbook of Switzerland*, Federal Statistical Office, Bern, 1991; *Foreign Labor Trends*, U.S. Department of Labor, 1991–1992.
Notes: *participation rate is for 1990; **participation rate is for 1989.

Earlier analysts have examined the links between national industrial relations systems and macro-economic outcomes (Bruno and Sachs, 1985; Calmfors and Driffill, 1988; and Crouch, 1985; Freeman, 1988b; and Pohjola, 1989). There is no truly accepted typology of national industrial relations systems, and Soskice (1990) has provided a lucid critique of some authors' claims, but three main classifications of centralization have been used: a corporatist/non-corporatist dichotomy developed by Colin Crouch and used by Bruno and Sachs, an earlier classification by Blyth (1979), and a 1988 classification by Calmfors and Driffill. Crouch (1985) classified Austria, the Netherlands, the Federal Republic of Germany, Norway, and Switzerland as corporatist and Canada, Italy, the United Kingdom, and the United States as noncorporatist. Blyth (1979) classified Austria and Norway as countries with high centralization, the Federal Republic of Germany as a country with medium centralization, and Canada, the Netherlands, Italy, the United Kingdom, and the United States as countries with low centralization. Calmfors and Driffill (1988) classified Austria, the Federal Republic of Germany, and Norway as highly centralized countries, the

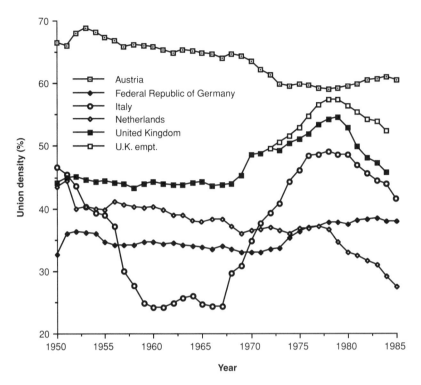

Figure 7.1
Union density: 1950–1985

Netherlands as countries with medium centralization, and Canada, Italy, Switzerland, the United Kingdom, and the United States as countries with low centralization. There is common agreement that the United Kingdom, the United States, Italy, and Canada are noncorporatist and that Austria is corporatist. There is disagreement over the appropriate way to classify the industrial relations systems in Germany and the Netherlands.

Notwithstanding the taxonomic difficulties, there is some evidence in the literature that unions retained numbers in countries with centralized as opposed to decentralized wage-setting systems in the 1970s and 1980s (Blanchflower and Freeman, 1992). Freeman's (1990a) regressions suggest that this is unaffected by controls for macroeconomic conditions across countries.

Table 7.4 sets out standardized unemployment rates by country. With the exception of Korea, these nations experienced substantial increased

Table 7.4
Country unemployment rates (%)

	1979	1981	1983	1985	1987	1989	1991	1993 (April)
Australia	5.8	5.8	10.0	8.3	8.1	6.2	9.6	10.7
Austria	2.0	2.4	4.5	4.8	5.6	3.1	3.3	4.8
Canada	7.4	7.5	11.9	10.5	8.9	7.5	10.3	11.3
Germany	3.8	5.5	9.1	9.3	8.9	7.9	6.7	10.1**
Ireland	9.3	10.1	14.7	17.7	18.8	15.6	15.8	16.9
Italy	7.7	8.4	9.9	10.3	11.9	12.0	11.0	9.1
Korea	3.8	4.5	4.1	4.0	3.1	2.6	2.3	n/a
Netherlands	5.1	7.0	13.9	12.9	11.5	8.0	7.0	8.2
Norway	2.0	2.0	3.4	2.6	2.1	4.9	5.9	5.9
Switzerland	0.4	0.2	0.9	1.0	0.8	0.6	1.1	4.6
United Kingdom	5.3	10.4	11.6*	11.9	10.6	6.3	8.3	10.5
United States of America	5.8	7.5	9.5	7.1	6.1	5.2	6.7	6.9

Sources: *Yearbook of Labour Statistics*, ILO, various years; *OECD Employment Outlook*, July 1993, table 1.3; *Employment Gazette*, July 1993, table 2.18.
Note: *change in method of calculating rates occurred here; **includes East Germany

joblessness between 1980 and 1982. Unemployment generally remained high during the 1980s but showed some signs of decline at the end of the decade. During the 1980s, Italy, the Netherlands, the UK and Canada all experienced unemployment rates of over 10%. The unemployment rate in Korea and Austria was below 6% through the 1980s.

The movement of consumer prices, monthly earnings, industrial production, and employment (manufacturing employment in the case of Korea) are graphed in figures 7.2 to 7.13. This is for the period from 1980 to 1992. As is well known, Korea has had dramatic growth in industrial production. Between 1985 and 1988, for example, industrial production increased by 62% in Korea, compared with 6% in Austria, 12% in Canada and Italy, 1% in the Netherlands, 6% in the Federal Republic of Germany, and 10% in the United Kingdom and the United States. Price inflation was highest in Italy and lowest in the Netherlands over the same period (16.5% and 0.1% respectively). Real earnings declined in the United States and Canada, but rose in the other countries, especially in South Korea where real monthly earnings between 1985 and 1988 went up over 32%.

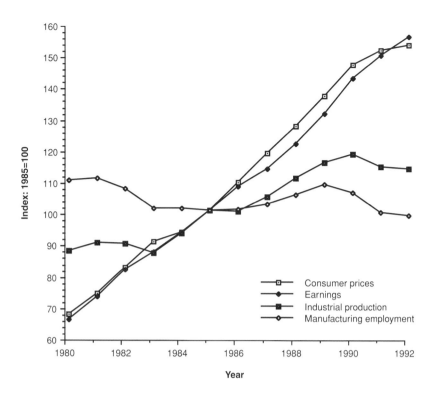

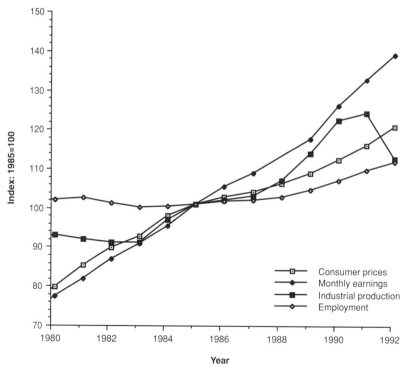

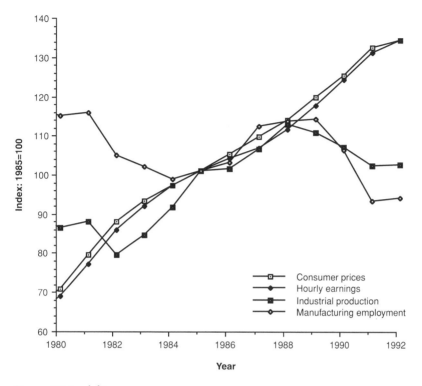

Figure 7.2 (top left)
Economic indicators in Australia: 1980–1992

Figure 7.3 (bottom left)
Economic indicators in Austria: 1980–1992

Figure 7.4 (above)
Economic indicators in Canada: 1980–1992

7.2 The West German Labor Market

By 1985 West German GDP was, at U.S. $612 billion, noticeably higher than any other OECD country except the United States and Japan. Inflation remained low throughout the 1980s; between 1975 and 1984 the annual increase of consumer prices was 4.5%, less than in all other OECD countries except Japan. By 1985 the German rate had fallen to 3.9%, the same rate as Japan. For a discussion of German economic policy in the 1970s and 1980s, Hellwig and Neumann (1987) is a useful source.

Although Germany experienced a relatively greater increase in unemployment than most other countries (1971: 0.6%; 1984: 7.7%), unemploy-

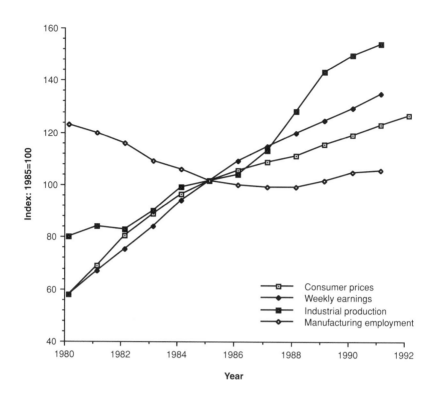

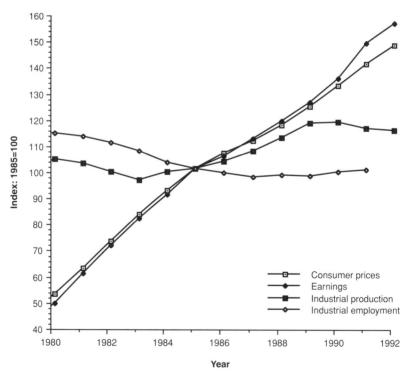

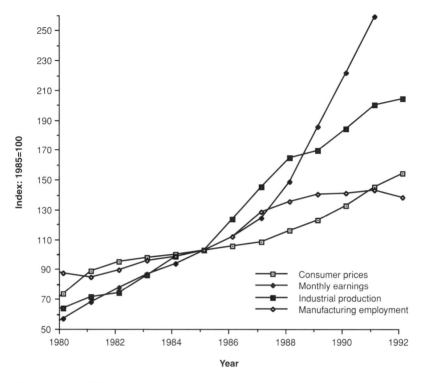

Legend:
- □ Consumer prices
- ◆ Monthly earnings
- ■ Industrial production
- ◇ Manufacturing employment

Figure 7.5 (top left)
Economic indicators in Republic of Ireland: 1980–1992

Figure 7.6 (bottom left)
Economic indicators in Italy: 1980–1992

Figure 7.7 (above)
Economic indicators in South Korea: 1980–1992

ment levels have generally been lower than in their trading partners. This is despite the size of unemployment benefits in Germany, which appear to be generous (Soltwedel, 1988). According to OECD (1982) estimates, for an average single (married) income earner, the effective loss of income in 1978 for an unemployment spell of three months was roughly 4% (6%). An income loss of 32% would only be incurred for a spell of unemployment of over one year. These replacement rates were reduced slightly in 1982 and 1986.

Out of a total population in 1988 of approximately sixty-one million, approximately 40% of Germans were in civilian employment. Relatively more people are employed in industry than in any other OECD country

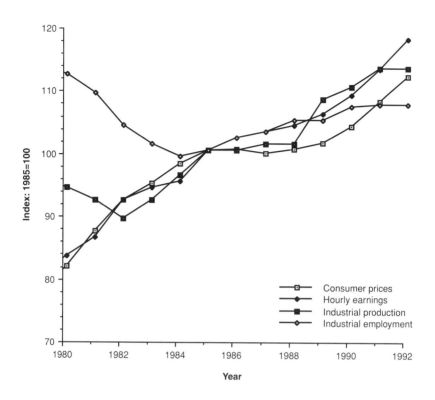

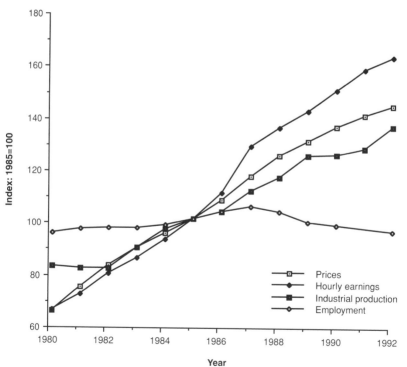

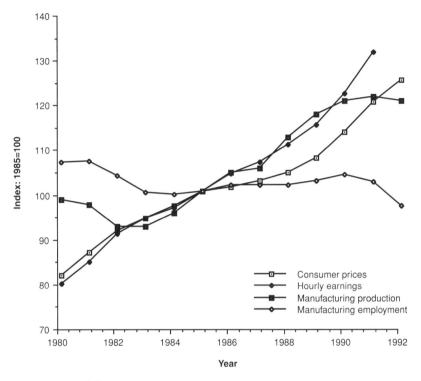

Figure 7.8 (top left)
Economic indicators in Netherlands: 1980–1992

Figure 7.9 (bottom left)
Economic indicators in Norway: 1980–1992

Figure 7.10 (above)
Economic indicators in Switzerland: 1980–1992

(41% compared, for example, with 29.4% in the United Kingdom, 26.5% in the Netherlands and 32.6% in Italy). The service sector employs 54.5% (68.3% in the United Kingdom, 65% in the Netherlands, and 57.5% in Italy). (Eurostat, 1990). In 1983, foreign guest-workers made up approximately 8.5% of the labor force.

In contrast to the United States and the United Kingdom, union density in the Federal Republic of Germany remained more or less constant between 1975 and 1989 at approximately 38% of employees (see Visser, 1989; U.S. Department of Labor, 1992b). For a discussion of the determinants of union density in Germany, see Carruth and Schnabel (1990) and Schmidt and Zimmermann (1993). German unions appear to exert an influ-

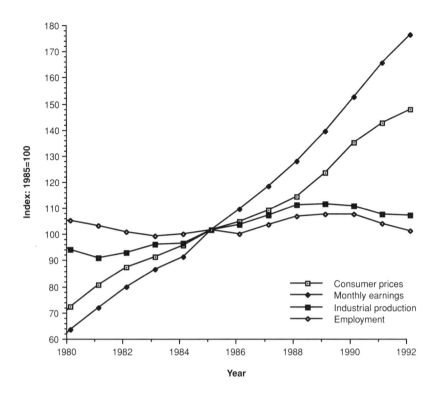

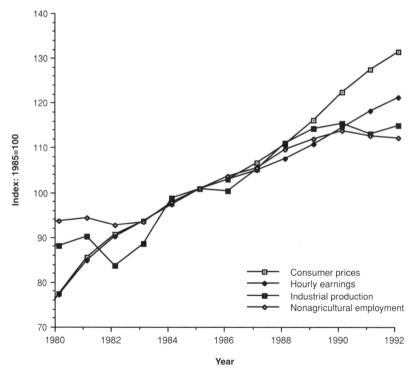

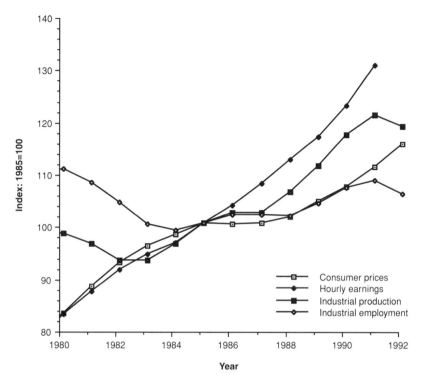

Figure 7.11 (top left)
Economic indicators in United Kingdom: 1980–1992

Figure 7.12 (bottom left)
Economic indicators in United States: 1980–1992

Figure 7.13 (above)
Economic indicators in Federal Republic of Germany: 1980–1992

ence on political and social life. Collective bargaining between unions and managers is limited to one level and is highly bureaucratic and legalistic. There is little national wage bargaining, very little company bargaining, and almost no local bargaining. The general practice is to have bargaining at the state level between an industry employers' association and the industry union. Under German law the union and the employers association have the power to agree on a new contract without referring it for ratification to the employees or the employers. Once a pay agreement is reached in one state, it commonly becomes the basis for settlement in other states. The contract between union and employers' association can be declared compulsory for the whole industry by the Federal Minister of Labor if one or both parties apply for it (Soltwedel, 1988:175).[4]

The scope of bargaining tends to be limited because social legislation covers many fringe benefits. Many local plant matters are settled by the employers with work councils. Works councils have rights to information, consultation, and codetermination. The 1972 Works Constitution Act, for example, allows work councils to regulate work discipline, hours and breaks, short-time or overtime work, piece rates, pay systems, suggestion schemes, holiday schedules, monitoring of employee performance, safety regulations, welfare services in the establishment, and the administration of works housing for employees. The state-wide wage agreements are limited to minimum wage standards and a few other major matters. Each company is free to pay higher rates, so significant wage drift often occurs. This is potentially important for the later estimation of a wage curve.[5]

The German apprenticeship system is a central plank in the German labor market system.[6] Annually almost 80% of the young people not destined for university enter; this provides them with on-the-job training and some formal schooling each week. The apprenticeships normally begin at age fifteen to twenty and last for three years. During that time the apprentice is paid an allowance, which averages 20% of the adult rate in the first year but which increases in subsequent years. National standards for every occupation are enforced. Firms involved in the various training programs develop a written curriculum. These curricula are reviewed and certified by the appropriate chambers of industry and commerce, with examinations validated by outside experts.

There has, of course, been previous work on the wage determination process using individual data for Germany. It has concentrated primarily on measuring male-female wage differentials (Gerlach, 1987; Schasse, 1986), rates of return to human capital (Lorenz and Wagner, 1994; Wagner and Lorenz, 1988, 1991; Krueger and Pischke, 1993), interindustry wage differentials (Hubler and Gerlach, 1990; and Wagner, 1990), earnings inequality (Abraham and Houseman, 1994; Blau and Kahn, 1993; Krueger and Pischke, 1994), the earnings of immigrants (Schmidt, 1992, 1993), and

---

4. Christoph Schmidt has pointed out to us that under the Allgemeinverbindlichkeitsklauseln, as it is called, contracts can be declared compulsory only under one further qualification. This is that the workers already covered by the contract constitute a substantial fraction of their industry's workforce.

5. For further details of the German system of industrial relations, see Kennedy (1980: chapter 5), IDE (1981), Soltwedel (1988), Bratt (1986), Streeck (1988), and Fuerstenberg (1987).

6. This section draws on U.S. Department of Labor (1992b).

Table 7.5
German wage curve: 1986–1991 monthly earnings

	(1)	(2)	(3)	(4)
Log U_t^r	−.0129	−.2596		
Log U_t^a	(0.81)	(4.04)	−.0041	−.1303
			(0.25)	(1.75)
Region dummies		10		10
$\bar{R}^2$	.5141	.5174	.5140	.5159
F	77.49	68.04	77.47	67.66
DF	4,564	4,554	4,564	4,554

Source: International Social Survey Program.
Notes: In all cases there are 4,629 observations. The following control variables were also included: (1) three marital status dummies, (2) union dummy, (3) seven highest qualification dummies, (4) five year dummies, (5) gender dummy, (6) six age dummies, (7) part-time dummy, (8) nine occupation dummies, and (9) self-employment dummy and a constant.
The unemployment rates U are measured across 11 regions—Source: Eurostat, *Statistical Yearbook—Regions*, (various years). Data are by (1) gender (U_t^r), and (2) age (U_t^a) − < 24 years and ≥ 25 years.
The dependent variable is the log of monthly earnings.
t-statistics are in parentheses.

firm-size differentials (Schmidt and Zimmermann, 1991; Gerlach and Schmidt, 1989). A number of early papers use time-series (see, for example, Franz and Konig, 1986, and Franz and Schafer-Jackel, 1990) or industry level data (Neumann et al., 1990, and Holmlund and Zetterberg, 1991) to estimate wage level or wage change equations.

A recent paper by Wagner (1994) obtains estimates of the unemployment elasticity of pay using micro-data from two sources for the years 1979 to 1990. His results are discussed in more detail later in this chapter.

Table 7.5 uses pooled data from the ISSP surveys of 1986 to 1991 to estimate log earnings equations that include a vector of personal and workplace controls.[7] It was not possible to include 1985 data: regions were not identified in that survey. Unemployment rates are mapped separately by gender and age (under and over twenty-five) across the eleven regions (Schleswig-Holstein; Hamburg; Niedersachsen; Bremen; Nordrhein-Westfalen; Hessen; Rheinland-Pfalz; Baden-Württemberg; Bayern; Saarland and Berlin) for each of the six years of data.[8] In both cases there are 132

---

7. Lorenz and Wagner (1993) previously estimate a (fairly restricted) wage equation for men using the 1987 ISSP data, but do not include industry or locational controls.
8. Although we have ISSP data on East Germany for 1990 and 1991, we have been unable to obtain regional unemployment rates, and so restrict the analysis to West Germany.

Table 7.6
German wage curve: 1986–1991 monthly earnings

	(1)	(2)	(3)	(4)
$1/U_t^r$	.0674	.4578	—	—
	(0.99)	(2.67)		
$1/U_t^a$	—	—	.0165	.2182
			(0.20)	(0.79)
Region dummies	—	10	—	10
$\bar{R}^2$	.5141	.5164	.5140	.5157
F	77.50	68.04	77.47	67.66
DF	4,564	4,554	4,564	4,554

Source: International Social Survey Program.
Notes: In all cases there are 4,629 observations. The following control variables were also included: (1) three marital status dummies, (2) union dummy, (3) seven highest qualification dummies, (4) five year dummies, (5) gender dummy, (6) six age dummies, (7) part-time dummy, (8) nine occupation dummies, and (9) self-employment dummy and a constant.
The unemployment rates are measured across eleven regions—Source: Eurostat, *Statistical Yearbook—Regions*, (various years). Data are by (1) gender (U_t^r), and (2) age (U_t^a) − < 24 years and ≥ 25 years.
The dependent variable is the log of monthly earnings.
t-statistics are in parentheses.

Table 7.7
German wage curve: 1986–1991 monthly earnings

	(1)	(2)	(3)	(4)
U_t^r	− .0012	− .0176	—	—
	(0.40)	(1.89)		
U_t^a	—	—	− .0006	− .0140
			(0.22)	(1.46)
Region dummies	—	10	—	10
$\bar{R}^2$	.5140	.5160	.5140	.5159
F	77.48	67.68	77.47	67.63
DF	4,564	4,554	4,564	4,554

Source: International Social Survey Program.
Notes: In all cases there are 4,629 observations. The following control variables were also included: (1) three marital status dummies, (2) union dummy, (3) seven highest qualification dummies, (4) five year dummies, (5) gender dummy, (6) six age dummies, (7) part-time dummy, (8) nine occupation dummies, and (9) self-employment dummy and a constant.
The unemployment rates are measured across eleven regions—Source: Eurostat, *Statistical Yearbook—Regions*, (various years). Data are by (1) gender (U_t^r), and (2) age (U_t^a) − < 24 years and ≥ 25 years.
The dependent variable is the log of monthly earnings.
t-statistics are in parentheses.

Table 7.8
German wage curve: 1986–1991 monthly earnings

	(1)	(2)	(3)	(4)
U_t^r	−.0193	−.1113	—	—
	(1.70)	(4.61)		
$(U_t^r)^2$	.0014	.0050	—	—
	(1.66)	(4.21)		
U_t^a	—	—	−.0041	−.0842
			(0.25)	(2.46)
$(U_t^a)^2$			.0004	.0036
			(0.43)	(2.14)
Region dummies	—	10	—	10
$\bar{R}^2$	.5142	.5178	.5139	.5162
F	76.36	67.25	76.2	66.85
DF	4,563	4,553	4,563	4,553

Source: International Social Survey Program.
Notes: In all cases there are 4,629 observations. The following control variables were also included: (1) three marital status dummies, (2) union dummy, (3) seven highest qualification dummies, (4) five year dummies, (5) gender dummy, (6) six age dummies, (7) part-time dummy, (8) nine occupation dummies, and (9) self-employment dummy and a constant.
The unemployment rates are measured across eleven regions—Source: Eurostat, *Statistical Yearbook—Regions*, (various years). Data are by (1) gender (U_t^r), and (2) age (U_t^a) − <24 years and ≥ 25 years.
The dependent variable is the log of monthly earnings.
t-statistics are in parentheses.

separate unemployment observations. The distribution of the regional unemployment rates is reported in appendix C1.

Wages in Germany appear to be determined statistically by forces similar to those in the United Kingdom and the United States. Gender, marital status, age, qualifications, part-time work, and union membership all have a significant influence on pay levels. Blanchflower and Oswald (1989b) and Blanchflower and Freeman (1992) find small but significant union/nonunion wage differentials for Germany using these ISSP data for only 1985 to 1987. In these studies a more limited set of control variables was used to allow comparability with other countries. The estimates here, of between 3.5% and 4.5%, are smaller than their estimates of 6% to 8%. Estimates of a comparable magnitude to those reported here are discovered by Schmidt (1992).

In columns 1 and 3 of table 7.5, the two unemployment rates are included separately in log form without any controls for regional fixed effects. The unemployment coefficients are both insignificantly different from zero. In columns 2 and 4, ten regional dummies are added. The

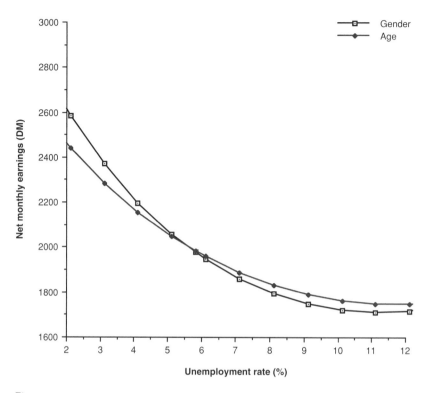

Figure 7.14
Federal Republic of Germany wage curve: 1986–1991

coefficients are large in absolute terms and significantly different—though borderline for column 4—from zero. In tables 7.6 to 7.8, a variety of nonlinear specifications of the unemployment rate are checked. Table 7.6 has the reciprocal of the unemployment rates included: only in column 2 is the coefficient significant. The unemployment rate as a level is given in table 7.7: the coefficients never reach significance at conventional levels whether or not regional fixed effects are included. Finally, table 7.8 tests for both the level of unemployment and its square. In columns 1 and 3 of the table, which do not include fixed effects, the unemployment terms are insignificant. However, when fixed effects are added in columns 2 and 4, the level and the square are both significant. Using the estimates in columns 2 and 4 of table 7.8, the minimum of the estimated wage curve occurs at 11% unemployment (using the estimates from column 2), and 12% in column 4. Looking at the distribution of the unemployment rates, only 0.5% of the distribution of both unemployment rates are higher than these

Table 7.9
Wagner's West German wage curves

| | 1979 and 1985 | | 1984–1990 | |
	(1)	(2)	(3)	(4)
Log regional unemployment	−.025	−.130	−.049	−.060
	(3.45)	(2.84)	(5.38)	(0.87)
Regional fixed effects	No	Yes	No	Yes
$\bar{R}^2$	.382	.384	.507	.511
N	20,565	20,565	7,429	7,429

levels. In figure 7.14 the two wage curves obtained from columns 2 and 4 of table 7.8 are plotted. The dependent variable and both unemployment rates are set at their means, and solved for the constant. Various unemployment values are inserted into the resulting equations. Taking antilogs, the equations are:

1. "Gender" wage curve $= 8.052 - .1113U + .0050U^2$.

2. "Age" wage curve $= 7.946 - .0842U + .0036U^2$.

By construction the two wage curves pass through the intersection of the means of the wage and unemployment series. The curves are over the range of unemployment rates present in the data. They are of broadly similar shape, and minimize at approximately 11% unemployment.

Wagner (1994) applies individual data from two series of individual-level micro surveys to test for the existence of wage curves in West Germany. Figures for the years 1979 and 1985 are taken from data collected for the Bundesinstitut für Berufsbildung (BIBB) and the Institut für Arbeitsmarkt und Berufsforschung ($n = 20,565$). The first seven sweeps of the German Socio-Economic Panel (SOEP) are used for the years 1984 to 1990 ($n = 7,429$). The samples consist of German men working full-time as blue- or white-collar workers, not in nonprofit organizations or the public sector. Unemployment is measured at the level of the region and is for males only. The wage level is measured as gross monthly earnings. Personal controls (schooling, experience and its square, tenure, disability, hours of work, firm size, and industry dummies) plus a group of year dummies are included. Equations estimated with the BIBB data also have five dummies for various kinds of working conditions.

Wagner's main results are reported above. The first two columns use the BIBB data and the last two the SOEP data. The specifications include the natural log of regional unemployment, both with and without controls for regional fixed effects.[9]

In the case of the regressions using BIBB data there is evidence of a wage curve even in the presence of fixed effects. In column 2 the unemployment elasticity is approximately -0.13. For the later period, the coefficient on unemployment is significant without the fixed effects, but is insignificant when the region dummies are included. It should be noted, however, that the coefficient rises somewhat in column 4 (from -0.049 to -0.06). The coefficient of -0.06 is not significantly different from zero, nor, of course, from -0.1. Wagner speculates that the difference in findings for the two periods could be because of the different macroeconomic situations in the periods covered by the two series of microdata. The BIBB data are from the peak of a boom to the end of a downswing, while the SOEP data cover a period of recovery from the depths of a recession in 1985. One possible explanation for the finding of an insignificant coefficient on the unemployment rate, on the basis of the evidence reported earlier, is that the log transformation may not be the right functional form in the second half of the 1980s.

7.3   The Austrian Labor Market

Austria is a latecomer to the international movement towards improving the functioning of markets. It appears to be one of the more regulated economies in the OECD area. This in part reflects the institutional set-up. The strong corporatist leaning—while having served to maintain both inflation and unemployment below the average of trading-partner countries—has favored the maintenance of barriers to entry and collusive behavior. This is perhaps most evident in the sheltered parts of business, notably the liberal professions, crafts, domestic transportation and the distribution sector (*OECD Economic Surveys: Austria, 1989/1990:72*).

Austria had a population in 1987 of 7.6 million people, of whom 2.79 million were in employment. Only 38.8% of the employed population worked in industry; approximately 10% of workers were self-employed. In 1983 5.4% of the workforce were guest workers, mostly from Turkey and Yugoslavia. Their numbers increased from 1985 after a period of decline in the years from 1981. As Pichelmann and Wagner (1986:77) have pointed out, however, "foreign workers are the most conspicuous of the flexible components of Austrian labor supply, but they are not the only such

---

9. The results are essentially the same when the unemployment rate is included in levels or as a reciprocal.

component. During slumps participation rates drop, whereas the share of self-employed people decreases at a significantly slower pace." Evidence in Christl (1982) also indicates that there is a substantial discouraged-worker effect in Austria.

Over the last two decades, the rate of unemployment in Austria has been relatively low. Following the first oil crisis of 1973 to 1974, unemployment increased at a slower rate than was generally the case elsewhere. As a proportion of the total labor force, between 1960 and 1982, unemployment averaged below 2% compared with 4.2% in the OECD as a whole. Though remaining low by international standards since then, unemployment steadily increased to 5.6% in 1987, but then fell back slightly to 5.4% in 1990. Part of this increase is due to an influx of workers from Eastern Europe. The incidence of long-term unemployment, that is, those unemployed for at least twelve months, more than doubled from 1982. However, at 13% in 1986 its share is lower than in other OECD countries. A discussion of Austria's unemployment problem is provided in OECD (1988a).

The maintenance of satisfactory labor market conditions is an element in Austria's system of social partnership. As part of fiscal support to employment, expenditures on active labor market policies have risen since the 1968 Labor Market Promotion Law. Labor market policies purportedly aim at:

1. achieving higher efficiency in the matching of job-offers and job-seekers at the labor exchanges;

2. increasing the mobility of the labor force, both geographically and vocationally

3. alleviating long-term unemployment through intensive retraining and financial incentives to employers;

4. restraining labor supply by limiting the intake of foreign workers and inducing the long-term unemployed to enter early retirement schemes.

Over 60% of Austrian workers are members of trade unions. Although this is lower than in the 1950s and 1960s, the unionization rate remained more or less constant through the 1980s (Visser, 1989). The proportion of workers covered by collective agreements is higher. One central trade union organization, the Osterreichischer Gewerkschaftsbund (OGB) negotiates on behalf of 95% of all employees (Bratt, 1986). The federation of the highly concentrated and centralized Austrian trade unions sets wage guidelines.

The level of target wages is set in real terms, although there are no formal COLA clauses in collective bargaining agreements, which normally last twelve months. The federal government itself takes a relatively favorable view of the wage determination process between unions and employers' associations. Pichelmann and Wagner argue that the government

considers itself a third partner in a neo-corporatist arrangement, in which exchange rate and incomes policies are designed to keep inflation down without distorting (on average) either Austria's international competitiveness or the balance between domestic demand and supply. In return for the unions' and employers' submission to (implicit) incomes policy guidelines, the government has to guarantee full employment (Pichelmann and Wagner 1986:79).

Despite this highly institutionalized framework for wage bargaining, wage drift is built into the system. At the level of the firm, supplementary terms to the central agreements are negotiated. In recent years the need for wage moderation was apparently accepted by the social partners, and the terms of trade loss caused by the oil price rises was not offset by higher nominal agreements. Austria belongs to the group of countries, which include Japan and Italy, where real wages in the business sector might be thought to be comparatively flexible and where employment is rather resilient to changes in output growth (OECD, 1988a). These beliefs can be tested by estimating wage curves.

A "solidaristic" orientation would thus typify Austria as it would the Scandinavian countries: organized labor may be willing to abstain from using its full bargaining power in wage negotiations in return for influence in economic policy. Labor organizations have tended to favor long-term employment rather than the short-term exploitation of tight labor market conditions. As mentioned in the previous section, people in the Federal Republic of Germany practice a type of social democracy comparable to that in Austria, which apparently delivers a high standard of living, social protection, and a considerable degree of social consensus.

A number of papers have estimated wage (change) equations for Austria using time series data.[10] Only two studies seem to use micro-data to estimate wage equations for Austria. Christl (1982) estimates a conventional human capital earnings equation on a sample of around 5,000 Austrian males in 1981. The rate of return to schooling is estimated at 9.4%. Age earnings profiles have the conventional shape, reaching a maximum at 34

---

10. For example, see Pollan (1980), Neusser (1986), Stiassny (1985), OECD (1988a), and Pichelman and Wagner (1986).

years of experience. Blau and Kahn (1994) use ISSP data for 1985 to 1987, and focus on an examination of gender earnings gaps.

Earlier papers reported log earnings equations using ISSP data for Austria.[11] The papers' purpose was to estimate equivalent equations across countries, and this meant that relatively small numbers of control variables had to be included. No measure of outside unemployment was used as an explanatory variable. Subsequently, Lorenz and Wagner (1993) estimated an earnings equation with 1987 ISSP data for a sample of 229 males. Their equation has three regressors—years of schooling, experience, and its square. Their coefficients on these variables are similar to ours.

Table 7.10 estimates a monthly earnings equation for Austria for the years 1986 and 1989.[12] There are 1,587 observations: 829 from 1989 and 362 and 396 from the 1985 and 1986 surveys respectively. The unemployment variable is measured at the level of the region, of which there are nine, and separately by gender. This gives thirty-six data points on unemployment. As shown in the appendix, even though the jobless rate in Austria is low by Western standards, there is a good deal of variation both by region and by gender.[13]

The first column of table 7.10 includes the log of the unemployment rate without controls for regional fixed effects. Experimentation could find no compelling evidence to support the inclusion of higher order terms. In column 2 the presence of eight regional dummies drives the log unemployment term to insignificance. It would probably be a mistake to make much of this insignificance, because the coefficient, at -0.08, is exactly like that found in many other nations. Column 3 groups four of the regions together on the basis of F-tests. They are Oberöstereich, Kärnten, Steiermark, and Niederöstereich. The log unemployment variable now has a coefficient of -0.09 and a t-statistic on the border of significance. Appendix C2 contains the full equation estimated in column 3 of table 7.10, plus a summary of variable means. Despite the high levels of union membership and coverage in Austria, being a member of a union apparently conveys a pay differential of approximately 15%.

---

11. Blanchflower and Oswald (1989b) and Blanchflower and Freeman (1992).

12. Traditionally, apparently, workers in Austria receive fourteen wage payments per annum (Christl, 1982). Data from the 1985, 1986, and 1989 surveys are employed to obtain the estimates. The reason for this is that the interviews for the 1985 ISSP were conducted in May and June 1986. Each of the questionnaires was administered to a random half of the sample. It was not possible to use the 1988 survey because it did not contain data on regions.

13. Rudolf Winter-Ebmer generously provided these data.

Table 7.10
Austrian wage curve: 1986 and 1989 monthly earnings

	(1)	(2)	(3)	(4)	(5)	(6)
Log U	-.1403	-.0773	-.0908	-.1517	-.2134	-.0926
	(3.18)	(0.72)	(1.59)	(3.22)	(1.49)	(1.62)
Long-term U	—	—	—	.0015	.0165	.0014
				(0.69)	(1.36)	(0.56)
Region dummies	—	8	3	—	8	3
$\bar{R}^2$	.5152	.5158	.5172	.5150	.5160	.5170
DF	1,561	1,553	1,558	1,560	1,552	1,557
F	68.41	52.19	61.68	65.78	50.74	59.54

Source: International Social Survey Program.
Notes: In all cases there are 1,587 observations. Unless stated otherwise the following control variables were included: (1) union membership dummy, (2) four marital status dummies, (3) nine occupation dummies, (4) year dummy, (5) gender dummy, (6) age and its square, (7) part-time dummy, and (8) five qualification dummies and a constant.
Unemployment is measured at the level of the region (9) across the two years.
The dependent variable is the log of monthly earnings.
t-statistics are in parentheses.

Winter-Ebmer (1994) takes micro-data at the level of the individual from the 1983 Austrian Microzensus to check for the existence of wage curves. He estimates a series of log hourly wage equations. These include unemployment rates at the level of the occupation (31 observations) or the region (99 observations) for males. In total there are 7,587 observations. To try to control for fixed effects, a series of region and occupation dummies are included. These are at a higher level of aggregation than is used to map in the unemployment rates (fifteen occupation dummies and nine region dummies). The author finds signs of a negatively sloped wage curve, with the strongest evidence obtained from the regional unemployment variable. The unemployment elasticity of pay is estimated at between -0.02 and -0.07 using the regional unemployment rates, and between -0.01 and -0.02 using the occupational rates. Nonlinear unemployment terms are significant, although unemployment duration effects turn out to be a positive and significant influence. These results are robust to the simultaneous inclusion of regional and occupational unemployment rates. In order to examine these claims, in columns 4 to 6 of table 7.10, following Layard and Nickell (1987), an independent variable is incorporated for the proportion of the unemployed who had been continuously unemployed for at least one year (Rudolph Winter-Ebmer generously supplied these). This information is available by gender across the nine regions. Statistically, it is found to be insignificantly different from zero. The variable's presence has little or no effect on the coefficient on the unemployment variable itself, although it might be argued that it has the sign expected.

7.4   The Italian Labor Market

From a small industrial base at the end of the second World War, the Italian economy grew rapidly. By the 1990s it had become a major European economy of equivalent status to the United Kingdom and France. There is, however, high unemployment, and there are major obstacles to an economic takeoff in the south (the *Mezzogiorno*). The 1974 oil shock had a damaging effect on Italy because of its dependence on imported energy. The mid-1970s was a period of crisis on several fronts: inflation, balance of payments crises, runs on the lira, public sector borrowing, and militant trade unions. A period of respite was achieved from 1976 to 1979 by cooperating with the communists, and thereby with the unions. The breakdown of this compromise in 1979 and the second oil shock led to further problems. The first half of the 1980s brought recovery to the private sector's profitability. The Italian economy experienced substantial growth in the second half of the 1980s. Price inflation came down from 15% in 1983 to 5% in 1988. In 1988, for the fifth consecutive year, GDP growth was one of the highest in Europe. The unemployment rate has stabilized, albeit at a level which is high (12% in 1988).

Italy's agricultural sector (10.5%) has large employment in comparison with most other Western countries, even though its scale has declined from 34% of total employment in 1959. The nation has a higher proportion of its workforce employed in industry (32.6%) than the United Kingdom (29.8%), the United States (27.1%), and Netherlands (25.5%), but less than Austria (37.7%) and Germany (40.5%).

Wage bargaining in Italy has long been characterized by a three-tiered process, involving negotiations at national, sectoral, and firm level. National bargaining is concerned in part with negotiations about the cost-of-living indexation scheme (the *scala mobile*). Industry-level agreements are signed by national unions and cover various segments of the economy. Wage increases and conditions of employment are handled by the union representing workers in a particular industry and the corresponding employers' association. Many labor contracts are negotiated every three years. Contracts signed by unions and employers' associations are applicable to all workers in a particular industry. Wages and working conditions are negotiated at local and firm level, which results in some wage drift over the industry-level agreements. In 1991, 15% of workers were dues-paying union members. Nevertheless, the three main confederations of labor unions—the Christian Democrat Italian Confederation of Labor Unions (CSL), the former Communist-dominated Italian General Confederation of Labor (CGIL), and the Socialist-led Union of Italian Labor (UIL)—apparently negotiate on behalf of all workers, unionized or not (U.S. Department of Labor 1992c). They sign national labor contracts by sector which are applicable nationwide and cover all workers. Basic salaries fixed with the unions act as a de facto minimum wage. Discussions of the Italian industrial relations system can be found in OECD (1986), Bratt (1986), Pellegrini (1987), Santi (1988), Perulli (1990), and Kennedy (1980).

Male unemployment in Italy has risen more slowly than in most other nations; in 1988 it was 8%. In contrast, female and youth unemployment is great: in 1988 the rates were 18.6% and 34.5% respectively. Unemployment in the South (Abruzzi, Molise, Campania, Puglia, Basilicata, Calabria, Sicilia, and Sardinia) is particularly high at 20.6% overall, compared with 9.8% in the Center (Toscana, Marche, Umbria, and Lazio) and 6.4% in the

North (Piemonte, Valle d'Aosta, Lombardia, Liguria, Trentino-Alto, Adige, Veneto, Friuli-Venezia Guilia, and Emilia-Romagna). See OECD (1990b).[15] Apart from the East European countries, Italy is believed to have Europe's most extensive hidden or black economy, involving some 3.5 million workers. Unemployment at 2.87 million in 1989 or 12% of the workforce may therefore be less believable than the statistics suggest.

Research estimating wage equations for Italy has generally used time-series data (Modigliani et al., 1986; Modigliani and Tarentelli, 1977; Bean et al., 1986; and Dreze and Bean, 1990). Dell'Aringa and Lucifora (1990) estimate cross-section earnings equations on individual workers. Their concern is to test for interindustry and occupational wage differentials. Lorenz and Wagner (1993) use the 1987 ISSP data to examine, for Italian males, rates of return to schooling and experience-earnings profiles. Antonelli (1987) also estimates a log annual earnings equation and finds a rate of return to schooling of 4.6%. A quadratic experience/earnings profile is observed, which maximizes at approximately 31 years. Two recent papers, Blau and Kahn (1994) and Erickson and Ichino (1994), use micro data to look at aspects of earnings inequality.

In table 7.11, monthly earnings equations for Italy (for the years 1986 and 1989) are summarized. These are the only years with usable earnings information for which area unemployment data are available. There is only aggregate information on the area in which the individual lives (source: *Regions—Statistical Yearbook*, 1988 and 1990, published by Eurostat). The surveys only distinguish whether the individual lives in the North West, the North East, Center, or South, and Islands. Due to the small number of unemployment observations, unemployment rates are mapped in by sex by region.

Column 1, table 7.11, reveals what happens when a log unemployment term is included. It is significantly different from zero with a coefficient of -0.12. This is, again, the -0.1 outcome that is now familiar from earlier countries. The addition of three regional dummies in column 2 makes the coefficient insignificant, but reduces the $\bar{R}^2$. The lack of significance of these variables presumably is because of the small numbers of degrees of freedom available(4 regions*2 years*2 sexes). Hence in what follows they are omitted. In column 3 the cube of the log of unemployment is a regressor, but this does not work as well as the specification with the simple log formulation. Table 7.12 tries alternative specifications. These include the unem-

---

15. For a discussion of the economic causes of the regional differentials in unemployment rates, see Caroleo (1990).

Table 7.11
Italian wage curve: 1986 and 1989 monthly earnings

	(1)	(2)	(3)
Log U	−.1235	−.1052	−.1230
	(3.32)	(0.63)	(1.23)
Log U^3			−.0000
			(0.01)
Region dummies	—	3	—
$\bar{R}^2$	.5233	.5230	.5229
DF	1,002	999	1,001
F	31.05	28.81	30.22

Source: International Social Survey Program.
Notes: In all cases there are 1,041 observations. The following control variables were also included: (1) two marital status dummies, (2) two schooling dummies, (3) two year dummies, (4) gender dummy, (5) five age dummies, (6) part-time dummy, and (7) nineteen occupation dummies.
Unemployment rates are measured by sex by region (4). Source: Eurostat, *Regions—Statistical Yearbook*, (various years).
The dependent variable is the log of monthly earnings.
t-statistics are in parentheses.

ployment rate without any regional fixed effects. Both the reciprocal and the level of joblessness are significantly different from zero, but the specification explains a smaller proportion of the variance than the log in column 1 of table 7.11. The square of unemployment is insignificant.

In summary, once again a negatively-sloped wage curve is found. The unemployment elasticity of pay for Italy is estimated at −0.12.

7.5   The Labor Market in the Netherlands

This relatively small country, on the western edge of Europe, exports and imports over 50 percent of GDP, making the Netherlands one of the most trade-dependent economies in Europe. Per-capita GNP during the period 1970 to 1976 grew at 2.6%, a higher rate than Germany (2.0%), Great Britain (1.7%), or the United States (1.7%). Toward the end of the 1970s the economy experienced a period of slow growth. In the early 1980s the world recession produced two consecutive years of negative GDP growth. By 1984 the economy had picked up again, recording GDP growth of 3.2%. Further measures to tackle domestic economic imbalances contributed to another decline of growth, which reached only 1.5% in 1987.

Table 7.12
Italian wage curve: 1986 and 1989 monthly earnings

	(1)	(2)	(3)
$1/U$	.8453		
	(2.99)		
U		−.0091	−.0247
		(2.96)	(2.45)
U^2			.0004
			(1.62)
$\bar{R}^2$	.5223	.5223	.5230
DF	1,002	1,002	1,001
F	30.93	30.92	30.24

Source: International Social Survey Program.
Notes: In all cases there are 1,041 observations. The following control variables were also included: (1) two marital status dummies, (2) two schooling dummies, (3) two year dummies, (4) gender dummy, (5) five age dummies, (6) part-time dummy, and (7) nineteen occupation dummies.
Unemployment rates are measured by sex by region (4). Source: Eurostat, *Statistical Yearbook—Regions*, (various years).
The dependent variable is the log of monthly earnings.
t-statistics are in parentheses.

A recovery has occurred since that time (OECD, 1990c): in 1989 real GDP grew by over 4%.

Public spending as a proportion of GDP is relatively high in the Netherlands. The ratio rose steadily through much of the post-war period to 62.2% in 1983, the highest figure after Sweden in the OECD (1989a). Subsequently, government policy has been directed at reducing the share of expenditure and the deficit in GDP. Government consumption spending has fallen from 17.9% of GDP in 1980 to 15.1% in 1989. Three-quarters of this decline is in social security spending. Net lending has fallen from 6.4% of GDP in 1983 to 5.8% in 1989.

As in many countries, Dutch labor-market performance started to worsen in the early 1970s. From 1979 to 1983 the Netherlands recorded among the sharpest rises in the unemployment rate and in the number of long-term unemployed in the OECD (1989a). These developments reflected both a decline in employment and an increase in the labor force. The response of wages to higher rates of unemployment appeared to be weak. Centralized wage negotiations were supplemented by additional wage demands in the stronger industries. Labor market regulations may have limited the flexibility of Dutch firms in hiring and firing.

Active labor market policies shifted emphasis, during the 1980s, towards the goal of improving labor-market flexibility. The budget for these policies remained broadly unchanged over the period from 1982 to 1986. However, training rose from 30% of spending to almost 60%. The end to investment subsidies and changes in social security contributions in 1988 led to a fall in the relative cost of labor. The reduction in the minimum wage relative to the average wage may have increased the employment prospects of the lower paid. These factors combined with increased part-time work and some shortening of the working week led, in the OECD's (1989a:58–64) opinion, to growth in employment.

Pay and other terms of employment are normally regulated by collective agreements at industry-level between unions and employers' associations (Crul, 1990). The negotiations are handled by the two sides independently, but the government still has powers to intervene. Between 1970 and 1986–1987, union membership in the Netherlands fell from 36.5% to 27.5% of total employees (figure 7.1). However, collective agreements still cover some 60% of the labor market. For further discussion of the Dutch system of industrial relations, see Kennedy (1980), Bratt (1986), and Industrial Democracy in Europe International Research Group (1981).

Similarly to the other countries examined in this chapter, there is a small time-series literature estimating wage change equations (see Driehuis, 1986; Graafland, 1989, 1990, 1991; Bean et al., (1986); and Dreze and Bean, 1990). A number of earlier papers have used micro data on the Netherlands to examine rates of return to human capital (Hartog, 1986, 1988, 1989; Lorenz and Wagner, 1993; Theeuwes et al., 1985; Wagner and Lorenz, 1991), public-private sector wage differentials (Hartog and Oosterbeek, 1989), and earnings inequality (Gottschalk and Joyce, 1991). None of these studies, however, estimates unemployment effects or wage curves.[16]

Table 7.13 presents the results from estimating a monthly earnings equation on a sample of 1,867 adults—separately and pooled—for the years 1988, 1989 and 1991. The unemployment rate is measured by gender at the level of the region, of which there are twelve (Groningen, Friesland, Drenthe, Overjissel, Gelderland, Utrecht, Noord-Holland, Zuid-Holland, Zeeland, Noord-Brabant, Flevoland, and Limburg) and by year, giving us seventy-two unemployment rates in all. The unemployment rates are summarized in appendix C4.

---

16. Layard et al. (1991), however, estimate time-series wage equations for virtually all OECD countries.

Table 7.13
The Netherlands wage curve: 1988, 1989 and 1991 monthly earnings

	(1) 1988	(2) 1989	(3) 1991	(4) 1988–1991	(5) 1988–1991
Log U	−.2458 (2.62)	−.3309 (3.91)	−.3575 (2.39)	−.3032 (4.84)	−.0576 (0.33)
Regional dummies					11
$\bar{R}^2$	.5184	.5474	.2138	.4634	.4678
DF	600	615	589	1,844	1,833
N	621	636	610	1,867	1,867
F	34.37	39.40	9.28	74.26	50.70

Source: International Social Survey Program.
Notes: The following control variables were also included: (1) seven age dummies, (2), (3) union membership dummy, (4) two marital status dummies, (5) one occuptation dummy for farmer, (6) gender dummy, (7) age and its square, (8) part-time dummy, (9) six qualification dummies, and (10) two year dummies.
Regional unemployment rates are measured by gender across twelve regions—Source: Eurostat, *Basic Statistics of the Community*, 26th, 27th, and 29th editions.
The dependent variable is the log of net monthly earnings.
t-statistics are in parentheses.

In columns 1 through 3 of table 7.13 the log of the unemployment rate, with no regional dummies, is incorporated for each year in turn, and in column 4 for all three years together. There is evidence of a downward-sloping wage curve. The size of the elasticity is rather large, at around −0.3. It might be thought implausibly large. Table 7.14 experiments with the level of unemployment along with ten regional dummies, but that variable has an insignificant coefficient.

Columns 2 through 4 of table 7.14 report the results of some experiments with the regional dummies. In four cases (Flevoland, Zeeland, Noord-Holland, and Geldrland) the coefficients are large—around 0.25—and insignificantly different from each other. They are then combined to form one dummy variable, alongside the remaining six dummies.[17] Now the coefficient on the log unemployment variable is significant with a coefficient of −0.17. Analogously in column 3 the level of unemployment is also significant. No support could be found for higher-order terms in unemployment (column 4).

17. Our institutional knowledge is insufficient to be able to say whether these regions would be thought of as similar in other ways.

Table 7.14
The Netherlands wage curve: 1988–1991 monthly earnings

	(1)	(2)	(3)	(4)
Log U		−.1687		
		(2.35)		
U	−.0045		−.0124	−.0304
	(0.38)		(2.31)	(0.70)
U^2				.0006
				(0.42)
Regional dummies	10	7	7	7
$\overline{R}^2$	.4678	.4687	.4687	.4684
DF	1,833	1,837	1,837	1,836
N	1,867	1,867	1,867	1,867
F	50.70	57.76	57.75	55.81

Source: International Social Survey Program.
Notes: The following control variables were also included: (1) seven age dummies, (2), (3) union membership dummy, (4) two marital status dummies, (5) one occupation dummy for farmer, (6) gender dummy, (7) age and its square, (8) part-time dummy, (9) six qualification dummies, and (10) two year dummies.
Regional unemployment rates are measured by gender across twelve regions Source: Eurostat, *Basic Statistics of the Community*, 26th, 27th, and 29th editions.
The dependent variable is the log of net monthly earnings.
t-statistics are in parentheses.

In a response to Blanchflower and Oswald (1990b), Groot et al. (1992) analyze micro-data for the Netherlands. They use three waves of individual-level data, for the years 1985, 1986, and 1988, taken from the labor market surveys of the Organization of Strategic Labour Market Research (OSA). The data sets contain 2,261, 2,391, and 2,479 observations respectively. The dependent variable is net weekly pay. Estimation is done separately for each year; no fixed effects are included. The equations include a series of control variables (tax regime dummies, education, gender, marital status, public sector, age, number supervised, tenure, and experience and the squares of the last two terms). The unemployment rate is defined first at the level of the region, of which forty are identified, and second at a more highly disaggregated level. The authors distinguish forty-six homogenous occupational groups across forty regions, five age categories and two genders. This gives 18,400 unemployment rates, but the authors' data set is not as large as this, so they must have aggregated (dramatically) somehow.

Groot et al. (1992) include as regressors the level of unemployment, and its square, to test for nonlinearities in the wage curves.[18] Using the more aggregated of these two measures, the authors argue that there are significant unemployment effects for 1986, but not for 1985 or 1988. When the highly disaggregated unemployment rates are employed, however, they find a U-shaped relationship between wages and unemployment for both men and women. In the case of women this only occurs when the wage equation is estimated as a system along with a sample-selection/ participation equation. The unemployment effect minimizes at between 13% and 33% for women and between 22% and 34% for men. They also report a series of elasticities by gender in the range of between −0.05 and −0.08 for men and −0.0005 to −0.17 for women. Unfortunately the authors do not provide information on how these elasticities are calculated; the reason this is an issue is that the only specifications they present include the level of unemployment and its square. It is difficult to evaluate the argument that it is crucial to include a selection term for women. The authors do not pool years, nor control for region-specific fixed effects. There appears to be some evidence in support of a negatively sloped wage curve for the Netherlands.

7.6   The Irish Republic's Labor Market

Ireland is a small country: in 1989 it had 3.5 million inhabitants (source: Central Statistics Office). It is also a comparatively poor country by European standards. Real GDP per head is lower than in other OECD countries except Greece, Turkey, Portugal, and Spain.

GDP growth averaged 4% per annum between 1970 and 1982. From 1982 to 1986, however, real GNP in Ireland fell by over 4%. More recently, the performance of the Irish economy has improved significantly. Strong growth resumed in 1987 when GNP grew by 4.2% while exports increased by 13.3%, at constant 1980 prices. Consumer prices rose at an average rate of 16.2% per annum between 1975 and 1983, reaching a peak of 20.4% in 1981. Since 1981 the rate of increase has slowed significantly to only 3.1% in 1987 and 2.1% in 1988. The rate of inflation rose to 4.1% in 1989.

---

18. The authors do not report any other specifications for the unemployment rate. However, they state that they experimented with a variety of other specifications and the results were very close to those reported here.

Ireland's population is young by European standards. In 1986 46% of the population was estimated to be aged twenty-five or younger. Ireland has historically possessed a rate of population growth well above that of most of its European neighbors, registering at more than 20 births per thousand over the three decades from 1950 to 1980. In the 1970s Ireland experienced an influx of able-bodied adults as a result of an unusually bountiful market for employment. Currently, however, the Irish labor market sees large numbers of young workers emigrating or remaining at school, in response to limited nonagricultural employment opportunities.

For much of the 1960s and 1970s, the unemployment rate in Ireland followed a pattern similar to that found in most other Western countries. Like most of the world's economy, Ireland suffered a surge of unemployment and inflation following the first oil shock in the mid-1970s, with unemployment reaching 9% in 1976. Since the 1979 cyclical low, policies to reverse the increase have failed, and unemployment has continued to climb, reaching nearly 18% in recent years. During the 1980s an increasing proportion of these unemployed had been out of work for more than a year. Indeed, in 1985, more than 30% had been continuously unemployed for at least three years (OECD, 1988b). Unemployment has been especially high amongst the young.

The industrial relations system in Ireland is similar to that in the United Kingdom.[19] Even though it experienced a similar 1980s recession, it did not pass new laws to weaken unions (see Freeman and Pelletier, 1990). In contrast to the United Kingdom, where union density fell during the 1980s, in Ireland it continued the gradual upward trend it had followed during the whole of the postwar period. In 1980, for example, Freeman and Pelletier estimate union density in the United Kingdom at approximately 52% compared with 42% in Ireland. In 1985 the figures were 44% and 49% respectively (Freeman and Pelletier, 1990:143). There has been some previous work estimating Phillips curves for Ireland (for example, Newell and Symons, 1990; OECD, 1988b). Recent research by Reilly (1987, 1990) uses cross-section data on young people for 1982 to estimate a series of wage equations. Although these equations include regional and industry controls, they do not contain unemployment rates.

The wage equations presented in table 7.15, for the years 1988, 1989, and 1990, confirm the existence of a negatively sloped wage curve.[20]

---

19. For a discussion of the similarities between the two systems see Ross (1988).
20. There was no separate survey in 1990; the 1990 ISSP module was asked alongside the Religion module, to the same group of respondents in 1991.

Table 7.15
Irish wage curve: 1988, 1989, and 1991 monthly earnings

	(1)	(2)	(3)	(4)	(5)
Log U	−.3633	−1.4307			
	(1.92)	(2.66)			
$1/U$			26.6042		
			(2.38)		
U				−.0746	−.1867
				(1.78)	(0.47)
U^2					.0029
					(0.28)
Regional dummies	No	Yes	Yes	Yes	Yes
$\bar{R}^2$	.4058	.4326	.4326	.4326	.4322
DF	1,349	1,341	1,341	1,341	1,340
F	72.53	50.45	50.45	50.49	48.13

Source: International Social Survey Program.
Notes: In all cases there are 1,363 observations. The following control variables were also included: (1) supervisor dummy, (2) union membership dummy, (3) three marital status dummies, (4) gender dummy, (5) age and its square, (6) part-time dummy, (7) years of schooling, and (8) ten year dummies.
Regional unemployment is measured over seven regions across three years—Source: *Live Register*, p. 194.
The dependent variable is the log of net monthly earnings.
t-statistics are in parentheses.

However, the coefficients on the unemployment rate in levels (column 4 of table 7.15) and on the log of the unemployment rate (column 2 of table 7.15) are unstable and abnormally large. This is especially true when regional dummies are added. It is hard to believe these numbers. The data are suspect. Possible explanations for the unusually large coefficients include the small number of regional observations available, and the fact that the unemployment rate in the Irish Republic is high (19.1% in 1991). Moreover, the unemployment rate is high across all nine provinces; the lowest rate observed is 15.6% in the Midlands in 1988 and the highest an astounding 23.2% in the North-West and Donegal in 1991.

These estimates, because of their instability (possibly because of the small variation over time in unemployment), are perhaps best treated with suspicion. They are included here for reasons of completeness.

7.7   The Labor Market in Switzerland

Switzerland is slightly larger than Ireland and Norway, which are the other two small countries studied in this chapter. The country has three official languages: German, French, and Italian. The country is highly decentralized, with 26 cantons and more than 3,000 local authorities that have a high degree of independence. Through frequent referenda, individual citizens can participate in decisions on many issues.

Switzerland has one of the highest levels of per capita income of any country in the world: at current prices and current exchange rates GDP per capita in 1987 was $25,848, compared with $18,338 in the United States, $18,280 in West Germany, $15,470 in Austria, $13,224 in Italy, $14,530 in the Netherlands, and $11,765 in the United Kingdom (OECD, 1990d). The country's prosperity is derived principally from technological expertise in manufacturing and a highly developed service sector, particularly tourism, banking, and insurance.

Switzerland is economically strong; both the current external account and the general government financial balance are in surplus. However, average annual growth rates of GDP in Switzerland are unremarkable—2.5% from 1977 to 1980, 0.3% from 1981 to 1983, and 2.7% from 1984 to 1989. The rate of inflation is low but not especially so: over the period 1979–1988 prices in Switzerland rose an average of 3.6% per annum.[21] What is unusual is the performance of the labor market. Over the period from 1979 to 1988, when most countries experienced severe unemployment (see table 7.4), the annual unemployment rate in Switzerland was never higher than 1%, and averaged 0.5% (though Layard et al., 1991, argue that the true figure is three times this). There was little regional variation in unemployment. Because the demand for labor could not be met fully by domestic supply the Swiss looked elsewhere for labor and permitted a large influx of foreign workers.[22] By 1989, 23.3% of the economically active population and 41.1% of the unemployed were foreigners.[23] The OECD estimate the NAIRU for Switzerland at 0.7% (OECD 1990d:128).

A low degree of union membership has been the tradition in Switzerland. As can be seen from table 7.3, union density was 30% in 1991. The

---

21. The price rise is measured as the change in the GDP price deflator (OECD 1990d:128).

22. For a discussion of the Swiss experience with foreign workers, see Clark (1983).

23. Weck-Hanneman and Frey (1985) argue that few of these foreign workers work in the shadow economy. Compared with other countries they estimate that the shadow economy in Switzerland is small.

negotiating system is highly decentralized.[24] Collective agreements are reached at a union or company level where the practical negotiating work takes place. The period of an agreement normally varies between two and five years. It normally covers general terms of employment and procedural issues such as the handling of disputes. Employees who do not belong to a union are not automatically covered by a collective agreement. Pay is often agreed individually between employer and employee. The average length of the working week is the longest in the Western world with an average of over forty-three hours.

A number of earlier papers have estimated wage equations for Switzerland using time-series data (see, for example, Grubb et al., 1983, Grubb et al., 1984; Bean et al., 1986; and Newell and Symons, 1985). Grubb et al. (1983) claim that Switzerland has a very high degree of wage flexibility (measured by the coefficient on the unemployment rate in a wage change equation). Indeed, it is second only to Japan in the OECD in the extent of this flexibility. Apart from the earlier papers Blanchflower and Oswald (1989b) and Blanchflower and Freeman (1992), there do not seem to be any published microeconometric wage studies on Switzerland.

Switzerland is not currently a member of ISSP, but a team at the Soziologisches Institut der Universität Zurich has replicated the 1987 module and kindly provided us with the data.[25] We are thus able to estimate a series of earnings equations for Switzerland for one year.[26] There are 645 observations. In an earlier paper (Blanchflower and Oswald, 1989b) we also used these data to estimate an earnings equation, but a limited number of control variables were included to permit comparisons to be drawn with other ISSP countries.[27] Moreover, in that paper we did not include an unemployment rate. Table 7.16 includes thirty-nine independent variables—personal controls, occupation and industry dummies, in addition to various specifications of the regional unemployment rate.

In column 1 of table 7.16 the level of unemployment is significantly negative; so too is the log form in column 2. Both the log and its cube are significant in the preferred specification in column 3. When the level and its

---

24. This section draws heavily on Bratt (1986).

25. Blau and Kahn (1994) also use these data to estimate gender earnings gaps.

26. In an earlier paper (Blanchflower and Oswald, 1989b) we reported on the details of this survey. We found an unemployment rate of 0.9%, a union membership rate of 36% and a self-employment rate of 23%.

27. The controls included were age and its square, gender, union member, marital status, part-time, and years of schooling. Earnings followed a quadratic in age ($w = .0465{*}age -$ $.0005{*}age2$) The rate of return to a year of schooling was 1.05%. No significant union wage effect was found.

Table 7.16
Swiss wage curve: 1987 monthly earnings

	(1)	(2)	(3)	(4)
U	−.1608			
	(4.35)			
Log U		−.1184	−.2100	
		(3.62)	(4.44)	
Log U^3			.0554	
			(2.67)	
$1/U$				.0317
				(1.96)
Constant	5.5210	5.3236	5.3553	5.3054
	(26.75)	(25.91)	(26.15)	(25.26)
$\bar{R}^2$	.5452	.5409	.5455	.5339
DF	605	605	604	605
F	20.33	19.99	19.88	19.47

Source: International Social Survey Program.
Notes: In all cases there are 645 observations. The following control variables were also included: (1) supervising dummy, (2) union membership dummy, (3) three marital status dummies, (4) seven occupation dummies, (5) gender dummy, (6) age and its square, (7) part-time dummy, (8) seven qualification dummies, (9) public sector dummy, (10) self-employment dummy, and (11) fourteen industry dummies.
Regional unemployment is measured over twenty-five regions.
The dependent variable is the log of net monthly earnings.
t-statistics are in parentheses.

square were included together, neither was significantly different from zero (results not reported). Finally, the reciprocal of the unemployment rate is significantly positive and significant in column 4, but is dominated statistically by the specification in column 3 of the table. Over the range of unemployment rates we have available to us, there is evidence of a negatively sloped wage curve for Switzerland.

7.8 Norway's Labor Market

Norway is an oil-producing country with a population of 4.2 million in 1990. Over the past decade GDP and employment growth have been among the greatest, and unemployment among the lowest, in the OECD. Living standards are also among the highest in the OECD, measured both by per capita income and by other indicators such as infant mortality rates and life expectancy. However (as Asbjørn Rødseth has pointed out to us), on the basis of purchasing power parity calculations of the OECD, private consumption in Norway is at a par with Spain and much below Britain.

Norway possesses substantial oil and gas reserves. Oil was first discovered in 1968 and production started in 1971. Norway became a net exporter of oil in the middle of the 1970s. The growth of the oil sector allowed Norway to maintain high spending and employment levels in the decade to the mid-1980s. From 1980 to 1986 the value of oil and gas exports was equal to or greater than that of all other merchandise exports combined. The oil price collapse of 1985–1986 produced a dramatic fall in Norway's real disposable income of approximately 10% of GDP; this was a much bigger supply shock than in any other OECD country (see OECD, 1989b). After the 1986 price falls, oil and gas fell to half the size of manufacturing industry in terms of contribution to GDP, but recovered to two thirds of that size by 1989. The 1990 surge in oil prices has resulted in a further strengthening of the country's external position.

The average unemployment rate in the period 1960 to 1986 in Norway was only 1.6% compared with 6% in the United States, 1.8% in Japan, 2.9% in Germany, 2.2% in Austria, and 5% in the OECD as a whole (OECD, 1989b). This record of low and broadly stable unemployment was achieved in spite of a strong growth in both the labor force and in the labor force participation rate. Although unemployment has risen in recent years, it is still relatively low by international standards. Perhaps partly as a consequence of this policy of full employment, price inflation has been high since the 1970s. Inflation peaked in 1981 when consumer price rises reached 13.6%. The rate of inflation has declined steadily since 1987 from 8.7% to 4.1% in 1990.

Another notable feature of the Norwegian labor market has been the rapid growth in part-time employment, which as a proportion of total employment is the highest in the OECD. The number of part-time jobs increased by approximately 50% between 1975 and 1986. By 1989 part-timers made up 36% of total employment and nearly 49% of female employment.

A characteristic of the Norwegian labor market is the high degree of centralization in collective bargaining. In 1985 approximately 65% of employees (Visser, 1989) were union members.[28] Unions are affiliated to one of three major union confederations: Landsorganizasjonen i Norge (LO), Yrkesorganizasjonens Sentralforbund (YS), and Akademikernes Fellesrogaisasjon (AF). On the employers' side there are two major federations, with

---

28. Rødseth and Holden (1990) estimate that 59 percent of employees were union members in 1985. In a private communication dated 24 October 1991, Asbjørn Rødseth pointed out to us that this discrepancy probably arises because Visser overlooked the fact that many union members are pensioners.

the major one operating in the private sector—Norsk Arbeidsgiverforening (NAF)—with members mainly in manufacturing and a coverage of 22% of all employees. Local authorities also have their own negotiating organization.

Bargaining occurs centrally between employers associations and union confederations. LO/NAF agreements play a role as pace-setters in bargaining rounds. Once a LO/NAF settlement has been struck, bargaining starts in the public sector, with outcomes influenced by LO/NAF agreements. Settlements reached between LO and NAF are also extended to all nonunion workers in establishments affiliated to NAF. Moreover, this agreement is frequently taken over by nonmember firms whether or not their workers are unionized. Wage contracts are sometimes one year, but more frequently for two years. In the latter case there are always negotiations about wage increases in the mid-year. Strikes and lockouts cannot be used during these mid-year negotiations (Hersoug et al., 1986). As in Austria, trade unions have pursued solidaristic wage policies, which attempt to even out disparities in personal income. The inclusion of wage compression clauses in central wage agreements has had the effect of reducing income inequality, particularly between men and women. This effect is most pronounced in the public sector.

Despite the centralized bargaining system, a considerable part of wage increases tend to be determined outside bargaining between unions and employer federations. Local bargaining has been introduced widely since the 1960s, making all central wage agreements minimum contracts. Wage drift varies significantly between industries. Since the 1960s wage drift in manufacturing has on average accounted for more than half of total annual wage increases and over the last decade it has contributed more than three-quarters (OECD, 1989b). Manning rules and other regulations affecting employment are not covered by central bargaining but are frequently included in local bargaining agreements. Wage drift is largely absent in the public sector.

Norwegian governments have operated various types of incomes policy. On occasions they have offered increased public spending and tax benefits in exchange for moderate wage settlements between LO and NAF. For example, in 1988 the government offered greater availability of housing loans, lowering of some mortgage interest rates, an extension of maternity leave and early retirement provisions in return for an agreement limiting total wage increases to less than 5%. Perhaps more importantly, the government by law extended the contract between LO and NAF to all other sectors, thus removing LO's fears that by showing moderation they would lose out to other unions. On other occasions, governments have introduced legislation with the purpose of limiting the extent of wage increases and industrial unrest.

A small time-series literature estimates real wage equations for Norway. This includes Kjær and Rødseth (1987), Hoel and Nymoen (1988), Rødseth and Holden (1990), Alogoskoufis and Manning (1988), Bean et al. (1986), and Newell and Symons (1987). The last three papers argue that a change in aggregate unemployment has a larger effect on the real wage in Norway than in most other OECD countries. For example, Bean et al. (1986:18) say the results "support the idea that the functioning of the labour market is related to the degree of corporatism. Wages in the more corporatist economies display a greater response to unemployment in both the long and (especially) the short run.... Finally, adjustment not only of wages but especially of the labour market as a whole, is faster in corporatist environments."

Most of the studies conducted by Norwegians (e.g. Rødseth and Holden, 1990; Hersoug et al., 1986; Hoel and Nymoen, 1988) often find a small and frequently statistically insignificant effect.[29] We owe this point to Rødseth. Many of the international studies use data that stopped in the early or mid 1980s. In these samples there were two extreme observations, the wage explosion in 1974–1975 and the wage freeze of 1978–1979. The first followed what was then relatively high unemployment. Results appear to depend very much on whether one excludes the wage freeze observation and on how price expectations in 1974–1975 are modeled. Indeed, Kjær and Rødseth (1987:3) argue that it is difficult to model wage formation in Norway using time-series data because small changes in the way variables are measured produces disturbingly different results. They warn that "results should serve as a warning against drawing too strong policy conclusions from other estimated wage equations or from casual evidence on wage formation."

Table 7.17 gives earnings equations using micro-data at the level of the individual for the years 1989 to 1991. The dependent variable in the regressions is the log of yearly earnings before taxes. The earnings variable is reported in bands. In 1989 there are twelve, but only seven in 1990 and

---

29. In his introduction to a volume on wage formation in the Nordic countries where the paper by Rødseth and Holden was published, Lars Calmfors (1990:45) argues that "our most controversial result is probably the difficulty of finding a wage-unemployment relation for Norway."

Table 7.17
Norwegian wage curve: 1989–1991

	(1) 1989	(2) 1990	(3) 1991	(4) 1989–91	(5) 1989–91	(6) 1989–91
Log U	−.1321	−.0406	−.0722	−.1003	−.0134	−.0833
	(2.74)	(0.59)	(0.68)	(2.64)	(0.12)	(2.19)
Regional dummies					18	4
Year dummies				2	2	2
$\bar{R}^2$	.3915	.3303	.3016	.3526	.3688	.3688
F	46.63	33.66	28.01	95.34	47.00	80.23
DF	909	862	800	2,583	2,565	2,579
N	923	862	813	2,599	2,599	2,599

Source: International Social Survey Program.
Notes: The following control variables were also included: (1) two marital status dummies, (2) eight age dummies, (3) gender dummy, and (4) three qualification dummies.
Regional unemployment is measured over twenty regions across three years. In column 6 the regional dummies are for Hedmark, Oslo, Nord Trondelag, and Vest-Agder.
The dependent variable is the log of gross yearly income.
t-statistics are in parentheses.

1991. Bands are treated by using mid-points. In 1989 the top category was 401,000 Norwegian Kroner and more. This was given an imputed value of 450,000 (seventeen cases). In 1990 and 1991 the top open-end was 300,000 NK and over, to which we imputed values of 400,000 (sixty-three cases and seventy cases respectively). The unemployment rate is measured across 20 regions.[30] The first three columns of table 7.17 report the coefficient on the log of the unemployment rate for each year in turn. We experimented with other formulations for the unemployment rate without success. For 1989 the coefficient is − 0.13 and significantly different from zero; for the other two years the coefficients are around − 0.05 but are not significant. In column 4 we pool the years together and once again find an elasticity of − 0.1. In column 5 we add eighteen regional dummies and this drives the unemployment term to insignificance. Only four of these regional dummies were found to be significantly different from the remaining fifteen dummies. In column 6 we thus include just these four dummies (Hedmark, Oslo, Nord Trondelag, and Vest-Agder), and the coefficient on the unemployment rate is significant again with a coefficient of − 0.08.

The estimated unemployment elasticity of pay for Norway is, according to the tables, consistent with estimates for the other countries examined in the book. These micro-based estimates are out of line with some findings from time-series analysis.

7.9 Conclusions

Even if it were true, as has been asserted in chapters 4 to 6, that Britain and the United States have the same kind of wage curve, there would be no particular reason to believe that that pattern would be found elsewhere. The labor markets across the nations of Europe, for example, differ dramatically among themselves and in comparison to Anglo-American labor mar-

---

30. We are grateful to Steiner Holden and Hege Torp for their help in obtaining these data. The source of data is the register of the unemployed run by the Directorate of Labor. This is the only source from which it is possible to calculate "regional" unemployment rates. Hege Torp pointed out to us, in private communication dated 30 August 1993, that there are discrepancies between this rate and the ones obtained from the monthly Labor Force Surveys. Traditionally the latter source gives higher unemployment numbers, in part because, Torp argues, people on labor market program report themselves as unemployed and in part because students and housewives do not register. The rates from the two sources over the last few years are reported next in percent.

	1985	1986	1987	1988	1989	1990	1991	1992
Survey	2.6	2.0	2.1	3.2	4.9	5.2	5.5	5.9
Register	2.5	1.8	1.5	2.3	3.8	4.3	4.7	5.4

kets. A new tradition of research, recently granted orthodoxy,[31] says that the different institutional structures across Europe play a key role in explaining their labor markets' different performances. Experience dictates, moreover, that in this subject first-glance regularities disintegrate under closer inspection. That is why, the usual argument goes, economics books do not look like mechanics books.

Despite such cogent skepticism, it seems that the seven nations studied in this chapter all have a wage curve. Still less predictably, the elasticity in each case is reasonably close to -0.1. To show this, the chapter applies the same methods as before. It draws upon computerized information about randomly sampled individuals, in this instance from the International Social Survey Programme. Although still not well-known to most social scientists, this source has the advantage that, by design, it asks the same questions of samples of people from different countries. The ISSP data-files offer details about the pay and characteristics of 4,629 Germans, 1,041 Italians, 1,587 Austrians, 1,867 Netherlanders, 1,349 Irish, 605 Swiss, and 2,599 Norwegians. These are small numbers when compared to the samples used in earlier chapters for the United States and Great Britain, but not by the usual standards of economic research. Microeconometric earnings equations are estimated in which, together with conventional personal control variables, a local unemployment rate is entered as an independent variable. No instrumenting is done in this chapter. Not every t-statistic on unemployment turns out to be well defined. Some drop below unity. It could be argued, on top of this, that even these t-statistics may be biased upwards by common group errors. In addition, adding dummies for regional fixed effects in some instances generates unconvincing results (though Germany, for example, is strong). What is noticeable, however, is the common message from the different data sets, the rough similarity in estimated logarithmic coefficients, and the continued lack of empirical support for the first and most basic tenet of Harris-Todaro reasoning. Of the fifty-two estimated equations reported in the chapter, every one finds a negative coefficient on the local rate of unemployment.

If the previous chapters take us two large steps, this one takes us seven small ones. It discovers wage curves in the data of Germany, Italy, Austria, Holland, Switzerland, Ireland, and Norway.

---

31. A review, with many interesting criticisms, is provided by Calmfors (1993). Like this book, Calmfors has some doubts about the orthodox view that unemployment elasticities are deeply affected by the degree of corporatism.

8

Canada, South Korea, Australia, and Other Nations

Occasionally experience casts up evidence that is about as direct, dramatic, and convincing as any that could be provided by controlled experiments.

Milton Friedman (1953)

As perhaps befits a penultimate chapter, this part of the book travels far afield. It begins with an analysis of data on 80,000 Canadians, 8,000 Australians, and 1.4 million South Koreans. For Canada, some of the econometric findings discussed here are due to others, including Louis Christofides, David Card, and Thomas Lemieux, but the chapter also gives new unpublished results. The chapter ends with a description of some other researchers' results based on data from Côte d'Ivoire, India, Japan, and Sweden. The object in this chapter is to assess the remaining evidence about the nature of the wage curve across the globe.

8.1   Canada, Australia, and Korea

Canada

A number of earlier studies have used micro data to estimate earnings equations for Canada. This work has tended to concentrate on measuring gender differentials (Gunderson, 1979; Miller, 1987), union-nonunion wage differentials (Simpson, 1985; Robinson and Tomes, 1984; Robinson, 1989; Grant et al., 1987; Swidinsky and Kupferschmidt, 1991), rates of return to human capital (Dooley, 1985; Bar-Or et al., 1992), public-private sector differentials (Shapiro and Stelcner, 1989), earnings inequality (Blackburn and Bloom, 1991b; Freeman and Needels, 1993; DiNardo and Lemieux, 1993; Lemieux, 1993; Burbidge et al., 1993), and the earnings of minorities (Bloom and Grenier, 1991; Christofides and Swidinsky, 1994). Despite this large body of literature, there appears to have been little previous work estimating earnings equations from micro-data for Canada in which a disaggregated unemployment rate is a regressor. An exception, discussed in chapter 2, is Card (1990a, 1990b), who finds a statistically significant negative effect of provincial unemployment upon the real wage from a sample of contracts written between 1966 and 1982.

This section reports a series of estimates of wage curves for Canada. These are obtained from two main sources. The first is a sample of union labor contracts for the years 1978 to 1984, examined by Christofides and Oswald (1992). The second results are from a number of micro-data files at the level of the individual for the whole Canadian economy. They cover the years 1973 to 1987.

Christofides and Oswald (1992) use data made available by Labour Canada[1] on labor contracts reached between 420 establishments and 68 unions across a variety of Canadian industries.[2] These contracts involve 500 or more employees and are for the private noncontrolled sector between 1978Q1 and 1984Q4.[3] The data tape contains information on 1,015 contracts: usable responses are available on only 595 contracts. The authors' main results are reported in table 8.1. The dependent variable is the change in the log of real wages.[4] Included as explanatory variables are a number of features of the contract, including the real wage rate at the end of the previous contract, the duration of the contract, the expected inflation rate in the contract, and the CPI. A number of variables are included that were appended to the data file from outside sources including various measures of industry level profits, product prices, the province-industry specific real outside wage rate, as well as the national and regional unemployment rates.

Column 1 of table 8.1 includes a set of year dummies. These pick up all aggregate influences on Canadian real wages, such as the real productivity of the economy, the influence of wage-controls, and the state of the

1. Christofides et al. (1980), Christofides and Wilton (1985), and Card (1990a, 1990b) also analyze data drawn from this source.
2. These include Mining, Logging, and several aspects of Manufacturing, Trade, and Services. Data on the construction industry are not available prior to 1983 and are not included in this sample.
3. During 1982Q3 to 1983Q4, a number of federal and provincial programs attempted to regulate pay in the public and para-public (i.e., Education, Health, Federal and Provincial Administration, and parts of Transportation, Communications, and Utilities) sectors. All agreements subject to such controls were excluded from the present sample by Labour Canada. Nevertheless, these programs may have had an impact on wage determination in the private sector, a possibility captured by the use of year-effect dummies.
4. For details of precisely how the dependent variable was constructed, see Christofides and Oswald (1992:990–991).

Table 8.1
Canadian wage curves: 1978Q1–1984Q4

	(1)	(2)	(3)	Means
Regional unemployment rate	−.036		−.027	10.112
	(4.64)		(3.12)	
National unemployment rate		−.038	.004	9.685
		(5.30)	(0.24)	
Long term unemployment/ total unemployment			−.0250	.398
			(1.26)	
Last contract wage	.524	.533	.535	9.151
	(22.10)	(21.61)	(21.26)	
$\bar{R}^2$	.209	.175	.190	
N	595	595	595	
$SSE*100$	.101	.105	.103	

Notes: Estimated by GLS: MA(1) Process. Dependent variable is $\Delta\ln$ real wage. All independent variables except the year dummies are entered as changes in their logarithms.
Controls in column 1: (a) profits/employment, (b) outside wage, (c) unemployment benefit/wage, (d) CIP, (e) year dummies, and (f) industry prices. In columns 2 and 3 the CPI and the unemployment benefit/wage ratio and the year dummies are excluded.
t-statistics are in parentheses.
Source: Christofides and Oswald (1992): Table III.

aggregate labor market. Nevertheless, there is a statistically significant role for local unemployment. When entered at the provincial level, the regional unemployment rate—in the area in which the labor contract was signed— is negative and significant in the wage equations. Because the variables are in logarithms, the unemployment elasticity of real pay can be read directly from the tables. Correcting for the effect of the lagged dependent variable, column 1 of table 8.1 suggests that the long-run elasticity of wages is approximately −0.08. This estimate of the unemployment elasticity of pay is stable across a range of specifications.

Column 2 of table 8.1 enters the national Canadian unemployment rate, in logarithmic form, as an additional regressor (there are no year dummies). It has a coefficient of approximately −0.04 and an absolute t-statistic of more than 5. The national unemployment elasticity of the real wage is therefore approximately equal to −0.08. It is interesting to note that the simultaneous inclusion of regional and national unemployment, as in column 5, drives the latter to insignificance. This is consistent with the plausible idea that labor market negotiators pay more attention to the unemployment rate exisiting within their members' area than to that in the whole Canadian economy.

Column 3 performs a simple test of the Layard and Nickell (1986, 1987) hypothesis that wage pressure depends on the amount of long-term unemployment in the economy. The authors' hypothesis can be captured by testing whether the coefficient on the ratio of long-term unemployment is positive in a wage equation that includes the level of unemployment as an additional independent variable. As explained earlier, this long-term proportion will enter positively if, for example, short-term unemployed people are more tenacious job-seekers than those who have been unemployed for a long time, or if employers discriminate against the latter group. Layard and Nickell favor specifications in which the definition of long-term unemployment is a spell of joblessness of either six months or one year. The Canadian data mean it is necessary to use the much shorter period of unemployment of fourteen weeks or more. The coefficient on the proportion of long-term unemployment is not statistically significant and has the wrong sign for the Layard-Nickell hypothesis. This could, of course, be because of the different definition of long-term unemployment.

Unlike the estimates described earlier, which are restricted to contracts in the union sector, those reported next—new results produced by us for this book—use data about individuals in the economy as a whole. The analysis is based on the Statistics Canada census family tapes which contain data collected in the Survey of Consumer Finances (Economic Families) for the years 1973, 1980, 1987 and 1988.[5] We use data on individuals aged between sixteen and seventy who report positive earnings in the year prior to interview.[6] Hence, as with the estimates in earlier chapters using the CPS in the United States, the 1973 survey, for example, provides earnings data for 1972.

The dependent variable in the regressions is the natural log of annual earnings. The following set of personal controls is included: age and its square, six schooling dummies, two marital status dummies, a gender dummy, part-time status, nine occupation dummies, and an immigrant dummy. The unemployment rate is measured at the level of the province, of which Ontario, Quebec, and British Columbia are the largest. Further details of the survey plus definitions of variables, sample means and a complete listing of the result reported in column 2 of table 8.3 are presented in the

---

5. Data from this source were also used by Dooley (1985) Bar-Or et al. (1992), and Burbidge et al. (1993), although for different years.

6. The 1973, 1978, and 1987 data are taken from the "Economic Families" files. The 1986 data are taken from the 1987 "Individuals" files and includes heads of households and non-heads. These were the only files available. Omitting the 1986 data has little effect on the results reported here.

Table 8.2
Canadian wage curves, 1972, 1979, 1986, and 1987

	1972 (1)	1979 (2)	1986 (3)	1987 (4)
Log U	−.1740 (9.83)	−.1117 (10.26)	−.1944 (12.09)	−.1796 (15.98)
Regional dummies	No	No	No	No
Year dummies	No	No	No	No
$\overline{R}^2$	.3663	.2700	.4189	.3077
F	417.45	356.95	896.68	462.20
DF	15,107	21,146	23,589	22,809
N	15,129	21,169	23,619	22,832

Source: Survey of Consumer Finances, 1973, 1980, 1987, and 1988.
Note: All equations also include the following controls for (1) age and its square, (2) six schooling dummies, (3) two marital status dummies, (4) gender dummy, (5) part-time status, (6) nine occupation dummies, and (7) immigrant dummy plus a constant. All unemployment rates and the dependent variable (annual earnings) are in natural logarithms.
t-statistics are in parentheses.

Table 8.3
Canadian wage curves with alternative specifications of the unemployment rate: 1972–1987

	(1)	(2)	(3)	(4)	(5)
Log U	−.1629 (23.65)	−.0953 (6.11)	−.0175 (0.59)		
$(\text{Log } U)^3$			−.0072 (3.11)		
U				−.0130 (7.00)	
$1/U$					.4092 (2.64)
Regional dummies	No	Yes	Yes	Yes	Yes
Year dummies	Yes	Yes	Yes	Yes	Yes
$\overline{R}^2$	.4738	.4783	.4783	.4784	.4782
F	2,980.95	2,231.81	2,168.56	2,232.48	2,168.71
DF	82,713	82,704	82,703	82,704	82,704
N	82,739	82,739	82,739	82,739	82,739

Source: Survey of Consumer Finances, 1973, 1980, 1987, and 1988.
Notes: All equations also include the following controls for (1) age and its square, (2) six schooling dummies, (3) two marital status dummies, (4) gender dummy, (5) part-time status, (6) nine occupation dummies, and (7) immigrant dummy plus a constant. All unemployment rates and the dependent variable (annual earnings) are in natural logarithms.
t-statistics are in parentheses.

appendix. Empirical results for separate years are in table 8.2. In each case there is a significant negative coefficient that varies in size from -0.19 in 1986 to -0.11 in 1978.

Table 8.3 pools the four years of data, adds three year-dummies, and experiments with various specifications of the local unemployment rate. In column 1 the log of the unemployment rate is included without any region fixed effects and has a coefficient of -0.16. The addition of nine province dummies reduces the coefficient to -0.095. Similar results are presented using the log of U and its cube (column 3), the unemployment rate as a level (column 4), and the reciprocal (column 5). As there is little to choose between these various specifications, table 8.4 uses the log of the unemployment in various exploratory disaggregated equations. In all cases the unemployment rate is the total for the region; the sample is simply restricted to individuals with that particular characteristic. As was found earlier, for the United States and the United Kingdom, the unemployment elasticity is higher in absolute terms for the young and the least schooled. It is also relatively high for those working in agriculture, in mining and quarrying, in construction, and for those workers who are single.

Thomas Lemieux of the University of Montreal kindly estimated some other wage curves to check these results, and his findings are summarized here. He uses individual-level data from two surveys harnessed by Di-Nardo and Lemieux (1993)—the 1981 Survey of Work History and the 1988 Labour Market Activity Survey. In addition, Lemieux draws upon the 1986 Labour Market Activity Survey. These surveys ask retrospective questions on earnings in the previous year. The sample sizes are around 40,000 observations. In the first stage, Lemieux estimates a log wage equation with age, education, industry, occupation, part-time, and union status, plus province dummies for men and women in each of the three years. He then runs the estimated province effects on the provincial unemployment rates for men and women separately, which is roughly equivalent to including the unemployment rates directly. This means that each province is given an equal weight. Unfortunately, unemployment rates are unavailable in Prince Edward Island in 1981, so only fifty-eight observations are available. The unemployment rate is included as a level rather than as a log, with a mean of 10.02.

Lemieux's results are reported in table 8.5. Evaluated at the mean, the estimates of the unemployment elasticity of pay are -0.17 in 1980, -0.14 in 1985 and -0.20 in 1987. When the years are pooled, without

Table 8.4
Disaggregated estimates of the unemployment elasticity of pay in Canada: 1972–1987

	Coefficient	t-statistic	N
All	−.0953	6.11	82,739
No qualifications	−.2228	4.84	12,266
University degree	−.0650	1.63	8,290
<25 years	−.1689	3.42	11,638
25–44 years	−.0620	3.17	46,247
45–64 years	−.0946	3.42	23,900
65–70 years	−.0880	0.43	954
Canadian	−.0971	5.65	70,798
Immigrant	−.0736	1.99	11,941
Managerial and administrative	−.0406	1.04	10,008
Professional	−.1019	2.64	12,038
Clerical	−.0043	0.09	9,660
Sales	.0271	0.52	7,549
Services	−.1258	2.04	9,359
Farming	−.2481	2.20	2,563
Mining & quarrying	−.1595	3.47	7,654
Product fabricating	−.1208	2.67	8,528
Construction	−.1470	3.09	6,874
Transport equipment	−.0666	1.49	8,507
Married	−.0900	5.32	59,442
Other	−.0607	1.11	7,263
Single	−.1338	3.16	16,034

Source: Survey of Consumer Finances, 1973, 1980, 1987, and 1988.
Notes: All equations also include the following controls for (1) age and its square, (2) six schooling dummies, (3) two marital status dummies, (4) gender dummy, (5) part-time status, (6) nine occupation dummies, and (7) immigrant dummy plus a constant. All unemployment rates and the dependent variable (annual earnings) are in natural logarithms.
t-statistics are in parentheses.

the fixed effects, the elasticity is −0.17. With them it is −0.10.[7] These numbers are close to the ones obtained above using the Surveys of Consumer Finances, and so seem to offer valuable corroboration.

---

7. Just before this book went to press, in a private communication dated 24 September 1993, Tom Lemieux reported to us that when he used the population in the province as weights the elasticities were −0.11 without province dummies and −0.14 with them. He also redid the analysis by directly including the unemployment rate in the micro-wage equation and obtained estimates of −0.10 and −0.12 respectively.

Table 8.5
Lemieux's wage equations for Canada: 1980–1987

	1980	1985	1987	1980–7	1980–7
U	−.0172	−.0144	−.0202	−.0171	−.0096
	(3.70)	(3.88)	(4.45)	(7.09)	(3.35)
Year dummies	No	No	No	Yes	Yes
Province dummies	No	No	No	No	Yes
$\overline{R}^2$	.4082	.4594	.5015	.4957	.9252
N	18	20	20	58	58

Calculations performed by Thomas Lemieux, University of Montreal.
Source: Survey of Work History, 1981; Labour Market Activity Survey, 1986, 1988.
t-statistics are in parentheses.

Australia

In 1991 Australia had a population of 17.4 million, 71% of whom lived in twelve cities of over 100,000 residents. Over three quarters of the population live in the three east-coast states of New South Wales, Victoria, and Queensland.

The Australian system of industrial relations is highly centralized. Trade unions in Australia appear to be strong. Unlike unions in most other developed countries they do not have to overcome employers' anti-union campaigns in order to represent workers. Union organizers have to persuade tribunals that their union should represent a group of workers. The system is characterized by local and industry-wide awards, which are negotiated by company, union, and government officials and then submitted to the federal Industrial Relations Commission (IRC) for ratification or resolution of differences.[8] These awards establish minimum wages and working conditions for specific categories of workers in each industry or enterprise. Individual companies may then negotiate supplementary "over award" wage benefits. Approximately half of awards are company-based and half industry-based. Accordingly, wage increases to one group of skilled or unskilled workers have tended to be followed by increases for others doing the same work elsewhere in the economy. In 1985 the pay of about 85% of wage earners was regulated in this way (Australian Bureau of Statistics, 1988).

---

8. This section draws heavily on U.S. Department of Labor (1992a).

There seem to be no previous studies for Australia that incorporate an unemployment rate into a micro-earnings equation. Previous work estimating earnings equations from micro data has tended to concentrate on examining (1) the effects of trade unions (Mulvey, 1992; Miller and Mulvey, 1991; Blanchflower and Oswald, 1990b); (2) rates of return to education (Vella and Gregory, 1992; Wagner and Lorenz, 1991), (3) gender differentials (Miller and Rummery, 1991; Chapman and Miller, 1986), (4) youth wages (Chapman and Tan, 1992), (5) the earnings of immigrants (Chiswick and Miller, 1992, 1993; Beggs and Chapman, 1988), and (6) earnings inequality (Gottschalk and Joyce, 1991; Davis, 1992). Pissarides (1991) finds that the rate of unemployment is weak in an aggregate real wage equation for 1966–1986, but concludes that participation captures that role.

The data used here are taken from the Income Distribution Survey of Australia for 1986. These data have been used previously by Blackburn and Bloom (1991a) and Blau and Kahn (1994). The sample consists of those whose main current activity is employment. The dependent variable is current usual weekly income from wages or salary from the main job and is expressed in natural logarithms. When missing values are omitted we have 8,429 observations. The unemployment rate is measured by state and mapped in separately by gender. In total there are only fourteen separate unemployment observations (seven states by two sexes). We only have one year of data, so are unable to control for area-specific fixed effects in the empirical analysis. Further details of the survey, plus definitions of variables, sample means, and a complete listing of the results reported in column 1 of table 8.6, are presented in the appendix.

Table 8.6 sets out the main results. There is a wage curve. Both the log of the unemployment rate and the level (columns 1 and 3) are highly significant. There is no evidence that higher-order terms should be included. The reciprocal explains a slightly greater proportion of the variance, but as the difference is so small that for ease of exposition in what follows the log formulation is adopted. In table 8.7 there are disaggregated estimates. These are of interest because in a number of cases the pattern of the elasticities is almost the reverse to that reported earlier for the United States, the United Kingdom, and Canada. In the case of Australia, the unemployment elasticity of pay is higher in absolute terms for managers and professionals, and those individuals with the most education, whether education is measured by years of schooling or by highest qualification. The elasticity is relatively low for the young, part-time workers and foreign-born individuals. These results are somewhat different from those for other nations, and it is not easy to know why.

Table 8.6
Australian wage curves: 1986

	(1)	(2)	(3)	(4)	(5)
Log U	−.1947	−.4609			
	(5.79)	(1.60)			
$(\text{Log } U)^3$		.0217			
		(0.93)			
U			−.0248	−.0742	
			(5.65)	(1.78)	
U^2				.0031	
				(1.20)	
1/U					1.4559
					(5.89)
$\bar{R}^2$	.5851	.5851	.5851	.5851	.5852
F	205.95	202.47	205.88	202.43	206.0
DF	8,370	8,369	8,370	8,369	8,370
N	8,429	8,429	8,429	8,429	8,429

Source: Income Distribution Survey, 1986.
Notes: All equations also include the following controls for (1) fourteen age dummies, (2) six schooling dummies, (3) two marital status dummies, (4) gender dummy, (5) part-time status, (6) nine occupation dummies, (7) seven country of birth dummies, (8) eleven industry dummies, and (9) self-employment dummy plus a constant. The dependent variable (current usual weekly income from wages or salary from main job) is in natural logarithms. U is regional unemployment.
t-statistics are in parentheses.

South Korea

Over the past thirty years, South Korea, a country of forty-three million people, has achieved rapid economic growth. This has been accompanied by a move from a largely rural economy to an industrial one.

In 1970, 50% of the population worked in agriculture, compared with 20% in 1990, and 25% in manufacturing (Kim and Topel, 1994). In 1992, about three-quarters of Korea's population lived in urban areas, compared with only 41% in 1970 and 57% in 1980 (see U.S. Department of Labor, 1992d). Unemployment has been low: in 1991 it was recorded at just 2.3%. By some international standards, however, wages are low, hours are long, and employment conditions are poor (Bauer and Lee, 1989). Job security is limited. Lifetime or permanent employment such as that in Japan is apparently not a significant feature of the Korean economy. Only management and skilled workers generally qualify for any sort of lifetime employ-

Table 8.7
Unemployment elasticities of pay for Australia: 1986

	Coefficient	t-statistic	$\bar{R}^2$	N
1. All	−.1947	5.79	.5851	8,429
2. Males	−.2100	5.99	.5083	4,961
3. Females	−.2003	2.78	.5340	3,468
4. Age ≤24 years	−.1385	2.00	.5739	1,969
5. Age 25–49 years	−.2146	5.20	.5707	5,275
6. ≥50 years	−.2013	1.94	.5354	1,185
7. Part-time	−.1494	1.01	.1761	1,597
8. Full-time	−.2020	7.24	.4532	6,832
9. Married or separated	−.2129	5.39	.5811	6,022
10. Single	−.1929	3.00	.5713	2,407
11. Australian born	−.2132	5.44	.5973	6,350
12. Foreign born	−.1212	1.83	.5365	2,079
13. No qualifications	−.1299	2.17	.5350	3,357
14. Completed secondary	−.2048	2.17	.6167	1,179
15. Certificate or diploma	−.1853	3.55	.5143	2,911
16. Degree or higher	−.3071	3.53	.5368	874
17. <15 years of schooling	−.2252	2.34	.5822	1,120
18. 15 or 16 years of schooling	−.1448	2.99	.5764	4,315
19. 17 or more years of schooling	−.2628	4.88	.5950	2,994
20. Manufacturing/utilities & construction	−.2292	4.35	.5195	2,079
21. Services*	−.1485	2.54	.5994	3,068
22. Public administration**	−.2174	3.60	.5887	2,926
23. Self-employed	−.4444	1.84	.2475	400
24. Employee	−.1788	5.40	.6128	8,029
25. Managers/professionals/ para/professionals	−.2749	4.55	.4590	2,239
26. Tradespersons/clerks/ salespersons/operators & drivers/laborers	−.1510	3.73	.5645	6,190

Notes: The dependent variable and the unemployment rate are in natural logarithms. All equations also include the following controls for (1) fourteen age dummies, (2) six schooling dummies, (3) two marital status dummies, (4) gender dummy, (5) part-time status, (6) nine occupation dummies, (7) seven country of birth dummies, (8) eleven industry dummies, and (9) self-employment dummy plus a constant. The dependent variable (current usual weekly income from wages or salary from main job) is in natural logarithms.
*=Wholesale & retail trade, transport, communication & financial services.
**=All includes community services & recreation, personal & other services.

ment. The majority of workers have high turnover rates of around 5% per month (Lindauer, 1984). In manufacturing, 60% of all new jobs end in the first year (Kim and Topel, 1994).

Women account for just over 40% of Korea's economically active population. Traditionally they work in labor-intensive manufacturing sectors such as textiles, apparel, footwear, and electronics. Over the last five years they have increasingly taken jobs in the service sector. However, females do not enjoy equal rights at work. Normally women quit working after marriage, or at least after the birth of the first child. The average female worker's wage is half that of the average male worker.•

Kim and Topel (1994) show that the growth of manufacturing was accompanied by a wholesale shift out of agriculture. Workers of all ages appear to have left the farms. The authors find "scant" evidence that manufacturing drew on agriculture or any other sector as a source of labor supply. Instead, "virtually all of manufacturing's growth was accomplished by hiring ever larger numbers of new entrants to the labor force, who then stay in the sector over their careers. In the manufacturing sector there was virtually no net hiring of workers over age 25. In a sort of "musical chairs" process, migrants from agriculture entered the non-manufacturing sector, replacing the young workers who were hired into manufacturing" (Kim and Topel 1994:3). Kim and Topel report that wage inequality fell during Korea's industrialization. The 90-10 log wage differential dropped from 1.683 in 1971 to 1.219 in 1989. From its peak in 1976, the college-elementary school wage differential fell by nearly fifty log points in thirteen years. The college-high school differential went down by by twenty-five log points over the period. The growth of education caused a convergence of schooling levels, which seems to have reduced inequality. The labor force's share of unskilled workers fell, which raised their relative price. Similar points are made by Kwark and Rhee (1991).

The Korean labor movement historically has been controlled by the government. The result is that union members traditionally accounted for a small proportion of total employment. Union density as a proportion of all employment was 5% in 1970, and just under 10% as a proportion of nonagricultural employment. From 1987, as a response to widespread pro-democracy protests, there has been a relaxation of government restrictions on collective bargaining. The unionization rate increased to 14% in 1989 but fell back to 12% in 1991. The number of unionized employees grew from one million in 1986 to nearly two million by 1991 (U.S. Department of Labor, 1992d).

Does Korea have a wage curve? It is only possible, in this book, to address that issue with industry-unemployment data. Korean statistics on regional joblessness could not be unearthed.

The next table estimates wage curves for South Korea using data from the Occupational Wage Surveys (OWS), which is a random sample conducted annually by the Korean Ministry of Labor. This survey offers wage, employment, and demographic information on about five million workers per year.[9] Government workers are excluded. The sampling units are firms not individuals. Firms report wage and demographic data for a random sample of their workers aged sixteen to sixty-four, but only firms with ten or more employees are included in the survey. This omits roughly one-third of all the nonagricultural workforce in a typical year. Because manufacturing firms are larger than those in other sectors, and they employ younger workers, this has the effect of giving greater weight to young workers who work in manufacturing (Kim and Topel, 1993). These data have also been used by Bauer and Lee (1989), Kim and Topel (1993), Davis (1992), and Kwark and Rhee (1991). Data are available for 1971, 1983, and 1986. Industry unemployment rates were mapped in at the one-digit level. Earnings regressions with the log of regular monthly earnings as the dependent variable are estimated. A variety of controls, such as age, gender, occupation, location, education, and job tenure are included in the regressions.

Table 8.8 sets down wage curves—the dependent variable is the log of net monthly earnings—for 1971, 1983, and 1986. There are nearly 200,000 observations in 1971 and approximately 500,000 for 1983 and 1986. In column 1 the log of the (industry) unemployment rate has a coefficient of +0.0399 for 1971. However, for 1983 it is −0.11, and −0.04 for 1986 in column 3. Columns 4 and 5 pool the three years of data together, giving more than 1.3 million observations. Without industry dummies (column 4) the unemployment elasticity of pay is estimated at −0.06 with a t-statistic of 70. Once industry fixed effects are included in column 5, it is −0.04 with a t of nearly 26.

Disaggregated estimation using the same dependent variable is in table 8.9. Only small differences by age or gender exist. As for the United States, the United Kingdom, and Canada, wages of the least-skilled and least-

---

9. These data were kindly supplied by John Bauer. Each of the tapes has around 500,000 observations (200,000 in 1971) that are randomly sampled from the original survey. We also thank Chang Jee Kim, Executive Director of the Ministry of Labor, Republic of Korea, for giving us permission to use these data and Professor Sookon Kim of Kyung Hee University, Seoul, for help in obtaining this permission.

Table 8.8
Korean wage curve: 1971, 1983, and 1986

	(1) 1971	(2) 1983	(3) 1986	(4) 1971–86	(5) 1971–86
Log U	.0399	−.1077	−.0439	−.0630	−.0403
	(8.14)	(73.11)	(41.96)	(70.35)	(25.67)
Industry dummies					8
$\bar{R}^2$	.5988	.7293	.7404	.8941	.8965
F	10,980.3	60,849.9	63,726.72	330,400.72	327,216.98
DF	191,218	587,125	580,963	1,359,358	1,359,350
N	191,245	587,152	580,990	1,359,387	1,359,387

Source: Korean Occupational Wage Surveys, 1971, 1983, and 1986.
Notes: The following control variables were also included: (1) nine occupation dummies, (2) nine region dummies, (3) three level of education dummies, (4) gender dummy, (5) age and its square, and (6) years of tenure in current job plus a constant and in columns 4 and 5, two year dummies. The unemployment rate, U, is at the one-digit industry level. Source: *ILO Yearbook of Labor Statistics*, various years. The dependent variable is log of regular monthly payments/earnings (in won). t-statistics are in parentheses.

Table 8.9
Unemployment elasticities from disaggregated Korean wage curves: 1983–1986 (with industry dummies)

	Coefficient	t-statistic	$\bar{R}^2$	N
1. All	−.0403	25.67	.8965	1,359,350
2. Males	−.0435	25.05	.8804	848,744
3. Females	−.0774	17.90	.9051	510,643
4. ≤25 yrs	−.0191	5.36	.9041	561,677
5. 26–35 yrs.	−.0593	25.90	.8782	460,479
6. 36–50 yrs.	−.0462	16.16	.8650	301,284
7. ≥51 yrs.	−.0187	1.88	.7328	35,934
8. Primary school	−.1418	24.84	.9104	203,344
9. Middle school	−.0618	15.22	.8729	469,715
10. High school	−.0281	13.47	.8449	496,035
11. College	−.0103	3.37	.8414	190,293
12. Tenure <1 year	−.1301	20.36	.8845	246,366
13. Tenure 1–5 years	−.0770	33.42	.8930	820,310
14. Tenure 6–9 years	−.0329	10.34	.8315	185,083
15. Tenure ≥10 years	−.0123	3.84	.8148	107,628
16. Professional	+.1706	6.03	.8796	26,514
17. Administrative	+.0105	1.10	.7704	32,487
18. Clerical	−.0240	9.08	.8893	270,175
19. Production workers	−.2723	53.32	.9106	396,314

Notes: In all cases the dependent variable and the industry unemployment rate are in natural logarithms. All equations also include age, age squared, nine occupation dummies, two year dummies, nine region dummies, gender dummy, years of tenure, three education dummies, and nine industry dummies plus a constant.

educated are the most flexible. The unemployment elasticity of pay of those with primary school education is −0.14 compared with a mere −0.01 for those with a college education. There are large differences in this elasticity by tenure and occupation: the shorter the length of time the worker has been employed at the firm the higher in absolute terms is the elasticity of pay. For example, for individuals who have been employed less than one year it is −0.13 compared to −0.01 for those employed for more than ten years. Analogously, the elasticity is high for production workers (−0.27) but apparently non-negative for professional and administrative workers who are subject to the lifetime employment provisions discussed earlier.

8.2   Other Investigations

It is natural to wonder if a wage curve exists also in labor markets that are very different from those found in the industrialized nations. A painstaking and original study by Hoddinott (1993) appears to be one of the first to examine this issue for a developing country.

Hoddinott takes data from the 1985, 1986, and 1987 Living Standard Survey of the Côte d'Ivoire, in western Africa. The survey is a rolling panel and, in each sweep, provides information on approximately 1,600 urban and rural households. The survey seems to provide reliable data about people's earnings, employment status, and search behavior while unemployed. Just under half of male individuals are in paid employment as employees. Because this is low by Western standards, the author argues that it is likely to be important to control for sample selection bias. The paper estimates a logit participation equation and then uses a Heckman procedure to correct an earnings equation.

Apart from the inverse Mill's ratios, the earnings function includes variables such as age, occupational type, whether the individual is related to workers in the employing enterprise, whether parents did the same kind of work, and the individual's level of education and marital status. This wage equation also incorporates a measure of the unemployment rate in the region (or "cluster"). Hoddinott notes that unemployment may be endogenous, and suggests that the use of lagged local unemployment, which ought to be closer to a pre-determined variable, should reduce the extent of any simultaneity bias. The unemployment rates for thirty-one areas are used in the initial estimation. The author's equations explain more than half of the variance in individuals' earnings, and the structure of the equations is demonstrated to be broadly similar to that found in data from developed countries.

Hoddinott begins by leaving out controls for regional fixed effects. Current unemployment enters the author's most basic wage specification with a negative coefficient and an elasticity of -0.056. This equation pools the three years of observations, with year dummies, and is for a sample of 813 male employees. The t-statistic on local unemployment is just over unity. This is consistent with the existence of a wage curve, and offers little direct proof for a Harris-Todaro locus, but, as the null of zero is not rejected, is too weak a result to allow confident conclusions either way. The author re-estimates with lagged unemployment instead of current unemployment. The point elasticity jumps to -0.13 with a t-statistic of 2.9. As the author is aware, this is uncannily similar to the numbers generated on Western data. When location dummies are excluded, the lagged-unemployment elasticity is -0.08 with a t-statistic of 2.09.

The author does a number of further tests. Re-estimation with OLS, and with different identifying assumptions in the Heckman Tobit, gives almost identical results. There is some evidence for higher-order nonlinearities. The sample is disaggregated into private-sector and public-sector employees. Separate wage curves are estimated for each subsample using OLS, a generalized Tobit, and an endogenous switching model. All three estimation methods generate the same result. The unemployment elasticity of pay is higher in a subsample of private sector employees. The sample is also disaggregated by age of worker. The unemployment elasticity of wages is significantly higher for younger workers. These conclusions are reminiscent of those described for other countries in earlier chapters.

To allow for the Moulton (1986) bias caused by group errors, the estimation is redone on mean private-sector values by region. A Hausman test rejects a fixed effects model in favor of a random effects specification. As might be expected, given the relatively small sample, the levels of significance fall. The unemployment elasticity becomes -0.08, with a t-statistic of 1.3, in a linear specification. With a quadratic form, the level is statistically significant and the square has a t-statistic of 1.5. This implies that there is slight, but not clinching, support for a U-shape. The unemployment elasticity of wages at the mean is -0.20. This is comparable to Hoddinott's pooled results for the private sector, which have an elasticity of -0.22. The substantive implications remain unchanged by these checks.

Bhalotra (1993) studies the relationship between local wages and local unemployment using data from urban India. She begins by noting the great disparity in rates of joblessness across space: the (daily status) unemployment rate varied in 1987–1988, for example, from 22% in Kerala to 5% in Uttar Pradesh. Although not her sole focus, the author estimates earnings equations using data on regions (states) from the ASI and NSS surveys of the Indian Central Statistical Office. This information provides fifty-six quinquennial data points, namely, statistics on fourteen major geographical areas over the four years of 1972–1973, 1977–1978, 1983, and 1987–1988. This is, as Bhalotra is aware, a small sample. It is not greatly smaller than some of the earlier work for other countries based upon regional cell-means, however, and the author has the advantage—denied to almost all other investigators—that there are consumer price indices by region for India so that real wages can be calculated explicitly. The wage variable is defined as annual manufacturing-sector wage earnings in the organized sector. Control variables include regional literacy rates, youth proportions, caste proportions, productivity, and political and amenity variables. The author also includes year dummies.

The real wage equations estimated by Bhalotra suggest that the area unemployment elasticity of pay in India is negative and large. In a two-stage least squares framework, to allow for the endogeneity of unemployment, the unemployment rate (entered as a level rather than a log) is negative and statistically significant. The unemployment elasticity of pay, at the mean, is estimated at -0.38 with a t-statistic of 4.8. This implies an enormous effect: a doubling of regional unemployment would reduce pay by 38%. It may be that India really has wages that are much more responsive than elsewhere. An alternative possibility is that the omission of regional dummies from the wage equation, which Bhalotra believes is justified by a Basmann test and by the fact that some of the controls are slow-moving compositional factors, is partly responsible for estimates that are out of line with those from most other nations.

The author reports that the unemployment elasticity falls dramatically when a region dummy for each area is included among the regressors. After a full set of region dummies is included, the unemployment elasticity of pay, at the mean, is -0.13 with a t of 1.6. Similar results are obtained by the author when a different measure of unemployment, "usual status" unemployment, is used as the regressor. This Indian estimate of the key elasticity is, of course, again close to the minus-point-one rule.

Wage curves have recently been estimated for Japan in an important paper by Montgomery (1994). Like Bhalotra, he has regional averages rather than micro-data, and again the focus of the paper is not entirely upon wages. Montgomery's main purpose is to ask whether Japan's labor market is really more flexible than that of the United States. His answer, backed up by the data, is surprising: if anything, Japan seems less flexible.

Montgomery estimates a regional log monthly earnings equation for Japan, and a similar manufacturing wage equation for the states of the United States. The former equation has 139 degrees of freedom and is constructed by pooling forty-six Japanese regions ("prefectures") for the years 1970, 1975, 1980, and 1985. To control for year effects, the equation is estimated with all regional variables as deviations from national means. Region dummies, regional employment change, unemployment, price indices, and unionization rates are all included. A lagged dependent wage variable is insignificant, which again seems bad news for the Phillips curve.

Local unemployment enters negatively in Montgomery's estimated Japanese pay equations, with a t-statistic in some cases above 3. He does not use a double logarithmic form for the equation, so the unemployment elasticity of pay cannot be read directly from the tables. Because the dependent variable is the logarithm of earnings, Montgomery enters the mean values of the independent unemployment variable to calculate the implied unemployment elasticity of pay for Japan. It is -0.15. In other specifications in the paper this estimate falls to slightly below -0.1 and is less well-determined. These numbers are again comparable to the estimates for other nations. Montgomery's paper, which includes U.S. results, neatly illustrates this: the state unemployment elasticity of wages is -0.11. Japan, it seems, has the same kind of wage curve as elsewhere.

Similar findings have been produced independently by Rebick (1993). He estimates similar equations using data from the Wage Census of Japan. Rebick time-differences the data to eliminate regional fixed effects, and regresses the change in log hourly average wages (including overtime) on the change in prefectural unemployment, on year dummies, and on firm size controls. There are 414 observations. Unemployment enters the equations negatively. It is strongest in the small-firm sector. Rebick concludes that the pay of large firms is less elastic.

Edin and Holmlund (1989) and Edin et al. (1993) examine whether there is evidence for the existence of a wage curve in Sweden (Holmlund and Skedinger's 1990 results, discussed in chapter 2, uncover a wage curve for the Swedish wood industry). Sweden, a so-called corporatist country, has been famous historically for its low rate of joblessness. Given the nature of its wage-setting system, and its unions' desire for nation wage parity, Sweden is not necessarily a country that might be thought likely to exhibit signs of a regional wage curve.

Edin and Holmlund (1989) is a clear and careful test. It was designed principally as a check, for the Swedish case, on claims made about the UK in a 1988 working paper version of Blanchflower and Oswald (1990a).[10] Edin and Holmlund use household (HUS) surveys in 1984 and 1986. When pooled, the total number of observations is approximately 2,500 individual workers. There are twenty-four counties in Sweden. For each of their two cross-sections, the authors enter the county unemployment rate in an otherwise conventional kind of microeconometric earnings equation. The dependent variable is the log of the hourly wage rate. The independent variables in the regression are experience and its square, years of job ten-

---

10. At a conference in 1988, our old friend Bertil Holmlund was unpersuaded, to put it in a diplomatic way, that a wage curve would be visible in the data for his country. Holmlund and colleagues' work eventually suggested that it seems to be.

ure, age, gender, a dummy for white-collar, a dummy for non-Swede, plant size, dummies for various kinds of shift-working and evening work, dummies for receiving different sorts of piece-rate pay, and industry dummy variables at the two-digit level. In 1984 a linear unemployment term is negative but not strong (a t-statistic of 1.26), but the additional inclusion of a quadratic term produces a well-defined U-shaped wage curve. The 1984 survey gives still stronger results. The unemployment rate enters negatively with a t-statistic of 2.30. There again appear to be important nonlinearities in the data. An unemployment squared term has a t-statistic of 2.38 and the level unemployment term continues to be easily significant at the 5% level. Without controls for regional fixed effects, the unemployment elasticity at the mean is -0.06.

Edin and Holmlund are then able to allow for regional fixed effects. This is also done in Edin et al. (1993), who estimate first-differenced equations with a panel from the engineering industry by pooling their two years of data and including twenty-three regional dummy variables. The authors find that, although the standard errors worsen slightly, this allowance for fixed effects has little effect. The authors conclude as follows. "We find strong evidence in favor of a Swedish wage curve. The log of the hourly wage rate is initially decreasing in regional unemployment rates. The minimum occurs at unemployment rates between 3% and 4%, less than a percentage point above the national unemployment rate. Above these rates, there is a marked tendency to an upward sloping wage curve. These results hold for both the 1984 and 1986 samples."

The later work by Edin et al. (1993) does not state the estimated unemployment elasticity, because the focus of their paper is elsewhere, but the authors report wage equations—estimated on approximately 77,000 observations over a ten year period—that contain a statistically significant and negative effect from local unemployment.[11]

8.3   Conclusions

Another tranche of empirical work has been summarized in this chapter. It is not easy to believe that the findings would have been predicted by the most prescient observer of labor market behavior. Each country, it seems, has a declining function, or wage curve, in wage and unemployment space. More striking is the apparent similarity across a diverse group of nations that are routinely thought of as quite different in their cultures and in-

---

11. As this book was going to press, papers arrived from Blomskog (1993) and Wulfsberg (1993) disputing this for Sweden and Norway, so matters are not yet settled.

stitutions. There is a wage curve in the Côte d'Ivoire that seems to have the same curvature as that in Germany. South Korea emerges as not terribly different from the United States. Sweden and Canada are apparently alike. Japan, contrary to the view that permeates most of Western economics, and the mind-sets of a generation of TV politicians, has a degree of wage responsiveness that is similar to that in Britain or Australia.

This chapter gives new estimates for Canada, Korea, and Australia. It also discusses Canadian results produced by Christofides and Oswald (1992) and by Thomas Lemieux (in table 8.5). The chapter summarizes recent work by other researchers using the data of four further nations. The key papers are Hoddinott (1993) for the Côte d'Ivoire, Bhalotra (1993) for India, Rebick (1993) and Montgomery (1993) for Japan, and Edin and Holmlund (1989) and Edin et al. (1994) for Sweden. For all these cases, there is evidence, usually of a statistically significant kind, for the existence of a downward-sloping wage curve. The responsiveness of log wages to the log of the local rate of joblessness, or unemployment elasticity of pay, is estimated at -0.08 for Canada, -0.04 for Korea, -0.19 for Australia, -0.13 for the Côte d'Ivoire, -0.36 for India, and up to -0.15 for Japan. The larger estimates here are for India and Australia, and are not strictly comparable to the others, because they omit regional dummies. Once region dummies are included for India, the unemployment elasticity is again -0.1. The Australian data set does not allow this check to be done.

It may be reasonable to think of the elasticity in these nations as approximated by the same number as found in the rest of the book. Future work, however, will have to begin to test for statistically significant differences among numbers that lie in a rough band from -0.05 to -0.20. It would probably be unwise to treat the minus-point-one rule as more than one of thumb.

9   Summary and Conclusions

This book is a study of labor markets. Random samples of individuals, from twelve nations, are used in the analysis. These samples record statistical information about three and a half million people.[1] Earlier chapters probably contain more tables and equations than a lay reader will find useful, but the book's message is a simple one. There seems to be a curve linking wages to the local rate of unemployment. It slopes down: higher joblessness in a region or industry means lower pay in that region or industry. The nature of this relationship—the wage curve—is almost identical across the countries of the world. It is also present, within nations, across different periods of time. Empirical regularity here, as so often, leads to theoretical points. There are reasons to believe that the existence of this curve throws into doubt the relevance of the textbook model of the labor market. By contrast, the curve seems to be like that predicted by a newly emerging kind of macroeconomic theory.

Earlier pages try to fuse elements from macroeconomics, labor economics, and regional economics. The reason for studying wages and unemployment is that people care about them. These variables stand at the influential but still poorly understood border between macroeconomics and microeconomics. The wage rate is the price of labor. It is a natural measure of individual prosperity, and a force shaping not only firms' choices about how many workers to hire but also people's choices about where and when to supply their labor. Both the level of pay and its dispersion stir emotions, and the structure of wages plays a role in the determination of the distribution of income. Unemployment is seen by some as still more significant —as an indicator of waste in modern economies. Psychological research

---

1. However, the largest single regression equation in the book uses 1.7 million observations.

reveals the damage that joblessness causes to feelings of self-worth; economic research points to its role in the creation of poverty; criminological research hints at further losses to society. Pay and joblessness also matter to voters. As a glance at newspapers from Ottawa to Oslo confirms, this makes these issues of particular interest to politicians. Reasonably enough, those politicians expect economists to be able to offer explanations and remedies.

The dictionary defines science as a branch of study concerned with a connected body of demonstrated truths or with observed facts systematically classified and which includes trustworthy methods for the discovery of new truth.[2] This book may or may not be science, but it tries to be systematic, and, by marshaling the facts, attempts to demonstrate a kind of truth that others can check. Moreover, its methods—the creation and use of internationally comparable micro data sets—can be harnessed by future researchers and re-fashioned to other topics. A subplot here, distinct from the book's overt message, is about how to contribute to a set of research procedures for the next century.

Some economists may look upon this methodological approach as unconvincing. They may see it as overly ambitious or as mistaken in principle. Economics textbooks, according to a common point of view, do not write down empirical discoveries. The subject is about how to think; economics is more like history than engineering; it is not about the detection of empirical regularities; there will never be a Boyle's law or a coefficient of friction, and to believe otherwise is to deny people their humanity. These views, which may have been conveyed unconsciously in some university economics courses over the last few decades, are out of step with the philosophy underlying the book. In a sense, the work reported here is an attempt to prove them wrong.

It may be useful to summarize the main conclusions from earlier chapters.

1. A wage curve exists. Employees who work in areas of high unemployment earn less, other things constant, than those who are surrounded by low unemployment.

2. A picture of this downward-sloping locus can be drawn with either regional unemployment or industry unemployment on the horizontal axis.

3. Approximately the same curve holds in data from the United States, Great Britain, the former Federal Republic of Germany, Canada, Austria,

---

2. Verbatim from the *Oxford English Dictionary*, 1973 edition, Clarendon Press.

the Netherlands, Switzerland, South Korea, Norway, Ireland, Italy, Japan, Australia, the Côte d'Ivoire, Sweden, and India.

4. The idea of a Phillips curve may be inherently wrong. Using microeconomic data, and controlling for fixed effects, the autoregression found in macroeconomic wage equations tends to disappear.

5. In the countries studied in this book, the estimated unemployment elasticity of pay is approximately -0.1. This uniformity runs counter to orthodox teaching (based on time-series analysis).[3]

6. Harris-Todaro orthodoxy, which says that regional wages are positively correlated with regional unemployment, is misleading.

7. Bargaining and efficiency wage models, because they give the correct prediction, are consistent with the pattern discovered in the data.

8. It is difficult to see how the wage curve can be compatible with the textbook competitive model of the labor market.

9. The wage curve helps to provide the missing empirical foundation for a new class of noncompetitive macroeconomic models (it is the 'missing' flat quasi-supply curve discussed by Woodford, 1992). The evidence suggests that it is not a labor supply curve.

10. Microeconomic data drawn from internationally comparable random samples provide economists with a rich resource for testing hypotheses. Ours is the first generation of economists to have this advantage.

Few monographs in economics talk of discoveries and empirical laws. The book's unusual claim stems from an analysis of survey information on individual workers, establishments, and labor contracts. Earnings equations are estimated in which conventional control variables—age, gender, education, among others—are included. A measure of the local rate of unemployment is introduced as an independent variable on the right hand side of these wage equations. In most instances, this local rate is the degree of joblessness within the geographical area where the individual employee works. In a few cases, such as the United States and South Korea, data are available for the industry rate of unemployment. Unemployment is usually entered as a logarithm in the wage equations, so that, because the dependent variable is also in logs, its coefficient can be read off as an elasticity. The unemployment elasticity of pay is the obvious name to describe this

---

3. It should be noted, however, that by using time dummies the book implicitly controls for macroeconomic forces, so it might be argued that the two ways to measure the unemployment elasticity of wages are not strictly comparable.

number. It is negative and close to one tenth. This implies that a doubling of unemployment is associated with a fall of ten percentage points in the level of pay. A representative table of unemployment elasticities derived from the book's chapters is given in table 9.1.

Britain, Canada, and the United States produce similar results. The estimates of the unemployment elasticity of pay lie in a range from -0.08 to -0.11 in almost all the specifications reported in chapters 4 to 8. For the U.S. data it is important to control for regional fixed effects, that is, to include a set of region dummies or to difference the data. Once this is done, Hall's (1970,1972) positive spatial correlation between pay and joblessness becomes strongly negative. The twelve coefficients summarized in table 9.1 are negative and in most cases well-defined. For some nations there are few years of data across which to pool, and it is then to be expected that the inclusion of regional dummies will lead to low t-statistics. Ireland is the analysis's only real outlier. Its coefficient is so unstable that the results were almost left out; they should be treated skeptically. South Korea, for which an industry wage curve alone can be estimated, has a low unemployment elasticity of -0.04. Future research, no doubt, will aim to chart divergences from the minus-point-one rule.

Some economists have estimated wage curves for other nations. In an iconoclastic paper Montgomery (1994) obtains an unemployment elasticity of pay for Japan of -0.15 or less. He finds little sign—contrary to popular preconceptions—that Japan's labor market is unusually flexible. Rebick's (1993) new Japanese results are similar. Hoddinott (1993) produces an estimate of -0.13 for the Côte d'Ivoire. This is doubly interesting, because it is one of the first estimates of the local unemployment elasticity of pay for a developing country, and because the calculated number is so like that in the industrialized West. Bhalotra (1993) finds a negative effect for India. Although the coefficient is not always well-determined, once regional dummies are included the estimated elasticity at the mean is, remarkably, again -0.1. Edin and Holmlund (1989), Holmlund and Skedinger (1990), and Edin et al. (1993) estimate a small but well-determined negative coefficient for regional unemployment in Sweden.

To economists raised on the Harris and Todaro (1970) and Hall (1970, 1972) models, the results given in this book may be a surprise. Those models predict that, by the requirement for a spatial equilibrium in which all regions provide the same expected utility, high-unemployment areas ought also to be high-wage regions. In other words, the wage locus should slope up. This hypothesis is as decisively rejected by the international microeconomic data as it is possible to imagine. That does not mean that

Table 9.1
International wage curves

Country	Dependent variable is Log of:	Data set	Coefficient of log U	t-statistic	Fixed effects	Sample size
1. United States	Annual earnings	Current Population Survey 1963–90	−.10	Up to 25	Yes	1,730,175
2. Britain	Monthly earnings	General Household Survey 1973–90	−.08	6.23	Yes	175,500
3. Canada	Gross annual earnings	Survey of Consumer Finances, 1972–87	−.09	6.1	Yes	82,739
4. S. Korea	Gross monthly earnings	Occupational Wage Surveys 1971–86	−.04*	25.7	Yes	1,359,387
5. Austria	Gross monthly earnings	ISSP, 1986 & 89	−.09	1.59	Some	1,587
6. Italy	Gross monthly earnings	ISSP, 1986–9	−.10	0.63	Yes	1,041
7. Holland	Net monthly earnings	ISSP, 1988–91	−.17	2.35	Some	1,867
8. Switzerland	Net monthly earnings	ISSP, 1987	−.12	3.6	No	645
9. Norway	Gross yearly earnings	ISSP, 1989–91	−.08	2.19	Some	2,599
10. Ireland	Net monthly earnings	ISSP 1988–91	−.36	1.92	No	1,363
11. Australia	Weekly income	IDS 1986	−.19	5.8	No	8,429
12. Germany	Gross monthly earnings	ISSP, 1986–91	−.13	1.75	Yes	4,629

Notes: Log U is defined as the logarithm of an area unemployment rate at various levels of disaggregation in different countries. Where indicated by a *, unemployment is measured at the industry level.

The dependent variable, pay, is in natural logarithms. "Fixed effects" refers to controls for regions or industries.

In all equations, personal variables (gender, race, age, schooling, etc.) are included as controls. Some countries' unemployment coefficients weaken when full regional dummies are added. Ireland's results are unstable and should be treated with caution. Some countries' unemployment coefficients weaken when full regional dummies are added. This table is meant only to be representative. More complete results are discussed in the text.

the idea of compensating differentials is wrong or irrelevant. The theoretical framework of chapter 3 shows how actual wages can be negatively correlated with actual unemployment while at the same time "permanent" unemployment, put loosely, is positively related to "permanent" wages. The mistake that the early empirical literature made was to omit controls for regional fixed effects.

Three potential criticisms of the wage curve are taken up in chapters 4, 5, and 6. First, chapter 5 checks the hypothesis that, because unemployment depends upon pay (perhaps through the functioning of a downward-sloping labor demand curve), OLS estimation of the wage curve is flawed by a lack of allowance for simultaneity bias. Attractive though such thinking is theoretically, little support for it could be found empirically. In U.S. data, instrumenting regional unemployment by weather variables, military spending, industry mix, or lagged unemployment produces estimates of the unemployment elasticity of pay that are only fractionally higher than those from OLS methods. Unemployment apparently has the characteristics of a predetermined variable. Second, chapters 4 and 6 show that, for Britain and the United States, it is necessary to correct the standard errors —for bias caused by common group effects—in estimation where the independent variable is more highly aggregated than the dependent variable. The nature of the difficulty, which is routinely ignored in empirical research, is explained in sources such as Moulton (1986). When a correction is done, the book's substantive findings remain unchanged. Third, regional consumer price data are available for only one country, but theory suggests that it is real wages that are depressed by local unemployment. Although undesirable, there are reasons to think that this problem is not too serious. First, controlling for regional prices in the British case leaves the wage curve intact. Second, nominal wages are likely to be sufficient whenever year dummies and regional dummies can be, as for most countries here, included in the regression equations. Third, the evidence for an industry wage curve is presumably immune to the criticism. Fourth, if prices depend dominantly upon wages and a constant, they can be substituted out to leave a nominal reduced-form wage equation.

Demand-and-supply models struggle to make sense of these data.[4] A textbook account of unemployment as the gap between demand and supply incorrectly predicts that wages will be positively correlated with the

---

4. As the quote at the opening of chapter 3 indicates, Robert Solow, for one, is unlikely to be surprised: "Our preoccupation with price-mediated market clearing...may be a serious error" (Solow, 1986:S33). Solow (1990) continues the theme.

level of joblessness. Some will say that a disequilibrium interpretation of unemployment is the wrong one, and that it is necessary to think in terms of equilibria. As the most famous diagram in economics has a line that slopes up and another that slopes down, a believer can twist the picture to any problem. If, however, unemployment plays the role of mismeasured labor supply in the book's estimated wage equations, then variables like participation, which are presumably less error-ridden measures of the aggregate desire to work, should out-perform unemployment in the regressions. They do not do so. The wage curve may be a labor supply curve, but this book cannot find evidence to support such an interpretation.

A few economists, particularly those convinced that it makes sense to use the same model when studying the labor market as when studying the market for strawberries, may look at the correlation reported in the book and shake their heads. These readers may see the wage curve as an inexplicable reduced-form equation—a twist of demand, a dash of supply, a statistical pattern from nowhere. Where, they are likely to ask, are the structural neoclassical model and the supply-demand specification that any satisfactory research must, surely, contain? This is a sensible reaction, and one that has probably helped the discipline of economics to advance. But in the 1990s it is dictated by habit. It carries with it the danger that the idea of the wage curve will be pushed aside because it is outside our pre-set mental pictures. First, the pattern documented in this book is not going to melt away if we close our eyes. Second, the regularity in the international data seems too uniform to be plausibly interpreted as a chance correlation, some statistical serendipity, caused by an identification problem. Third, the monograph's purpose is, among other things, to question the notion that labor market outcomes are usefully viewed as cutting-points on graphs inscribed with demand functions and supply functions. The book constructs alternative models with predictions that seem to fit the facts. It would not make sense, therefore, to glance into the monograph and ask to be shown the underlying demand-supply framework behind the data's configuration. In the models of chapter 3, the wage curve replaces the labor supply curve.

Bargaining and efficiency wage models are consistent with the observed patterns. Before getting swept away by this fact, however, one should bear in mind that the test is not a sharp one. These models predict a downward sloping locus in wage-unemployment space, and there appears to be one. There may, however, be other as yet undiscovered explanations for the pattern. Little has been said here about the noncompetitive restrictions and monitoring assumptions underlying these models. The book's aim has not been to provide definitive proof of the relevance of bargaining or efficiency wage models, and should not be interpreted as such. It is simply consistent with one prediction they make. Can any more than this be said? The statistical significance of profit-per-employee alongside unemployment in a wage equation is in the spirit of bargaining theory. Moreover, "weak" bargaining groups—the young and relatively unskilled and nonunion—might be predicted by this model to have the greatest responsiveness to unemployment. As the book's disaggregated unemployment elasticities of pay confirm, that is an almost universal characteristic of the data. For all nations except Australia, the unskilled, the nonunion, and the young seem to have relatively high unemployment elasticities of pay.

The wage curve does not seem to be an illusion caused by some kind of composition effect. It is not because people's incomes drop when they lose their jobs, nor that in a recession there is downward-bumping to junior posts, nor that hours fall in a recession, nor that low-paid workers are forced to stay in depressed areas because mobility costs are prohibitive. The result is robust to the removal from the samples of all people with an unemployment spell in the period. It is robust to a correction for the numbers of hours worked. It holds, as chapter 6 shows, for a cross-section of plant wage levels and not just for individuals' income levels.

Recent literature has begun to ask whether wage-curve equations should include independent variables for either the proportion of the jobless who are long-term unemployed or for polynomial terms in the level of unemployment. This book has not found a great deal of evidence—once regional dummies are included—for either idea. A simple logarithmic function of unemployment seems to do a reasonable job of capturing the patterns in the data. For example, the British experiments in chapter 6 do not find t-statistics approaching two on either long-term unemployment or on highly nonlinear unemployment terms. More research will be needed, however, before definite conclusions can be drawn.

Over the last few years, a small tide of new macroeconomics papers has swelled to become a movement to be taken seriously. Rowthorn (1977), David Soskice's unpublished Oxford lectures in the 1970s, Shapiro and Stiglitz (1984), Layard and Nickell (1986), Carlin and Soskice (1990), Layard et al. (1991), Lindbeck (1993), and Phelps (1990, 1992, 1993, 1994) have constructed macroeconomic models in which an aggregate wage curve, in the language of this book, not only appears but plays the principal role that marks the approach as different from convention. Hoon and Phelps (1992:889) call it a new paradigm in the economics of booms and slumps: the "hallmark of this theoretical approach is a labor market that exhibits involuntary unemployment." Lindbeck (1993) lucidly chronicles a similar framework. The crucial constituent in these analyses, which are longer on theoretical ideas than on empirical proof, is what Phelps (1992) describes as a quasi-labor supply curve or equilibrium wage locus. In Europe, perhaps because persistent unemployment has become part of the wall-paper, this way of thinking is better developed than in the United States. Layard and Nickell's (1986) paper makes an influential contribution. The authors bring data, as well as new theory, to bear on the problem. Yet it is difficult, and some might say impossible, for aggregate time-series correlations to be decisive. This book could be viewed as an attempt to establish the existence of a relationship between pay and joblessness in a manner more compelling than can be achieved—no matter how carefully executed—by time-series methods. Chapter 1's parallel with the study of data on smokers is again relevant. Richard Doll's society-shaking proof grew out of a co-movement between smoking and lung cancer that was first observed as a vague association over time but could never be proved by that observation.

Those who shape economic policy are also likely to ask what there is to learn from a wage curve. That is a legitimate question, but not one that this book can answer in a detailed way. The analysis propounded in the last eight chapters is consistent with the view that governments should see involuntary unemployment as existing in equilibrium, and that they should consider whether it is possible to alter beneficially the slope of the wage curve. The book, however, is more about how things work than about what governments should do.

This book is not a study of inflation or the Phillips curve. Economists from areas outside labor economics and macroeconomics may find this hard to fathom: the wage curve surely looks much like Phillips's (1958) locus. To recapitulate, however, the Phillips curve is a disequilibrium adjustment-process linking wage change to unemployment and is routinely estimated on macro data. The wage curve is none of these things. A. W. Phillips's curve, this book suggests, is, if anything at all, a kind of misspecified aggregate wage curve. The autoregression—indeed unit root—imposed by Phillips seems largely to disappear when micro data are used.[5] Tables such as 4.36 for the United States and 6.20 for Britain estimate the lagged dependent variable at zero. Paradoxically, the use of macroeconomic data may have done macroeconomists a disservice.

---

5. A similar tale is told by Goodfriend (1985) about lagged dependent variables in money demand equations.

A methodological message runs beneath the surface of the monograph. It is that international microeconomic data—comparable random samples from many nations—offer opportunities that were out of the reach of Marshall and Hicks. The reason for these surveys' availability is not that the current generation of economists is more diligent or far-sighted than earlier ones, nor that economists now believe that their subject needs to use facts more often and theory less often, but rather that a new breed of computer designers and government statisticians has changed the raw material with which social scientists can work.[6] This study probably only scratches the surface of what might be achieved with the test-bed of international survey data.

---

6. Morgan (1988) calculates that more than 50% of economics-journal articles use no data, whereas the figures for physics and chemistry journals are, respectively, 12% and approximately 0%. Stafford (1986), Hamermesh (1988), and Oswald (1992) discuss related issues. Morishima (1992:74), a theorist, is critical of a new generation of economists who "regard as their inferiors those who contend the need to observe the real world. This phenomenon is a palpable symptom of scientific degeneration." Leontief (1971, 1982) is even harsher. Although economics in the twentieth century may be passing through an extreme phase, most disciplines face tensions between theoretical and applied research. The way to convince theorists of the value of data is, presumably, to show them image-breaking facts.

Appendix A:
U.S. Data Files

A1 The General Social Surveys, 1972–1988

The General Social Surveys have been conducted by the National Opinion Research Center at the University of Chicago since 1972. Interviews were undertaken during February, March, and April of 1972, 1973, 1974, 1975, 1976, 1977, 1978, 1980, 1982, 1983, 1984, 1985, 1986, 1987, and 1988. There were no surveys in 1979 and 1981. There are a total of 23,356 completed interviews (1,613 in 1972, 1,504 in 1973, 1,484 in 1974, 1,409 in 1975, 1,499 in 1976, 1,530 in 1977, 1,532 in 1978, 1,468 in 1980, 1,506 in 1982, 354 in 1982 black oversample, 1,599 in 1983, 1,473 in 1984, 1,534 in 1985, 1,470 in 1986, 1,466 in 1987, 353 in 1987 black oversample, and 1,481 in 1988). The median length of the interview has been about one and a half hours. Each survey is an independently drawn sample of English-speaking persons eighteen years of age or over, living in noninstitutional arrangements within the United States. Block quota sampling was used in 1972, 1973, and 1974 surveys and for half of the 1975 and 1976 surveys. Full probability sampling was employed in half of the 1975 and 1976 surveys and the 1977, 1978, 1980, and 1982 through 1988 surveys. In this book we make use of data from 1974, because of the unavailability of earnings data in 1972 and 1973.

The initial survey, 1972, was supported by grants from the Russell Sage Foundation and the National Science Foundation (NSF). NSF has provided support for the 1973 through 1978, 1980, and 1982 through 1987 surveys. NSF continued to support the project through 1991. Supplemental funding for the years 1984 to 1991 comes from Andrew M. Greeley.

The items appearing on the surveys are one of three types: Permanent questions that occur on each survey, rotating questions that appear on two out of every three surveys (1973, 1974, and 1976, or 1973, 1975, and 1976), and a few occasional questions such as split ballot experiments that occur in a single survey. In recent years the GSS has expanded in two significant ways. First, it has added annual topical modules that explore new areas or expand existing coverage of a subject. Second, it expanded its cross-national collaboration. Bilateral collaboration with the Zentrun fuer Unfragen, Methoden and Analysen in the Federal Republic of Germany dates from 1982. In 1985 the first multinational collaboration was carried out with the United States, Britain, Germany, Italy, and Australia. The 1985 topic was the role of government and included questions on (a) civil liberties and law enforcement, (b) education and parenting, (c) economic regulation, and (d) social welfare and inequality. The 1986 topic was social support covering information of contact with family and friends and hypothetical questions about where one would turn for help when faced with various problems. The 1987 topic was social inequality dealing with social mobility, intergroup conflicts, beliefs about reasons for inequality, and perceived and preferred income differentials between occupations. We make use of these international data, known as the International Social Survey Program (ISSP), in subsequent chapters of this book.

In section A we report variable definitions along with the means and standard deviations of the variables used in our earnings equations. In section B we report an earnings equation using these data.

A)   Variable Definitions, Means and Standard Deviations

		Mean	S.D.
Dependent variable			
Earnings	Log of annual earnings over the year prior to the date of interview	9.237	1.075
Independent variables			
Union member	a (1,0) dummy if respondent a union member	.142	.349
Children	a (1,0) dummy if respondent has children	1.838	1.769
Experience	Age (years of schooling + 5)	21.334	13.994
Male	a (1,0) dummy if respondent is male	.544	.498
Redundancy expected	a (1,0) dummy if respondent expected to lose their job in the next period	.057	.232
Years of schooling	Highest year of school completed	12.947	2.937
Unemployed five years	a (1,0) dummy if respondent had been unemployed in last five years	.136	.343
Unemployed ten years	a (1,0) dummy if respondent had been unemployed in last ten years	.231	.421
Self-employed	a (1,0) dummy if respondent was self-employed	.124	.330

Married	a (1,0) dummy if respondent was married	.618	.486
Separated	a (1,0) dummy if respondent was separated	.035	.184
Divorced	a (1,0) dummy if respondent was divorced	.115	.319
Nonmanual	a (1,0) dummy if respondent was white-collar worker	.688	.463
Industry unemployment	2 digit industry log unemployment rate	1.784	.500
Regional unemployment	area log unemployment rate	1.955	.264
Black	a (1,0) dummy if respondent was black	.129	.335
Brown	a (1,0) dummy if respondent was other nonwhite	.019	.137
Part-time	a (1,0) dummy if respondent was a part-time worker	.156	.363
Supervisor	a (1,0) dummy if respondent was a supervisor	.261	.439
REG2	a (1,0) dummy if respondent lived in Middle Atlantic region	.155	.362
REG3	a (1,0) dummy if respondent lived in East North Central region	.202	.402
REG4	a (1,0) dummy if respondent lived in West North Central region	.080	.271
REG5	a (1,0) dummy if respondent lived in South Atlantic region	.181	.385
REG6	a (1,0) dummy if respondent lived in East South Central region	.064	.245
REG7	a (1,0) dummy if respondent lived in West South Central region	.085	.279
REG8	a (1,0) dummy if respondent lived in Mountain region	.051	.220
REG9	a (1,0) dummy if respondent lived in Pacific region	.126	.332
Year74	a (1,0) dummy if respondent was interviewed in 1974	.066	.248
Year75	a (1,0) dummy if respondent was interviewed in 1975	.068	.252
Year76	a (1,0) dummy if respondent was interviewed in 1976	.065	.246
Year77	a (1,0) dummy if respondent was interviewed in 1977	.066	.248
Year78	a (1,0) dummy if respondent was interviewed in 1978	.077	.267
Year80	a (1,0) dummy if respondent was interviewed in 1980	.072	.259
Year82	a (1,0) dummy if respondent was interviewed in 1982	.090	.287

Year83	a (1,0) dummy if respondent was interviewed in 1983	.080	.272
Year84	a (1,0) dummy if respondent was interviewed in 1984	.078	.268
Year85	a (1,0) dummy if respondent was interviewed in 1985	.081	.273
Year86	a (1,0) dummy if respondent was interviewed in 1986	.076	.265
Year87	a (1,0) dummy if respondent was interviewed in 1987	.100	.300
SIC1	a (1,0) dummy if respondent was employed in Agriculture, Forestry or Fishing	.028	.166
SIC2	a (1,0) dummy if respondent was employed in Mining	.013	.111
SIC3	a (1,0) dummy if respondent was employed in Construction	.057	.232
SIC4	a (1,0) dummy if respondent was employed in Lumber and Wood	.005	.069
SIC5	a (1,0) dummy if respondent was employed in Furniture	.005	.070
SIC6	a (1,0) dummy if respondent was employed in Stone, Clay and Glass	.007	.081
SIC7	a (1,0) dummy if respondent was employed in Primary Metals	.014	.116
SIC8	a (1,0) dummy if respondent was employed in Fabricated Metals	.013	.114
SIC9	a (1,0) dummy if respondent was employed in Machinery (except Electrical)	.029	.167
SIC10	a (1,0) dummy if respondent was employed in Electrical Machinery	.018	.133
SIC11	a (1,0) dummy if respondent was employed in Motor Vehicles	.014	.116
SIC12	a (1,0) dummy if respondent was employed in Aircraft and Other Transportation	.011	.103
SIC13	a (1,0) dummy if respondent was employed in Photographic	.010	.101
SIC14	a (1,0) dummy if respondent was employed in Food	.018	.134
SIC15	a (1,0) dummy if respondent was employed in Misc. Manufacturing	.008	.090
SIC16	a (1,0) dummy if respondent was employed in Textiles	.008	.086
SIC17	a (1,0) dummy if respondent was employed in Apparel	.013	.113

SIC18	a (1,0) dummy if respondent was employed in Paper	.007	.083
SIC19	a (1,0) dummy if respondent was employed in Printing	.016	.126
SIC20	a (1,0) dummy if respondent was employed in Chemicals	.018	.134
SIC21	a (1,0) dummy if respondent was employed in Petroleum	.008	.086
SIC22	a (1,0) dummy if respondent was employed in Rubber	.005	.071
SIC23	a (1,0) dummy if respondent was employed in Leather	.003	.055
SIC24	a (1,0) dummy if respondent was employed in Transport	.029	.167
SIC25	a (1,0) dummy if respondent was employed in Communications, Utilities and Sanitary	.034	.182
SIC26	a (1,0) dummy if respondent was employed in Wholesale Trade	.028	.166
SIC27	a (1,0) dummy if respondent was employed in Retail Trade	.129	.335
SIC28	a (1,0) dummy if respondent was employed in Banking	.062	.241
SIC29	a (1,0) dummy if respondent was employed in Professional Services	.221	.415
SIC30	a (1,0) dummy if respondent was employed in Business and Repair Services	.095	.294

Notes: Excluded Categories: Public Administration, New England, and 1988.
N of cases = 10,639

B) Regression Equation—GSS, 1974–1988

	Coefficient	t-statistic
(Log industry unemployment)^3	.0086	1.36
Log industry unemployment	−.1025	1.24
Log regional unemployment	−.3726	2.05
(Log regional unemployment)^3	.0308	1.93
Schooling	.0870	27.16
Experience	.0432	20.09
Experience squared	−.0006	15.93
Separated	.0530	1.22
Divorced	.1489	5.27
Other nonwhite	.0084	.15
Black	−.0674	2.89

Unemployed last ten yrs.	−.1781	7.76
Unemployed last five yrs.	−.1964	7.00
Self-employed	.0861	3.54
Redundancy expected	−.1748	5.30
Part-time	−1.0235	6.97
Children	−.0143	2.77
Union member	.1571	6.83
Supervisor	.2011	30.11
Married	.0874	4.31
Nonmanual	.0752	3.53
SIC1	.3479	4.46
SIC2	−.0005	0.00
SIC3	−.0937	0.76
SIC4	−.0676	0.57
SIC5	.1479	1.41
SIC6	.2503	3.02
SIC7	.1157	1.37
SIC8	.1828	3.03
SIC9	.1125	1.55
SIC10	.2776	3.31
SIC11	.0543	.66
SIC12	.0833	1.03
SIC13	−.0008	0.00
SIC15	−.1051	1.13
SIC16	.1359	1.40
SIC17	−.0145	.20
SIC18	.1935	2.98
SIC19	.0573	.49
SIC20	.0765	.53
SIC21	.1196	2.17
SIC22	.2266	4.69
SIC23	.0125	.20
SIC24	−.1940	3.34
SIC25	.0372	.87
SIC26	−.1359	3.69
SIC27	−.2519	4.13
SIC28	−.0746	.92
SIC29	.0201	.20
SIC30	.1535	1.88
REG2	.0166	.41
REG3	−.0246	.60
REG4	−.0830	1.99

REG5	−.1022	2.64
REG6	−.1442	3.01
REG7	−.1177	2.69
REG8	−.0969	1.99
REG9	.0007	.01
Year74	−.9428	3.84
Year75	−.8304	17.39
Year76	−.7853	17.26
Year77	−.6281	14.68
Year78	−.5477	14.45
Year80	−.3922	9.35
Year82	−.3549	6.74
Year83	−.1081	2.06
Year84	−.2080	4.82
Year85	−.1962	4.72
Year86	−.0131	.32
Year87	−.1377	3.78
Constant	8.4310	34.99
$\bar{R}^2$	.51312	
F	158.904	
N	10,615	

Note: SIC1−30 and REG1−9 defined above in section A, which reports means and standard deviations.

A2   The Current Population Surveys, 1964−1991

The Current Population Survey (CPS) is the source of the official government statistics on employment and unemployment. The CPS has been conducted monthly for over forty years. Currently, about 56,500 households are interviewed monthly, scientifically selected on the basis of area of residence to represent the nation as a whole, individual states, and other specified areas. Each household is interviewed once a month for four consecutive months in one year, and again for the corresponding time period a year later. This technique enables month-to-month and year-to-year comparisons to be obtained at a reasonable cost while minimizing the inconvenience to any one household.

Although the main purpose of the survey is to collect information on the employment situation, a secondary purpose is to collect information on the demographic status of the population, information such as age, sex, race, marital status, educational attainment, and family structure. From time to time additional questions are included on such subjects as health, education, income, and previous work experience. The statistics resulting from these questions serve to update similar information collected once every ten years through the decennial census, and are used by policymakers and legislators as indicators of the economic situation, in the United States, and for planning and evaluating many government programs.

The CPS provides current estimates of the economic status and activities of the population of the United States. Because it is not possible to develop one or two overall figures (such as the number of unemployed) that would adequately describe the whole complex of labor market phenomena, the CPS is designed to provide a large amount of detailed and supplementary data. Such data are made available to meet a variety of needs on the part of users of labor market information.

Thus, the CPS is the only source of monthly estimates of total employment (both farm and nonfarm); nonfarm self-employed persons, domestics, and unpaid helpers in nonfarm faily enterprises; wage and salary employees; and, finally, estimates of total unemployment. It provides the only available distribution of workers by the number of hours worked (as distinguished from aggregate or average hours for an industry), permitting separate analyses of part-time workers, workers on overtime, and so on. The survey is also the only comprehensive current source of information on the occupation of workers and the industries in which they work. Information is available from the survey not only for persons currently in the labor force but also for those who are outside the labor force. The characteristics of such persons, whether married women with or without young children, disabled persons, students, older retired workers, and so on, can be determined. Information on their current desire for work, their past work experience, and their intentions as to job seeking are also available.

The March CPS, also known as the Annual Demographic File, contains the basic monthly demographic and labor force data described earlier, plus additional data on work experience, income, noncash benefits, and migration.

In section A we report the variable definitions used in our reported regressions along with the means and standard deviations. In section B we report the complete results from one earnings equation using these variables and over 1.5 million data points for the years 1963 through 1987. In section C we report the coefficients on the various personal controls for the 1960s, 1970s, and 1980s, while in section D we do the same for the regional and industry dummies

A)   Variable Definitions, Means, and Standard Deviations

		Mean	S.D.
Dependent variable			
Pay	Log of annual earnings (over the preceeding year)	8.532	1.431
Independent variables			
Experience	Number of years of experience	18.388	15.212
Schooling	Number of years of schooling	13.284	2.935
Private sector	a (1,0) dummy if respondent worked in the private sector	.823	.382
Part-time	a (1,0) dummy if respondent worked less than 30 hours per week	.168	.374
Married	a (1,0) dummy if respondent was married	.558	.497
Divorced	a (1,0) dummy if respondent was divorced	.077	.267
Male	a (1,0) dummy if respondent was male	.551	.497
Black	a (1,0) dummy if respondent was black	.094	.292
Nonwhite	a (1,0) dummy if respondent was other nonwhite	.021	.143
Separated	a (1,0) dummy if respondent was separated	.022	.146
Widowed	a (1,0) dummy if respondent was widowed	.030	.170
Regional unempt.	Log of regional unempt. (21 areas for years 1968–1972 and in 50 states in other years)	1.756	.361
Industry unempt.	Log of 2 digit industry unemployment	1.701	.508
ST2	a (1,0) dummy if respondent lived in Connecticut	.012	.110
ST3	a (1,0) dummy if respondent lived in New York	.072	.259
ST4	a (1,0) dummy if respondent lived in New Jersey	.034	.182
ST5	a (1,0) dummy if respondent lived in Pennsylvania	.049	.215
ST6	a (1,0) dummy if respondent lived in Ohio	.046	.209
ST7	a (1,0) dummy if respondent lived in Indiana	.022	.146
ST8	a (1,0) dummy if respondent lived in Illinois	.046	.211
ST9	a (1,0) dummy if respondent lived in Michigan or Wisconsin	.056	.230
ST10	a (1,0) dummy if respondent lived in Minnesota, Missouri, Iowa, North Dakota, South Dakota, Nebraska, or Kansas	.082	.274
ST11	a (1,0) dummy if respondent lived in Delaware, Maryland, Virginia, or West Virginia	.062	.241
ST12	a (1,0) dummy if respondent lived in Washington, D.C.	.007	.084
ST13	a (1,0) dummy if respondent lived in North Carolina, South Carolina, or Georgia	.060	.237

ST14	a (1,0) dummy if respondent lived in Florida	.034	.180
ST15	a (1,0) dummy if respondent lived in Kentucky or Tennessee	.028	.164
ST16	a (1,0) dummy if respondent lived in Alabama or Mississippi	.025	.156
ST17	a (1,0) dummy if respondent lived in Arkansas, Louisiana, or Oklahoma	.039	.193
ST18	a (1,0) dummy if respondent lived in Texas	.052	.222
ST19	a (1,0) dummy if respondent lived in Montana, Arizona, Idaho, Wyoming, Colorado, New Mexico, Utah, or Nevada	.076	.265
ST20	a (1,0) dummy if respondent lived in California	.092	.289
ST21	a (1,0) dummy if respondent lived in Washington, Oregon, Alaska, or Hawaii	.048	.214
IND2	a (1,0) dummy if respondent worked in Mining	.011	.106
IND3	a (1,0) dummy if respondent worked in Construction	.054	.227
IND4	a (1,0) dummy if respondent worked in Lumber & Wood	.008	.088
IND5	a (1,0) dummy if respondent worked in Furniture	.003	.053
IND6	a (1,0) dummy if respondent worked in Stone, Clay, and Glass	.008	.087
IND7	a (1,0) dummy if respondent worked in Primary Metals	.012	.109
IND8	a (1,0) dummy if respondent worked in Fabricated Metals	.017	.129
IND10	a (1,0) dummy if respondent worked in Machinery excl. electrical	.025	.155
IND11	a (1,0) dummy if respondent worked in Electrical Machinery	.022	.147
IND12	a (1,0) dummy if respondent worked in Motor Vehicles or Other Transport	.011	.102
IND13	a (1,0) dummy if respondent worked in Aircraft	.013	.114
IND15	a (1,0) dummy if respondent worked in Photographic	.002	.039
IND17	a (1,0) dummy if respondent worked in Misc. Manufacturing, Toys and Metals N.E.S.	.006	.079
IND18	a (1,0) dummy if respondent worked in Food	.022	.147
IND19	a (1,0) dummy if respondent worked in Tobacco	.001	.026
IND20	a (1,0) dummy if respondent worked in Textiles	.011	.102
IND21	a (1,0) dummy if respondent worked in Apparel	.016	.124
IND22	a (1,0) dummy if respondent worked in Paper	.008	.092
IND23	a (1,0) dummy if respondent worked in Printing	.014	.119
IND24	a (1,0) dummy if respondent worked in Chemicals	.013	.113

IND25	a (1,0) dummy if respondent worked in Petroleum	.005	.068
IND26	a (1,0) dummy if respondent worked in Rubber	.006	.079
IND27	a (1,0) dummy if respondent worked in Leather	.003	.055
IND28	a (1,0) dummy if respondent worked in Transportation	.038	.191
IND29	a (1,0) dummy if respondent worked in Communications	.014	.119
IND30	a (1,0) dummy if respondent worked in Utilities and Sanitary	.016	.126
IND31	a (1,0) dummy if respondent worked in Wholesale Trade	.047	.212
IND32	a (1,0) dummy if respondent worked in Retail Trade	.160	.367
IND33	a (1,0) dummy if respondent worked in Banking	.023	.151
IND34	a (1,0) dummy if respondent worked in Insurance and Real Estate	.028	.166
IND35	a (1,0) dummy if respondent worked in Private Household Services	.026	.159
IND36	a (1,0) dummy if respondent worked in Business Services	.024	.154
IND37	a (1,0) dummy if respondent worked in Repair Services	.010	.099
IND38	a (1,0) dummy if respondent worked in Personal Services excl. Private	.025	.157
IND39	a (1,0) dummy if respondent worked in Entertainment	.016	.124
IND40	a (1,0) dummy if respondent worked in Hospitals	.037	.190
IND41	a (1,0) dummy if respondent worked in Health excl. Hospitals	.033	.178
IND42	a (1,0) dummy if respondent worked in Education	.081	.273
IND43	a (1,0) dummy if respondent worked in Social Services	.007	.083
IND44	a (1,0) dummy if respondent worked in Other Professional Services	.035	.183
IND45	a (1,0) dummy if respondent worked in Forestry and Fishing	.001	.026
IND46	a (1,0) dummy if respondent worked in Public Administration	.053	.225
YEAR65	a (1,0) dummy if respondent was interviewed in 1965	.017	.130
YEAR66	a (1,0) dummy if respondent was interviewed in 1966	.037	.189

YEAR67	a (1,0) dummy if respondent was interviewed in 1967	.024	.153
YEAR68	a (1,0) dummy if respondent was interviewed in 1968	.036	.185
YEAR69	a (1,0) dummy if respondent was interviewed in 1969	.041	.197
YEAR70	a (1,0) dummy if respondent was interviewed in 1970	.040	.195
YEAR71	a (1,0) dummy if respondent was interviewed in 1971	.040	.196
YEAR72	a (1,0) dummy if respondent was interviewed in 1972	.038	.192
YEAR73	a (1,0) dummy if respondent was interviewed in 1973	.038	.191
YEAR74	a (1,0) dummy if respondent was interviewed in 1974	.033	.179
YEAR75	a (1,0) dummy if respondent was interviewed in 1975	.033	.180
YEAR76	a (1,0) dummy if respondent was interviewed in 1976	.028	.165
YEAR77	a (1,0) dummy if respondent was interviewed in 1977	.046	.209
YEAR78	a (1,0) dummy if respondent was interviewed in 1978	.045	.208
YEAR79	a (1,0) dummy if respondent was interviewed in 1979	.046	.209
YEAR80	a (1,0) dummy if respondent was interviewed in 1980	.054	.227
YEAR81	a (1,0) dummy if respondent was interviewed in 1981	.054	.226
YEAR82	a (1,0) dummy if respondent was interviewed in 1982	.048	.214
YEAR83	a (1,0) dummy if respondent was interviewed in 1983	.047	.211
YEAR84	a (1,0) dummy if respondent was interviewed in 1984	.047	.212
YEAR85	a (1,0) dummy if respondent was interviewed in 1985	.048	.214
YEAR86	a (1,0) dummy if respondent was interviewed in 1986	.047	.213
YEAR87	a (1,0) dummy if respondent was interviewed in 1987	.047	.212
YEAR88	a (1,0) dummy if respondent was interviewed in 1988	.048	.213

N of Cases = 1,534,093

B) CPS Earnings Equation, 1963–1987

	Coefficient	t-statistic
Log industry unemployment	−.10931	35.19
Log regional unemployment	−.09874	24.83
Year dummies		
Year65	.0117	1.44
Year66	.0409	5.79
Year67	.0785	10.03
Year68	.0644	8.62
Year69	.1106	15.13
Year70	.1434	19.30
Year71	.2732	39.86
Year72	.3796	52.70
Year73	.2666	37.69
Year74	.5380	74.39
Year75	.6329	87.74
Year76	.6271	77.93
Year77	.7280	103.11
Year78	.7735	111.52
Year79	.8482	122.94
Year80	.9230	136.82
Year81	1.0498	153.40
Year82	1.0996	148.62
Year83	1.1332	162.06
Year84	1.2604	171.09
Year85	1.2667	180.90
Year86	1.3121	188.21
Year87	1.3393	193.10
Year88	1.3630	198.66
Industry dummies		
Mining	.8230	99.79
Construction	.6277	119.48
Lumber & wood	.5772	60.95
Furniture	.6421	43.59
Stone, clay & glass	.7367	76.79
Primary metals	.8178	99.79
Fabricated metals	.7070	99.86
Machinery excluding electrical	.7578	113.24
Electrical machinery	.7252	107.91
Motor vehicles	.8963	104.05
Aircraft	.7633	96.68

Photographic	.7969	40.12
Miscellaneous manufacturing	.6141	59.29
Food	.6181	95.22
Tobacco	.7277	24.92
Textiles	.6897	80.44
Apparel	.5275	71.83
Paper	.6880	73.30
Printing	.4914	63.00
Chemicals	.7780	95.20
Petroleum	.8432	70.65
Rubber	.6385	61.38
Leather	.4667	32.73
Transport	.7265	121.82
Communications	.8345	96.69
Utilities and sanitary	.6858	86.65
Wholesale trade	.5872	106.59
Retail trade	.3811	82.49
Banking	.6800	96.02
Insurance and real estate	.5474	81.26
Private household services	−.6205	97.16
Business services	.3489	54.32
Repair services	.4747	55.15
Personal serv./excl. priv.	.3107	48.89
Entertainment	.2321	31.12
Hospitals	.7239	120.36
Health excl. hospitals	.4556	70.98
Education	.3645	61.00
Social services	.1431	13.69
Other professional servs.	.4571	72.34
Forestry and fishing	.2311	7.84
Public administration	.5202	73.50
Regional dummies		
Connecticut	.0754	10.37
New York	.1172	30.00
New Jersey	.1126	19.30
Pennsylvania	.0065	1.48
Ohio	.0038	0.86
Indiana	−.0397	6.89
Illinois	.0997	22.74
Michigan/Wisconsin	.0283	6.58
Min/Miss/Iowa/ND/SD/Neb/Kan	−.0955	25.23
Del/Mary/Virg/W.Virg	.0087	2.26
Washington, D.C.	.2603	27.59

N & S. Carolina/Georgia	−.0797	20.27
Florida	−.0464	9.62
Kentucky/Tennessee	−.1062	20.11
Alabama/Mississippi	−.1535	27.54
Arkansas/Louisiana/Oklahoma	−.1055	22.73
Texas	−.0272	6.48
Mon/Ariz/Id/Wy/Col/NM/UT/NV	−.0819	21.43
California	.1163	31.17
Washington/Oregon/Alaska/Hawaii	.0483	10.86
Personal variables		
Married	.1948	92.03
Divorced	.0205	6.56
Widowed/widower	.1441	28.87
Separated	.0880	16.19
Other nonwhite	−.0869	16.05
Black	−.1076	39.35
Experience	.0713	400.09
Experience squared	−.0011	314.10
Part-time	−1.2065	540.85
Male	.5358	312.31
Years of schooling	.1043	335.33
Private sector	−.0109	3.48
Constant	5.9393	471.73
$\bar{R}^2$	.5757	
F	20,606.93	
N	1,534,093	

Notes: Excluded categories: New England, Agriculture, and 1964.

C) Coefficients, 1963–1987—Personal Characteristics

	1963–1987	1963–1968	1969–1978	1979–1987
Personal characteristics				
Married	.1948	.1594	.3566	.2474
Other nonwhite	−.0869	.0095*	.0372	−.1244
Black	−.1076	−.1186	−.0785	−.1306
Experience	.0713	.0813	.0645	.0592
Experience squared	−.0011	−.0012	−.0010	−.0009
Part-time	−1.2065	−.6624	−1.1594	−1.4319
Male	.5358	.7204	.6108	.4172
Years of schooling	.1043	.0901	.1015	.1100
Private sector	−.0109	−.0324	−.0230	.0034*

* Not significantly different from zero at 1% (two-tailed)

D) Coefficients, 1963–1987—Industry and Regional Dummies

	1960s	1970s	1980s	All
Industries				
Mining	1.3324	.7396	.7144	.8230
Construction	1.1518	.5669	.4829	.6277
Lumber & wood	1.0042	.5094	.4687	.5772
Furniture	1.2210	.5754	.4365	.6421
Stone, clay & glass	1.3067	.6449	.5886	.7367
Primary metals	1.3525	.7181	.7285	.8178
Fabricated metals	1.3116	.5760	.6000	.7070
Machinery excl. electrical	1.3550	.6512	.5851	.7578
Electrical machinery	1.3363	.6269	.5623	.7252
Motor vehicles	1.4692	.7958	.7574	.8963
Aircraft	1.3880	.6254	.5958	.7633
Photographic	1.3686	.6953	.6010	.7969
Miscellaneous manufacturing	1.1322	.4930	.4669	.6141
Food	1.1502	.5167	.4960	.6181
Tobacco	1.2191	.5923	.6990	.7277
Textiles	1.3040	.6057	.4952	.6897
Apparel	1.1712	.4597	.3349	.5275
Paper	1.1141	.6565	.5722	.6880
Printing	1.0451	.3935	.3106	.4914
Chemicals	1.3640	.6753	.5832	.7780
Petroleum	1.3477	.7647	.8169	.8432
Rubber	1.1687	.5466	.5178	.6385
Leather	1.1642	.4192	.2846	.4667
Transport	1.2643	.6292	.5646	.7265
Communications	1.5039	.7789	.5370	.8345
Utilities/sanitary	1.2714	.6169	.4215	.6858
Wholesale trade	1.1972	.5153	.3957	.5872
Retail trade	.8329	.3111	.2611	.3811
Banking	1.4292	.6543	.3730	.6800
Insurance/real estate	1.2495	.4600	.3011	.5474
Private household services	−.0918	−.7353	−.6751	−.6205
Business services	1.0731	.1557	.2537	.3489
Repair services	1.0512	.4008	.3195	.4747
Personal services	.7731	.1489	.2603	.3107
Entertainment	.5485	.2377	.0720	.2321
Hospitals	1.1516	.6671	.5872	.7239
Health excluding hospitals	1.0176	.4224	.1957	.4556
Education	1.0243	.3389	.0895	.3645
Social services	.7086	.1286	.1119	.1431

Other professional services	1.1532	.4012	.1961	.4571
Forestry and fishing	.7745	.2653	.1088	.2311
Public administration	1.1811	.4424	.2372	.5202
Regions				
Connecticut	.0580	.0694	.0945	.0754
New York	.1228	.1302	.1194	.1172
New Jersey	.1073	.1115	.1272	.1126
Pennsylvania	−.0273	.0024	.0625	.0065
Ohio	−.0186	.0053	.0412	.0038
Indiana	−.0447	−.0402	−.0109	−.0397
Illinois	.0689	.1216	.1283	.0997
Michigan/Wisconsin	.0226	.0284	.0625	.0283
Min/Miss/Iowa/ND/SD/Neb/Kan	−.0828	−.0810	−.0865	−.0955
Del/Mary/Virg/W.Virg	.0131	.0126	.0273	.0087
Washington, D.C.	.1972	.2927	.3118	.2603
N & S. Carolina/Georgia	−.1184	−.0754	−.0577	−.0797
Florida	−.0694	−.0575	−.0264	−.0464
Kentucky/Tennessee	−.1495	−.1025	−.0775	−.1062
Alabama/Mississippi	−.2614	−.1607	−.0760	−.1535
Arkansas/Louisiana/Oklahoma	−.0894	−.1338	−.0765	−.1055
Texas	−.0657	−.0588	.0214	−.0272
Mon/Ariz/Id/Wy/Col/NM/Ut/NV	−.0493	−.1017	−.0644	−.0819
California	.1180	.0736	.1559	.1163
Washington/Oregon/Alaska/Hawaii	−.0050	.0383	.0892	.0483

Appendix B:
British Data Files

B1   Workplace Industrial Relations Survey, 1980 (WIRS1)

The 1980 Workplace Industrial Relations Survey (henceforth WIRS1), was sponsored by the Department of Employment, the Policy Studies Institute and the Social Science Research Council. The survey is based upon a representative sample of 3,309 working establishments distributed throughout England, Scotland, and Wales. The sample was drawn from the 1977 Census of Employment: to be included in the sample an establishment had to have twenty-five or more employees (both full and part-time) at the time of the 1977 Census and at the time of the survey (April to September 1980). Hence new establishments and those whose size increased from below twenty-five to above twenty-five and those that declined below twenty-five in the years 1977 to 1980 were excluded from the sample. Omitting these establishments, a response rate of 76.3% was achieved, giving 2,040 observations in the data set. The sample includes establishments drawn from both manufacturing and nonmanufacturing, private as well as public sectors, although it does exclude agricultural and farming establishments and coalmining (see Daniel and Millward, 1983:5).

This survey was the first of a series designed to provide information about a broad range of topics within the industrial relations field. The survey incorporated interviews both with management and work representatives, with the senior manager at the establishment who deals with industrial relations or nonindustrial establishments, staff or employee relations. In certain cases (165 cases out of 2,040) the responsibility for industrial relations rests in more than one centre and in such cases a secondary management interview was also undertaken. In addition, at each establishment interviews were undertaken with worker representatives (who were nominated by management respondents) up to a maximum of three. In total 2,439 interviews with worker representatives are included in the data set. This book restricts itself to data drawn from the management questionnaire (plus that from the "Basic Workforce Data Sheet," a self-completion questionnaire received by respondents prior to the interview) because all questions used were asked of the management respondents, whereas only relatively few were asked of the worker representatives. The sample design incorporated the use of variable sampling fractions according to the number of employees at the Census Unit, which is essentially the number of employees working at the same address who are paid from the sample place. In general there was a sufficient degree of correspondence between Census Units and establishments to serve as a frame from which the sample could be drawn. In order to ensure that large establishments were numerically well represented in the sample, variable sampling fractions were used. This necessitated a weighting of the data to adjust for the inequalities of selection that were introduced because of the differential sampling of the size bands. All regressions use unweighted data.

Here we present variable definitions and means of the variable used in our earnings regressions. We then give an example of such an equation for semi-skilled manual workers.

A)   Variable Definitions, WIRS1

		Mean
Wages	log of weekly earnings—semi-skilled	4.161
	log of weekly earnings—skilled	4.541
	log of weekly earnings—clerical workers	4.190
	log of weekly earnings—middle managers	4.826
Part-time	the percentage of the labor force that work part-time ($<$ 30 hrs/week)	19.90
Female manuals	the percentage of manual workers that are female	22.00
Manual	the percentage of the labor force that are manual workers	60.4
Skilled	the percentage of those workers in the labor force who have received formal training (apprenticeship or equivalent)	17.5
Shiftworking	a (1,0) dummy if there is any shift work the establishment	.410
Performance above average	(1,0) dummy if the financial performance of the establishment compared with other firms/establishments in the same industry was assessed as being better than average	.287

Performance below average	(1, 0) dummy if the financial performance of the establishment compared with other firms/establishments in the same industry was assessed as being below average	.038
Performance not possible	(1, 0) dummy if it was not possible to compare the financial performance of the establishment with other firms/establishments in the same industry	.027
Performance about average	the financial performance of the establishment compared with other firms/establishments in the same industry was assessed as about average—excluded category	.65
Size of establishment	the number of employees at the establishment (full + part-time)	131.5
Under 3 years old	(1,0) dummy if the establishment first engaged in its main activity within the preceding 3 years	.022
3–5 years old	(1,0) dummy if the establishment first engaged in its main activity ≥ 3 and < 5 years ago	.037
5–10 years old	(1,0) dummy if the establishment first engaged in its main activity ≥ 5 and ≤ 10 years ago	.142
10–25 years old	(1,0) dummy if the establishment first engaged in its main activity ≥ 10 and < 25 years ago	.281
25 + years old	if the establishment first engaged in its main activity 25 years ago or more—excluded category	.518
Union recognition	a (1,0) dummy for the existence of manual union(s) recognised for negotiating the pay and conditions of employment of their members	.565
Pre-entry closed shop	(1,0) dummy if any manual workers at the establishment held jobs where union membership was required before starting work	.049
Post-entry closed shop	(1,0) dummy if any manual workers at the establishment held jobs where union membership was required once they had started work	.177
Unemployment	Total unemployment rate in the county, 1980 (Data supplied by the Department of Employment)	7.106
Private sector	a (1,0) dummy if the establishment is in the private sector	.724
Scotland	a (1,0) region dummy	.135
North	a (1,0) region dummy	.010
Yorks & Humberside	a (1,0) region dummy	.096
North West	a (1,0) region dummy	.109
West Midlands	a (1,0) region dummy	.081

East Midlands	a (1,0) region dummy	.071
East Anglia	a (1,0) region dummy	.055
South West	a (1,0) region dummy	.082
Greater London	a (1,0) region dummy	.133
Wales	a (1,0) region dummy	.037
Industry dummies	50 industry dummies	

B) Earnings Equation—Semi-skilled Manuals (WIRS1)

Variable	Coefficient	t-statistic
Workplace Controls		
Size of establishment * 10^4	.5894	4.214
(size of establishment) * 10^8	−.3187	2.020
Proportion skilled	−.0012	3.077
Proportion part-time	−.0045	8.282
Proportion manual	.0041	10.790
Proportion female manuals	−.0053	10.622
Shiftworking	.0363	2.220
Foreign owned	.0763	3.178
Performance above average	.0299	1.835
Performance below average	−.0093	0.290
Performance not possible	.0848	2.409
Union recognition	.0757	3.967
Pre-entry closed shop	.0860	3.393
Post-entry closed shop	−.0002	0.016
Age of plant <3 yrs.	.1004	1.630
Age of plant ≥3 & <5 yrs.	.0346	0.797
Age of plant ≥5 & <10 yrs.	.0029	0.135
Age of plant ≥10 & <25 yrs.	.0408	2.470
Log of unemployment rate	−.1091	3.144
Private sector	.1701	4.781
Regional dummies		
Scotland	.0483	1.363
North	.1161	0.869
Yorkshire & Humberside	.0731	2.215
North West	.0409	1.222
West Midlands	.0012	0.039
East Midlands	.0430	1.420
East Anglia	.0273	0.769
South West	−.0578	1.803
Greater London	.0432	1.734
Wales	.0416	0.973

Industry dummies

Food	.0684	1.320
Drink and tobacco	.1449	2.198
Chemicals	.0949	1.774
Metal manufacture	.0769	1.369
Mechanical engineering	.0101	0.220
Instrument engineering	.0310	0.420
Electrical machinery, etc.	−.0148	0.221
Other electrical engineering	.0163	0.313
Shipbuilding	−.0316	0.353
Motor vehicles and tractors	−.0097	0.166
Other vehicles	.0293	0.444
Metal goods n.e.s.	.0291	0.569
Man-made fibers, spinning, etc.	−.0663	0.673
Other textiles and leather	.0090	0.162
Clothing and footwear	−.0248	0.377
Bricks, pottery, and glass	.0887	1.392
Timber and furniture	.0196	0.311
Paper	.0642	0.983
Printing	.1145	1.851
Other manufacturing	.0726	1.223
Mining, quarrying, and construction	.0007	0.018
Gas, electricity, and water	.1999	4.369
Road transport	.1079	2.030
Rail, sea, and air transport	.0683	1.442
Wholesale distribution	.0603	1.117
Retail food	−.0010	0.018
Other retail distribution	.0126	0.240
Dealing in materials	.0975	1.427
Insurance	−.0040	0.034
Banking	−.0145	0.174
Other business services	−.0448	0.628
Education	−.0048	0.132
Other professional services	−.0720	1.064
Hotels and pubs	−.1654	3.047
Other miscellaneous services	−.0170	0.332
Other services	.0442	0.755
Medical services	.2077	5.413
(Constant)	4.1693	65.641
$\bar{R}^2$	.4965	
F	23.1688	
DF	1,439	

B2   The Workplace Industrial Relations Survey of 1984 (WIRS2)

The British Workplace Industrial Relations Survey of 1984 (WIRS2) was sponsored by the Department of Employment, the Policy Studies Institute, the Economic and Social Research Council, and the Advisory, Conciliation, and Arbitration Service. The sampling frame used was the 1981 Census of Employment. To be included in the survey an establishment had to have at least twenty-five employees (full or part-time) both in 1981 and 1984. The survey covered England, Scotland, and Wales and its industrial coverage was all manufacturing and services, both public and private sectors.

A sample of 2,019 establishments (defined as "places of employment at a single address or site") was drawn. Establishments were selected differentially across establishment size bands, with large establishments over-sampled. Hence in order to make the estimates nationally representative of the population of surviving establishments with at least twenty-five workers in 1981 and 1984, the data must be weighted to compensate for these inequalities of selection. The survey incorporated interviews with the senior manager responsible for dealing with employee relations, industrial relations, or personnel matters, plus interviews with worker representatives and, where appropriate, with works managers. This book restricts itself to data obtained from the senior manager's interview. For details of the weighting scheme, and the design and selection of the sample, see Millward and Stevens (1986: Technical Appendix).

In section A we present variable definitions and means of the variable used in our earnings regressions. We then present an example of such an equation for semi-skilled manual workers.

A)   Key to Variables in WIRS2

		Mean
Independent variables		
Performance a lot above average	A dummy variable where the manager reported that the establishment had performed a lot better than average compared with other establishments/firms in the same industry	.159
Performance a little above average	A dummy variable where the manager reported that the establishment performed a little better than average compared with other establishments/firms in the same industry.	.157
Performance a little below average	A dummy variable where the manager reported that the establishment had performed a little below average compared with other establishments/firms in the same industry.	.023

Performance a lot below average	A dummy variable where the manager reported that the establishment had performed a lot below average compared with other establishments/firms in the same industry.	.027
Performance not possible	A dummy variable where managers reported that no comparison of the performance of the establishment was possible with other establishments/firms in the same industry.	.087
Few competitors	A dummy variable where there were five or less competitors in the market for the main product or service of the organization.	.279
Empt.change 1 yr.	Percentage change in employment at the establishment, 1983–1984.	2.548
Union recognition	A dummy variable if recognized union (manual)	.645
Pre-entry closed shop	A dummy variable if all or some manual workers were required to be union members before starting work.	.061
Post-entry closed shop	A dummy variable if all or some manual workers were required to be union members after starting work.	.189
County unempt. rate	The percentage of the workforce who were unemployed county in 1984—in natural logarithms. (Source: *Regional Statistics*, 1985)	2.521
% part-time	The percentage of workers who were part-time.	16.511
% manual	The percentage of the workforce who were manual.	61.486
Majority male	A dummy variable if the majority of the unskilled/ semi-skilled/skilled workforce were male.	.750
% unskilled	The percentage of manuals who were unskilled.	57.63
% semi-skilled	The percentage of manuals who were semi-skilled.	24.50
% skilled	The percentage of those in the workforce who had received formal training through an apprenticeship or equivalent.	25.12
Foreign-owned	A dummy variable for a foreign owned establishment.	.050
Shiftworking	A dummy variable for the existence of shift work at the establishment.	.457
Single independent	A dummy variable for a single establishment.	.204
Size of establishment	The number of workers (full and part-time).	133.885
Wales	a (1,0) regional dummy	.034
North	a (1,0) regional dummy	.067
North West	a (1,0) regional dummy	.079
Yorks & Humberside	a (1,0) regional dummy	.087
East Midlands	a (1,0) regional dummy	.099
West Midlands	a (1,0) regional dummy	.103
East Anglia	a (1,0) regional dummy	.049
South West	a (1,0) regional dummy	.107
London	a (1,0) regional dummy	.124

| Scotland | a (1,0) regional dummy | .073 |
| Industry dummies | 50 2-digit industry dummies | |

Dependent variables

Unskilled wage	Typical level of gross (weekly) pay of unskilled manual workers (in natural logarithms).	4.281
Semi-skilled wage	Typical level of gross (weekly) pay of semi-skilled manual workers (in natural logarithms).	4.587
Skilled wage	Typical level of gross (weekly) pay of skilled manual workers (in natural logarithms).	4.827
Clerical wage	Typical level of gross (weekly) pay of skilled manual workers (in natural logarithms).	4.350
Foreman wage	Typical level of gross (weekly) pay of skilled manual workers (in natural logarithms).	4.965

B) Earnings Equation: Semi-Skilled Manuals—WIRS2

	Coefficient	t-statistic
Workplace controls		
Establishment size * 10^4	.5627	3.55
Establishment size^2 * 10^8	−.4303	2.72
1 year employment change	−.0006	1.47
% of workforce semi-skilled	.0001	0.45
Single independent	−.0486	1.77
Foreign owned	.0601	2.13
Age of plant < 3 yrs	−.0311	0.44
Age of plant ≥ 3 & < 5 yrs	.0927	1.82
Age of plant ≥ 5 & < 10 yrs	−.0011	0.03
Age of plant ≥ 10 & < 25 yrs	.0117	0.63
Performance very high	.0719	2.89
Performance quite high	.0292	1.27
Performance quite low	−.0088	0.20
Performance very low	−.0787	1.45
Performance not possible	.0410	1.43
Profit sharing	.0163	0.69
Shiftworking	.0960	5.09
Majority male	.2912	13.33
Few competitors	.0298	1.57
% part-time	−.0036	6.08
% total manual	.0010	2.29
Log of unemployment rate	−.0030	0.06
Nationalized industry	.0868	1.47
Public sector	−.0863	2.27
Manual union recognition	.0327	1.35

Manual post-entry closed shop	.0089	0.42
Manual pre-entry closed shop	.0885	3.03
Regional dummies		
Wales	−.0524	1.06
North	−.0409	0.86
North West	−.0041	0.11
Yorkshire & Humberside	.0291	0.78
East Midlands	−.0400	1.21
West Midlands	−.0161	0.45
East Anglia	−.0020	0.05
South West	−.0286	0.89
London	.1177	4.14
Scotland	.0088	0.22
Industry dummies		
Extraction mineral oil & gas	.4301	2.50
Mineral oil processing	.2103	1.70
Nuclear fuel production	−.3774	1.54
Electricity & gas prodn. & distrib.	−.0410	0.54
Water supply	−.0333	0.19
Metal manufacture	−.1584	2.54
Extraction of minerals n.e.s.	.0022	0.01
Manufacture of non-metal minerals	−.0105	0.17
Chemicals	−.0445	0.77
Production of man-made fibers	−.3911	2.33
Metal goods n.e.s.	−.0454	0.81
Mechanical engineering	−.1581	3.19
Office machinery etc.	−.4064	1.73
Electrical engineering	−.1520	2.89
Manufacture motor vehicles & parts	−.1576	2.42
Manufacture other transportation equipment	−.2191	3.18
Instrument engineering	−.1793	1.97
Food, drink & tobacco	−.1157	2.24
Textiles	−.1774	2.83
Manufacture of leather etc.	−.2101	1.51
Footwear & clothing	−.1553	2.09
Timber & wooden furniture	.0651	0.72
Paper & printing	−.0136	0.24
Processing of rubber & plastics	.0049	0.06
Other manufacturing	−.2618	1.56
Wholesale distribution	−.0719	1.31
Dealing in scrap & waste materials	.2711	1.14
Retail distribution	−.1147	2.10
Hotels & catering	−.3087	4.58

Repair of consumer goods	−.1944	1.78
Railways	.0814	0.55
Other inland transport	−.0710	1.12
Sea transport	−.0558	0.33
Air transport	.1566	0.92
Supporting services for transport	−.0101	0.08
Miscellaneous transport & storage	.0679	0.61
Postal services & telecoms.	−.1404	1.77
Banking & finance	.0495	0.63
Insurance	−.1185	1.22
Business services	−.1594	2.30
Renting of movables	−.1796	1.07
Owning & dealing in real estate	−.1195	0.51
Public administration	−.1977	3.36
Sanitary services	−.1579	1.63
Education	−.1292	2.22
Research & development	−.1448	1.65
Medical services	−.1128	1.89
Other services to general public	−.2139	2.84
Recreational services	−.0821	1.29
Personal services	−.2193	2.01
(Constant)	4.4205	35.13
$\bar{R}^2$	.5136	
F	12.871	
DF	891	

B3 Workplace Industrial Relations Survey, 1990 (WIRS3)

The sample design for the 1990 main survey broadly followed that developed for previous surveys. The sampling frame was the Employment
Department's 1987 Census of Employment; for the 1984 survey it was the
census conducted in 1981, and for the 1980 survey it was the census
conducted in 1977. As in previous surveys, all census units recorded as
having twenty-four or fewer employees were excluded, as were units falling within Agriculture, Forestry, and Fishing (Division 0) of the Standard
Industrial Classification (1980). Otherwise all sectors of civil employment
in England, Scotland, and Wales were included in the sampling universe—
public and private sector, manufacturing, and service industries. In 1990, as
in previous surveys, larger units (on the basis of number of employees)
were oversampled.

A census unit is in most cases a number of employees working at the
same address who are paid from the same location by the same employer.

The requirement of the survey design was for a sample of establishments, that is of individual places of employment at a single address and covering all the employees of the identified employer at that address. In general there is a sufficient degree of correspondence between census units and establishments for the census to serve as a viable sampling frame for the survey series. However, some census units have been found to refer to more than one establishment and in others to just part of an establishment.

At the time of the design of the 1990 sample, the 1987 Census of Employment file contained just over 142,000 units with twenty-five or more employees, slightly more than the 135,000 in the 1981 census used for the 1984 survey. From this file a stratified random sample totaling 3,577 units was drawn; in 1984 the figure was 3,640 units and in 1980 the figure was 3,994 units. The selected sample was smaller in 1990 for two reasons. First, the number of establishments at which interviews were required was 1,870, as against 2,000 in the first survey. Second, as none of the "reserve pool" of nearly 500 units had been used in 1984 and the 1984 experience gave a good guide to the extent of out-of-scope and nonresponding addresses, the size of the reserve pool in 1990 could be reduced. In the event none of the 358 units selected for the 1990 reserve pool were used.

The selection of units from the census file involved an initial division of the file into seven files, each containing units within a size range: twenty-five to forty-nine employees, fifty to ninety-nine employees, and so on. Within each file the census units were then reordered by the proportion of male employees, within the proportion of full-time employees, within the Activities of the Standard Industrial Classification (SIC). Differential sampling fractions were applied to the six lower size bands, the seventh (top) band having the same sampling fraction as the sixth band. From the reordered lists, samples were selected by marking off at intervals from a randomly selected starting point, the list being treated as circular.

The range of sampling fractions employed has been progressively increased during the course of the series. Partly this was because the number of large units in the population has declined and we still wanted to have sufficient large establishments of different sizes. It also reflected an increased emphasis on estimates focusing on employees rather than establishments. Analysis of the 1980 results had shown that employee estimates could be improved with little loss of accuracy on establishment estimates if the sample contained more large, and fewer small, units.

Besides the withdrawal of the ten per cent of addresses for the reserve pool, the sample selected in 1990 was also reduced by a further 210 addresses from SIC Classes 91, 93, and 95. This innovation was made because analysis of the previous surveys had demonstrated that there was less variation within these easily identifiable parts of the public sector on most of the matters of interest in the surveys. It seemed advisable, therefore, to spread the survey resources that could be saved by undersampling these sectors over the remaining sectors of the population. The result of these two types of withdrawal from the selected sample—the reserve pool and the undersampling of Classes 91, 93, and 95—was to bring the number of units in the initial sample down to 3,009.

In 1984, all addresses in the deep coal-mining industry had been withdrawn from the sample prior to fieldwork, owing to the industry-wide dispute current at the time. In 1990 the deep coal-mining industry was again excluded so that the industrial coverage of the three surveys in the series would be identical.

Interviewing started in late January, shortly after the main interviewer briefings, and continued until September 1990, with the bulk of interviews taking place in February to April. The median date for the main management interviews was late March, compared with May for the two previous surveys.

For further details of the survey, see Millward et al. (1992).

A)   Key to Variables in WIRS3

		Mean
Independent variables		
Union recognition	A dummy variable if recognized union (manual)	.373
Unemployment	The log of the percentage of the workforce unemployed in each travel-to-work-area	1.63
% part-time	The percentage of workers who were part-time.	25.46
% manual	The percentage of the workforce who were manual.	61.38
% female	The percentage of workers who were female.	25.62
Size of establishment	The number of workers (full and part-time).	122.97
(Size of establishment)^2	Square of establishment size.	79,738.14
Partnership	a (1,0) dummy if a partnership or self-proprietor	.03
Trust	a (1,0) dummy if a company limited by guarantee/trust/friendly society/charity	.04

Cooperative	a (1,0) dummy if a cooperative	.003
State owned ltd co.	a (1,0) dummy if state or govt owned ltd. company	.002
Nationalized industry	a (1,0) dummy if trading public corporation	.027
Non-trading pub corp.	a (1,0) dummy if non-trading public corporation	.004
QUANGO	a (1,0) dummy if a quasi autonomous governmental organisation	.003
Local/central govt.	a (1,0) dummy if local/central govt. (including national health service/local education authorities	.295
Specialist	a (1,0) dummy if specialist industrial relations respondent	.911
Majority female	a (1,0) dummy if majority unskilled manuals female	.514
Extraction mineral oil & gas	a (1,0) industry dummy	.001
Mineral oil processing	a (1,0) industry dummy	.000
Electricity & gas	a (1,0) industry dummy	.008
Water supply	a (1,0) industry dummy	.008
Metal manufacture	a (1,0) industry dummy	.007
Extraction of minerals n.e.s.	a (1,0) industry dummy	.004
Non-metal minerals	a (1,0) industry dummy	.018
Chemicals	a (1,0) industry dummy	.014
Man made fibers	a (1,0) industry dummy	.014
Metal goods n.e.s.	a (1,0) industry dummy	.015
Mechanical engineering	a (1,0) industry dummy	.034
Office machinery etc.	a (1,0) industry dummy	.001
Electrical engineering	a (1,0) industry dummy	.019
Motor vehicles & parts	a (1,0) industry dummy	.003
Other trans. equipt.	a (1,0) industry dummy	.005
Instrument engineering	a (1,0) industry dummy	.005
Food	a (1,0) industry dummy	.012
Drink & tobacco	a (1,0) industry dummy	.012
Textiles	a (1,0) industry dummy	.008
Manufacture of leather, etc.	a (1,0) industry dummy	.002
Footwear & clothing	a (1,0) industry dummy	.016
Timber & wooden furniture	a (1,0) industry dummy	.018
Paper & printing	a (1,0) industry dummy	.033
Rubber & plastics	a (1,0) industry dummy	.028
Other manufacturing	a (1,0) industry dummy	.002
Construction	a (1,0) industry dummy	.053
Wholesale distribution	a (1,0) industry dummy	.053
Retail distribution	a (1,0) industry dummy	.041
Motor vehicle distrib., etc.	a (1,0) industry dummy	.042

Hotels & catering	a (1,0) industry dummy	.068
Repair of consumer goods	a (1,0) industry dummy	.006
Railways	a (1,0) industry dummy	.006
Sea transport	a (1,0) industry dummy	.016
Air transport	a (1,0) industry dummy	.000
Other transport	a (1,0) industry dummy	.006
Misc. transport & storage	a (1,0) industry dummy	.003
Postal services & telecoms.	a (1,0) industry dummy	.020
Banking & finance	a (1,0) industry dummy	.006
Insurance	a (1,0) industry dummy	.005
Business services	a (1,0) industry dummy	.027
Renting of movables	a (1,0) industry dummy	.003
Owning/dealing in real estate	a (1,0) industry dummy	.012
Public administration	a (1,0) industry dummy	.033
Sanitary services	a (1,0) industry dummy	.010
Education	a (1,0) industry dummy	.186
Research & development	a (1,0) industry dummy	.002
Medical services	a (1,0) industry dummy	.032
Other services	a (1,0) industry dummy	.067
Recreational services	a (1,0) industry dummy	.029
Personal services	a (1,0) industry dummy	.001
Dependent variable		
Unskilled wage	Gross annual earnings of unskilled manual workers (in natural logarithms).	8.548

B)   Earnings Equation: Unskilled Manuals—WIRS3

	Coefficient	t-statistic
Log of unemployment rate	−.0916	3.93
Union recognition	.0951	2.91
% part-time	−.0072	8.69
% manual	.0019	3.06
% female	.0002	0.18
Size of establishment	.0002	5.59
(Size of establishment)^2 * 10^7	−.2133	3.57
Partnership	.0459	0.47
Trust	−.1413	1.76
Cooperative	−.0039	0.02
State owned ltd co.	.0697	0.58
Nationalized industry	.0623	0.67
Non-trading pub corp.	.0288	0.22
QUANGO	.0894	0.58
Local/central govt.	−.2269	3.56

Specialist	− .0135	0.50
Majority female	− .3611	11.07
Extraction mineral oil & gas	.8079	2.91
Mineral oil processing	.4111	1.08
Electricity & gas	.2963	2.60
Water supply	.2777	1.59
Metal manufacture	.2059	1.63
Extraction of minerals n.e.s.	.4497	1.63
Non-metal minerals	.3134	2.52
Chemicals	.3527	3.31
Man made fibers	.4428	1.16
Metal goods n.e.s.	.2665	2.22
Mechanical engineering	.2199	2.13
Office machinery etc.	.2437	1.31
Electrical engineering	.1258	1.26
Motor vehicles & parts	.2749	1.90
Other trans. equipt.	.0776	0.65
Instrument engineering	.3329	2.16
Food	.4013	3.66
Drink & tobacco	.4512	4.12
Textiles	.2011	1.58
Manufacture of leather, etc.	.0231	0.08
Footwear & clothing	.1350	1.09
Timber & wooden furniture	.2039	1.63
Paper & printing	.3799	3.66
Rubber & plastics	.3180	2.83
Other manufacturing	.4242	1.56
Construction	.2722	2.84
Wholesale distribution	.4426	4.42
Retail distribution	.4254	4.56
Motor vehicle distrib etc.	.3551	3.81
Hotels & catering	.1359	1.42
Repair of consumer goods	.1022	0.51
Railways	.2217	1.33
Sea transport	.6234	1.64
Air transport	.3094	0.81
Other transport	.3222	2.63
Misc. transport & storage	.3712	2.67
Postal services & telecoms.	.2269	1.89
Banking & finance	.1541	1.02
Insurance	.3703	2.46
Business services	.2390	2.13

Renting of movables	.3983	1.45
Owning/dealing in real estate	.0254	0.16
Public administration	.1029	1.53
Sanitary services	−.0920	0.20
Research & development	.1523	1.17
Medical services	.5126	8.51
Other services	.5763	7.02
Recreational services	.3135	3.64
Personal services	.6129	2.23
Constant	8.7031	92.36
$\bar{R}^2$	.5466	
F	20.92	
DF	1,040	
N	1,108	

Notes: Excluded categories: limited company: education.

B4   The National Child Development Study, 1958–1981

The National Child Development Study is a longitudinal study that takes as its subjects all those living in Great Britain who were born between March 3 and 9, 1958. The survey has been sponsored by five government departments—the Departments of Health and Social Security (DHSS), Education and Science (DES), Employment (DE), Environment (DOE), and the Manpower Services Commission (MSC). Since the original Perinatal Mortality Study was undertaken in 1958, the National Children's Bureau has sought to monitor the social, economic, educational, and health circumstances of the surviving subjects. To this end major surveys were carried out in 1965 (NCDS1), 1969 (NCDS2), 1974 (NCDS3), and 1981 (NCDS4). Details of response rates, etc., are contained in table B4.

For the purposes of the first three surveys, the birth cohort was augmented by including those new immigrants born in the relevant week and information was obtained separately from parents, teachers, and doctors as well as members of the NCDS cohort. The 1981 survey differs in that no attempt was made to include new immigrants since 1974 and information was obtained from the subject only.

The 1981 survey contained a total of 12,537 interviews or approximately 76% of the original target sample and 93% of those traced and contacted by interviewers. The interview survey was carried out between August 1981 and March 1982. For further details of the survey, see Elias and Blanchflower (1989).

Table B.4
Responses to the National Child Development Study

Source	Birth 1958	Seven 1965	Eleven 1969	Sixteen 1974	1978	Twenty-three 1981	Thirty-three 1991
Parents	Interview	Interview	Interview	Interview			
Medical	Records	Examination and history	Examination history	Examination and history			
Schools	Questionnaire	Questionnaire	Questionnaire	Questionnaire	Exam results (CSE, O-levels and A-levels)		
Subjects		Tests	Tests	Tests		Tests	
Subjects			Questionnaire	Questionnaire		Interview	Interview
						Census-based area data	
Spouses							Interview
Children							Tests
N	18,559	15,468	15,503	14,761	14,370	12,537	15,000 (?)

A)   Variable Definitions

		Mean
Wage	log of weekly earnings	4.508
Higher degree	(1,0) dummy if highest qualification a higher degree.	.001
First degree	(1,0) dummy if highest qualification a first degree.	.070
Teaching qualification	(1,0) dummy if highest qualification a teaching qualification.	.005
HNC/HND/ BEC/TEC	(1,0) dummy if highest qualification a HNC/HND/BEC/TEC higher award.	.065
Nursing qualification	(1,0) dummy if highest qualification a nursing qualification.	.033
2 + "A" level	(1,0) dummy if highest qualification 2 or more "A" levels.	.057
1 "A" level	(1,0) dummy if highest qualification 1 "A" level or ONC/OND or BEC/TEC Lower.	.132
5 + "O" levels	(1,0) dummy if highest qualification 5 or more "O" levels or craft qualification.	.153
1–4 "O" level + clerical	(1,0) dummy if highest qualification 1–4 "O" levels plus a clerical qualification.	.033
1–4 "O" levels	(1,0) dummy if highest qualification 1–4 "O" levels.	.165
Clerical qual.	(1,0) dummy if highest qualification clerical–no "O" levels.	.018
CSE grades 2–5	(1,0) dummy if highest qualification CSE grades 2–5.	.001
Apprenticeship	(1,0) dummy if highest qualification an apprenticeship.	.015
Other qual.	(1,0) dummy if highest qualification a qualification not itemized previously.	.019
Numeracy problem	(1,0) dummy if the respondent reported that they had ever experienced problems with numeracy.	.012
Literacy problem	(1,0) dummy if the respondent reported that they had ever experienced problems with literacy.	.024
Disabled	(1,0) dummy if the respondent is registered as a disabled person.	.005
Excellent health	(1,0) dummy if the respondent reported being generally in excellent health.	.464
Good health	(1,0) dummy if the respondent reported being generally in good health.	.455
Fair health	(1,0) dummy if the respondent reported being generally in fair health.	.075
Poor health	if the respondent reported being generally in poor health—excluded category.	.006
Fairly secure job	(1,0) dummy if the respondent reports that their current job is fairly secure.	.380
Very secure job	(1,0) dummy if the respondent reports that their current job is very secure.	.496

Not very secure	if the respondent reports that their current job is not very secure—excluded category.	.124
Promotion prospects	(1,0) dummy if the respondent reports that the type of work done offers a career with prospects of promotion in the years ahead.	.639
Same employer	(1,0) dummy if the respondent reports that a year ahead they expected to still be working for the same employer.	.705
Female	(1,0) dummy if female.	.457
Have children	(1,0) dummy if has 1 or more children.	.151
Part-time	(1,0) dummy if part-time.	.053
Separated	(1,0) dummy if separated.	.020
Divorced	(1,0) dummy if divorced.	.011
Married	(1,0) dummy if married or living as married.	.424
Has Second job	(1,0) dummy if respondent has a second job.	.129
Unempt. ever	(1,0) dummy if respondent ever unemployed	.416
OLF ever	(1,0) dummy if the respondent has ever had a spell out of the labor force.	.336
Work unsocial hrs.	(1,0) dummy if the respondent regularly works evenings between 6–10 PM, at night after 10 AM, early in morning before 7 PM, Saturdays/Sundays	.525
No. of jobs held	Number of jobs held since leaving school.	3.005
Tenure current job	Number of months employed in current job.	36.325
Union member	(1,0) dummy if union member.	.463
Have been a picket	(1,0) dummy if served as a local union official or shop steward and/or stood on a picket line.	.050
Moved since 1974	(1,0) dummy if standard region of residence in 1981 different from that in 1974.	.235
Limited company	(1,0) dummy if employed by a limited company.	.630
Branch office	(1,0) dummy if place of work a branch of a larger organisation.	.174
10 workers or less	10 workers or less employed at the workplace—excluded category.	.091
11–25 workers	11–25 workers employed at the workplace.	.138
26–99 workers	26–99 workers employed at the workplace.	.156
100–499 workers	100–499 workers employed at the workplace.	.211
500 + workers	500 + workers employed at the workplace.	.404
Unemployment rate	Unemployment rate by county. (Data kindly supplied by the Department of Employment).	11.012
Wales	a (1,0) regional dummy	.049
North	a (1,0) regional dummy	.054
North West	a (1,0) regional dummy	.110
Yorks & Humberside	a (1,0) regional dummy	.086
East Midlands	a (1,0) regional dummy	.072
West Midlands	a (1,0) regional dummy	.097

East Anglia	a (1,0) regional dummy	.035
South West	a (1,0) regional dummy	.075
South East	a (1,0) regional dummy	.200
Scotland	a (1,0) regional dummy	.081
Industry dummies	50 industry dummies.	

B)   Earnings Equation: Twenty-three Year Olds—NCDS: 1981

	Coefficient	t-statistic
Log of regional unemployment	−.0643	2.657
Industry dummies		
Forestry	.0972	0.458
Fishing	.7476	4.288
Coal extraction	.2492	5.181
Coke ovens	.3487	3.909
Mineral oil processing	.2055	2.630
Nuclear fuel production	.0774	0.772
Electricity & gas distrib.	.2088	4.081
Water supply	.1118	1.674
Extraction metal ores	.5277	3.029
Metal manufacture	.1892	3.842
Extraction of minerals n.e.s.	.3319	2.429
Manufacture non-metal minerals	.0919	1.705
Chemicals	.1355	3.020
Man-made fibers	.2740	1.295
Metal goods n.e.s.	.0249	0.509
Mechanical engineering	.0978	2.413
Office machinery	.2654	4.010
Electrical engineering	.1069	2.608
Motor vehicles	.1358	3.046
Other transport equipment	.1447	2.974
Instrument engineering	.0834	1.380
Other manufacturing	.1263	1.765
Food, drink & tobacco	.1228	2.999
Alcohol	.3319	1.567
Textiles	.0560	1.045
Leather	−.1257	0.828
Footwear & clothing	.0032	0.068
Timber & furniture	.1623	3.207
Paper & printing	.1755	4.265
Rubber & plastics	.1097	2.187
Other manufacturing	−.0019	0.033
Construction	.1837	4.804

Wholesale distribution	.0324	0.765
Dealing in scrap & waste	−.0669	0.384
Commission agents	.0538	0.254
Retail distribution	−.0569	1.548
Hotels & catering	−.2220	5.365
Repairs	−.0690	1.437
Railways	−.0357	0.652
Other inland transport	.1622	3.447
Sea transport	.1601	2.421
Air transport	.2023	3.491
Transport services	.1727	2.642
Miscellaneous transport	−.0921	1.679
Posts & telecommunications	.1018	2.314
Banking & finance	.1062	2.683
Insurance	.0489	1.067
Business services	.1283	3.107
Renting of movables	.1544	2.250
Real estate	.0454	0.492
Other services	−.1226	2.274
Public administration	.0895	2.313
Sanitary services	−.0554	0.809
Education	.1257	2.890
Research & development	−.0833	1.061
Medical services	−.0240	0.598
Other services	−.0180	0.374
Recreation	.0297	0.681
Personal services	−.1328	2.615
Domestic services	−.3343	3.486
Highest qualification dummies		
Higher degree	.0791	0.531
First degree	.1591	7.295
Teaching qualification	.3064	5.223
HTEC/HND/HNC	.1463	7.755
Nursing qualification	.1251	4.590
≥2 "A" levels	.1219	6.035
1 "A" level	.1382	9.575
≥5 "O" levels	.0836	6.151
1–4 "O" levels + clerical qualification	.0646	2.845
1–4 "O" levels only	.0423	3.291
Clerical	.0305	1.057
CSE grades 2–5	−.1894	1.425
Apprenticeship	.1089	3.367
Other qualifications	.0373	1.313

Regional dummies

South East	−.1130	8.413
South West	−.1922	10.621
Wales	−.1521	6.043
West Midlands	−.1519	7.193
East Midlands	−.1638	8.513
East Anglia	−.1897	8.264
Yorkshire & Humberside	−.1830	9.046
North West	−.1461	6.941
North	−.1487	5.873
Scotland	−.1628	7.568

Size of workplace dummies

11−25 workers	−.0202	1.098
26−99 workers	.0645	3.698
100−499 workers	.0654	5.011
≥ 500 workers	.0902	7.222

Worker and workplace characteristics

Second job	−.0093	0.817
Disabled	−.2947	5.745
Separated	.0423	1.566
Divorced	.1315	3.553
Married	.0358	4.203
Children	−.0349	2.829
Female	−.2326	25.209
Fairly secure job	−.0125	0.961
Very secure job	.0119	0.883
OLF last five years	−.0301	3.605
Unemployed last 5 yrs.	−.0526	6.363
Same employer next year?	.0406	4.454
Moved region since 1974	.0151	1.316
Part-time	−.6798	35.496
Shift worker	.1075	12.593
Job prospects	.0791	8.995
Ltd. company	−.0156	1.249
Union membership	.0724	8.063
Picket	.0450	2.571
Branch of firm	.0185	1.391
Tenure (months)	.0009	4.972
Number of jobs	.0107	3.731
Maths test score	.0015	2.601
Reading test score	−.0003	0.328
Number problems	−.0950	2.699
Reading/writing problems	.0284	1.137

(Constant)	4.5046	67.760
$\bar{R}^2$	.5337	
F	63.854	
DF	6,255	

B5   British Social Attitudes Survey Series, 1983–1989

This series of surveys, core-funded by the Sainsbury Family Trusts, was designed to chart movements in a wide range of social attitudes in Britain and is similar to the General Social Survey carried out by NORC in the United States. The surveys were designed and collected by Social and Community Planning (SCPR) and derive from annual cross-sectional surveys from a representative sample of adults aged eighteen or over living in private households in Great Britain whose addresses were on the electoral register. The first three surveys involved around 1,800 adults; the numbers were increased to 3,000 in 1986. For the first time in 1989 interviews were also conducted in Northern Ireland.

The sampling in each year involved a stratified multi-stage design with four separate stages of selection. First, in each year approximately 120 (150 in 1986) parliamentary constituencies were selected, with probability of selection proportionate to size of electorate in the constituency. Then, for each constituency a polling district was selected also with probability of selection proportionate to the size of the electorate. Then, thirty addresses were selected at a fixed interval on the electoral register. Finally, at each sampled address the interviewer selected one respondent using a random selection procedure (a Kish grid). The majority of sample errors for each survey lie in the range 1.0 to 1.5; errors for subgroups would be larger. For further details of the survey designs, nonresponses, and so on, see *British Social Attitudes Technical Reports*, 1984, 1985, 1986, 1987, and 1989.

A)   Variable Definitions

		Mean
Wages	log of annual earnings	8.737
Employment rise expected	a (1,0) dummy variable if the respondent expected their workplace to increase its number of employees over the coming year.	.19
Employment fall expected	a (1,0) dummy variable if the respondent expected their workplace to decrease its number of employees over the coming year.	.25

Employment constant	if the respondent expected their workplace would keep constant its number of employees over the coming year—excluded category.	.56
Unemployed in previous five years	a (1,0) dummy variable if the respondent reported that they had ever been unemployed and seeking work in the preceding five years.	.19
Redundancy expected	a (1,0) dummy variable if the respondent expected that during the next year they would be declared redundant.	.05
Regional unemployment	Unemployment rate in the standard region.	9.92
Male	a (1,0) dummy variable for gender.	.55
Age	the respondent's age at the time of interview	38.71
Part-time	a (1,0) dummy variable if the respondent reported that they normally worked less than 30 hours per week.	.18
Separated	a (1,0) dummy variable if the respondent was separated or divorced.	.05
Widow	a (1,0) dummy variable if the respondent was widowed.	.02
Married	a (1,0) dummy variable if the respondent was married or living as married.	.72
Single	if the respondent had never been married—excluded category.	.21
School	number of years of schooling.	11.10
Private sector	if the respondent reported that they worked in the private sector.	67.20
Union recognized	a (1,0) dummy variable if trade unions or staff associations at the place of work recognized by management for negotiating pay and conditions.	.62
Supervisor	a (1,0) dummy variable if the respondent was a supervisor.	.35
Union member	a (1,0) dummy variable if the respondent was a member of a trade union or a staff association.	.47
Nonmanual	a (1,0) dummy variable if the respondent's occupation was non-manual.	.47
Self-employed in previous five years	a (1,0) dummy variable if the respondent reported that they had ever been self-employed over the previous five years as their main job.	.03
Year1984	(1,0) year dummy	.10
Year1985	(1,0) year dummy	.12
Year1986	(1,0) year dummy	.22
Year1987	(1,0) year dummy	.20
Year1989	(1,0) year dummy	.26
Wales	a (1,0) regional dummy	.043
North	a (1,0) regional dummy	.054
North West	a (1,0) regional dummy	.099
Yorks & Humberside	a (1,0) regional dummy	.087

East Midlands	a (1,0) regional dummy	.070
West Midlands	a (1,0) regional dummy	.093
East Anglia	a (1,0) regional dummy	.041
South West	a (1,0) regional dummy	.084
London	a (1,0) regional dummy	.109
Scotland	a (1,0) regional dummy	.082
Industry dummies	60 (1,0) dummy variables at the two digit SIC level	

B) Earnings Equation—BSA

	Coefficient	t-statistic
Log of regional unemployment	−.1232	5.33
Industry dummies		
Coal extraction	.2590	3.46
Coke ovens	−.0803	0.30
Mineral oil extraction	.6273	5.56
Mineral oil processing	.6106	4.08
Nuclear fuel processing	.1986	2.75
Energy production	.1447	1.43
Water supply	−.1943	0.42
Metal ore extraction	.0997	1.39
Metal manufacture	.1878	0.98
Mineral extraction	.1356	1.76
Non-metal prod. manufacture	.2699	4.57
Chemicals	.1623	0.35
Man-made fibers	.1516	2.46
Metal goods manufacture	.2125	4.00
Mechanical engineering	.2988	3.23
Office machine manufacture	.1800	3.35
Electrical engineering	.1589	2.70
Motor vehicles	.1604	2.52
Transport equipment manufacture	.1722	1.91
Instrument engineering	−.0148	0.06
Shipbuilding	.1806	3.36
Food, drink & tobacco	.0461	0.63
Textile industry	.3153	1.52
Leather goods	.0353	0.59
Footwear & clothing	.0521	0.76
Timber	.2007	3.56
Paper & printing	.2542	3.57
Rubber & plastic	.1763	1.72
Other manufacturing industry	.2149	4.51
Construction	.1482	2.80

Wholesale distribution	.0698	0.46
Scrap & waste	.3937	1.70
Commission agents	−.1215	2.56
Retail distribution	−.1523	2.84
Hotels & catering	.0263	0.42
Repair of goods	.0565	0.77
Railways	.1350	2.36
Other inland transport	.1763	1.23
Sea transport	.2566	2.11
Air transport	.3168	2.74
Transport support services	.1356	1.82
Misc. transport services	.1577	2.73
Post & telecommunications	.1365	2.44
Banking	.2661	4.21
Insurance	.1866	3.68
Business services	.0635	0.73
Renting of movables	−.0771	0.84
Real estate	.1516	2.46
Accountancy	.0871	0.42
Legal services	.1137	2.33
Public administration	−.1009	1.42
Sanitary services	.0709	1.46
Education	.1704	1.88
Research & development	.0813	1.64
Medical & veterinary	.0346	0.64
Other public services	−.0771	1.35
Recreational	−.0482	0.73
Personal services	−.2385	2.47
Domestic services	.2337	1.40
Year dummies		
Year84	.0811	3.50
Year85	.1506	6.68
Year86	.2297	11.42
Year87	.2817	13.74
Year89	.4132	18.39
Region dummies		
Scotland	−.0202	0.86
East Anglia	−.0611	2.10
Wales	−.0571	1.95
East Midlands	−.0709	3.07
North West	−.0369	1.66
South West	−.1369	6.41
North	−.0650	2.33

Yorkshire & Humberside	−.0452	2.03
West Midlands	−.0592	2.73
London	.0758	3.85
Worker and workplace controls		
Employment rise expected	.0843	6.05
Supervisor	.1895	15.55
Union member	.0909	6.27
Nonmanual	.2543	19.26
Unemployed last five yrs.	−.0970	6.74
Male	.4916	36.20
Union recognition	.0493	3.29
Part-time	−.8257	47.88
Separated	.0929	3.88
Widowed	.1389	3.70
Years of schooling	.0684	15.82
Experience	.0305	19.54
Experience^2	−.0005	17.48
Constant	7.1966	81.04
$\bar{R}^2$	.6607	
F	164.25	
DF	7,372	

B6   The General Household Survey Series, 1973–1989

The General Household Survey is a continuous multipurpose national sample survey based on private households selected from the Electoral Register. It originated in 1971 as a service to various government departments. Departmental interests change, and therefore, although there is substantial continuity in questions over time, new areas for questioning are introduced, for example, leisure in 1973 and 1977, and drinking in 1978, and the form of questions varies from year to year.

The sample remained largely unchanged between 1971 and 1974 and was designed to be representative of Great Britain in each calender quarter. The three-stage sample design involved the selection of 168 Local Authority areas as the primary sampling units (PSUs) by probability proportional to population size, after first stratifying Local Authority areas by (a) regions; (b) conurbations, other urban areas, semi-rural areas, and rural areas; and (c) average rateable value. Each year four wards (in rural areas, groups of parishes) are selected from each PSU with probability proportional to population size. The selected Local Authority areas are rotated such that a quarter are replaced every three months. Within each ward, twenty or twenty-five addresses are selected. A maximum of three households are interviewed at each address (and to compensate for additional households at an address a corresponding number are deleted from the interviewer's address list). This yielded a total effective sample of 15,360 households in 1973, for example.

Since 1975, in an attempt to reduce the effects of clustering, the sample design has been based on a two-stage sampling procedure with electoral wards as the PSUs. Geographically contiguous wards or parishes are grouped where necessary to provide a minimum electorate of 2,300 before selection. Wards are stratified by (a) regions, (b) metropolitan and non-metropolitan counties, and (c) percentage in higher or intermediate non-manual socio-economic groups, to produce 168 strata. Within these strata wards are listed by (d) percentage of households in owner occupation, before being systematically selected by probability proportional to size. Four wards are used from each stratum each year, with each selected ward in use for three years before being replaced. Selection of addresses within wards remains the same as before 1975, but addresses where there are multiple households are treated somewhat differently. The sample is not representative in each calender quarter after 1975.

Some households respond only partially, therefore response rates can be measured in a number of different ways:

1. The minimum response rate, defined as only completely cooperating households—70% in 1973.

2. The maximum response rate excludes only households where the whole household either refused or was not contacted—84% in 1973.

3. The middle response rate includes households where information is missing for certain questions but excludes those where information is missing altogether for one or more household member—81% in 1973. The middle response rate therefore includes the 6% (in 1973) of households in which information about one or more household member was obtained from someone else in the household (a "proxy"). Certain questions are not asked by proxy, for example, questions on income, educational qualifications, and opinion.

The data set is based on individuals (i.e., all adults and children in the sample households); that is, the case unit is an individual, not a household. The GHS defines a household as "a group of people living regularly at one address, who are all catered for by the same person for at least one meal a day."

Matching of Files

For the purposes of this book we have taken the 1973–1981–1990 surveys and put them on a comparable basis, merged them, and then aggregated them by year/region cell. For the years 1973 to 1986 the GHS was conducted in every month of the calendar year. Since 1987 the survey has been conducted during the financial year April to March: hence the 1987 survey contain nine monthly interviews in 1987 and three in 1988, and similarly for all subsequent surveys. The data for 1990 are taken from the 1989 survey and relate only to the first three months of 1990, hence the small sample size in that year.

The total sample is approximately one third of a million, which provides 175,946 employees with wage data. This means that, on average, there are approximately 10,000 observations per year. However, as seen here, sample sizes were reduced from 1982 onward.

Year	Sample size	Employees with wage data
1973	21,516	12,255
1974	19,884	11,434
1975	21,887	12,644
1976	21,653	12,061
1977	21,319	12,023
1978	21,165	11,802
1979	20,417	11,451
1980	21,087	11,597
1981	21,641	11,145
1982	18,339	9,137
1983	17,760	8,451
1984	16,947	7,966
1985	17,386	8,449
1986	17,704	8,763
1987	18,087	9,085
1988	13,058	6,524
1989	17,195	8,946
1990	4,356	2,213
Total	331,401	175,946

When aggregated this gives 198 observations (18 years*11 regions) for our analysis using cell means.

Pooling raises a number of issues about consistency over the period. There was a series of changes in the design of the survey over time as well as in the wording and coding of many of the relevant questions, plus changes in both the occupational and industry classifications.

For the years 1973 to 1977, respondents were asked to report both their earnings over the preceding twelve months and the number of weeks worked. In each survey after 1977 the following questions were asked of employees: (a) On what date were you last paid a wage or a salary, (b) how long a period did your last wage/salary cover, and (c) what was your gross pay last time before any deductions were made? These questions were used to construct the dependent variable: log weekly earnings. To control for a change in the nature of the earnings question in 1978 and onward, a series of eleven interaction terms were included in the regressions. These were interacted with each of the regional dummy variables with a dummy variable set to one if the data were taken from a survey prior to 1978 and to zero otherwise.

Appropriate data on unemployment rates, were mapped in from outside sources at various stages. Participation rates were constructed by the authors from the GHS files. The biggest problem came in obtaining a set of comparable industry codes through time. This was achieved in a reasonably satisfactory way using the relevant SIC codes. The biggest problem occurred in 1987 where the interviews conducted in the first quarter of the year used different codes to those in the following three quarters! Regional codes were broadly consistent—we everywhere excluded the Scottish Supplementary file on grounds of consistency. We also combined a series of highest qualification variables together in order to have a consistent basis through time.

Experience was calculated as age minus age completed full time education if this was less than twenty-seven. Where it was greater than twenty-six, and presumably where there was a broken spell of education, experience was calculated as age minus (age left full-time school + three). This was done because of a number of individuals reporting leaving full-time education in their forties, fifties, and even sixties.

Part-time status was defined as being where working hours were less than thirty. Individuals were classified as white or nonwhite. The self-employed were excluded from the analysis as were those individuals working on government schemes. The other variables—gender, marital status, and year dummies—were generated in the obvious way.

A) Variable Definitions

		Mean
1. Dependent variable		
Log of gross weekly earnings		4.09
2. Independent variables		
Log of regional unemployment		1.70
Year		
Year74	a (1,0) dummy if surveyed in 1974	.06
Year75	a (1,0) dummy if surveyed in 1975	.07
Year76	a (1,0) dummy if surveyed in 1976	.07
Year77	a (1,0) dummy if surveyed in 1977	.07
Year78	a (1,0) dummy if surveyed in 1978	.07
Year79	a (1,0) dummy if surveyed in 1979	.06
Year80	a (1,0) dummy if surveyed in 1980	.06
Year81	a (1,0) dummy if surveyed in 1981	.06
Year82	a (1,0) dummy if surveyed in 1982	.05
Year83	a (1,0) dummy if surveyed in 1983	.04
Year84	a (1,0) dummy if surveyed in 1984	.04
Year85	a (1,0) dummy if surveyed in 1985	.05
Year86	a (1,0) dummy if surveyed in 1986	.05
Year87	a (1,0) dummy if surveyed in 1987	.05
Year88	a (1,0) dummy if surveyed in 1988	.03
Year89	a (1,0) dummy if surveyed in 1989	.04
Year90	a (1,0) dummy if surveyed in 1990	.04
Month of interview		
January	a (1,0) month of interview dummy	.09
February	a (1,0) month of interview dummy	.08
March	a (1,0) month of interview dummy	.09
April	a (1,0) month of interview dummy	.08
May	a (1,0) month of interview dummy	.08
June	a (1,0) month of interview dummy	.08
July	a (1,0) month of interview dummy	.09
August	a (1,0) month of interview dummy	.08
September	a (1,0) month of interview dummy	.08
October	a (1,0) month of interview dummy	.08
November	a (1,0) month of interview dummy	.09
Highest qualification dummies		
Higher degree	a (1,0) qualification dummy	.01
First degree/diploma	a (1,0) qualification dummy	.05
Teaching qualification	a (1,0) qualification dummy	.02
HNC, HND, technical certificate	a (1,0) qualification dummy	.05

Nursing qualification	a (1,0) qualification dummy	.02
GCE "A" level, ONC, OND	a (1,0) qualification dummy	.08
GCE "O" level-5 or more	a (1,0) qualification dummy	.10
GCE "O" 1−4, + other quals.	a (1,0) qualification dummy	.02
GCE "O" 1−4 + no other quals.	a (1,0) qualification dummy	.07
Clerical qualifications	a (1,0) qualification dummy	.04
CSE	a (1,0) qualification dummy	.03
Apprenticeship	a (1,0) qualification dummy	.05
Any foreign qualification	a (1,0) qualification dummy	.01
Other qual.	a (1,0) qualification dummy	.02

Region dummies

North	a (1,0) region dummy	.06
Yorkshire & Humberside	a (1,0) region dummy	.09
North West	a (1,0) region dummy	.12
East Midlands	a (1,0) region dummy	.07
West Midlands	a (1,0) region dummy	.10
East Anglia	a (1,0) region dummy	.04
London	a (1,0) region dummy	.12
South East	a (1,0) region dummy	.19
South West	a (1,0) region dummy	.07
Wales	a (1,0) region dummy	.05
Scotland	a (1,0) region dummy	.10

Interaction terms

Int1	a (1,0) dummy if pre-1978 and North	.02
Int2	a (1,0) dummy if pre-1978 and Yorks/Humberside	.03
Int3	a (1,0) dummy if pre-1978 and North West	.04
Int4	a (1,0) dummy if pre-1978 and East Midlands	.02
Int5	a (1,0) dummy if pre-1978 and West Midlands	.03
Int6	a (1,0) dummy if pre-1978 and East Anglia	.01
Int7	a (1,0) dummy if pre-1978 and London	.04
Int8	a (1,0) dummy if pre-1978 and South East	.06
Int9	a (1,0) dummy if pre-1978 and South West	.02
Int10	a (1,0) dummy if pre-1978 and Wales	.02
Int11	a (1,0) dummy if pre-1978 and Scotland	.03

Industry dummies

SIC Order 1	a (1,0) industry dummy	.02
SIC Order 2	a (1,0) industry dummy	.04
SIC Order 3	a (1,0) industry dummy	.14
SIC Order 4	a (1,0) industry dummy	.12
SIC Order 5	a (1,0) industry dummy	.06

SIC Order 6	a (1,0) industry dummy	.16
SIC Order 7	a (1,0) industry dummy	.06
SIC Order 8	a (1,0) industry dummy	.07
SIC Order 9	a (1,0) industry dummy	.31
Personal controls		
Part-time	a (1,0) dummy if part-time	.21
Married	a (1,0) dummy if married	.70
Separated	a (1,0) dummy if separated	.01
Divorced	a (1,0) dummy if divorced	.03
Widowed	a (1,0) dummy if widowed	.02
Exp	years of experience	22.20
Exp^2	(years of experience)^2	699.59
Male	a (1,0) dummy if male	.55
Black	a (1,0) dummy if black	.03
School	years of schooling	10.49

B) Earnings Equation—GHS

Variable	Coefficient	T-statistic
Log of regional unemployment	−.082	6.22
Year74	.153	22.10
Year75	.410	61.92
Year76	.625	60.74
Year77	.718	67.43
Year79	.231	36.20
Year80	.413	66.24
Year81	.574	58.11
Year82	.669	57.59
Year83	.747	57.64
Year84	.790	59.68
Year85	.862	63.76
Year86	.936	68.64
Year87	.988	78.75
Year88	1.083	101.78
Year89	1.100	140.65
Year90	1.202	101.44
Month of interview		
January	−.130	22.66
February	−.115	19.55
March	−.095	16.54
April	−.084	14.51
May	−.076	13.11
June	−.067	11.73

July	−.045	7.82
August	−.054	9.40
September	−.042	7.32
October	−.032	5.62
November	−.020	3.48
Highest qualification dummies		
Higher degree	.727	53.03
First degree/diploma	.637	101.82
Teaching qualification—nongraduate	.820	92.26
HNC, HND, technical certificate	.387	63.93
Nursing qualification	.466	51.53
GCE "A" level, ONC, OND	.261	50.64
GCE "O" level 5 or more	.200	44.03
GCE "O" 1−4, with other qualifications	.208	24.60
GCE "O" 1−4, with no other qualifications	.119	22.57
Clerical qualifications	.100	15.96
CSE	.048	6.52
Apprenticeship	.100	18.28
Any foreign qualification	.180	15.06
Other qualifications	.123	15.47
Region dummies		
North	−.029	3.81
Yorkshire & Humberside	−.059	8.42
North West	−.024	3.86
East Midlands	−.074	8.55
West Midlands	−.050	7.22
East Anglia	−.078	6.85
London	.160	18.51
South East	−.002	0.15
South West	−.120	13.47
Wales	−.059	7.18
Interaction terms		
Int1	−.814	59.32
Int2	−.838	61.47
Int3	−.808	67.65
Int4	−.845	60.31
Int5	−.812	57.72
Int6	−.836	52.65
Int7	−.889	64.38
Int8	−.841	70.07
Int9	−.765	62.99
Int10	−.808	54.92
Int11	−.793	65.80

Industry dummies

SIC Order 1	.381	33.27
SIC Order 2	.345	33.61
SIC Order 3	.279	30.23
SIC Order 4	.271	29.19
SIC Order 5	.219	22.17
SIC Order 6	.086	9.39
SIC Order 7	.307	31.35
SIC Order 8	.298	30.31
SIC Order 9	.155	17.18

Personal controls

Part-time	$-.999$	290.53
Married	.086	23.54
Separated	.033	3.57
Divorced	.022	2.68
Widowed	$-.015$	2.73
Exp	$-.040$	113.24
$Exp^2 * 10^4$	.689	103.25
Male	.454	154.96
Black	$-.092$	13.17
School	.037	28.81
$\bar{R}^2$	.766	
F	7,029.0	
DF	175,485	
N	175,568	

Appendix C:
European Data Files

C1   West Germany

A)   Description of Survey

ALLBUS (Allgemeinen Bevoelkerungsumfrage der Sozialwissenschaften), has been conducted biennially since 1980: it is the West German general social survey and is a replicating time-series. It is the joint responsibility of the Zentrum fur Umfragen, Methoden und Analysen (ZUMA) in Mannheim and the ZentralArchiv fur Empirische Sozialforschung (ZA) at the University of Cologne.

Each survey is designed to be a representative sample of adults (aged 18 and over) living in private households in the Federal Republic and West Berlin. A three-stage stratified design is used: selection of sampling points; selection of households within those points by a random route method; and at each household the selection of an eligible West German national. The ISSP data are collected on a self-completion questionnaire, usually filled in following the main ALLBUS interview and returned by post.

Fieldwork was carried out as follows:

- Role of government module   May–August 1985
- Social networks module   March–May 1986
- Social inequality module   September–October 1987
- Women and the family module   April–July 1988
- Work orientations   November–December 1989
- Role of government II   March–May 1990
- Religion   May–July 1991

The table here shows the response rates achieved in each year. (The 1985 module was fielded on its own; the 1987 module was carried out as a supplement to another general social survey, Der Sozialwissenschaften-Bus.)

	1985		1986		1987		1988	
	N	%	N	%	N	%	N	%
Issued	2,704		5,512		2,896		4,620	
Adj. sample (elig.)	2,513	100	5,275	100	2,580	100	4,509	100
Achieved interviews	n/a		3,095	59	1,655	64	3,052	68
Completed ISSP questionnaires	1,048	42	2,809	53	1,397	54	2,994	66

	1989		1990		1991	
	N	%	N	%	N	%
Issued	3,360		5,204		2,900	
Adj. sample (elig.)	2,998	100	5,054	100	2,875	100
Achieved interviews	2,032	68	3,051	60	1,517	53
Completed ISSP questionnaires	1,575	53	2,812	56	1,346	47

Note: n/a = not applicable.
Telephone reminders were carried out to maximize response to the ISSP self-completion questionnaire. The 1985, 1987–1991 datasets were not weighted; the 1986 data were corrected by weighting for nonresponse.

Further information may be obtained from:

Dr. Peter Ph. Mohler
ZUMA
P.O. Box 5969
Mannheim
Federal Republic of Germany

B) Regression Results

	Coefficient	t-statistic	Mean
Unemployment rate	−.1113	4.61	5.98
(Unemployment rate)^2	.0050	4.20	42.18
Industry dummies			
Agriculture, forestry, etc.	−.1933	2.33	.02
Energy & water	.1432	2.06	.01
Mining	.1167	1.58	.01
Chemicals	.1322	2.70	.02
Plastics	.0989	1.33	.01
Stone and earth, ceramics & glass	−.0051	0.06	.01
Iron & metal production	.0210	0.49	.03
Mechanical engineering	.0746	2.01	.07

Electrical engineering	.0504	1.28	.05
Wood, paper & printing	.0125	0.25	.02
Textile mills	−.0961	1.67	.01
Food	−.0711	1.36	.02
Construction	.0422	0.96	.03
Industries related to construction	−.0293	0.59	.02
Wholesale trade	.0487	1.10	.03
Commercial & trade agency	.1222	1.17	.00
Retail business	−.0731	1.82	.07
Federal railways	.0043	0.05	.01
Post Office	−.0343	0.72	.02
Other transport & communication	.1242	2.28	.02
Banking, finance, and credit services	.0539	1.07	.02
Insurance	.1122	1.97	.01
Personal services	.0268	0.72	.09
Nonprofit organizations	−.0314	0.65	.02
Private households	−.1512	1.34	.00
Public services	.0404	1.19	.17
Social insurance	.0053	0.06	.01
Region dummies			
Schleswig-Holstein	−.1196	3.11	.05
Hamburg	.0037	0.08	.04
Niedersachsen	−.1232	3.87	.12
Bremen	−.1526	2.02	.01
Nordrhein-Westfalen	−.0879	2.96	.27
Hessen	−.2438	5.06	.09
Rheinland-Pfalz	−.2049	4.47	.05
Baden-Wuerttemberg	−.3023	4.86	.14
Bayern	−.2947	5.52	.17
Saarland	.0085	0.15	.02
Qualification dummies			
Lower secondary school	−.0691	1.25	.46
Middle school and vocational	.0283	.50	.28
Secondary technical or trade	.0784	1.21	.03
Abitur	.0293	.48	.08
Other school qualification	−.2261	1.72	.00
Higher degree below university	.2550	4.03	.04
University degree	.3606	5.94	.09
Occupation dummies			
Accountants, teachers, authors	.0143	0.54	.10
Administrative & managerial	.4331	8.90	.01
Clerical workers	.0308	1.53	.15
Sales workers	.0970	3.52	.09

Service workers	−.1284	4.83	.07
Agricultural workers	−.2161	3.23	.02
Production workers	.0013	0.04	.03
Shoemakers, fitters etc.	−.1106	5.00	.13
Laborers etc.	−.0918	3.49	.08
Personal controls			
Self-employed	.2120	8.65	.11
Widowed	.2684	5.82	.02
Separated	.1315	3.05	.02
Divorced	.1510	5.57	.07
Married	.1133	6.83	.61
Part-time	−.5225	26.64	.13
Male	.1929	5.67	.60
Age 25−34	.3319	16.02	.28
Age 35−44	.4399	18.66	.25
Age 45−54	.4600	18.88	.22
Age 55−64	.4586	16.08	.10
Age 65−74	.4283	4.96	.01
Age ≥ 75	.8979	4.93	.00
Union	.0404	2.93	.27
Year dummies			
Year 1987	.0999	4.33	.09
Year 1988	.0575	3.22	.23
Year 1989	.1230	3.24	.11
Year 1990	.0823	3.38	.24
Year 1991	.0910	2.63	.12
Constant	7.5801	46.62	
$\bar{R}^2$	.5154		
DF	4,554		
F	67.51		

Dependent variable:

Log of net monthly earnings   7.56

Excluded categories; age < 24: Berlin: Fishing and commercial animal husbandry; professional workers. All controls except the unemployment rates are (1,0) dummy variables.

C)   Unemployment Rates

	1986	1987	1988	1989	1990	1991
a) Males	5.5	5.4	n/a	4.7	3.9	3.6
Schleswig-Holstein	7.2	6.6	6.4	5.8	5.1	4.4
Hamburg	10.1	10.4	10.1	8.7	7.4	6.3
Niedersachsen	7.2	6.8	6.6	5.9	4.9	4.4
Bremen	10.7	10.5	9.9	9.6	9.0	7.3

Nordrhein-Westfalen	6.9	6.8	6.9	6.2	5.1	4.7
Hessen	3.9	3.8	3.8	3.4	2.9	2.8
Rheinland-Pfalz	4.8	4.5	4.2	3.7	3.1	2.8
Baden-Württemberg	2.9	2.7	2.8	2.5	2.1	1.9
Bayern	3.8	3.7	3.4	2.7	2.3	2.2
Saarland	9.0	9.3	8.6	7.8	6.1	5.6
Berlin	7.9	8.0	7.6	7.0	6.4	n/a
b) Females	8.2	7.8	n/a	7.3	7.2	5.2
Schleswig-Holstein	8.2	8.4	8.5	8.1	7.8	5.4
Hamburg	9.4	10.9	10.6	9.1	8.7	5.8
Niedersachsen	10.6	9.7	9.7	9.3	9.6	7.1
Bremen	10.4	13.3	13.1	13.0	12.5	8.6
Nordrhein-Westfalen	12.3	10.5	10.8	10.1	9.8	7.0
Hessen	6.7	6.3	6.2	5.9	6.0	4.3
Rheinland-Pfalz	8.3	7.6	7.3	6.8	6.8	4.7
Baden-Württemberg	5.0	4.7	4.7	4.4	4.3	3.1
Bayern	5.9	5.5	5.7	5.2	4.9	3.3
Saarland	12.1	12.0	10.7	10.1	9.2	7.0
Berlin	7.9	8.1	7.7	7.7	7.5	n/a
c) Total	6.6	6.3	6.3	5.7	5.2	4.2

Source: *Basic Statistics of the Community*: Eurostat. 24th–29th editions.

C2   Austria

A)   Survey Description

The Sozialer Survey Osterreich (SSOE) was first fielded in 1986, and the intention is to replicate it regularly in order to provide a time-series. The SSOE is conducted by the Institut fur Soziologie (IS) at the University of Graz and funded from various sources including the Social Science Foundation, the Austrian National Bank Jubilee Fund, the Ministry for Science and Research and the state government of Steiermark.

The sample, designed to be representative of adults in the Republic of Austria is three-stage:

• *Sampling points* are selected within each Bundesland (region) according to the population size of each point

• *Households* within each sampling point are selected using addresses drawn randomly from the electoral register

• *Individuals* (aged between sixteen and sixty-nine) are randomly selected for interview in each selected household, using a fixed random number

The main SSOE questionnaires for 1985 and 1986 were administered by face-to-face interview; the role of government and social networks ISSP questionnaires were administered, on a self-completion questionnaire (filled in after the interview) during May and June 1986; the social inequality and women and family modules were part of the SSOE questionnaire, conducted by personal interview in June and July 1988. The women and family module was fielded in April and May 1989. Response rates achieved on each interviewing round are shown here:

	1985 and 1986		1987 and 1988		1989	
	No	%	No	%	No	%
Issued addresses	2,820		1,400		2,840	
Adjusted sample (eligible)	2,763	100	1,361	100	2,772	
Achieved interviews	2,016	72	972	71	1,997	72
Completed ISSP questionnaires						
(i) Role of government module*	987					
(ii) Social networks module*	1,027					
(iii) Social inequality module**			972	71		
(iv) Women and the family**			972	71	1,997	72

The SSOE was not fielded in 1990 or 1991.
Notes: * = each was administered to a random half of those responding to the main SSOE questionnaire.
** = each was administered in 1988: each respondent had to answer both the 1987 and 1988 ISSP questionnaires.
These datasets contain weights that allow estimates to be obtained that represent the correct population proportions based on an achieved sample of 1,000 adults (IFES-weighting).

Further information may be obtained from:

Prof. Dr. Max Haller or Dr. Franz Hollinger
Sozialer Survey Osterreich
Institut fur Soziologie der Universitat Graz
Mariengasse 24
A-8020 Graz
Austria

B)   Regression Results

	Coefficient	t-statistic	Mean
Year 1985	−.0489	1.50	.228
Year 1989	.1114	3.99	.522
Personal controls:			
Compulsory school + Vocational training	.2924	9.39	.360

Middle school + Vocational training	.4461	12.01	.183
Matura-AHS	.5338	9.04	.050
Matura-BHS	.5518	10.98	.087
University	.6751	10.51	.050
Part-time	−.3787	9.92	.126
Widowers	.0712	0.79	.019
Separated	.1142	0.93	.009
Union member	.1423	5.96	.487
Male	.2653	9.37	.590
Age	.0795	11.54	36.614
Age^2	−.0008	9.78	1494.357
Occupation dummies:			
Accountants, jurists, teachers etc.	−.0410	0.68	.078
Administrative workers	.1684	1.94	.022
Clerical and related	−.1063	2.12	.221
Sales workers	−.0587	0.99	.092
Service workers	−.1458	2.58	.129
Agricultural workers	−.6285	9.44	.065
Production and related workers	−.1029	1.46	.046
Skilled manuals	−.1904	3.36	.139
Semi- and unskilled manuals	−.1136	1.99	.134
Log of regional unemployment rate	−.1421	3.22	1.600
Constant	7.3848	51.78	
$\bar{R}^2$	.5156		
DF	1560		
F	65.92		

Dependent variable:
Log of net monthly earnings   9.228

Excluded categories: Compulsory schooling only, Professional workers

Note: All variables except for the unemployment rate and age are (1,0) dummies.

C) Unemployment Rates (%)

Men	1985	1986	1987	1988	1989
Bergenland	10.9	10.1	10.1	8.9	7.7
Kärnten	7.1	7.7	8.2	7.4	6.2
Niederösterreich	5.2	5.4	5.6	5.0	4.3
Oberöstereich	3.9	4.0	4.4	4.1	3.3
Salzburg	4.0	4.3	4.1	3.5	3.1
Steiermark	5.5	6.0	6.3	6.1	5.5

Tirol	4.4	4.8	5.0	4.5	4.1
Vorarlberg	2.4	2.3	2.4	2.1	1.9
Wien	4.7	4.9	5.6	5.6	5.5
Österreich	4.9	5.1	5.5	5.1	4.6
Women	**1985**	**1986**	**1987**	**1988**	**1989**
Bergenland	6.2	6.6	6.9	6.6	6.4
Kärnten	6.8	7.8	8.5	8.1	7.9
Niederösterreich	5.5	5.9	6.3	6.0	5.6
Oberöstereich	4.4	4.9	5.3	5.2	4.8
Salzburg	3.7	4.2	4.3	3.8	3.6
Steiermark	5.1	6.1	6.7	6.9	7.0
Tirol	4.6	5.2	5.4	5.1	5.1
Vorarlberg	3.0	3.3	3.4	3.3	3.0
Wien	4.1	4.6	5.3	5.3	5.3
Österreich	4.7	5.1	5.7	5.6	5.5

C3   Italy

A)   Survey Description

The Indagine Sociale Italiana (ISI) is an annual series of surveys, carried out by the Ricerca Sociale e di Marketing (EURISKO) Institute in Milan. Since 1985, the surveys have included the ISSP questionnaire modules, administered either as a self-completion supplement to the main ISI interview or as an interviewer-assisted supplement.

The sample for each ISI survey is designed to be representative of the population of Italy aged between eighteen and seventy-four. A national multi-stage probability sample is used, with a quota-selection at the final stages, selecting:

• at the first stage, small geographical areas or administrative units to yield a probability sample of primary sampling units (PSUs), areas and units had been prestratified according to sex, age and population density;

• at the second stage, a prespecified number of households (or dwelling units) within each PSU;

• at the third stage, selection of an adult (aged 18–74) within each selected household according to pre-selected quota criteria.

Response rates are not available from the ZA Codebooks. Fieldwork was carried out as follows.

- Role of government module   September–October 1985
- Social networks module   March–April 1987
- Social inequality module   March–April 1987
- Women and the family module   no information available
- Work orientations   no information available
- Role of government II   April 1990
- Religion   April 1990

Please note that the social networks and social inequality modules were both conducted in 1987 and the role of government (II) and religion modules were conducted in 1990. In these cases the same individuals answered the two ISSP questionnaires.

Corrective weights were applied to the data for all of the surveys to adjust for population size, sex, age, and occupation (based on census estimates).

Further information may be obtained from:

Prof. Gabrieli Calvi or Dr. Paolo Anselmi
Ricerca Sociale e di Marketing (EURISKO)
Via Monte Rosa 15
20149 Milano, Italy

B)   Regression results

Variable	Coefficient	t-statistic	Mean
Log of regional unemployment rate	−.1234	3.32	2.15
Personal controls			
Male	.1156	2.26	.64
Divorced	−.1598	0.88	.01
Widowed	.2314	1.39	.01
Separated	.2457	1.88	.02
Married	−.0013	0.02	.69
Part-time	−.2924	4.31	.56
Self-employed	−.5479	1.39	.30
Union member	.0604	1.06	.14
Supervisor	.0432	1.05	.28
Public sector	.0617	1.28	.37
12 years of schooling	.0543	1.11	.32
13 years of schooling	.1238	2.13	.32
Age 25–34	.2221	3.32	.27
Age 35–44	.2497	3.29	.27

Age 45–54	.3616	4.55	.23
Age 55–64	.2902	3.31	.10
Age ≥ 65	.3973	2.07	.01
Year 1989	.7383	11.09	.53
Occupation dummies			
Entrepreneurs, manufacturers	1.0076	2.39	.02
Independent professionals	.7400	1.83	.05
Authors, writers, artists	.1854	0.39	.00
Proprietors, owners, drawers of rent	1.1281	2.03	.00
Managers, officials, civil servants	.4682	2.83	.01
Professors and teachers	.1776	2.64	.11
Journalists	−.5227	1.34	.00
Officers and NCOs in prof. army	.0329	0.21	.01
Chief clerks and supervisors	.2796	2.93	.04
Workers, operatives, etc.	−.0003	0.00	.22
Soldiers	−.3597	1.80	.01
Domestic servants, housemaids	−.1832	0.96	.01
Day laborers	−.0812	0.56	.02
Retail traders and salesmen	.6425	1.63	.11
Trade agents, salesmen (self-employed)	.8060	1.96	.02
Craftsmen	.6005	1.49	.05
Other self-employed laborers	.3380	0.85	.03
Family assistants	.7921	1.78	.01
Farmers, farm managers (nondependent)	.1043	0.24	.01
Constant	13.1000	88.14	1
$\bar{R}^2$	.5233		
DF	1,002		
F	31.05		

Dependent variable:
Log of monthly earnings   13.53

Note: all controls except for the unemployment rate are (1,0) dummies.

C) Unemployment Rates

	1986	1989
a) Males	7.1	7.4
North West	4.8	3.5
North East	4.8	3.7
Center	5.9	5.9
South & Islands	10.8	13.2

b) Females	17.0	17.0
North West	12.4	9.7
North East	12.1	9.7
Center	15.7	14.4
South & Islands	26.0	30.4
c) Total	10.6	10.9

C4   Netherlands

A)   Survey Description

The Netherlands has no single annual or biennial national survey on which to field the ISSP module. Instead, the Sociaal en Cultureel Planbureau (SCP) at Rijswijk regularly conducts surveys on social and cultural welfare in the Netherlands, as mandated by its terms of reference. In 1987, it fielded the Social Inequality module as a self-completion supplement to a nationwide personal interview survey among a full probability sample of Dutch adults aged between sixteen and eighty. No weights are applied to the data.

- Role of government module   no survey
- Social networks module   no survey
- Social inequality module   September–December 1987
- Women and the familymodule   November 1988–January 1989
- Work orientations   September 1989–January 1990
- Role of government II   March–May 1990
- Religion   throughout 1991

Responses were as follows

	1987	**1988**	**1989**	**1991**
Issued addresses	2,000	2,033	2,008	1,926
Completed ISSP questionnaire	1,638	1,737	1,690	1,635

Further information may be obtained from:

Dr. Carlo van Praag or Dr. Jos Becker
Sociaal en Cultureel Planbureau
JC van Markenlaan 3
Postbus 37
2280 AA Rijswijk
Netherlands

B)   Regression Results

Variable	Coefficient	t-statistic	Mean
Unemployment rate	−.0123	2.307	12.74
Male	.1815	7.222	.64
Married	.1660	6.088	.63
Divorced	.0910	1.690	.04
Widowed	.0741	0.512	.00
Union member	.0563	2.524	.30
Part-time	−.3572	11.882	.19
School	.0098	3.110	13.13
Age < 18	−1.0789	8.434	.01
Age 18–24	−.2179	6.262	.14
Age 35–44	.1091	4.098	.30
Age 45–54	.2114	6.509	.17
Age 55–64	.2171	4.484	.06
Age 65–74	.1166	0.882	.01
Primary and vocational training	.0723	1.553	.25
Extended	.2016	3.857	.11
Extended and vocational training	.2248	4.623	.22
Secondary	.2916	5.299	.10
Secondary and vocational training	.3338	6.196	.14
University	.4523	7.894	.13
Flevoland, Zeeland, Noord-Holland & Gelderland	.1994	3.269	.49
Friesland	.0636	0.850	.04
Drente	.0589	0.638	.02
Overijssel	.1219	1.708	.06
Zuid-Holland	.1487	2.323	.18
Noord-Brabant	.0232	0.266	.03
Limburg	.1147	1.842	.15
Year 1989	.0046	0.189	.33
Year 1991	.4386	13.987	.33
Constant	9.5363	76.483	1

Dependent variable

Log of monthly earnings			10.25
$\bar{R}^2$	.4687		
DF	1,837		
F	57.75		

Note: Excluded categories are age twenty-five to thirty-four; single; no qualifications; Groningen and 1988.
All variables except the unemployment rate are (1,0) dummies.

C) Unemployment Rates

	1988	1989	1991
a) Males	n/a	7.0	5.5
Groningen	11.1	11.4	11.1
Friesland	9.8	9.4	8.5
Drenthe	6.8	6.6	4.0
Overjissel	7.5	6.8	6.0
Gelderland	6.9	6.4	5.2
Utrecht	6.1	6.1	3.7
Noord-Holland	7.9	7.3	5.5
Zuid-Holland	7.4	7.3	5.8
Zeeland	5.0	4.5	3.7
Noord-Brabant	6.6	6.0	4.3
Limburg	7.6	7.0	6.1
Flevoland	6.9	6.7	6.1
b) Females	n/a	14.4	10.3
Groningen	19.2	20.6	15.0
Friesland	17.3	18.4	12.4
Drenthe	12.7	12.5	14.3
Overjissel	12.9	12.7	10.6
Gelderland	14.4	14.4	10.5
Utrecht	12.8	13.6	9.2
Noord-Holland	15.1	15.4	9.9
Zuid-Holland	12.7	13.1	10.4
Zeeland	10.6	10.7	8.8
Noord-Brabant	14.0	13.8	9.0
Limburg	16.2	15.7	9.9
Flevoland	17.9	18.0	12.4
c) Total	9.5	9.3	7.4

Source: *Basic Statistics of the Community*: Eurostat. 24th–29th editions.

C5 Republic of Ireland

A) Survey Description

Unlike the majority of ISSP member countries, the Republic of Ireland has no regular national survey on which to field the annual ISSP module. In 1988, however, the Women and the Family module was fielded as part of a nationwide attitude survey dealing with, among other issues, prejudice and tolerance.

A two-stage probability sample was drawn for the 1988 study, the first stage being District Electoral Divisions and the second, electors aged eighteen and over. A total of 1,290 addresses was issued and successful interviews carried out at 1,005 (a gross response rate of 78 percent). Fieldwork was carried out from November 1988 to February 1989. The Religion and Role of Government II modules were fielded to the same respondents from September to November 1991: 1575 addresses were issued and 1005 ISSP questionnaires were completed. Information was obtained through personal interview. The data were not weighted.

Further information may be obtained from:

Professor Conor K. Ward
Faculty of Philosophy and Sociology
University College Dublin
Dublin 4
Republic of Ireland

B)   Regression Results

Variable	Coefficient	t-Statistic	Mean
Male	.3058	9.02	.63
Age	.0406	5.66	37.90
Age squared	−.0004	5.30	1,610.5
Years of schooling	.0696	12.61	11.86
Married	.1577	4.29	.58
Separated	.2300	2.05	.02
Widowed	.3863	3.28	.02
Supervisor	.2368	6.53	.29
Part-time	−.4427	10.01	.16
Union member	.2640	8.35	.37
North West	.3001	1.40	.06
West	−.0550	0.77	.07
North East	.0553	0.42	.05
Midlands	−.1447	1.54	.10
East	.2308	3.17	.08
Dublin	.3025	5.39	.27
Mid West	.1593	2.40	.08
South East	.1828	1.69	.11
Log unemployment rate	−1.4307	2.66	2.91
Constant	5.3997	6.31	
$\bar{R}^2$	.4326		
DF	1,341		
F	50.45		
N	1,363		

C) Unemployment Rates (%)

	1988	1989	1990	1991
East	18.6	17.8	17.0	18.4
South East	19.7	18.7	18.5	20.5
North East	19.9	18.9	18.4	21.3
Midlands	15.6	15.7	14.5	16.7
South West	17.4	17.2	16.3	18.0
Mid West	17.4	17.5	17.1	18.7
West	17.6	17.3	17.0	20.3
North West	22.2	22.4	21.5	23.2
Total	18.4	17.9	17.2	19.1

Note: Thanks to Máire Nic Ghiolla Phádraig of University College, Dublin for providing us with these data.

C6 Switzerland

A) Survey Description

A two-stage stratified random sample of persons sixteen and over including foreign workers was conducted in Switzerland between October 1 and December 15, 1987, who could speak either German, French, or Italian. In 129 representative Swiss communities, addresses were selected "following instructions deducted from probability selection ('Select the fifth person after the one whose family name begins with MO')." A total of 2,046 addresses were issued and 987 interviews obtained. The survey was conducted by mail in two waves—a payment of fifty Swiss Francs was made if the questionnaire was completed and returned.

B) Regression Results

Variable	Coefficient	t-statistic	Mean
Log of regional unemployment	−.1183	3.618	−0.41
Male	.3064	5.633	.71
Marrieds	.1003	1.733	.60
Widowed	.0379	0.225	.02
Divorced	.0717	0.762	.06
Self-employed	.0239	0.478	.00
Public sector	−.0481	0.807	.23
Part-time	−.5552	6.713	.07
Supervisor	.1794	4.237	.45

Union	.0690	1.592	.36
Age	.0796	8.449	40.22
Age^2	−.0008	7.375	1,792.10
Secondary	.1627	2.635	.39
Incomplete middle school	.1674	1.972	.09
Technical qualification	.2649	3.769	.20
Complete middle school	.4389	2.944	.02
Teachers training	.4846	3.314	.02
Incomplete university	.4383	3.065	.02
Complete university	.5752	6.357	.10
Agriculture	−.2513	1.891	.03
Energy & water	−.7091	2.733	.01
Manufacturing	−.2266	2.286	.17
Wood, paper, and printing production	−.4041	2.906	.03
Food	−.3223	2.737	.06
Textile mills	−.3219	2.005	.02
Construction	−.3296	2.799	.06
Post Office	−.4836	2.765	.02
Wholesale & retail trade	−.0639	0.544	.06
Transportation incl. railways	−.2158	1.750	.05
Banking & insurance	−.1176	1.049	.07
Personal services	−.2328	1.816	.06
Nonprofit organizations	−.5111	2.344	.01
Public services and social insurance	−.2422	2.411	.28
Professional, technical & related	.5581	5.445	.18
Administrative & managerial	.5720	4.967	.11
Clerical & related	.7709	6.394	.06
Managers (wholesale & retail)	.5838	5.857	.18
Service workers	.6100	5.811	.11
Farm managers & supervisors	.3328	2.813	.08
Production−fitters, printers, etc.	.3784	3.827	.20
Constant	5.3235	25.909	1
$\bar{R}^2$	.5409		
DF	605		
F	19.99		

Notes: Excluded categories; mining, production and related; no qualifications.
With the exception of unemployment, age and its square, all variables are (1,0) dummies.

C)   Unemployment Rates (%)

Zurich	0.5
Bern	0.6
Luzern	0.7

Uri	0.1
Schwyz	0.2
Obwalden	0.2
Nidwalden	0.3
Glarus	0.2
Zug	0.5
Freiburg	0.8
Solothurn	0.6
Basel-Stadt	2.1
Basel-Land	1.1
Schaffhausen	0.9
Appenzell-Ar	0.3
St. Gallen	0.5
Graubuenden	0.4
Aargau	0.4
Thurgau	0.2
Tessin	2.2
Waadt	0.9
Wallis	1.2
Neuenburg	2.1
Genf	1.2
Jura	2.6
Total	0.8

C7   Norway

A)   Survey Description

The ISSP data are part of a survey called Work Conditions and Working Experience. The 1989 survey was conducted under the supervision of the National Committee for Survey Research and the Norwegian Social Science Data Services (NSD). The survey was financed by the Norwegian Council for Science and the Norwegian Council for Applied Social Research (NORAS). A two-stage sampling procedure was applied. Municipalities are the primary sampling units (psu's). They are divided into strata according to location, industrial structure and population size. Cities of more than 30,000 inhabitants formed separate strata. One psu is selected per stratum. For each of the municipalities selected at the first stage a register of households is established and a random sample of households is selected. The overall sampling probability is equal for all households. The survey is a random sample of people aged sixteen to seventy-nine. A total of 2,488 addresses were issued and 1,848 interviews were achieved. The fieldwork was conducted between April and May 1989. The ISSP data was collected by postal self-completion questionnaire. Labor force data was collected by telephone or personal interview.

In 1990 the data were collected as part of a survey called "Attitudes to the Government and the Civil Service." The survey was coordinated by the National Committee for Survey Research and financed by the Norwegian Council for Science and the Humanities (NAVF) and the Norwegian Council for Applied Social Research. The data were collected between February and July 1990 by postal self-completion questionnaire with one reminder being sent out early in March and two reminders later in March and late May. A total of 2,500 addresses were issued and 1,517 completed questionnaires received. No weights were applied.

In 1991 the Religion module was collected between February and June 1991. The sample was a simple random sample from the Central Register of Persons, aged sixteen to seventy-nine years. The data were collected using a mail survey. A total of 2,500 addresses were issued and 1,506 completed questionnaires were received.

For further information, contact:

Bjoern Henrichsen, Knud Knudsen or Vigdis Kvalheim
Hans Holmboesgt 22
N-5507 Bergen
Norway

B) Regression Results

	Coefficient	t-statistic	Mean
Log of the Unemployment rate	−.0832	2.19	1.39
Year 1989	−.1102	4.50	.44
Year 1990	−.0215	0.95	.29
Secondary school	.0403	1.14	.22
High school	.2000	5.93	.40
College or university	.4213	12.13	.27
Male	.4981	27.48	.56
Married	.0716	2.67	.74
Divorced/widowed/separated	.1607	3.70	.07
Age 18–24	.4308	2.47	.13
Age 25–34	.6664	3.82	.27
Age 35–44	.7819	4.48	.26
Age 45–54	.8202	4.70	.18
Age 55–64	.7695	4.39	.12

Age 65–74	.6898	3.73	.03
Oslo	.1604	5.17	.09
Hedmark	−.1487	3.10	.04
Vest-Agder	−.1643	2.93	.03
Nord-Trondelag	−.2025	3.61	.03
Constant	10.8102	59.31	1
$\bar{R}^2$	.3669		
DF	2,579		
F	80.23		

Note: Excluded category age under eighteen; primary school; single.

C) Unemployment Rates (%)

	1984	1985	1986	1987	1988	1989	1990	1991	1992
Ostfold	4.6	3.5	1.9	1.9	2.5	3.8	4.3	5.3	6.5
Akershus	1.2	0.8	0.4	0.3	0.6	2.1	2.7	3.3	4.1
Oslo	1.7	1.1	0.5	0.5	1.0	2.8	4.3	5.1	6.1
Hedmark	3.4	2.6	1.6	1.5	1.9	3.1	3.6	4.3	5.4
Oppland	3.9	3.0	1.9	1.6	2.0	3.3	4.2	4.6	5.4
Buskerud	2.4	1.7	0.9	0.9	1.4	2.8	3.5	3.8	4.7
Vestfold	2.5	2.0	1.5	1.4	2.1	3.8	4.2	4.4	5.4
Telemark	3.9	3.0	2.3	2.0	2.6	4.1	4.8	5.3	6.2
Aust-Agder	4.6	3.2	2.8	3.1	4.5	5.1	5.3	5.0	5.6
Vest-Agder	4.0	3.0	2.2	2.1	3.0	4.2	4.7	4.9	5.4
Rogaland	2.5	2.0	1.6	1.5	2.4	4.1	4.6	4.5	4.3
Hordaland	4.2	3.5	2.3	1.7	2.5	5.2	5.4	5.5	6.4
Sogn & Fjordane	3.1	2.0	1.6	1.3	1.9	2.7	2.7	3.2	3.2
Møre & Romsdal	4.1	2.8	2.1	1.8	3.2	4.7	4.5	4.7	4.9
Sør-Trøndelag	3.9	3.3	2.4	1.9	2.8	4.7	5.1	5.7	6.2
Nord-Trøndelag	4.0	3.8	3.0	2.9	3.5	4.4	4.2	5.0	5.6
Nordland	4.9	4.1	3.3	2.7	3.6	4.6	4.7	4.9	5.5
Troms	4.6	3.7	2.8	2.6	3.7	4.7	4.9	5.2	5.5
Finnmark	4.6	3.7	2.8	3.0	4.4	5.3	5.4	4.9	5.4

Appendix D:
Canadian, Australian, and
South Korean Data Files

D1 Canada

A) Survey Details

The data used in this section are taken from the Canadian Public Use Sample Tapes that are available from the Canadian Survey of Consumer Finances (SCF). (This section draws heavily on appendix B in Bar-Or et al., 1992). The SCF is an April-May supplement to the Canadian Labour Force Survey (LFS), which is now conducted annually (before 1981 it was biennial). The LFS is a monthly survey conducted by Statistics Canada for the purpose of collecting information about the labor force and is similar in many respects to the CPS. One major difference is that, just like the Labour Force Survey in the United Kingdom and other countries in the European Community, it does not provide any information on current earnings or income as does the CPS. The SCF seeks retrospective information on work activity, earnings, and income as well as other variables for the previous calendar year. In the 1970s the data are available only as family records, while in the 1980s the data are also available as files on individuals. The 1973, 1978, and 1987 data are taken from the "Economic Families" files. The 1986 data are taken from the 1987 individuals files. These were the only files available to us. Freeman and Needels (1993) report that differences between the two sets of tapes are tiny.

The universe is all individuals aged fifteen and over. Beginning in 1977, imputation of income data to income nonrespondents was incorpoated into the survey processing. The sample employed is a multistage stratified clustered probability sample. The sample is designed to represent 98% of the population. Excluded population groups are residents of the Yukon and Northwest territories, residents of Indian reservations, residents of military barracks, and inmates of institutions such as prisons, mental hospitals, orphanages, and homes for the elderly.

For further information on the surveys, contact:

Income and Housing Surveys Section, Household Surveys Division, Statistics Canada, 5th Floor, section D2, Jean Talon Building, Ottawa, Ontario K1A OT6: tel: 613 951-9775.

B)   Regression Results

	Coefficient	t-statistic	Mean
Log regional unemployment	−.0953	6.10	2.10
Male	.3905	55.30	.76
Age	.0923	67.96	37.93
Age^2	−.0010	61.38	1589.71
Married	.1827	25.59	.72
Separated/widowed/divorced	.0629	6.12	.09
Part-time	−.7434	82.34	.08
Canadian	.0568	8.33	.86
Year79	.6191	78.21	.25
Year86	.8815	70.50	.29
Year87	1.1944	110.41	.27
Prince Edward Island	−.0643	3.49	.02
Nova Scotia	.0357	2.38	.07
New Brunswick	.0462	3.16	.06
Quebec	.1181	8.10	.16
Ontario	.1620	8.23	.24
Manitoba	.0392	1.95	.07
Saskatchewan	.0317	1.49	.08
Alberta	.1497	8.25	.14
British Columbia	.1970	13.08	.11
Managerial & administrative	.1804	17.65	.12
Professional	.1248	11.98	.15
Clerical	−.0039	0.37	.12
Sales	−.0437	4.12	.09
Services	−.2847	27.93	.12
Agriculture	−.2698	18.11	.03
Mining & quarrying	.0465	4.47	.09
Product fabricating	−.0108	1.07	.10
Construction	−.0038	0.36	.08
High school not completed	.0847	10.29	.18
High school completed	.2329	29.70	.42
Some college	.2249	20.29	.07

University diploma or certificate	.2545	22.55	.07
University degree	.3986	35.54	.10
Constant	6.4051	132.15	1
$\bar{R}^2$	.4783		
F	2,231.82		
DF	82,704		
N	82,739		

Excluded categories: Newfoundland; transport equipment operation, materials handling, other crafts and equipment operations; education grade eight or less.

C) Unemployment Rates (%)

	1972	1979	1986	1987
Newfoundland	10.0	15.4	20	18.6
Prince Edward Island	9.6	11.3	13.4	13.3
Nova Scotia	6.6	10.2	13.4	12.5
New Brunswick	7.7	11.1	14.4	13.2
Quebec	6.8	9.6	11	10.3
Ontario	4.3	6.5	7	6.1
Manitoba	4.6	5.4	7.7	7.4
Saskatchewan	3.5	4.2	7.7	7.3
Alberta	5.3	3.9	9.8	9.6
British Columbia	6.7	7.7	12.6	12.0

D2 Australia

A) Regression Results

	Coefficient	t-statistic	Mean
Log of regional unemployment	−.1946	5.79	2.12
Age 15	−.9121	8.68	.02
Age 16−17	−.6027	18.14	.04
Age 18−20	−.3183	13.78	.06
Age 21−24	−.0567	2.89	.09
Age 30−34	.0534	2.96	.10
Age 35−39	.0835	4.49	.10
Age 40−44	.1085	5.49	.09
Age 45−49	.1088	4.93	.07
Age 50−54	.0832	3.50	.06
Age 55−59	.0551	2.06	.06
Age 60−64	−.0124	0.35	.06
Age 65−69	−.2398	2.41	.05
Age 70−74	−.0690	0.46	.04

Age ≥ 75	−.8723	4.43	.04
No qualifications since school	−.0015	0.08	.50
Completed highest year secondary	.0296	0.56	.11
Secondary qualification since school	.0741	4.68	.01
Trade certificate	.1124	6.89	.14
Other certificate or diploma	.2122	9.01	.15
Bachelor degree or higher	.0013	0.03	.07
Other qualification	−.2606	1.31	.01
< 14 years schooling	−.0983	3.42	.08
14 years schooling	−.0572	2.94	.16
15 years schooling	−.0010	0.07	.25
17 years schooling	.0097	0.65	.17
≥ 18 years schooling	−.0128	0.69	.12
U.K. born	−.0053	0.33	.09
Italy born	−.0155	0.41	.02
Other Europe born	−.0013	0.06	.07
Asian born	−.0435	1.54	.04
North/South American born	−.0709	1.26	.01
African born	−.0676	1.25	.01
Oceania born	.0083	0.24	.02
Professionals	−.0573	2.28	.12
Para-professionals	−.0964	3.54	.06
Tradespersons	−.2910	12.09	.17
Clerks	−.2155	9.41	.18
Salespersons & personal service workers	−.2637	10.88	.14
Plant machine operators & drivers	−.3008	11.33	.08
Laborers etc.	−.3880	16.45	.15
Defense forces	−.1931	2.60	.00
Mining	.6256	13.20	.01
Manufacturing	.2579	7.60	.16
Electricity, gas & water	.3204	7.08	.02
Construction	.3088	8.03	.07
Wholesale & retail trade	.1796	5.28	.21
Transport & storage	.3533	9.31	.06
Communication	.2608	5.86	.02
Finance, property & business services	.2849	7.97	.10
Public administration & defense	.2559	6.84	.06
Community services	.2273	6.59	.17
Recreational, personal & other services	.1041	2.78	.07
Married	.0789	5.37	.63
Separated	.0429	1.77	.11
Part-time	−.8989	63.33	.21
Male	.1662	12.49	.50

Self-employed	−.1841	7.72	.19
(Constant)	6.1200	71.31	1
Dependent variable—log weekly wage			5.69
$\bar{R}^2$	.5851		
F	205.95		
DF	8,370		
N	8,429		

Notes: Excluded categories are: age twenty-five to twenty-nine; never went to school; Australian born; agriculture, forestry, and fishing; managers and administrators; sixteen years schooling.

B)   Unemployment Rates: 1986 (%)

	Males	Females
New South Wales	8.2	9.4
Victoria	6.5	7.9
Queensland	8.9	10.1
South Australia	9.7	9.6
Western Australia	7.7	8.3
Tasmania	7.8	9.6
Northern Territories	6.3	9.0
ACT	4.2	4.7

Source: *Labour Statistics*, Australian Bureau of Statistics, No. 6101.0
Notes: In the data tape Northern Territories and ACT were classified as one category. According to the *Yearbook of Australia*, 1991, published by the Australian Bureau of Statistics, the populations of the two areas in 1986 were 154,421 and 258,910 respectively. In 1989 total employment figures were 61,500 and 124,500. On the basis of these numbers we decided to weight the unemployment rates by 1/3 for Northern Territories and 2/3 for ACT giving unemployment rates of 4.9% for men and 6.1% for women for the combined area.

D3   South Korea

A)   Regression Results

	Coefficient	t-statistic	Mean
Log unemployment rate	−.0403	25.67	1.23
Male	.3134	377.39	.62
Age	.0622	278.66	29.51
Age^2	−.0007	222.70	958.27
Year 1971	−2.4197	2143.69	.14
Year 1983	−.1882	214.81	.43
Middle school	.1084	110.91	.35

High school	.2168	201.61	.36
College	.5386	347.34	.14
Job tenure current firm (years)	.0322	336.47	3.59
Seoul	.0163	14.89	.31
Kyunggi	−.1061	86.68	.14
Kangwon	−.0804	70.35	.18
Chungcheongbuk	−.0745	33.13	.03
Chungcheongnam	−.0621	26.64	.02
Jeonrabuk	−.1190	66.54	.04
Jeonranam	−.1995	98.07	.03
Gyeongsangbuk	−.1201	61.61	.03
Gyeongsangnam	−.0649	49.49	.10
Professional, technical & clerical	.1559	58.19	.02
Administrative, managerial	.3355	140.70	.02
Clerical	−.0921	62.75	.02
Sales	−.1241	32.80	.01
Service	−.4007	187.12	.04
Agriculture	−.2878	34.36	.00
Production	−.2973	181.33	.29
Production related	−.3012	185.52	.21
Transportation	−.2291	134.90	.14
Mining & quarrying	.0830	10.00	.03
Manufacturing	−.0813	9.84	.70
Electricity, gas, & water	.0277	3.29	.01
Construction	.1114	12.11	.03
Wholesale & retail trade	.0392	4.72	.03
Transport, storage, & communication	−.0192	2.27	.09
Financing, insurance, real estate, etc.	.0964	11.90	.04
Community, special, & personal services	.0859	10.65	.06
Constant	10.8339	1,243.30	1
Dependent variable			11.73
$\bar{R}^2$	.8965		
F	327,217.0		
DF	1,359,350		
N	1,359,387		

Glossary of Data Sets

As an aid and reference to the tables, this glossary lists the book's principal sources of data, and gives for each the approximate number of regions or industries across which unemployment rates are available.

Number of Unemployment Rate Observations by Country

1. *United States*
a). GSS   13 years by 9 regions
                      13 years by 25 industries
b). CPS   19 years by 51 states (1963–1967, 1976–1990) and
                      9 years by 30 (approx.) regions (1968–1975)
                      25 years by 46 industries

Cell means

Regions   25 years by 21 areas
States   9 years by 51 states
Industry   25 years by 46 industries

2. *United Kingdom*
a). WIRS1   1 year by 65 counties
b). WIRS2   1 year by 65 counties
c). WIRS3   1 year by 322 Travel-to-Work-Areas
d). WIRS3   1 year by 280 Local Labor Market Areas
e). NCDS   1 year by 65 counties
f). BSA   6 years by 11 regions
g). GHS   18 years by 11 regions

3. *Germany*   6 years by 11 regions by male and female

4. *Austria*   5 years by 10 regions by male and female

5. *Australia*   1 year by 8 regions by male and female

6. *Korea*   3 years by 9 industries

7. *Canada*   4 years by 10 provinces

8. *Italy*   2 years by 4 regions by male and female

9. *Netherlands*　　　　3 years by 12 regions by male and female

10. *Switzerland*　　　　1 year by 25 counties

11. *Norway*　　　　　　3 years by 19 counties

12. *Eire*　　　　　　　4 years by 8 regions

Notes: The U.S. March CPS file from 1968 to 1975 identify a variety of different groupings of states. Where an individual state is identified, the state unemployment rate is used. When states are grouped, the weighted mean of their unemployment rates is used, with the relative labor force sizes as the weights. For example, in the 1968–1972 tapes, Arkansas and Oklahoma are included as one category with Louisiana as a separate category. However, in the 1973–1975 tapes, Arkansas, Louisiana, and Oklahoma are included together as one item. In the remaining tapes, states are identified separately.

References

Abowd, J. M. (1989). "The Effect of Wage Bargains on the Stock Market Value of the Firm." *American Economic Review* 79:774–800.

Abowd, J. M., and F. Kramarz (1992). "A Test of Negotiation and Incentive Compensation Models Using Longitudinal French Enterprise Data." Mimeo, INSEE and Cornell University, Ithaca, NY.

Abraham, K. G., and S. N. Houseman (1994). "Earnings Inequality in Germany." In *Differences and Changes in Wage Structures*, edited by Richard Freeman and Larry Katz. Chicago: University of Chicago Press and NBER. Forthcoming.

Adams, J. D. (1985). "Permanent Differences in Unemployment and Permanent Wage Differentials." *Quarterly Journal of Economics* 100:29–56.

Akerlof, G. A., and J. L. Yellen (1990). "The Fair Wage-Effort Hypothesis and Unemployment." *Quarterly Journal of Economics* 105:255–284.

Allen, S. G. (1992). "Updated Notes on the Interindustry Wage Structure." Mimeo, North Carolina State University, Raleigh.

Alogoskoufis, G., and A. Manning (1988). "On the Persistence of Unemployment." *Economic Policy* 7:427–469.

Andersen, T. M., and O. Risager (1990). "Wage Formation in Denmark." In *Wage Formation and Macroeconomic Policy in the Nordic Countries*, edited by L. Calmfors. Oxford: Oxford University Press. 137–181.

Antonelli, P. (1987). "Human Resources and Labour Incomes. Demand For Education, Supply of Labour and a Comparison Between the Private and Public Sector." *Labour* 1:153–190.

Arvan, L. (1993). "Why Explicit Performance Bonds are Absent from Employment Contracts." BEBR Faculty Working Paper 93-0119. Urbana-Champaign: University of Illinois.

Ashenfelter, O. C., and P. R. G. Layard (eds.) (1986). *Handbook of Labor Economics.* Amsterdam: North Holland.

Australian Bureau of Statistics (1988). *Incidence of Awards: May 1985.* Cat. No. 6315.0. Canberra: Australian Bureau of Statistics.

Azariadis, C. (1975). "Implicit Contracts and Underemployment Equilibria." *Journal of Political Economy* 83:1183–1202.

Baily, M. N. (1974). "Wages and Employment Under Uncertain Demand." *Review of Economic Studies* 41:37–50.

Bar-Or, Y., J. B. Burbidge, L. Magee, and A. L. Robb (1992). "Canadian Experience-Earnings Profiles and the Return to Education in Canada: 1971–1990." Working Paper 93-04. Hamilton, Ontario, Canada. Dept. of Economics, McMaster University.

Bartik, T. (1991). *Who Benefits from State and Local Economic Development Policies?* Kalamazoo, MI: Upjohn Institute for Employment Research.

Bauer, J. G., and C. H. Lee (1989). "Economic Development and Labor Market Segregation: The Case of Korea." Mimeo, East-West Center, University of Hawaii, Honolulu.

Bean, C. R. (1994). "European Unemployment: A Survey." *Journal of Economic Literature* 32:573–619.

Bean, C. R., P. R. G. Layard, and S. J. Nickell (1986). "The Rise in Unemployment: A Multi-Country Study." *Economica* 53:S1–S22.

Beckerman, W., and T. Jenkinson (1986). "What Stopped the Inflation? Unemployment or Commodity Prices?" *Economic Journal* 96:39–54.

Beckerman, W., and T. Jenkinson (1990). "Wage Bargaining and Profitability: A Disaggregative Analysis." *Labour* 4:57–77.

Beggs, J., and B. J. Chapman (1988). "Immigrant Wage Adjustment in Australia: Cross-Section and Time-Series Estimates." *Economic Record* 64:161–167.

Behman, S. (1978). "Interstate Differentials in Wages and Unemployment." *Industrial Relations* 17:168–188.

Bhalotra, S. (1993). "Geographical Differences in Unemployment and Wage Rates in India." Mimeo, Wolfson College, Oxford University, Oxford.

Bils, M. J. (1985). "Real Wages Over the Business Cycle: Evidence from Panel Data." *Journal of Political Economy* 93:666–689.

Binmore, K., A. Rubinstein, and A. Wolinsky (1986). "The Nash Bargaining Solution in Economic Modelling." *Rand Journal of Economics* 17:176–188.

Blackaby, D. H., R. C. Bladen-Hovell, and E. J. Symons (1991). "Unemployment, Duration and Wage Determination in the United Kingdom: Evidence from the FES, 1980–86." *Oxford Bulletin of Economics and Statistics* 53:377–399.

Blackaby, D. H., and L. C. Hunt (1992). "The 'Wage Curve' and Long-Term Unemployment." *Manchester School* 60:419–428.

Blackaby, D. H., and D. N. Manning (1987). "Regional Earnings Revisited." *Manchester School* 55:158–183.

Blackaby, D. H., and D. N. Manning (1990a). "Earnings, Unemployment and the Regional Employment Structure in Britain." *Regional Studies* 24:529–535.

Blackaby, D. H., and D. N. Manning (1990b). "The North-South Divide: Earnings, Unemployment and Cost of Living Differences in Great Britain." *Papers of the Regional Science Association* 69:43–55.

Blackaby, D. H., and D. N. Manning (1990c). "The North-South Divide: Questions of Existence and Stability." *Economic Journal* 100:510–527.

Blackaby, D. H., and D. N. Manning (1992). "Regional Earnings and Unemployment—A Simultaneous Approach." *Oxford Bulletin of Economic and Statistics* 54:481–503.

Blackaby, D. H., and P. D. Murphy (1991). "Industry Characteristics and Inter-Regional Wage Differences." *Scottish Journal of Political Economy* 38:142–161.

Blackburn, M. L., and D. E. Bloom (1991a). "Changes in the Structure of Family Income Inequality in the United States and Other Industrialized Nations During the 1980s." Mimeo, University of South Carolina.

Blackburn, M. L, and D. E. Bloom (1991b). "The Distribution of Family Income: Measuring and Explaining Changes in the 1980s for Canada and the United States." Working Paper No. 3659. Cambridge, MA: NBER.

Blanchard, O. J., and L. F. Katz (1992). "Regional Evolutions." *Brookings Papers on Economic Activity* 1:1–75.

Blanchard, O. J., and L. H. Summers (1986). "Hysteresis and the European Unemployment Problem." In *NBER Macroeconomics Annual*, edited by S. Fischer, 15–78. Cambridge, MA: MIT Press.

Blanchflower, D. G. (1984). "Union Relative Wage Effects: A Cross-Section Analysis Using Establishment Data." *British Journal of Industrial Relations* 22:311–332.

Blanchflower, D. G. (1986). "What Effect Do Unions Have on Relative Wages in Great Britain?" *British Journal of Industrial Relations* 24:196–204.

Blanchflower, D. G. (1991). "Fear, Unemployment and Pay Flexibility." *Economic Journal* 101:483–496.

Blanchflower, D. G., and R. B. Freeman (1992). "Going Different Ways: Unionism in the United States and Other Advanced OECD Countries." *Industrial Relations* 31:56–79.

Blanchflower, D. G., and R. B. Freeman (1993). "The Legacy of Communist Labor Relations." Working paper 4740 Cambridge, MA: NBER.

Blanchflower, D. G., and L. M. Lynch (1994). "Training at Work: A Comparison of U.S. and British Youths." In *International Comparisons of Private Sector Training*, edited by L. Lynch. Chicago: University of Chicago Press.

Blanchflower, D. G., and A. J. Oswald (1988). "Internal and External Influences Upon Pay Settlements." *British Journal of Industrial Relations* 26:363–370.

Blanchflower, D. G., and A. J. Oswald (1989a). "Comment." *Oxford Bulletin of Economics and Statistics* 51:137–143.

Blanchflower, D. G., and A. J. Oswald (1989b). "International Patterns of Work." *British Social Attitudes: Special International Report*, edited by R. Jowell, S. Witherspoon, and L. Brook. Aldershot: Gower Press.

Blanchflower, D. G., and A. J. Oswald (1990a). "The Determination of White Collar Pay." *Oxford Economic Papers* 42:356–378.

Blanchflower, D. G., and A. J. Oswald (1990b). "The Wage Curve." *Scandinavian Journal of Economics* 92:215–235.

Blanchflower, D. G., and A. J. Oswald (1993). "Testing for a U-Shaped Wage Curve: A Response." *Scandinavian Journal of Economics* 95:245–248.

Blanchflower, D. G., and A. J. Oswald (1994a). "Estimating a Wage Curve for Britain: 1973–1990." *Economic Journal* 104:1025–1043.

Blanchflower, D. G., and A. J. Oswald (1994b). "International Wage Curves." In *Differences and Changes in Wage Structures*, edited by R. Freeman and L. Katz. Chicago: University of Chicago Press. Forthcoming.

Blanchflower, D. G., A. J. Oswald, and M. D. Garrett (1990). "Insider Power in Wage Determination." *Economica* 57:143–170.

Blanchflower, D. G., A. J. Oswald, and P. Sanfey (1993). "Wages, Profits and Rent-Sharing." Mimeo, Centre for Economic Performance, LSE, London.

Blau, F. D., and L. M. Kahn (1994). "The Gender Earnings Gap: Some International Evidence." In *Differences and Changes in Wage Structures*, edited by R. Freeman and L. Katz. Chicago: University of Chicago Press. Forthcoming.

Blomskog, S. (1993). "Is There a Stable Swedish Wage Curve?" Mimeo, Swedish Institute for Social Research, Stockholm.

Bloom, D., and G. Grenier (1991). "The Earnings of Linguistic Minorities: French in Canada and Spanish in the United States." Working Paper No. 3660. Cambridge, MA: NBER.

Blyth, C. A. (1979). "The Interaction Between Collective Bargaining and Government Policies in Selected Member Countries." In *Collective Bargaining and Government Policies*. Paris: OECD, 59–94.

Booth, A. (1994). *The Economics of the Trade Union*. Cambridge: Cambridge University Press. Forthcoming.

Bover, O., J. N. Muellbauer, and A. Murphy (1989). "Housing, Wages and U.K. Labor Markets." *Oxford Bulletin of Economics and Statistics* 51:97–136.

Bowles, S. (1985). "The Production Process in a Competitive Economy: Walrasian, Neo-Hobbesian and Marxian Models." *American Economic Review* 75:16–36.

Bratt, C. (1986). *Labor Relations in 18 Countries*. Stockholm: Swedish Employers' Confederation.

Browne, L. E. (1978). "Regional Unemployment Rates: Why Are They So Different?" *New England Economic Review* July:5–26.

Bruno, M., and J. Sachs (1985). *Economics of Worldwide Stagflation*. Oxford: Basil Blackwell.

Burbidge, J. B., L. Magee, and A. L. Robb (1993). "On Canadian Wage Inequality: The 1970s and 1980s'." Working Paper 93–07. McMaster University, Department of Economic Hamilton, Ontario Canada.

Calmfors, L. (1990). "Introduction." In *Wage Formation and Macroeconomic Policy in the Nordic Countries*, edited by L. Calmfors. Oxford: Oxford University Press, 11–62.

Calmfors. L. (1993). "Lessons from the Macroeconomic Experience of Sweden." *European Journal of Political Economy* 9:25–72.

Calmfors, L., and J. Driffill (1988). "Bargaining Structure, Corporatism and Macroeconomic Performance." *Economic Policy* 6:13–61.

Calmfors, L., and H. Horn (eds.) (1986). *Trade Unions, Wage Formation and Macroeconomic Stability*. Houndsmill, England: Macmillan.

Calmfors, L., and R. Nymoen (1990). "Real Wage Adjustment and Employment Policies in the Nordic Countries." *Economic Policy* 11:397–448.

Card, D. (1990a). "Strikes and Wages: A Test of an Asymmetric Information Model." *Quarterly Journal of Economics* 105:625–660.

Card, D. (1990b). "Unexpected Inflation, Real Wages and Employment Determination in Union Contracts." *American Economic Review* 80:669–688.

Carlin, W., and D. Soskice (1990). *Macroeconomics and the Wage Bargain*. Oxford: Oxford University Press.

Caroleo, F. (1990). "Regional Differentials in Unemployment Rates." *Labour* 4:125–145.

Carruth, A. A., M. Hooker, and A. J. Oswald (1993). "Unemployment, Oil Prices and the Real Interest Rate: Evidence from Canada and the UK." Paper presented at a conference in memory of John Vanderkamp, University of Guelph, Ontario, Canada.

Carruth, A. A., and A. J. Oswald (1987a). "On Union Preferences and Labour Market Models: Insiders and Outsiders." *Economic Journal* 97:431–445.

Carruth, A. A., and A. J. Oswald (1987b). "Wage Inflexibility in Britain." *Oxford Bulletin of Economics and Statistics* 49:59–78.

Carruth, A. A., and A. J. Oswald (1989). *Pay Determination and Industrial Prosperity*. Oxford: Oxford University Press.

Carruth, A. A., A. J. Oswald, and L. Findlay (1986). "A Test of a Model of Trade Union Behaviour: The Coal and Steel Industries in Britain." *Oxford Bulletin of Economics and Statistics* 48:1–18.

Carruth, A. A., and C. Schnabel (1990). "Empirical Modelling of Trade Union Growth in Germany 1956–86: Traditional versus Cointegration and Error Correction Methods." *Weltwirtschaftliches Archiv* 126:326–346.

Champion, A., A. Green, D. Owen, D. Ellin, and M. Coombes (1987). *Changing Places: Britain's Demographic, Economic and Social Complexion*. London: Edward Arnold.

Chapman, B. J., and P. Miller (1992). "An Analysis of the Origins of Sex Differences in Australian Wages." *Journal of Industrial Relations* 28:504–520.

Chapman, B. J., and H. W. Tan (1992). "An Analysis of Youth Training in Australia, 1985–1988: Technological Change and Wages." In *Youth in the Eighties*, edited by R. Gregory and T. Karmel. CEPR, Australian National University, 99–124.

Chiswick, B., and P. Miller (1992). "The Determinants of Post-Immigrant Investments in Education." Working Paper No. 92.17. University of Western Australia, Department of Economics.

Chiswick, B., and P. Miller (1993), "The Endogeneity Between Language and Earnings: An International Analysis." Working Paper No. 93.03. University of Western Australia, Department of Economics.

Christl, J. (1982). "An Econometric Model of Labor Supply." *Empirica* 10:155–173.

Christofides, L. N., and A. J. Oswald (1991). "Efficient and Inefficient Employment Outcomes: A Study Based on Canadian Contract Data." *Research in Labor Economics* 12:173–190. Greenwich, CT: JAI Press.

Christofides, L. N., and A. J. Oswald (1992). "Real Wage Determination and Rent-Sharing in Collective Bargaining Agreements." *Quarterly Journal of Economics* 65:985–1002.

Christofides, L. N., and R. Swidinsky (1994). "Wage Determination by Gender and Visible Minority Status: Evidence from the 1989 LMAS." *Canadian Public Policy*. Forthcoming.

Christofides, L. N., R. Swidinsky, and D. A. Wilton (1980). "A Microeconometric Analysis of the Canadian Wage Determination Process." *Economica* 47:165–178.

Christofides, L. N., and D. Wilton (1985). "Wage Determination in the Aftermath of Controls." *Economica* 52:51–64.

Clark, A., and R. Layard (1989). *U.K. Unemployment*. London: Heinemann.

Clark, M. G. (1983). "The Swiss Experience With Foreign Workers: Lessons for the United States." *Industrial and Labor Relations Review* 36:606–623.

Coase, R. H. (1992). "The Institutional Structure of Production." *American Economic Review* 82:713–719.

Connolly, S., J. Micklewright, and S. J. Nickell (1992). "The Occupational Success of Young Men Who Left School at Sixteen." *Oxford Economic Papers* 44:460–479.

Cross, R. (ed.) (1988). *Unemployment, Hysteresis and the Natural Rate Hypothesis*. Oxford: Basil Blackwell.

Crouch, C. (1985). "Conditions for Trade Union Wage Restraint." In *The Politics of Inflation and Economic Stagnation*, edited by L. Lindberg, and C. S. Maier. Washington, D.C.: The Brookings Institution, 105–139.

Crul, P. W. (1990). "Pay-Service Investigations into Differences in the Evolution of Conditions of Employment and Pay Structures in the Netherlands." In *European Symposium on Wages*, vol. 4, 33–48. Paris: Centre d'Etude des Revenus et des Couts.

Daniel, W. W., and N. Millward (1983). *Workplace Industrial Relations in Britain*. Aldershot: Gower Press.

Davis, J. A., and R. Jowell (1989). "Measuring National Differences." In *British Social Attitudes: Special International Report*. edited by R. Jowell, S. Witherspoon, and L. Brook. Aldershot: Gower Press, 1–13.

Davis, S. (1992). "Cross-Country Patterns of Change in Relative Wages." In *NBER Macroeconomics Annual*, 239–292. Cambridge, MA: NBER.

Deery, S., and H. De Cieri (1991). "Determinants of Trade Union Membership in Australia." *British Journal of Industrial Relations* 29(1):59–74.

Del Boca, D. (1990). "Facts and Theories of the Italian Labour Market (1970–1985): A Time Series Analysis of Wages, Employment and Prices." *Labour* 4:163–179.

Dell'Aringa, C., and C. Lucifora (1990). "Wage Determination and Union Behaviour in Italy: An Efficiency Wage Interpretation." In *European Symposium on Wages*, vol. 4, 69–88. Paris: Centre d'Etude des Revenus et des Couts.

Denny, K., and S. Machin (1991). "The Role of Profitability and Industrial Wages in Firm-Level Wage Determination." *Fiscal Studies* 12:34–45.

Desai, M. (1975). "The Phillips Curve: A Revisionist Interpretation." *Economica* 42:1–19.

Desai, M. (1984). "Wages, Prices and Unemployment a Quarter Century After the Phillips Curve." In *Econometrics and Quantitative Economics*, edited by D. F. Hendry and K. F. Wallis. Oxford: Basil Blackwell, 253–274.

Dickens, W. T. (1990). "Error Components in Grouped Data: Is It Ever Worth Weighting?" *Review of Economics and Statistics* 72:328–333.

Dickens, W. T., and L. F. Katz (1987). "Inter-Industry Wage Differences and Industry Characteristics." In *Unemployment and the Structure of Labor Markets*, edited by K. Lang and J. S. Leonard. Oxford: Basil Blackwell, 48–89.

DiNardo, J., and T. Lemieux (1993). "Diverging Male Wage Inequality in the United States and Canada: Do Unions Explain the Difference?" Mimeo, Université de Montréal, Montréal.

Dooley, M. D. (1985). "The Overeducated Canadian? Changes in the Relationship among Earnings, Education and Age for Canadian Men." *Canadian Journal of Economics* 18:164–181.

Dreze, J. H., and C. R. Bean (1990). "European Unemployment: Lessons From a Multicountry Econometric Study." *Scandinavian Journal of Economics* 92:135–165.

Dreze, J. H., and C. R. Bean (1991). *Europe's Unemployment Problem.* Cambridge, MA: MIT Press.

Driehuis, W. (1986). "Unemployment in the Netherlands." In *The Rise in Unemployment*, edited by C. R. Bean, P. R. G. Layard, and S. J. Nickell. Oxford: Basil Blackwell, 297–312.

Eberts, R. W., and J. A. Stone (1992). *Wage and Employment Determination in Local Labor Markets.* Research Report. Kalamazoo: Upjohn Institute for Employment.

Economica (1986). Special issue on Unemployment Vol. 53.

Edin, P. A., and B. Holmlund (1989). "The Unemployment Elasticity of Pay: Evidence from Swedish Micro Data." Mimeo, University of Uppsala, Sweden.

Edin, P. A., B. Holmlund, and T. Ostros (1993). "Wage Behavior and Labor Market Programs in Sweden: Evidence from Micro Data." Working Paper 93-1. University of Uppsala, Sweden. Forthcoming, 1994, in *Labour Markets and Economic Performance: Europe, Japan and the United States*, edited by T. Tachibanaki. New York: Macmillan.

Elias, P., and D. G. Blanchflower (1987). "Local Labour Market Influences on Early Occupational Attainment." In *Unemployment, the Regions and Labour Markets: Reactions to Recession*, edited by I. Gordon. London: Pion Press, 158–171.

Elias, P., and D. G. Blanchflower (1989). *The Occupations, Earnings and Work Histories of Young Adults—Who Gets the Good Jobs?.* Research Paper No. 68. London: Department of Employment.

Eurostat (1990). *Basic Statistics of the Community.* Statistical Office of the European Communities, Luxembourg.

Erikson, C. L., and A. C. Ichino (1994). "Wage Differentials in Italy; Market Forces, Institutions, and Inflation." In *Differences and Changes in Wage Structures*, edited by R. Freeman and L. Katz. Chicago: University of Chicago Press and NBER. Forthcoming.

Farber, H. S. (1986). "The Analysis of Union Behavior." In *Handbook of Labor Economics*, edited by O. C. Ashenfelter, and P. R. G. Layard. Amsterdam: North-Holland. Vol. 2, 1039–1089.

Ferry, G. (1993). "No Smoke Without Fire: Sir Richard Doll." *Oxford Today* 5:11–12.

Fields, G. (1975). "Rural-Urban Migration, Urban Unemployment and Under-Employment, and Job Search Activity in LDCs." *Journal of Development Economics* 2:165–187.

Franz, W., and H. Konig (1986). "The Nature and Causes of Unemployment in the Federal Republic Of Germany Since the 1970s: An Empirical Investigation." In *The Rise in Unemployment*, edited by C. R. Bean, P. R. G. Layard, and S. J. Nickell. Oxford: Basil Blackwell, 219–244.

Franz, W., and E. Schafer-Jackel (1990). "Disturbances and Wages. A Theoretical and Empirical Analysis for the FRG." In *Economics of Wage Determination*, edited by H. Konig. Berlin: Springer-Verlag.

Freeman, R. B. (1982). "Economic Determinants of Geographic and Individual Variation in the Labor Market Position of Young Persons." In *The Youth Employment Problem: Its Nature, Causes and Consequences*, edited by R. B. Freeman and D. A. Wise. Chicago: University of Chicago Press, 115–148.

Freeman, R. B. (1988a). "Evaluating the European View That the United States Has No Unemployment Problem." *American Economic Review, Papers and Proceedings* 78:294–299.

Freeman, R. B. (1988b). "Labour Market Institutions and Economic Performance." *Economic Policy* 6:64–80.

Freeman, R. B. (1990a). "On the Divergence of Unionism Among Developed Countries." In *Labor Relations and Economic Performance*, edited by Brunetta, R. and C. Dell'Aringa. New York: Macmillan.

Freeman, R. B. (1990b). "Employment and Earnings of Disadvantaged Young Men in a Labor-Shortage Economy." Working Paper 3444. Cambridge, MA: NBER.

Freeman, R. B., and K. Needels (1993). "Skill Differentials in Canada in an Era of Rising Labor Market Inequality." In *Small Differences that Matter: Labor Markets and Income Maintenance in Canada and the United States*, edited by D. Card and R. Freeman. Chicago: University of Chicago Press, 45–68.

Freeman, R. B., and J. Pelletier (1990). "The Impact of Industrial Relations Legislation on British Union Density." *British Journal of Industrial Relations* 28:141–164.

Friedman, M. (1953). *Essays in Positive Economics*. Chicago: University of Chicago Press.

Fuerstenberg, F. (1987). "Industrial Relations in the Federal Republic of Germany." In *International and Comparative Industrial Relations*, edited by G. J. Bamber, and R. D. Lansbury. London: Allen and Unwin, 165–186.

Gerlach, K. (1987). "A Note on Male-Female Wage Differences in West Germany." *Journal of Human Resources* 22:584–592.

Gerlach, K., and E. M. Schmidt (1989). "Firm Size and Wages." Mimeo, University of Hannover, Germany.

Gilbert, C. L. (1976). "The Original Phillips Curve Estimates." *Economica* 43:51–57.

Goodfriend, M. (1985). "Reinterpreting Money Demand Regressions." In *Understanding Monetary Regimes*, edited by K. Brunner and A. H. Meltzer. Carnegie Rochester Conference Series, Vol. 22. Amsterdam: North Holland.

Gottfries, N., and H. Horn (1987). "Wage Formation and the Persistence of Unemployment." *Economic Journal* 97:877–884.

Gottschalk, P., and M. Joyce (1991). "Changes in Earnings Inequality: An International Perspective." Working Paper No. 66. Luxembourg: Luxembourg Income Study.

Graafland, J. J. (1989). "Can Hysteresis Explain Different Labour Market Operations Between Europe and the US?" *Applied Economics* 21:95–111.

Graafland, J. J. (1990). "Insiders and Outsiders in Wage Formation: The Dutch Case." Mimeo, Central Planning Bureau, The Hague, Netherlands.

Graafland, J. J. (1991). "On the Causes of Hysteresis in Long-term Unemployment in the Netherlands." *Oxford Bulletin of Economics and Statistics* 53:155–170.

Grant, E. K., R. Swidinsky, and J. Vanderkamp (1987). "Canadian Union/Non-union Wage Differentials." *Industrial and Labor Relations Review* 41:93–107.

Gray, W. B. (1989). "Industry Productivity Database." Mimeo, Clark University.

Green, A. E., C. Hasluck, and D. Owen (1991). *The Development of Local Labour Market Typologies: Classifications of Travel-To-Work-Areas.* Department of Employment Research Paper No. 84. London, England.

Greene, W. H. (1990). *Econometric Analysis.* New York: Macmillan.

Greenhalgh, C. (1980). "Male-Female Wage Differentials in Great Britain: Is Marriage an Equal Opportunity?" *Economic Journal* 90:751–775.

Greenwald, B. (1983). "A General Analysis of Bias in the Estimated Standard Errors of Least Squares Coefficients." *Journal of Econometrics* 22:323–328.

Greenwald, B., and J. E. Stiglitz (1993). "New and Old Keynesians." *Journal of Economic Perspectives* 7:23–44.

Greenwood, M. J. (1975). "Research on Internal Migration in the United States." *Journal of Economic Literature* 13:397–433.

Gregg, P., and S. Machin (1993). "Is the UK Rise in Inequality Different?" Mimeo, National Institute of Economic and Social Research, London.

Gregory, M., P. Lobban, and A. Thomson (1985). "Wage Settlements in Manufacturing, 1979–84: Evidence from the CBI Pay Databank." *British Journal of Industrial Relations* 23: 339–357.

Gregory, M., P. Lobban, and A. Thomson (1986). "Bargaining Structure, Pay Settlements and Perceived Pressures in Manufacturing 1979–1984: Further Analysis from the CBI Databank." *British Journal of Industrial Relations* 24:215–232.

Gregory, M., P. Lobban, and A. Thomson (1987). "Pay Settlements in Manufacturing Industry, 1979–1984: A Micro-Data Study of the Impact of Product and Labour Market Pressures." *Oxford Bulletin of Economics and Statistics* 49:129–150.

Gregory, R. G. (1986). "Wages Policy and Unemployment in Australia." *Economica,* Supplement, 53:S53–S72.

Groot, W., E. Mekkelholt, and H. Oosterbeek (1992). "Further Evidence on the Wage Curve." *Economics Letters* 38:355–359.

Groshen, E. L. (1991). "Sources of Intra-Industry Wage Dispersion: How Much Do Employers Matter?" *Quarterly Journal of Economics* 106:869–884.

Grossman, S. J., and O. D. Hart (1981). "Implicit Contracts, Moral Hazard and Unemployment." *American Economic Review, Papers and Proceedings*, 301–307.

Grubb, D. (1986). "Topics in the OECD Phillips Curve." *Economic Journal* 96:55–79.

Grubb, D., R. Jackman, and P. R. G. Layard (1983). "Wage Rigidity and Unemployment in OECD Countries." *European Economic Review* 21:11–39.

Grubb, D., P. R. G. Layard, and J. Symons (1984). "Wages, Unemployment and Incomes Policies." In *Europe's Stagflation*, edited by M. Emerson. Oxford: Clarendon Press, 57–88.

Gujarati, D. (1970a). "Use of Dummy Variables in Testing for Equality Between Sets of Coefficients in Two Linear Regressions: A Generalization." *American Statistician* 24:18–21.

Gujarati, D. (1970b). "Use of Dummy Variables in Testing for Equality Between Sets of Coefficients in Two Linear Regressions: A Note." *American Statistician* 24:50–52.

Gunderson, M. (1979). "Decomposition of Male/Female Earnings Differentials." *Canadian Journal of Economics* 12(3):479–485.

Hall, R. E. (1970). "Why is the Unemployment Rate So High at Full Employment?" *Brookings Papers on Economic Activity* 3:369–402.

Hall, R. E. (1972). "Turnover in the Labor Force." *Brookings Papers on Economic Activity* 3:709–756.

Hamermesh, D. S. (1988). "Data Difficulties in Labor Economics." In *Fifty Years of Economic Measurement*, edited by E. R. Berndt, and J. E. Triplett. NBER Research Studies in Income and Wealth 54. Chicago: University of Chicago Press.

Hamermesh, D. S. (1993). *Labor Demand*. Princeton, NJ: Princeton University Press.

Harberger, A. C. (1993). "The Search for Relevance in Economics." *American Economic Review, Papers and Proceedings*, 83:1–16.

Harris, J. R., and M. P. Todaro (1970). "Migration, Unemployment and Development: A Two-Sector Analysis." *American Economic Review* 60:126–142.

Hartog, J. (1986). "Earnings Functions: Beyond Human Capital." *Applied Economics* 18:1291–1309.

Hartog, J. (1988). "An Ordered Response Model for Allocation and Earnings." *Kyklos* 41:113–141.

Hartog, J. (1989). "Survey Non-Response in Relation to Ability and Family Background: Structure and Effects on Estimated Earnings Functions." *Applied Economics* 21:387–395.

Hartog, J., and H. Oosterbeck (1989). "Public and Private Sector Wages in the Netherlands or: the Vital Role of Unobserved Heterogeneity." Research Memorandum No. 8926. Amsterdam: University of Amsterdam, Department of Economics.

Hellwig, M., and M. J. M. Neuman (1987). "Economic Policy in Germany: Was There a Turnaround?" *Economic Policy* 5:105–145.

Hendry, D. F., and K. F. Wallis (eds) (1984). *Econometrics and Quantitative Economics*. Oxford: Basil Blackwell.

Hersoug, T., K. N. Kjaer, and A. Rødseth (1986). "Wages, Taxes and the Utility-Maximizing Trade Union: A Confrontation with Norwegian Data." *Oxford Economic Papers* 38:403–423.

Hicks, J. R. (1963). *The Theory of Wages*, 2d edition. London: Macmillan.

Hildreth, A. K. G., and A. J. Oswald (1993). "Rent-Sharing and Wages: Evidence from Company and Establishment Panels." Mimeo, Oxford University, Oxford.

Hoddinott, J. (1993). "Wages and Unemployment in Urban Cote d'Ivoire." Mimeo, Centre for the Study of African Economies, Oxford University, Oxford

Hoel, M., and R. Nymoen (1988). "Wage Formation in Norwegian Manufacturing: An Empirical Application of a Theoretical Bargaining Model." *European Economic Review* 32: 977–997.

Holmlund, B., and P. Skedinger (1990). "Wage Bargaining and Wage Drift: Evidence From the Swedish Wood Industry." In *Wage Formation and Macroeconomic Policy in the Nordic Countries*, edited by L. Calmfors. Oxford: Oxford University Press, 363–388.

Holmlund, B., and J. Zetterberg (1991). "Insider Effects in Wage Determination. Evidence From Five Countries." *European Economic Review* 35:1009–1034.

Holzer, H. J. (1991). "Employment, Unemployment and Demand Shifts in Local Labor Markets." *Review of Economics and Statistics* 73:25–32.

Hoon, H. T., and E. S. Phelps (1992). "Macroeconomic Shocks in a Dynamized Model of the Natural Rate of Unemployment." *American Economic Review* 82:889–900.

Hsiao, C. (1986). *Analysis of Panel Data*. New York, Cambridge.

Hubler, O., and K. Gerlach (1990). "Sectoral Wage Patterns, Individual Earnings and the Efficiency Wage Hypothesis." *Economics of Wage Determination*, edited by H. Konig. Berlin: Springer-Verlag.

Industrial Democracy in Europe (IDE) International Research Group (1981). *European Industrial Relations*. Oxford: Clarendon.

Jackman, R., P. R. G. Layard, and S. Savouri (1991). "Labour Market Mismatch: A Framework for Thought." In *Mismatch and Labour Mobility*, edited by F. Padoa Schioppa, Cambridge: Cambridge University Press, 44–101.

Jackman, R., R. Layard, and C. A. Pissarides (1990). "Labor Market Policies and Unemployment in the OECD." *Economic Policy* 11:449–490.

Jackman, R., and S. Savouri (1991). "Regional Wage Determination in Great Britain." CEP Discussion Paper 47. London: London School of Economics.

Johnston, J. (1992). "Econometrics: Retrospect and Prospect." In *The Future of Economics*, edited by J. D. Hey. Oxford: Basil Blackwell.

Jones, S. R. G. (1989). "Reservation Wages and the Cost of Unemployment." *Economica* 56:225–246.

Jowell, R., S. Witherspoon, and L. Brook (eds.). (1989). *British Social Attitudes: Special International Report*. Aldershot: Gower Press.

Jowell, R., L. Brook, and B. Taylor (eds.). (1991). *British Social Attitudes: The 8th Report*. Aldershot: Dartmouth Press.

Juhn, C., K. M. Murphy, and R. Topel (1991). "Unemployment, Non-Employment, and Wages: Why has the Natural Rate Increased Through Time?" *Brookings Papers in Economic Activity* 2:75–142.

Katz, L. F., and A. B. Krueger (1991a). "Changes in the Structure of Wages in the Public and Private Sectors." *Research in Labor Economics* 12:137–172. Greenwich, CT: Jai Press.

Katz, L. F., and A. B. Krueger (1991b). "The Effects of the New Minimum Wage Law in a Low-Wage Labor Market." Proceedings of the 43d annual meeting of IRRA, Washington, D.C., Dec 28–30, Madison, WI, 254–265.

Katz, L. F., and A. B. Krueger (1992). "The Effect of the Minimum Wage on the Fast Food Industry." *Industrial and Labour Relations Review* 46:6–21.

Katz, L. F., G. Loveman, and D. G. Blanchflower (1994). "A Comparison of Changes in the Structure of Wages in Four OECD Countries." In *Differences and Changes in Wage Structures*, edited by Richard Freeman and Larry Katz. Chicago: University of Chicago Press. Forthcoming.

Katz, L. F., and K. M. Murphy (1992). "Changes in Relative Wages, 1963–1987: Supply and Demand Factors." *Quarterly Journal of Economics* 107:35–78.

Katz, L. F., and L. H. Summers (1989). "Industry Rents: Evidence and Implications." *Brookings Papers on Economic Activity (Microeconomics)*, 209–275. Washington, D.C.: Brookings Institution.

Kennedy, T. (1980). *European Labor Relations*. Lexington, MA: Lexington Books.

Keynes, J. M. (1936). *The General Theory of Employment, Interest and Money*. London: Macmillan.

Kim, D. I., and R. Topel (1994). "Labor Markets and Economic Growth: Lessons from Korea's Industrialization, 1970–1990." In *Differences and Changes in Wage Structures*, edited by Richard Freeman and Larry Katz. Chicago: University of Chicago Press. Forthcoming.

Kjær, K., and A. Rødseth (1987). "Wage Formation in Norway: What Can Aggregate Time Series Tell Us?" Memorandum No. 6. Oslo: University of Oslo, Department of Economics.

Kloek, T. (1981). "OLS Estimation in a Model where a Microvariable is Explained by Aggregates and Contemporaneous Disturbances are Equicorrelated." *Econometrica* 49:205–207.

Krueger, A. B., and S. J. Pischke (1994). "A Comparative Analysis of East and West German Labor Markets: Before and After Unification." In *Differences and Changes in Wage Structures*, edited by R. Freeman and L. Katz. Chicago: University of Chicago Press. Forthcoming.

Krueger, A. B., and L. H. Summers (1987). "Reflections on the Inter-Industry Wage Structure." In *Unemployment and the Structure of Labor Markets*, edited by K. Lang and J. S. Leonard. Oxford: Basil Blackwell.

Krueger, A. B., and L. H. Summers (1988). "Efficiency Wages and the Inter-Industry Wage Structure." *Econometrica* 56:259–293.

Kwark, N. S., and C. Rhee (1991). "Educational Wage Differentials in Korea." Mimeo, Department of Economics, University of Rochester.

Kuhl, J. (1987). "Labour Policy in the Federal Republic of Germany: Challenges and Concepts." *Labour* 1:25–56.

Laidler, D. E., and J. M. Parkin (1975). "Inflation—A Survey." *Economic Journal* 85:741–809.

Lanot, G., and I. Walker (1993). "Alternative Estimators of the Union/Non-Union Wage Differential: UK Pooled Cross-Section Evidence." Mimeo, University of Keele, England.

Layard, R. (1986). *How to Beat Unemployment*. Oxford: Oxford University Press.

Layard, R., and C. R. Bean (1990). "Why Does Unemployment Persist?" In *The State of Macroeconomics*, edited by S. Honkapohja. Oxford: Basil Blackwell.

Layard, P. R. G., and S. J. Nickell (1986). "Unemployment in Britain." *Economica*, Supplement, 53:121–170.

Layard, P. R. G., and S. J. Nickell (1987). "The Labour Market." In *The Performance of the British Economy*, edited by R. Dornbusch and P. R. G. Layard. Oxford: Oxford University Press, 131–179.

Layard, P. R. G., S. J. Nickell, and R. Jackman (1991). *Unemployment: Macroeconomic Performance and the Labour Market*. Oxford: Oxford University Press.

Lee, K. C., and M. H. Pesaran (1993). "The Role of Sectoral Interactions in Wage Determination in the UK Economy." *Economic Journal* 103:21–55.

Lemieux, T. (1994). "Unions and Wage Inequality in Canada and the United States." In *Small Differences that Matter: Labor Markets and Income Maintenance in Canada and the United States*, edited by D. Card and R. Freeman. Chicago: University of Chicago Press. 69–108.

Leontief, W. (1946). "The Pure Theory of the Guaranteed Annual Wage Contract." *Journal of Political Economy* 54:76–79.

Leontief, W. (1971). "Theoretical Assumptions and Non-Observed Facts." *American Economic Review* 61:1–7.

Leontief, W. (1982). "Academic Economics." *Science* 217:104–107.

Lester, R. A. (1952). "A Range Theory of Wage Differentials." *Industrial and Labor Relations Review* 5:483–500.

Lillard, L., J. P. Smith, and F. Welch (1986). "What Do We Really Know About Wages? The Importance of Non-Reporting and Census Imputation." *Journal of Political Economy* 94:489–506.

Lindauer, D. L. (1984). "Labor Market Behavior in the Republic of Korea: An Analysis of Wages and Their Impact on the Economy." Staff Working Papers 641. Washington: World Bank.

Lindbeck, A. (1989). "Remaining Puzzles and Neglected Issues in Macroeconomics." *Scandinavian Journal of Economics* 91:495–516.

Lindbeck, A. (1992). "Macroeconomic Theory and the Labour Market." *European Economic Review* 36:209–235.

Lindbeck, A. (1993). *Unemployment and Macroeconomics*. Cambridge, MA: MIT Press.

Lindbeck, A., and D. J. Snower (1986). "Wage Setting, Unemployment and Insider-Outsider Relations." *American Economic Review, Papers and Proceedings* 76:235–239.

Lindbeck, A., and D. J. Snower (1987). "Union Activity and Wage-Employment Movements." Mimeo, Institute for International Economic Studies, Stockholm.

Lindbeck, A., and D. J. Snower (1988a). "Cooperation, Harassment and Involuntary Unemployment: An Insider-Outsider Approach." *American Economic Review* 78:167–188.

Lindbeck, A., and D. J. Snower (1988b). *The Insider-Outsider Theory of Employment and Unemployment.* Cambridge, MA: MIT Press.

Lipsey, R. G. (1960). "The Relation Between Unemployment and the Rate of Change of Money Wage Rates in the United Kingdom: A Further Analysis." *Economica* 27:1–31.

Lorenz, K. (1966). *On Aggression.* New York, NY: Harcourt Brace Jovanovich.

Lorenz, W., and J. Wagner (1993). "A Note on Returns to Human Capital in the Eighties: Evidence from Twelve Countries." *Jahrbücher für Nationalökonomie und Statistik* 211(1–2): 60–72.

McCormick, B., and S. Sheppard (1992). "A Model of Regional Contraction and Unemployment." *Economic Journal* 102:366–377.

McDonald, I. M., and R. M. Solow (1981). "Wage Bargaining and Employment." *American Economic Review* 71:896–908.

MacKay, D. I., D. Boddy, J. A. Diack, and N. Jones (1971). *Labour Markets Under Different Employment Conditions.* London: Allen and Unwin.

MacLeod, W. B., and J. M. Malcomson (1993). "Investments, Holdup, and the Form of Market Contracts." *American Economic Review.* 83:811–837.

MacLeod, W. B., J. M. Malcomson, and P. Gomme (1994). "Labor Turnover and the Natural Rate of Unemployment: Efficiency Wages vs Frictional Unemployment." *Journal of Labor Economics* 12:276–315.

MaCurdy, T. E., and J. H. Pencavel (1986). "Testing Between Competing Models of Wage and Employment Determination in Unionized Markets." *Journal of Political Economy* 94:S3–S39.

Manning, A. (1990). "Implicit-Contract Theory." In *Current Issues in Labour Economics,* edited by D. Sapsford and Z. Tzannatos. London: Macmillan.

Manning, A. (1993). "Wage Bargaining and the Phillips Curve: The Identification and Specification of Aggregate Wage Equations." *Economic Journal* 103:98–118.

Margo, R. A. (1993). "Employment and Unemployment in the 1930s." *Journal of Economic Perspectives* 7:41–60.

Marshall, A. (1961). *Principles of Economics,* 2 vol. London: Macmillan. Originally published 1890.

Marston, S. T. (1985). "Two Views of the Geographic Distribution of Unemployment." *Quarterly Journal of Economics* 100:57–79.

Marx, K. (1970). *Capital,* vol. 1. London: Lawrence and Wishart.

Meghir, C., and E. Whitehouse (1992). "The Evolution of Wages in the UK: Evidence from Micro Data." Working Paper 16. London: Institute for Fiscal Studies.

Micklewright, J. (1989). "Choice at Sixteen." *Economica* 56:25–39.

Miller, P. (1987). "Gender Differences in Observed and Offered Wages in Canada." *Canadian Journal of Economics* 20:225–244.

Miller, P., and C. Mulvey (1991). "Trade Unions, Collective Voice and Fringe Benefits." *Economic Record* 68:125–141.

Miller, P., and S. Rummery (1991). "Male-Female Wage Differentials in Australia: A Reassessment." *Australian Economic Papers* 30:50–69.

Millward, N., and M. Stevens (1986). *British Workplace Industrial Relations 1980–1984*. Aldershot: Gower Press.

Millward, N., and M. Stevens (1988). "Union Density in the Regions: Evidence from the 1984 WIRS and the British Social Attitudes Survey Series." *Employment Gazette* 96:286–295.

Millward, N., M. Stevens, D. Smart, and W. R. Hawes (1992). *Workplace Industrial Relations in Transition. The ED/ESRC/PSI/ACAS Surveys*. Aldershot: Dartmouth.

Modigliani, F., F. Padoa Schioppa, and N. Rossi (1986). "Aggregate Unemployment in Italy: 1960–83." In *The Rise in Unemployment*, edited by C. R. Bean, P. R. G. Layard, and S. J. Nickell. Oxford: Basil Blackwell, 245–274.

Modigliani, F., and E. Tarrantelli (1977). "Market Forces, Trade Union Action and the Phillips Curve in Italy." *Banca Nazionale del Lavoro* 30:3–36.

Montgomery, E. B. (1992). "Evidence on Metropolitan Wage Differences Across Industries and Over Time." *Journal of Urban Economics* 31:69–83.

Montgomery, E. B. (1994). "Patterns in Regional Labor Market Adjustment: The U.S. Versus Japan." In *Social Protection Versus Economic Flexibility Is There a Trade-off?* edited by R. Blank, Chicago: University of Chicago, 95–118.

Morgan, T. (1988). "Theory Versus Empiricism in Academic Economics: Update and Comparisons." *Journal of Economic Perspectives* 2(Fall):159–164.

Morishima, M. (1992). "General Equilibrium Theory in the Twenty-First Century." In *The Future of Economics*, edited by J. D. Hey. Oxford: Basil Blackwell.

Moulton, B. R. (1986). "Random Group Effects and the Precision of Regression Estimates." *Journal of Econometrics* 32:385–397.

Moulton, B. R. (1987). "Diagnostics For Group Effects in Regression Analysis." *Journal of Business and Economic Statistics* 5:275–282.

Moulton, B. R. (1990). "An Illustration of a Pitfall in Estimating the Effects of Aggregate Variables on Micro Units." *Review of Economics and Statistics* 72:334–338.

Mulvey, C. (1986). "Wage Levels: Do Unions Make a Difference?" In *Wage Fixation in Australia*, edited by J. Niland, 202–216. Sydney: Allen and Unwin.

Murphy, K. M., and R. H. Topel (1987). "Unemployment, Risk and Earnings: Testing for Equalizing Wage Differences in the Labor Market." In *Unemployment and the Structure of Labor Markets*, edited by K. Lang and J. Leonard. Oxford: Basil Blackwell, 103–140.

Murphy, K. M., and F. Welch (1992). "The Structure of Wages." *Quarterly Journal of Economics* 107:285–326.

Nash, J. F. (1953). "Two-Person Cooperative Games." *Econometrica* 21:128–140.

Neumann, M. J. ₁M., R. Schmidt, and E. Schulte (1990). "Determinants of Contract Wages in Germany." *European Economic Review* 34:1233–1245.

Neusser, K. (1986). "Time-Series Representations of the Austrian Labor Market." *Welwirtschaftliches Archiv* 122:292–312.

Newell, A. T., and J. S. Symons (1985). "Wages and Unemployment in the OECD Countries." Discussion Paper 219. London: Centre for Labour Economics, LSE.

Newell, A. T., and J. S. Symons (1987). "Corporatism, Laissez-Faire and the Rise in Unemployment." *European Economic Review* 31:567–601.

Newell, A., and J. S. Symons (1990). "The Causes of Ireland's Unemployment." *The Economic and Social Review* 21:409–429.

Nickell, S. J. (1981). "Biases in Dynamic Models with Fixed Effects." *Econometrica* 49:1399–1416.

Nickell, S. J. (1987). "Why is Wage Inflation in Britain so High?" *Oxford Bulletin of Economics and Statistics* 49:103–128.

Nickell, S. J. (1990). "Unemployment: A Survey." *Economic Journal* 100:391–439.

Nickell, S. J., and M. Andrews (1983). "Unions, Real Wages and Employment in Britain, 1951–1979." *Oxford Economic Papers*, Supplement, 35:183–206.

Nickell, S. J., and P. Kong (1992). "An Investigation into the Power of Insiders in Wage Determination." *European Economic Review* 36:1573–1601.

Nickell, S. J., and S. Wadhwani (1990). "Insider Forces and Wage Determination." *Economic Journal* 100:496–509.

Nickell, S. J., and S. Wadhwani (1991). "Employment Determination in British Industry: Investigations Using Micro Data." *Review of Economic Studies* 58:955–970.

OECD (1982). *Economic Surveys—Germany, 1981/2*, Paris, OECD.

OECD (1986). *Economic Surveys—Italy, 1985/1986*. Paris: OECD.

OECD (1988a). *Economic Surveys—Austria, 1987/1988*. Paris: OECD.

OECD (1988b). *Economic Surveys—Ireland, 1987/1988*. Paris: OECD.

OECD (1989a). *Economic Surveys—Netherlands, 1988/1989*. Paris: OECD.

OECD (1989b). *Economic Surveys—Norway, 1988/1989*. Paris: OECD.

OECD (1990a). *Economic Surveys—Austria, 1989/1990*. Paris: OECD.

OECD (1990b). *Economic Surveys—Italy, 1989/1990*. Paris: OECD.

OECD (1990c). *Economic Surveys—Netherlands, 1989/1990*. Paris: OECD.

OECD (1990d). *Economic Surveys—Switzerland, 1989/1990*. Paris: OECD.

Oswald, A. J. (1982). "The Microeconomic Theory of the Trade Union." *Economic Journal* 92:576–595.

Oswald, A. J. (1985). "The Economic Theory of Trade Unions: An Introductory Survey." *Scandinavian Journal of Economics* 87:160–193.

Oswald, A. J. (1986a). "Unemployment Insurance and Labor Contracts Under Asymmetric Information: Theory and Facts." *American Economic Review* 76:365–377.

Oswald, A. J. (1986b). "Wage Determination and Recession: A Report on Recent Work." *British Journal of Industrial Relations* 24:181–194.

Oswald, A. J. (1992). "Progress and Microeconomic Data." In *The Future of Economics*, edited by J. D. Hey. Oxford: Basil Blackwell.

Oswald, A. J. (1993). "Efficient Contracts are on the Labour Demand Curve: Theory and Facts." *Labour Economics* 1:85–114.

Oswald, A. J., and P. J. Turnbull (1985). "Pay and Employment Determination in Britain: What are Labour Contracts Really Like?" *Oxford Review of Economic Policy* 1:80–97.

Oswald, A. J., and I. Walker (1993). "Labor Supply, Contract Theory and Unions." Mimeo, LSE and University of Keele.

Paldam, M. (1980). "The International Element in the Phillips Curve." *Scandinavian Journal of Economics* 82:216–239.

Paldam, M. (1990). "Comment on The Wage Curve." *Scandinavian Journal of Economics* 92:237–242.

Pellegrini, C. (1987). "Italian Industrial Relations." In *International and Comparative Industrial Relations*, edited in G. J. Bamber and R. D. Lansbury. London: Allen and Unwin, 121–141.

Pencavel, J. H. (1984). "The Trade-off Between Wages and Employment in Trade Union Objectives." *Quarterly Journal of Economics* 99:215–232.

Pencavel, J. H. (1985). "Wages and Employment under Trade Unionism: Microeconomic Models and Macroeconomic Applications." *Scandinavian Journal of Economics* 87:197–225.

Pencavel, J. H. (1986). "Labor Supply of Men: A Survey." In *Handbook of Labor Economics*, vol. 1, edited by O. C. Ashenfelter and R. Layard. Amsterdam: North Holland, 3–102.

Pencavel, J. H. (1991). *Labor Markets Under Trade Unionism: Employment, Wages and Hours.* Oxford: Basil Blackwell.

Perulli, P. (1990). "Italian Unions as a Stabilising Force of the Political System." *Labour* 4:25–34.

Phelps, E. S. (1967). "Phillips Curves, Expectations of Inflation and Optimal Unemployment over Time." *Economica* 34:254–281.

Phelps, E. S. (1990). "Effects of Productivity, Total Domestic Product Demand and Incentive Wages on Unemployment in a Non-Monetary Customer-Market Model of the Small Open Economy." *Scandinavian Journal of Economics* 92:353–368.

Phelps, E. S. (1992). "Consumer Demand and Equilibrium Unemployment in a Working Model of the Customer-Market Incentive-Wage Economy." *Quarterly Journal of Economics* 107:1003–1032.

Phelps, E. S. (1993). "Foreign and Domestic Determinants of Unemployment Rates Through Real-Interest and Real-Exchange Rate Channels." Seminar paper presented at LSE, January.

Phelps, E. S. (1994). *Structural Slumps: The Modern Equilibrium Theory of Unemployment, Interest, and Assets*, Cambridge MA: Harvard University Press.

Phelps, E. S. et al. (1970). *Microeconomic Foundations of Employment and Inflation Theory.* New York: W.W. Norton.

Phelps, E. S., and S. G. Winter (1970). "Optimal Price Policy under Atomistic Competition." In *Microeconomic Foundations of Employment and Inflation Theory*, edited by E. S. Phelps, et al. New York: W. W. Norton, 309–337.

Phillips, A. W. (1958). "The Relation Between Unemployment and the Rate of Change of Money Wage Rates in The United Kingdom, 1861–1957." *Economica* 25:283–299.

Pichelmann, K., and M. Wagner (1986). "Labour Surplus as a Signal for Real-Wage Adjustment: Austria, 1968–1984." In *The Rise in Unemployment*, edited by C. R. Bean, P. R. G. Layard, and S. J. Nickell, Oxford: Basil Blackwell, 75–88.

Pigou, A. C. (1927). *Industrial Fluctuations.* London: Macmillan.

Pissarides, C. A. (1990). *Equilibrium Unemployment Theory.* Oxford: Basil Blackwell.

Pissarides, C. A. (1991). "Real Wages and Unemployment in Australia." *Economica* 58:35–56.

Pissarides, C. A., and I. McMaster (1990). "Regional Migration, Wages and Unemployment: Empirical Evidence and Implications for Policy." *Oxford Economic Papers* 42:812–831.

Pissarides, C. A., and R. Moghadam (1990). "Relative Wage Flexibility in Four Countries." In *Wage Formation and Macroeconomic Policy in the Nordic Countries*, edited by L. Calmfors. Oxford: Oxford University Press, 417–442.

Pohjola, M. (1989). "Corporatism and Wage Bargaining." Discussion Paper No. 85. Helsinki: Labour Institute for Economic Research, Finland.

Pollan, W. (1980). "Wage Rigidity and the Structure of the Austrian Manufacturing Industry—An Econometric Analysis of Relative Wages." *Welwirtschaftliches Archiv* 116: 697–728.

Rayack, W. (1987). "Sources and Centers of Cyclical Movement in Real Wages: Evidence From Panel Data." *Journal of Post Keynesian Economics* 10:3–21.

Rebick, M. (1993). "The Persistence of Firm-Size Earnings Differentials and Labor Market Segmentation in Japan." *Journal of the Japanese and International Economies* 7:132–156.

Reilly, B. (1987). "Wages, Sex Discrimination, and the Irish Labour Market for Young Workers." *The Economic and Social Review* 18:307–314.

Reilly, B. (1990). "Occupational Endogeneity and Gender Wage Differentials For Young Workers: An Empirical Analysis Using Irish Data." *The Economic and Social Review* 21:311–318.

Reza, A. M. (1978). "Geographical Differences in Earnings and Unemployment Rates." *Review of Economics and Statistics* 60:201–208.

Roback, J. (1982). "Wages, Rents, and Quality of Life." *Journal of Political Economy* 90:1257–1278.

Robertson, D., and J. Symons (1990). "The Occupational Choice of British Children." *Economic Journal* 100:828–841.

Robinson, C. (1989). "The Joint Determination of Union Status and Union Wage Effects: Some Tests of Alternative Models." *Journal of Political Economy* 97:639–667.

Robinson, C., and N. Tomes (1984). "Union Wage Differentials in the Public and Private Sectors: A Simultaneous Equations Specification." *Journal of Labor Economics* 2:106–127.

Rødseth, A. (1990). "Comment on The Wage Curve." *Scandinavian Journal of Economics* 92:243–245.

Rødseth, A., and S. Holden (1990). "Wage Formation in Norway." In *Wage Formation and Macroeconomic Policy in the Nordic Countries*, edited by Lars Calmfors. Oxford: Oxford University Press.

Rosen, S. (1985). "Implicit Contracts: A Survey." *Journal of Economic Literature* 23:1144–1175.

Ross, M. (1988). "Standard European-Type Institutions in a Developing Economy: The Case of Ireland." In *The Search for Labour Market Flexibility*, edited by R. Boyer. Oxford: Clarendon Press, 81–95.

Rowlatt, P. A. (1987). "A Model of Wage Bargaining." *Oxford Bulletin of Economics and Statistics* 49:347–372.

Rowthorn, R. E. (1977). "Conflict, Inflation and Money." *Cambridge Journal of Economics* 1:215–239.

Sanfey, P. (1991). "Insider-Outsider Models and Wage Determination: Theory and Evidence From US Manufacturing Industries." Mimeo, Yale University, New Haven, CT.

Sanfey, P. (1992). "Insiders and Outsiders in Union Models: Theory and Evidence for the US and the UK." Ph.D. dissertation, Yale University, New Haven, CT.

Sanfey, P. (1993). "Wages and Insider-Outsider Models: Theory and Evidence for the US." Mimeo, University of Kent, Canterbury, England.

Santi, E. (1988). "Ten Years of Unionization in Italy, 1977–1986." *Labour* 2:153–182.

Sargan, J. D. (1964). "Wages and Prices in the United Kingdom: A Study in Econometric Methodology." Reprinted in D. F. Hendry and K. F. Wallis (eds.) (1984). *Econometrics and Quantitative Economics*. Oxford: Basil Blackwell.

Schasse, U. (1986). "Male-Female Wage Differences in West Germany: Empirical Evidence, Causes and Implications." Mimeo, Institut fur Quantitative Wirtschaftsforschung, Universitat Hannover, Germany.

Schmidt, C. M. (1991). "Empirical Analyses of the German Labor Market: Unions, Unemployment and Wages." Ph.D. Dissertation, Princeton University, Princeton, NJ.

Schmidt, C. M. (1992). "Country-of-Origin Differences in the Earnings of German Immigrants." Discussion Paper 92–29. Munich: Münchener Wirtschaftswissenschaftliche Beiträge, Ludwig-Maximilians University of Munich, Germany.

Schmidt, C. M. (1993). "The Earnings Dynamics of Immigrant Labour." Discussion Paper 763. London: Centre for Economic Policy Research.

Schmidt, C. M., and K. F. Zimmermann (1991). "Work Characteristics, Firm Size and Wages." *Review of Economics and Statistics* 73:705–710.

Schmidt, C. M., and K. F. Zimmermann (1993). "Unemployment, Real Wages and Union Membership." Discussion Paper 93–07. Munich: Münchener Wirtschaftswissenschaftliche Beiträge, Ludwig-Maximilians University of Munich, Germany.

Schmitt, J. (1994). "The Changing Structure of Male Earnings in Britain: 1974–88." In *Differences and Changes in Wage Structures*, edited by Richard Freeman and Larry Katz. Chicago: University of Chicago Press. Forthcoming.

Schultze, C. L. (1985). "Microeconomic Efficiency and Nominal Wage Stickiness." *American Economic Review* 75:1–15.

Sessions, J. (1993). "An Exposition on the Nature of the Wage Curve." *Scandinavian Journal of Economics* 95:239–244.

Shapiro, C., and J. E. Stiglitz (1984). "Equilibrium Unemployment as a Worker Discipline Device." *American Economic Review* 74:433–444.

Shapiro, D. M., and M. Stelcner (1989). "Canadian Public-Private Sector Earnings Differentials, 1979–1980." *Industrial Relations* 28:72–81.

Simpson, W. (1985). "The Impact of Unions on the Structure of Canadian Wages: An Empirical Analysis with Microdata." *Canadian Journal of Economics* 18:164–181.

Slichter, S. H. (1950). "Notes on the Structure of Wages." *Review of Economics and Statistics* 32:80–91.

Sneesens, H. R., and J. H. Dreze (1986). "A Discussion of Belgian Unemployment Combining Traditional Concepts and Disequilibrium Econometrics." *Economica*, Supplement, 53: S89–S119.

Solow, R. M. (1985). "Insiders and Outsiders in Wage Determination." *Scandinavian Journal of Economics* 87:411–428.

Solow, R. M. (1986). "Unemployment: Getting the Questions Right." *Economica* 53:S23–S34.

Solow, R. M. (1990). *The Labor Market as a Social Institution.* Oxford: Basil Blackwell.

Soltwedel, R. (1988). "Employment Problems in West Germany—The Role of Institutions, Labor Law, and Government Intervention." *Carnegie-Rochester Conference Series on Public Policy* 28:153–220.

Soskice, D. (1990). "Wage Determination: The Changing Role of Institutions in Advanced Industrialized Countries." *Oxford Review of Economic Policy* 6(Winter):36–61.

Sparks, G. R., and D. A. Wilton (1971). "Determinants of Negotiated Increases: An Empirical Wage Analysis." *Econometrica* 39:739–750.

Stafford, F. (1986). "Forestalling the Demise of Empirical Economics: The Role of Microdata in Labor Economics Research." In *Handbook of Labor Economics*, edited by O. C. Ashenfelter and P. R. G. Layard, Amsterdam: North-Holland. Vol. 1, 387–423.

Stewart, M. B. (1987). "Collective Bargaining Arrangements, Closed Shops and Relative Pay." *Economic Journal* 97:140–156.

Stiassny, A. (1985). "The Austrian Phillips Curve Reconsidered." *Empirica* 12:43–66.

Storer, P. (1992). "The Wage and Unemployment Relationship in a Multi-Sector Search Model." Mimeo, University of Quebec at Montreal, Canada.

Streeck, W. (1988). "Industrial Relations in West Germany, 1980–1987." *Labour* 2:3–44.

Summers, L. H. (1991). "The Scientific Illusion in Empirical Macroeconomics." *Scandinavian Journal of Economics* 93:129–148.

Swidinsky, R., and M. Kupferschmidt (1991). "Longitudinal Estimates of Union Effects on Wages, Wage Dispersion and Pension Fringe Benefits." *Relations Industrielles* 46:819–837.

Symons, E., and I. Walker (1988). "Union/Non-Union Wage Differentials, 1979–1984: Evidence from the U.K. Family Expenditure Surveys." Mimeo, Keele University, Keele, England.

Theeuwes, J., C. C. Koopmans, R. Van Opstal, and H. Van Reijn (1985). "Estimation of Optimal Human Capital Accumulation Parameters for the Netherlands." *European Economic Review* 29:233–257.

Topel, R. H. (1986). "Local Labor Markets." *Journal of Political Economy*, Supplement, 94: 111–143.

U.S. Department of Labor (1992a). *Foreign Labor Trends—Australia*. FLT 92-56. Washington, D.C.: U.S. Department of Labor.

U.S. Department of Labor (1992b). *Foreign Labor Trends—Germany*. FLT 92-51. Washington, D.C.: U.S. Department of Labor.

U.S. Department of Labor (1992c). *Foreign Labor Trends—Italy*. FLT 92-58. Washington, D.C.: U.S. Department of Labor.

U.S. Department of Labor (1992d). *Foreign Labor Trends—Korea*. FLT 92-57. Washington, D.C.: U.S. Department of Labor.

Vella, F., and R. Gregory, (1992). "Are We Over-Educating Young Australians? Human Capital Investment and Self-Selection." In *Youth in the Eighties*, edited by R. Gregory and T. Karmel. CEPR, Australian National University, Canbern. 125–151.

Visser, J. (1989). *European Trade Unions in Figures*. Deventer, Netherlands: Kluwer.

Wadhwani, S. (1985). "Wage Inflation in the United Kingdom." *Economica* 52:195–207.

Wagner, J. (1990). "Earnings Functions Under Test: Evidence From Five Countries." *Economie et Prevision*, 92:61–66.

Wagner, J. (1994). "German Wage Curves: 1979–1990." *Economics Letters*. Forthcoming.

Wagner, J. (1993). "An International Comparison of Sector Wage Differentials." *Economics Letters* 34:93–97.

Wagner, J., and W. Lorenz (1988). "The Earnings Function Under Test." *Economics Letters* 27:95–99.

Wagner, J., and W. Lorenz (1991). "An International Comparison of the Rates of Return to Human Capital: Evidence From Five Countries." *Research in Economic Inequality* 3. Greenwich CN: JAI Press.

Weck-Hannemann, H., and B. S. Frey (1985). "Measuring the Shadow Economy: The Case of Switzerland." In *The Economics of the Shadow Economy*, edited by W. Gaertner and A. Wening. Berlin: Springer-Verlag.

Willis, R. J. (1986). "Wage Determinants: A Survey and Reinterpretation of Human Capital Earnings Functions." In *Handbook of Labor Economics*, edited by O. C. Ashenfelter and P. R. G. Layard. Amsterdam: North Holland.

Winter-Ebmer, R. (1994). "Unemployment and Individual Pay: Wage Curve or Compensating Differentials?" *Labour Economics*. Forthcoming.

Woodford, M. (1992). A Book Review, "Seven Schools of Macroeconomic Thought," by E. S. Phelps, *Journal of Economic Dynamics and Control* 16:391–398.

Wulfsberg, F. (1993). "An Application of Wage Bargaining Models to Norwegian Panel Data." Mimeo, University of Oslo, Norway.

Index